GLOBAL ISSUES

D0170878

HUMAN RIGHTS

Faith Merino

Foreword by Brian E. Klunk
University of the Pacific

Facts On File
An Infobase Learning Company

GLOBAL ISSUES: HUMAN RIGHTS

Facts On File, Inc.
An imprint of Infobase Learning
132 West 31st Street
New York NY 10001

Library of Congress Cataloging-in-Publication Data

Merino, Faith.
    Human rights / Faith Merino ; foreword by Brian E. Klunk.
        p. cm.—(Global issues)
    Includes bibliographical references and index.
    ISBN 978-0-8160-8261-2
    1. Human rights. 2. Human rights—Case studies. I. Title.
    JC571.M441 2011
    323—dc22   2010032501

Facts On File books are available at special discounts when purchased in bulk quantities for businesses, associations, institutions, or sales promotions. Please call our Special Sales Department in New York at (212) 967-8800 or (800) 322-8755.

You can find Facts On File on the World Wide Web at http://www.infobaselearning.com

Text design by Erika K. Arroyo
Illustrations by Dale Williams
Composition by Publication Services, Inc.
Cover printed by Yurchak Printing, Inc., Landisville, Pa.
Book printed and bound by Yurchak Printing, Inc., Landisville, Pa.
Date printed: June 2011
Printed in the United States of America

10 9 8 7 6 5 4 3 2 1

This book is printed on acid-free paper.

CONTENTS

PART III: Research Tools

Foreword

When I was in college in the mid-1970s studying international relations, the topic of human rights was scarcely addressed. On those rare occasions when human rights were discussed, the principal message was that students striving for a sophisticated understanding of international relations and foreign policy should not distract themselves from the truly important concerns of arms-control negotiations, Middle East peace talks, and the endgame of the wars in Southeast Asia then still being played out in Cambodia and Vietnam.

In my first international relations course, a very colorful professor who frequently reached for outrageously vivid images to make her points imagined a country given to cannibalism in order to emphasize the importance of sovereignty and the limited appropriate scope of foreign policy. Sovereignty is the first rule of international law. Since the end of the Thirty Years' War in 1648, sovereign states have been recognized in international law as the primary legitimate actors in international relations. The rule of sovereignty means that states are free to decide for themselves how to act in foreign policy and free to carry out life within the state however they see fit, without interference from any outside force. My international relations professor put it this way, "If another country wants to round up its people, boil them in a pot, and serve them up for supper, they are free to do so. Other countries should only care about that country's *foreign policy* and whether the cannibalistic state's international activities affected their national interests."

When Jimmy Carter was elected president of the United States in 1976 and came to office proclaiming that U.S. foreign policy would reflect a preference for societies that respect individual rights, another professor, this time a very distinguished Soviet foreign-policy expert, was quick to point out the new president's naïveté. In this professor's view, Carter's commitment to human rights as the "soul of our foreign policy" was another example of unfortunate American idealistic tendencies in foreign policy. It was too easy in the United States, he argued, for foreign policy amateurs like Carter to rise to national leadership. More experienced, professional diplomats in Europe would not take Carter or his human rights goals seriously, damaging U.S. leadership in addressing really important security and economic issues. We students, who imagined ourselves headed for important careers in government service, research, and teaching, got the message: Don't waste your time worrying about human rights.

As it turns out, my professors underestimated the importance of human rights. Thirty-five years later, we can no longer imagine foreign policy or the study of international relations without attention to human rights. Almost nobody bat an eye in 2010 when Secretary of State Hillary Clinton said that human rights concerns are always on the diplomatic agenda. Those sophisticated Europeans have developed some of the world's most effective human rights institutions. It was European states that led the creation of the International Criminal Court, which is intended to provide a venue for trying and punishing the worst violators of human rights. During the mid-1970s, the most popular college international relations textbooks—such as Hans J. Morgenthau's *Politics Among Nations*—were silent about human rights. In 2010, few professors would assign a textbook that did not have at least a chapter on human rights.

The essence of the idea of human rights is that human dignity can be protected and advanced by taking as fact that every person is endowed with certain freedoms and entitlements, some that should be protected and some that may need to be provided. Ironically, the idea of the sovereign state with unlimited authority to govern its people and territory and immunity from outside interference plays a key role in the success of human rights. In international law it is common to imagine the state as a legal person who can claim the sovereign right to govern its own body politic free from the control of either emperor or pope. This notion translates naturally to actual persons. If states enjoy a territorial zone of sovereignty, should not human individuals be free to rule themselves in their own persons? Should not sovereign individual persons enjoy reasonable protections against interference from their own governments as well as their compatriots? The very sovereignty argument that supported my professor's cannibalism proposition also tends to subvert it. You cannot very well defend the sovereignty of individual states while denying the sovereignty of individual persons.

However, as this volume points out, while human rights is a very convincing idea, it is also a very complicated idea. At every turn, hard questions loom, and easy answers are scarce. Are human rights best thought of as protections against interference, as in the rights protected by the U.S. Constitution's First Amendment? Should we concentrate on protecting individuals' free expression, religious freedom, and similar fundamental liberties? Or do human rights include entitlements to goods such as education and health care that would seem to be necessary for human dignity to develop and flourish? Can only individual persons claim rights, or can groups of people claim human rights as a group? Humans are naturally social, and we can only develop our individuality within groups of people. But does this mean that groups can claim human rights? Social groups, whether they are based on race, ethnicity, language, religion, or some other factor, are ultimately imagined communities without clear definitions or borders. When a group claims rights, for whom is it claiming them?

The subject of cultural relativism and human rights is discussed extensively in this volume. No question about human rights has received more attention from scholars and diplomats. While essentially all countries have accepted the idea of rights, how to interpret and apply specific human rights certainly varies from one culture to another. One does not have to believe that human rights are an idea imposed on much of the world by European and American colonial powers in order to cement their global dominance to understand that politically, economically, and culturally powerful countries like the United States often will have the greatest impact on how human rights questions are treated in international affairs. On the other hand, claims of cultural relativism cannot explain or excuse all inhumane actions. To understand is not always to justify or forgive. Not every awful practice can be explained away as culturally normal. The tragedy of important moral values such as promoting human dignity or respecting cultural differences is that noble ideals can be used and manipulated for political advantage.

One more matter that can bewilder the student who tries to learn more about human rights is the question of responsibility. If most of us agree about the meaning and importance of human rights and most countries have signed an array of international agreements promising to observe human rights, it is still not always clear who is responsible for ensuring that human rights are respected and promoted. The frustrating answer may be everybody. International organizations like the United Nations have some responsibility for human rights, and the UN has established an array of human rights commissioners, councils, and committees. But international organizations are ultimately tools of the states that created them and belong to them. International organizations can do no more than their most powerful members want them to do.

Countries like the United States may claim to be committed to human rights, but countries will always face competing priorities in their foreign policies. Security and economic interests constantly tempt countries to compromise on human rights. Accordingly, human rights activists have created nongovernmental organizations like Amnesty International and Human Rights Watch to keep attention on human rights abuses and push governments to improve human rights. Global corporations can play an important human rights role in their investment and labor practices. Even high-profile individuals can play a role, as the rock singer Bono and the Irish band U2 do when they perform their song "Walk On" in tribute to the Burmese activist Aung San Suu Kyi, who has spent most of the last two decades under house arrest. Ultimately, though, it is those still sovereign states that must first and foremost be responsible for their citizens' human rights.

This is why political scientists who study human rights have focused their gaze on what goes on inside individual states. To what extent does a country's political culture support the idea of human rights? Do governments go beyond just signing and ratifying human rights treaties? Do they change domestic laws and regulations to conform to the treaties they have signed? Learning more about whether and how states accommodate themselves to human rights expectations should help us answer many of the questions mentioned here.

Finally, human rights is both a very depressing and quite hopeful subject. The ease with which normal decency breaks down in Bosnia or Rwanda or even Murfreesboro, Tennessee, reminds us that the power of human rights can be severely limited any time people see others, whether they are Croats or Tutsis or Muslims, as not fully human. On the other hand, we can be hopeful because small improvements can have big impacts. Any time a country stops torturing prisoners or disappearing political opponents human rights have improved. The trick may be for us to keep our eye on the small improvements.

This book will be useful to students interested in learning more about human rights as a global issue. Part I introduces the subject of human rights and shows how the idea of human rights has developed since ancient times. The case studies in Part I come from the United States and other countries, including Iran and the Democratic Republic of the Congo. The case studies make clear how important basic human rights concerns are and yet how difficult it is to manage them. Parts II and III have many resources, including primary documents, short biographical sketches, and an annotated bibliography, to guide those who want to explore this compelling issue at greater length.

—Brian E. Klunk
University of the Pacific
Stockton, California

List of Maps, Tables, and Charts

PART I

At Issue

1

Introduction

In 1689, the English philosopher John Locke proposed a controversial theory of what life would be like without government: existence in a state of "perfect freedom" and equality.[1] If we were to revert to life before the development of government and political systems, Locke theorized, we would exist in a state of nature, which would render every human being equal under God and free to defend his or her right to life, liberty, and estate (or property).[2] Such a wide-sweeping notion of human equality was a radical affront to the customs of 17th-century English society, which reserved civil and political rights to the elite.

The concept of human rights is relatively new and yet to be universally accepted. When Thomas Jefferson penned the Declaration of Independence in 1776, he opened the second paragraph with: "We hold these truths to be self-evident, that all men are created equal, that they are endowed by their Creator with certain unalienable Rights, that among these are Life, Liberty and the pursuit of Happiness."[3] But how self-evident are such rights when societies throughout history have spent years trying to understand what rights really are? Are human rights self-evident when they need to be out-lined in a formal declaration?

The notion of innate human rights has had a rocky history throughout the world as scholars, politicians, religious leaders, and community members have debated the legitimacy of individual and group rights, who is entitled to rights, and how to protect rights. Today, rights continue to evolve around the world, and various organizations have developed to encourage freedom and equality worldwide.

This book discusses the way in which different societies have approached human rights throughout history, how rights are viewed and acted upon around the world today, and disputes over the nature of human rights and where they come from.

HISTORY OF HUMAN RIGHTS

The idea that every person has a right to life, liberty, and the pursuit of happiness requires as its foundation the concept that every person has an innate worth as a human being. Respect for an individual's basic rights hinges on a respect for the inherent dignity of the individual. Many past and current societies have grappled with the concept of human dignity and have attempted to clarify rights while maintaining social order. Although the general concept of human rights may be self-evident to many, respect for the rights of specific individuals is to a large extent dependent on the views of those in power. Thus, the history of thought on human rights chronicles the public discussions of the social elite regarding how much freedom to allow members of the lower classes.

Near Eastern Thought

Ancient texts evidence few if any references to human rights, but nevertheless many societies developed various theories of justice and were concerned with the protection of the weak and vulnerable. The earliest known legal code is the Code of Ur-Nammu, written in the Sumerian language between 2112 and 2095 B.C.E., in what is now Iraq. While the code made provisions for the protection of orphans and widows, the protection of individual rights was peripheral to the protection of Sumerian social order. Murder, theft, and rape were punishable by death; however, the severity of a punishment depended on the respective social classes of the victim and the perpetrator. Furthermore, crimes were considered within the context of who had been wronged, according to those judging the situation. Rape, while not considered a crime in and of itself, was considered a crime if one man raped another man's wife. The underlying understanding was that a woman's husband had a right to her body as his property.[4]

This basic approach to justice and social harmony was common throughout ancient Mediterranean societies, and many of the ancient legal codes of this region are virtually identical. Mirroring the denunciation of rape in the Code of Ur-Nammu, the later Old Testament Book of Deuteronomy clarifies that in legal terms, rape consists of one man raping another man's wife. In this context, the perpetrator will be put to death for his crime against another male citizen. However, if a slave is raped, the offender must compensate the slave's owner in the form of a monetary fine. The books of Genesis, Exodus, and Deuteronomy all proclaim that if one citizen rapes the daughter of another, but swears at the sanctuary gate that he was not aware that she was a daughter of the household, he will not be found guilty.[5]

While such laws do not appear to have much in common with modern notions of human rights, they are more easily understood when considered in the context of protecting the rights of citizens and thereby protecting a particular social order. In these ancient societies, only adult, free males qualified as citizens.

The Babylonian Code of Hammurabi, as proclaimed by King Hammurabi around 1780 B.C.E., is the oldest complete code of law known to date, and it was unique in its aim for accountability among citizens as well as the government. Much of the code was set within a framework of social equality, treating one's neighbors as one would like to be treated, as well as holding every citizen responsible for crimes he commits against his neighbors.[6] Punishment was largely based on the *lex talionis* system, otherwise known as the principle of "an eye for an eye," that is retribution equal to the committed offense. When a person fell victim to a crime, it was common for the victim's family to seek their own form of retribution, which could far exceed the violence of the offense. Babylonian law was designed to limit the severity of the punishment, but this principle applied only to social equals. A person of the lower classes who committed an offense against a person of higher social standing often faced punishment that far outweighed the nature of the crime.

Another key element of the Code of Hammurabi is its emphasis on the king's role as a servant of the gods and the community. The preamble of the code begins:

> When Anu the Sublime, King of the Anunaki, and Bel, the lord of Heaven and earth, who decreed the fate of the land, assigned to Marduk, the overruling son of Ea . . . they called Babylon by his illustrious name, made it great on earth, and made an everlasting kingdom in it . . . then Anu and Bel called by name me, Hammurabi, the exalted prince, who feared God, to bring about the rule of righteousness in the land, to destroy the wicked and evil-doers; so that the strong should not harm the weak; so that I should rule over the Black Headed people like Shamash, and enlighten the land, to further the well-being of mankind.[7]

Thus, Hammurabi presents himself as a king who has been assigned by the gods the duty of protecting his people and fostering their spiritual, intellectual, and physical development to better the human population as a whole. Further emphasizing the fundamental and unalterable nature of the laws, the code was transcribed onto an eight-foot-tall stone pillar, in full view of all, making the law absolute, accessible, and applicable to all.[8] This can be interpreted as one of the earliest expressions of a people's civil rights.

Old Testament Hebrew Bible texts reflect many of the positions taken in the Code of Hammurabi concerning peace and justice. Contemporary scholars debate the biblical foundations of human rights; while some argue that the very concept of human rights is rooted in the Jewish tradition and the Ten Commandments, others contend that Jewish law as detailed in the Old Testament was heavily influenced by the Code of Hammurabi.[9] Still others contend that the Hebrew laws were specifically meant to protect and uphold the identity and survival of the group as distinct from other groups.

Judaism, Christianity, and Islam are the three major monotheistic traditions that form the Abrahamic religions, so called because each one traces its heritage back to Abraham as its founder. The Jewish (and Christian) lineage is believed to follow from Abraham through his son Isaac, while the Islamic tradition is believed to have continued though Abraham's other son, Ishmael, who is known in Islam as Father of the Arabs.

While the Islamic faith finds its origins in Abraham, the tradition became organized under the name "Islam," which translates to "submission," in 610 C.E. by the Muslim prophet Muhammad, who collected his revelations from God in the Quran. The Quran emphasizes unity and surrendering to God's will, which Muhammad demonstrated in 622 C.E., when he drafted a constitution that would settle disputes between Muslim, Jewish, and pagan tribes in the region of Medina. Known as the Constitution of Medina, the body of laws that Muhammad put forth not only established rules and guidelines for civil interactions but also outlined the individual rights of the people residing in Medina, including the rights of Jews and other non-Muslims. It posits: "The Jews of B. 'Auf are one community with the believers (the Jews have their religion and the Muslims have theirs). . ."[10] Islam is credited with implementing a number of social reforms that revolutionized the Arab world and improved the lives of women, children, the poor, and even slaves. While Muhammad did not expressly forbid slavery, he encouraged the freeing of slaves as a praiseworthy deed in itself.

Classical and Christian Thought

In addition to Jerusalem, western philosophy is traditionally traced back to ancient Greece, which, like most other ancient societies, had no concept of human rights as they are known today. Philosophers did, however, link justice and the functioning of society to respect for the rights of others. Plato's *Republic* (ca. 380 B.C.E.) expertly dissects the concepts of state, citizenship, and justice to arrive at the conclusion that a state or society is composed of a number of individuals assuming diverse and specialized roles to support the whole. In questioning the nature of justice, Glaucon, one of the principal speakers in the *Republic,* presents the story of the Ring of Gyges. One day, the shepherd Gyges finds a dead body, which is naked except for a ring. In taking and wearing the ring, Gyges discovers that he can turn invisible, and he sets out to court, where he seduces the queen, murders the king, and seizes the throne. Glaucon uses the story to back up his argument that 1) human beings are, by nature, unjust (immoral) and behave justly only under threat of punishment, and 2) if a man finds an unjust advantage over his peers (as Gyges finds in the ring), he should use it for his own benefit. Socrates counters this argument by assessing the nature of the state and the basic fact that a society that embraces such a belief system would destroy itself; thus, it is better for individuals as well as society as a whole to behave justly, regardless of the threat of punishment. Further, Socrates argues, ". . . haven't we found that justice itself is the best thing for the soul itself, and that the soul should do what is just, whether it has Gyges' ring or not, or even the cap of Hades [the god of the underworld] as well?"[11] Socrates' argument that all individuals have an innate awareness of what is just and are, in fact, predisposed to behave justly, is a precursor to later enlightenment thought on human nature and rights.

Plato's famous pupil Aristotle (384–322 B.C.E.) took a less idealistic approach toward the concept of justice and equality. Human rights scholar Gary Herbert states that Aristotle had a practical grasp of everything within a means/ends relationship, particularly in his belief that the "lower" always exists for the "higher." Human beings are unequal in society, according to Aristotle, because they are unequal in nature. Aristotle believed that "a natural commensurability exists between natural abilities and natural rights; those who have greater abilities have correspondingly greater rights."[12] The slave, according to Aristotle, is, by nature, an "animated tool" who is "nothing of himself, but totally another's," and therefore is not entitled to rights because his very existence is defined by his master's ownership of him.[13]

A major concept that arose out of the Greek school of Stoicism (ca. third century B.C.E.) was the notion of natural reason. If man can reason, then man can know truth. Because the theory of natural reason posits an objective, natural truth that exists exclusive of human creation or influence, the concept easily lends itself to the theory of natural law, which states that the truths of nature are, in fact, laws of nature that can be accessed and understood through natural reason. In other words, if man can reason, then man can know truth, and thus man can live according to that truth. Virtually all of the classical scholars developed upon the concept of reason being the critical human capacity, which would later go on to form the foundation of the Enlightenment in the 17th century. Around 43 B.C.E., the Roman statesman and writer Cicero theorized that "True law is Reason, right and natural, commanding people to fulfill their obligations and prohibiting and deterring them from doing wrong. Its validity is universal; it is immutable and eternal."[14] The early Roman Christians developed this theory of natural law by defining it as instinctively understood by the conscience, which brought law and justice into the realm of human nature. The writings of Paul of Tarsus, otherwise known as Saint Paul (10–67 C.E.), played a large role in the new understanding of natural law and thus natural rights. In the Epistle of Saint Paul to the Galatians, Paul explained all people's equality in Christ:

> For you are all the children of God by faith, in Christ Jesus. For as many of you have been baptized in Christ, have put on Christ. There is neither Jew nor Greek: there is neither bond nor free: there is neither male nor female. For you are all one in Christ Jesus. And if you be Christ's, then you are the seed of Abraham, heirs according to the promise.[15]

Paul presented a new perspective on society: equality in fraternity. This can be seen as a variation of the rights of citizens, the unique distinction being the fact that anyone can be a Christian. Historically, this has been truer in theory than in practice. Nevertheless, the ideal of a society based on unity and equality was a revolutionary new theory that exalted the dignity of the individual human being and had a large-scale effect on global history, particularly when Christianity was officially adopted by the Roman emperor Constantine in the early fourth century.

At the time of Paul's writing, Roman philosophers and statesmen, such as Cicero and Seneca, were developing the concept of *humanitas,* which refers to a way of life wherein citizens develop a natural incentive, through education and training, to behave justly and avoid violent behavior toward other human beings. The concept of *humanitas* emphasizes respect for the dignity of other human beings, which is a key element in understanding human rights. But this was only applicable insofar as it benefited the state. The state was of primary importance, and the rights of citizens could be subverted where the state was concerned. According to Cicero, "Mildness and clemency are only to be practiced if they can be replaced by *severitas* when the interests of the state require it."[16] The rise of the cult of Christianity, as well as other cults of the time, may be viewed as a response to this view of human rights. What kind of worth and dignity can be ascribed to the individual human being if that worth can be devalued according to the interests of the state? In this light, Christianity, as it was developed by Paul, can be considered a social movement.

Introduction

History teems with social revolutions that have helped shape the modern world. While governments throughout history have framed rights within the context of maintaining peace and order within the kingdom, people's movements have responded to authoritarian regimes to define and protect individual rights. Some movements have blended the goals of establishing individual rights and maintaining peace. Magna Carta is considered the result of the first major rights movement in the Western world. In 1215, the barons of England forced King John to proclaim the rights of freemen as well as a limitation to his own will by the law. According to Magna Carta, "We have also granted to all freemen of our kingdom, for us and our heirs forever, all the underwritten liberties, to be had and held by them and their heirs, of us and our heirs forever." Such liberties included inheritance rights, rights of widows, and reasonable taxation.[17]

Theories of conscience and justice continued to develop with the evolution of Christianity into the medieval period, when Thomas Aquinas undertook the cause of investigating natural law, or *ius* (justice). In the 13th century, Thomas Aquinas posited that *ius,* or that which is just, is the natural good, while written law is the human expression of that good.[18] According to Gary Herbert, "Drawing on 'The Philosopher,' the name used by medievalists to refer to Aristotle, Aquinas reintroduced nature into the human."[19]

Deriving his own school of thought from that of Aristotelian philosophy, Thomas Aquinas was one of several philosophers of this period who rediscovered the value of classical thought. In 1330, the Italian poet and scholar Petrarch termed the years between the fall of Rome and his own present day the "Dark Ages," a period he considered devoid of cultural achievement. Petrarch theorized that the solution to this cultural drought was a return to the writers of classical antiquity, particularly Cicero, whom he considered a master rhetorician. Petrarch is today considered the founder of Renaissance humanism, a movement that emphasized the importance of developing well-rounded, eloquent citizens who were capable of full and informed participation in civic life. The literary arts were heavily emphasized, and the term *umanista* came to refer to the study of philosophy, history, poetry, rhetoric, and grammar. While many of the Renaissance humanists, including Petrarch, were ordained priests, the humanist movement was neither a line of Christian philosophy nor an anti-Christian doctrine. The humanist movement took the position that the development of the human mind should not be constrained by a particular religious allegiance, nor strict secular utility. Rather, the humanists argued, the individual human mind is innately deserving of development for its own sake.

The new free flow of humanist thought was coupled with the 15th-century development of the printing press, which allowed for the outward spread of Italian humanism into other parts of Europe. This, consequently, paved the way for the Protestant Reformation, the large-scale revolt against both the decadence of the Roman Catholic Church and the tenets of the Catholic faith. Martin Luther, a 16th-century German monk, is best known for nailing his Ninety-five Theses on the door of All Saints' Church in Wittenberg in 1517, in which he not only disparaged the Catholic Church's sale of indulgences (remissions of punishment for sins) but also argued with the church's approach to concepts such as absolution and baptism. Of particular concern to Luther was his fundamental belief that man is saved through faith alone, while the Catholic Church taught that man is saved through good works which had been conflated with the purchase of indulgences (though in recent years the two sects have agreed that they are not truly divided on a perceived opposition between faith and works). One of the most notable cultural achievements to come out of the Protestant Reformation was Luther's translation of the Bible into German vernacular, which not only emphasized the responsibility of the individual to cultivate an unmediated relationship with God but also standardized the German language.[20]

Martin Luther was consequently excommunicated, and the Catholic Church responded to the Protestant Reformation by organizing a Catholic revival. In the mid-16th century, the Council of Trent convened and reexamined the state of Catholicism, addressing the abuses that Luther had argued against, such as the sale of indulgences. While the Council of Trent refused to compromise on the tenets of Catholicism, particularly Luther's contention that man is saved through faith alone, it was forced to reevaluate the current condition of the church and reform accordingly. Thus, the Reformation, like other social movements and revolutions, revived the inherent integrity and rights of the individual against the political superstructure (as the Catholic Church of the Renaissance and Reformation periods was, undoubtedly, a daunting political force). In emphasizing the innate value of the individual, Renaissance humanism and the Protestant Reformation laid the groundwork for later theories on the individual right to self-fulfillment and self-determination, which would come to prominence in the coming years.

The Age of Enlightenment

Western Europe saw a range of political conflicts and cultural innovations in the 17th century that spurred many scholars to reconsider common conceptions of justice and authority. John Locke was born in 1632, during a particularly turbulent era in English history, in which struggles for power crystallized in the struggle between the Catholic Church and the Church of England. In 1649, following a long, exhausting battle between Charles I and Parliament over the king's negligent and abusive reign, as well as his apparent sympathy for the Catholics, the king was executed for treason. He was replaced by the puritan Oliver Cromwell, after whose death in 1658 the throne was restored to the Anglican Charles II. He was, in turn, succeeded by the Catholic King James II. In 1689, the Glorious Revolution saw the overthrow of King James II and the ascent of Anglican William of Orange. It was during this time that John Locke anonymously published his *Two Treatises of Government,* in which he proposed a natural, universal state of equality and human rights.

An empiricist (one who emphasizes the importance of sensory understanding as the primary path to knowledge, as opposed to intuition or idealism), Locke broke down the concept of government and society in his *Two Treatises of Government* to arrive at the conclusion that all men are fundamentally equal, which logically suggests that no man *naturally* has power over another. All men, Locke theorized, are born with equal power to not only govern themselves, but to govern their neighbors, who, in turn, have the same power. Locke wrote:

> . . . all power and jurisdiction is reciprocal, no one having more than another; there being nothing more evident, than that creatures of the same species and rank, promiscuously born to all the same advantages of nature, and the use of the same faculties should also be equal one amongst another without subordination or subjection. . . .[21]

Government arises from the need to maintain order, which, according to Locke, is every man's responsibility. Locke argues that law is not only applicable to every man, but also within every man's power to execute, and would be meaningless otherwise. Locke states unequivocally:

> And if any one in the state of nature may punish another for any evil he has done, every one may do so: for in that state of perfect equality where naturally there is no superiority or jurisdiction over another, what any may do in prosecution of that law, every one must needs have a right to do.[22]

Government, thus, is an expression of the people (as a collection of individuals rather than a community) and, by nature, intended to function for the people. A community consents to the rule of a governmental body, and in return, the governmental body executes the will of the community.[23]

Locke's theory of government as a social contract would later be instrumental in establishing a basis of republican government following the American Revolution.

Like other scholars of his time, Locke distinguished between those eligible for equality and those who were ineligible. Equality among men expressly referred to propertied men, excluding men who did not own property, women, and slaves. Such individuals were not created on the same level as men of property and therefore fall into the realm of property, themselves, according to Locke, who writes: ". . . the power of a magistrate over a subject may be distinguished from that of a father over his children, a master over his servant, a husband over his wife, and a lord over his slave."[24] Such individuals, Locke reasoned, do require an authoritarian ruler, regardless of whether or not they consent to be governed.

Another major philosopher of human rights, Jean-Jacques Rousseau, took up the theory of the social contract in the mid-18th century in France. In his 1762 book, *The Social Contract*, Rousseau's famous opening words read: "Man is born free; and everywhere he is in chains."[25] It was Rousseau's position that man was in his ideal form in the state of nature, before the development of society. In this state, man was peaceful, free, and happy; it was a state of animalistic primitivism, when man was an amoral creature, driven by instinct and appetite. Inequality developed,

> the moment one man began to stand in need of the help of another; from the moment it appeared advantageous to any one man to have enough provisions for two, equality disappeared, property was introduced, work became indispensable, and vast forests became smiling fields, which man had to water with the sweat of his brow . . .[26]

It was at this point of passing from nature into society that man entered the social contract, wherein men traded unlimited personal freedom for protection of their property. *The Social Contract* is widely credited with coining the term *rights of man*, which was soon embedded in the French lexicon. Opposition to authoritarian rule was fermenting in the Western world. Rousseau's *Social Contract* was published in 1762, a mere 14 years before the Declaration of Independence was written.

Thomas Paine, a British intellectual who moved to the American colonies shortly before the revolution, succinctly summed up the need for change in the introduction to his highly influential pamphlet titled *Common Sense:* "a long habit of not thinking a thing wrong, gives it a superficial appearance of being right, and raises at first a formidable outcry in defense of custom."[27]

Introduction

Thomas Paine, a failed excise officer and lay minister, met Benjamin Franklin in London in 1774. Impressed with Paine, Franklin encouraged him to relocate to the American colonies and wrote him a letter of recommendation. Once in America, Paine anonymously published *Common Sense* as a pamphlet. The pamphlet, written in clear, accessible language that was understandable to the common man, was wildly successful, selling out almost immediately after its release in January 1776.

Common Sense placed the blame for the colonies' problems on the British monarchy and openly called for a break from England, claiming Americans' need to defend their natural rights. Paine also suggested a new way of considering government as a body distinct from society. "Society," Paine writes, "is produced by our wants, and government by our wickedness; the former promotes our happiness positively by uniting our affections, the latter negatively by restraining our vices."[28] Like Rousseau, Paine chronicled the human past by projecting a possible new society, beginning with one man's need for help from his neighbor, leading to the coalescing of a society, and the necessary establishment of government to restrain those who would take advantage of his peers. In this ideal society, the people themselves would be the government. "In this first parliament," Paine explained, "every man by natural right will have a seat."[29] As the society grows and legislation cannot accommodate every individual, the parliament will then be staffed by elected officials who will act according to the will of their constituency.

Declaration of Independence, 1776

Scholars debate how much of an effect Thomas Paine's *Common Sense* had on catalyzing the American Revolution, but it is widely accepted that Paine played a key role in bringing anti-Crown sentiment to the forefront of international discussion. Resentment toward British rule had been brewing in the colonies for many years. In 1750, the British Parliament passed the Iron Act, which sought to suppress the development of the iron industry in the American colonies to bolster the iron industry in England. The act stirred up bitterness, which was later compounded by the Sugar Act of 1764, which exclusively taxed the American colonies for sugar imports to fund the British military. Also in 1764, Parliament passed the Currency Act, which banned the American colonies from printing their own money. An act forcing colonial families to house and feed British soldiers further fanned the flames of discontentment.

Tensions came to a head in 1770, when British soldiers opened fire on an unarmed mob, killing five and injuring six others. The situation found an uneasy resolution with two soldiers being found guilty of murder, but the conviction did little to quell resentment among the American colonialists. In

1773, the Tea Act—which granted the British East India Company a monopoly on exporting tea to the colonies—prompted a number of angry Bostonians disguised as Mohawk Indians to board British import ships and dump 342 containers of tea into the harbor.

In 1775, British troops set out to destroy the American military supplies in Concord, Massachusetts. Paul Revere, a strong supporter of American independence, rode through the streets at midnight to alert the town. When an armed militia met the British soldiers, eight Americans were killed and 10 others were injured. It was reportedly this event that convinced Thomas Paine that a break from England was necessary.[30] But he did not stop at merely demanding America's right to self-governance; he typified the American cause as a human cause, urging his readers to see the American right to freedom from oppression as a basic human right to life. Therefore, America's declaration of its rights, according to Paine, was a logical response to England's declaration of "war against the natural rights of all mankind."[31]

The following year, George Mason drafted the Virginia Declaration of Rights, the first paragraph of which reads:

That all men are by nature equally free and independent, and have certain inherent rights, of which, when they enter into a state of society, they cannot, by any compact, deprive or divest their posterity; namely, the enjoyment of life and liberty, with the means of acquiring and possessing property, and pursuing and obtaining happiness and safety.[32]

Among the rights outlined in the document is the right to a government created by, and for, the people, the right to a fair and speedy trial, as well as reasonable punishment, freedom of the press, the right to organize a trained militia, and freedom of religion.[33] The Declaration was adopted by the Virginia Convention of Delegates in June of 1776.

The universality of rights was a revolutionary theory, and in his Declaration of Independence, published on July 4, 1776, Thomas Jefferson followed the train of logic to the furthest extent possible, given the historical context. According to the modern European history scholar Lynn Hunt, "Human rights require three interlocking qualities: rights must be *natural* (inherent in human beings); *equal* (the same for everyone); and *universal* (applicable everywhere.)"[34] Jefferson is well known today as a champion for human rights at a time when rights were reserved for freeborn, propertied, white men. Among the rights he envisioned in a new, free American society were religious freedom, women's right to file for divorce, and the abolition of slavery.

The Declaration of Independence as it is known today went through several edits and revisions. In the rough draft, the second paragraph opened: "We

14

hold these truths to be sacred and undeniable." Later on, Jefferson revised this to say: "We hold these truths to be self-evident." This is a telling revision as it speaks to Jefferson's awareness that to defend or justify rights is to open the door to debate about rights. "We hold these truths to be sacred" could easily be read to emphasize the subjectivity of the colonies' declaration, for what is "sacred"? The term *sacred* is relative not only to a belief in God but to religious persuasion as well as culture. That which is held to be sacred by one community may not be held sacred by another. The term *undeniable* also invites debate, particularly when one considers that Jefferson was posing these statements to King George III. In the 18th-century British world order, nothing was "undeniable" by the monarch, who had inherited the throne by divine right and was thus entrusted to rule by God's own will. Changing the statement to "We hold these truths to be self-evident" effectively eliminated the possibility of negotiation or debate. That which is self-evident cannot be explained or debated. The new phrase was therefore the equivalent of saying "it is what it is." The document goes on to list the human and civil rights that King George III violated, in effect stating the king's failure to comply with the terms of the social contract as the colonies' reason for dissolving the contract. This approach is unique in its underlying assumption that the colonies are on equal footing with the king and therefore have a right to judge his actions.

Not everyone in Congress agreed with the rights that Jefferson outlined in the Declaration. In addition to listing the king's crimes against the American colonies, the first draft also included an attack on the king's crimes against humanity for his participation in the slave trade, writing:

> . . . he has waged cruel war against human nature itself, violating its most sacred rights of life & liberty in the persons of a distant people who never offended him, captivating & carrying them into slavery in another hemisphere, or to incur miserable death in their transportation thither. This piratical warfare, this opprobrium of infidel powers, is the warfare of the CHRISTIAN king of Great Britain. Determined to keep open a market where MEN should be bought & sold, he has prostituted his negative for suppressing every legislative attempt to prohibit or to restrain this execrable commerce . . .[35]

Jefferson worded this passage carefully, and records show that he was very conscientious of how it would be interpreted by his other slave-owning peers. In the rough draft, the line reading "determined to keep open a market where MEN should be bought & sold" was bracketed, possibly suggesting that this sentence could appear to be inflammatory. After several edits, Jefferson eliminated the brackets and submitted the passage in its original form, but it was ultimately struck out by Congress altogether. This hiccup in the evolution of human rights in America presents a unique problem with the act of declaring rights: To "declare" rights is to announce the objective, unwavering existence of rights as distinct from the subjective opinions of the writers. But as we see in the rough draft of the Declaration of Independence, one strike of the pen eliminated one group of people's rights entirely, thereby undermining the power of the written word and the act of declaring.

It is important to recognize the historical context of the Declaration of Independence, and the fact that the men declaring universal human rights were, themselves, white, Christian, and propertied (many were also slaveholders), and were thus acting from a social perspective that precluded any recognition of the rights of African-American slaves and women. The Declaration of Independence was a singular, history-making document. The act of declaring one's rights to one's ruler and subsequently emancipating oneself from that rule presented a new institutionalized approach to politics and government. So how do we reconcile the revolutionary act of declaring universal human rights with the fact that, just as easily as declaring those rights, the same men could wipe some rights from historical record altogether? Who creates rights and who "gives" rights?

Declaration of the Rights of Man and Citizen, 1789

In 1787, a French Calvinist pastor named Jean-Paul Rabaut Saint-Étienne wrote a letter to the king regarding the Edict of Toleration for Protestants. In a nation largely dominated by Catholicism, French Protestants had faced centuries of cruel persecution for their faith, and the edict promised to allow some new freedoms. Until the edict's registration by the French Parliament in 1788, Protestant marriages were considered invalid because they were not performed in the Catholic Church. The edict proposed civil marriages for Protestants, as well as allowances for registration of Protestant births and deaths. Nevertheless, the edict reemphasized Catholicism as the French national religion, and Protestants were still barred from holding public positions.

In his letter to the king, Rabaut Saint-Étienne wrote: "[W]e know today what natural rights are, and they certainly give men much more than the edict accords to Protestants . . . The time has come when it is no longer acceptable for a law to overtly overrule the rights of humanity that are very well known all over the world." As Lynn Hunt comments in her book *Inventing Human Rights*, "everything depended—as it still does—on the interpretation given to what was 'no longer acceptable.'"[36] Basing rights on what is "acceptable," as Rabaut Saint-Étienne does in his letter, frames the concept of human rights within the context of an emerging awareness of rights.

Introduction

The American Declaration of Independence became a source of inspiration and hope to French reformers, who sought to establish a more inclusive, rights-based government. Between 1776 and 1783, the American Declaration of Independence appeared in France in nine different translations.[37]

By the 1780s, France was facing an unprecedented financial crisis that was compounded by a poor harvest that resulted in mass hunger and malnutrition among peasants throughout the country. The nobility, however, maintained their elaborate displays of consumption and decadence, which only served to intensify resentment among the peasantry. Finally, in May 1789, the crisis called for a meeting of the Estates General—the first one since 1614. The Estates General consisted of three estates: the clergy, the nobility, and the common classes, and each estate was entitled to one vote, despite the fact that the common classes far outnumbered the nobility and the clergy. When negotiations between the three estates became burdensome, the Third Estate met in June 1789 and declared itself the National Assembly. King Louis XVI's attempts to keep the assembly from meeting prompted the group to convene at an indoor tennis court, where they took the Tennis Court Oath, in which they agreed not to disband until they had produced a constitution for France.

While the king made some concessions, the mounting tension among the masses led him to increase the numbers of mercenary troops just outside of Paris, which, in turn, led to louder protests.

Several liberal-leaning members of the clergy and nobility joined the National Assembly, and a committee of 30 was selected to draft a constitution. The marquis de Lafayette, a friend of Thomas Jefferson and a French soldier who had fought under George Washington during the American Revolution, played a key role in the creation of the Declaration of the Rights of Man and Citizen, with notable influences from the American Declaration of Independence.

In July 1789, following the dismissal of the popular Protestant minister Jacques Necker for allegedly advising the king to limit his levels of consumption to assist in the success of the national budget, a mob of angry Parisians attacked the Bastille, demanding its store of gunpowder and ammunition. A symbol of monarchical authoritarianism, the Bastille was a fortress that also served as a prison where King Louis XIII had once sent political enemies in a shroud of secrecy. When the Bastille was attacked on July 12, it housed seven prisoners and it could not hold against the raging mob. The Parisians took the Bastille and brutally murdered and decapitated governor Bernard-René de Launay, whose head was stuck to the end of a pike and paraded through the streets.

The following August, the Declaration of the Rights of Man and Citizen was officially adopted by the National Assembly. Both Thomas Jefferson and Thomas Paine supported the Declaration, which, like the American Declaration of Independence, outlined the universal rights of all French citizens and men alike (making no mention of women or slaves). This necessarily paved the way for a reevaluation of a number of institutions, including religion, patriarchy, wealth, and slavery. Feudal privileges held by the nobility and clergy were abolished, and all church property was seized. In 1790, religious orders were banned, along with inherited aristocratic titles.

In 1791, Thomas Paine addressed the French Revolution in his book *Rights of Man*, asserting that the people of France had determined that "ignorance, neglect, or contempt of human rights, are the sole causes of public misfortunes and corruptions of Government." He went on to outline the key tenets of the French Declaration of Rights, including freedom and equality among all men, government and law as derived expressly from the will of the people, and political liberty.[38]

Despite the new international language of rights, not everyone agreed with the revolutionary movements. Jeremy Bentham, the father of utilitarianism, rejected any notion of natural rights, asserting in response to the French Declaration of the Rights of Man and Citizen: "Natural rights is simple nonsense: natural and imprescriptable rights, rhetorical nonsense, nonsense upon stilts."[39] Bentham argued against the grounding of human rights upon nature and instead proposed the principle of utility, which prioritized the greatest happiness for the greatest number of people. Bentham created an elaborate scientific calculation that weighed pleasures against pains to determine the best outcome for the largest number of people. Bentham was not necessarily inveighing against the concept of rights, but rather he argued against basing a notion of rights on the belief in a natural, shared human conscience. Bentham's principle of utility separated rights from sentiment and grounded them in mathematical calculations and scientific fact.

Another outspoken opponent of the French Revolution was Edmund Burke. An Irish-born Catholic in England, Burke spent much of his own life as an outsider, facing various prejudices, and was thus sympathetic to the American colonies to a certain extent, which may have been influenced by his friendship with Thomas Paine. He was, nevertheless, deeply disturbed and angered by the French Revolution, which he considered a perversion of "the natural order of things."[40] In *Reflections on the Revolution in France*, Burke writes:

> The occupation of a hair-dresser, or of a working tallow-chandler, cannot be a matter of honor to any person—to say nothing of a number of

Introduction

other more servile employments. Such descriptions of men ought not to suffer oppression from the state, but the state suffers oppression if such as they, either individually or collectively, are permitted to rule. In this, you think you are combating prejudice, but you are at war with nature.[41]

Thus, Burke turned the theory of natural rights on its head by characterizing the act of revolting against social and customary norms as, itself, unnatural. While Burke explained that he did not consider aristocratic or hereditary titles a reasonable system of government, he insisted that the pendulum had swung too far in the opposite direction. "Woe to that country too, that passing into the opposite extreme, considers a low education, a mean, contracted view of things, a sordid mercenary occupation, as a preferable title to command."[42]

Social order, according to Burke, reflected natural order, and those individuals born into a state of "natural subordination" must not only accept their lot in life, but must accept the fact that they will inevitably face injustice and inequality, and must therefore set their sights on the glory of heaven. He went further in positing that human society's survival in general and European civilization in particular was a direct result of government based on tradition and chivalry:

This mixed system of opinion and sentiment had its origin in the ancient chivalry; and the principle, though varied in its appearance by the varying state of human affairs, subsisted and influenced through a long succession of generations, even to the time we live in. If it should ever be totally extinguished, the loss, I fear, will be great. It is this which has given its character to modern Europe.[43]

Thomas Paine responded with outrage and reminded Edmund Burke in *Rights of Man* that in the Glorious Revolution of 1688 the people of England rose up against their government for the sake of protecting their rights. Furthermore, while Burke had argued that the Glorious Revolution of 1689 had established a binding, eternal pact of submission and loyalty between the English citizens and the government, Paine countered that,

There never did, there never can, and there never will exist a parliament, or any other description of men, in any country, possessed of the right or the power of binding and controuling posterity to the "end of time," or of commanding for ever how the world shall be governed, or who shall govern it; and therefore all such clauses, acts or declarations by which the makers of them attempt to do what they have neither the right nor the power to do, nor the power to execute, are in themselves null and void.[44]

Later, in the 19th century, Karl Marx, the architect of communism, would emerge as another vehement critic of human rights. Human rights as declared by the French and the Americans, according to Marx, could never be universal because they operated exclusively in a free-market, capitalistic society. Human rights, according to Marx, are little more than political fictions created by capitalistic governments to urge on production at the expense of the weak and vulnerable. Capitalism essentially encourages competition and production in a free market by promising individuals the right to claim ownership of the products of their labor. Thus, entrepreneurs are driven to compete with their peers, leading to an egoism that separates man from the community and creates "an individual withdrawn into himself, his private interest and his private desires and separated from the community."[45] Marx became one of the most vehement critiques of the preeminence of the individual over community.

SOCIAL MOVEMENTS BASED IN HUMAN RIGHTS
Abolition and the Civil Rights Movement

The American Declaration of Independence and the French Declaration of the Rights of Man and Citizen opened the channels for discourse on a range of subjects concerning human rights and their violations. One such topic was the slave trade. Thomas Jefferson was an outspoken advocate for abolition, despite owning slaves himself. Explaining the apparent contradiction in a letter, Jefferson wrote: "As far as I can judge from the experiments which have been made, to give liberty to, or rather to abandon persons whose habits have been formed in slavery is like abandoning children."[46] The claim that freeing one's slaves was akin to abandoning a child was an argument frequently made to justify slave-ownership in the 18th and 19th centuries. It is also well known today that Jefferson fathered six children with his quadroon slave, Sally Hemings, and later freed several of them; however, they were the only slaves on his Monticello estate to be freed.

Nonetheless, as far as politics was concerned, Jefferson championed abolition of both the slave trade and the institution of slavery as a whole, stating definitively: "Nobody wishes more ardently to see an abolition, not only of the trade, but of the condition of slavery; and certainly, nobody will be more willing to encounter every sacrifice for that object."[47]

Introduction

The Society for the Abolition of the Slave Trade was formed in London in 1787 (a mere two years before the Declaration of the Rights of Man and Citizen). Previously, those calling for the abolition of slavery were largely Quakers from England and America, but the new group consisted of both Quakers and Anglicans. The group pressed for reform by exposing the brutality of the slave trade via pamphlets and petitions, as well as personal accounts of freed slaves. One such account was *The Interesting Narrative of the Life of Olaudah Equiano, or Gustavus Vassa, the African, Written by Himself.* Kidnapped as a child by slave traders in Africa, Equiano miraculously survived the torturous Middle Passage and arrived in Virginia, where he became a slave to a succession of different owners and was renamed several times. During his lifetime, he learned to read and write, became a skilled seaman and trader, and was eventually able to save up enough money to buy his freedom, at which point he left the Americas, never to return. Upon moving to England, Equiano became involved in the abolitionist movement and published his memoir in 1789. He also proved to be a charismatic speaker, and he shocked listeners and readers alike with his tragic account of being separated from his family as a child and enduring the heartaches and tortures of the Middle Passage. He also made a point of noting that he was only one of millions of Africans who had suffered in such a manner, writing:

> I believe there are few events in my life which have not happened to many: it is true the incidents of it are numerous; and, did I consider myself an European, I might say my sufferings were great: but when I compare my lot with that of most of my countrymen, I regard myself as a *particular favourite of Heaven,* and acknowledge the mercies of Providence in every occurrence of my life.[48]

The Slave Trade Act of 1807 abolished the kidnapping and importation of slaves throughout the British Empire. The act did not abolish the institution of slavery, however, and slaves living within the British Empire at the time of the act were not affected. The slave trade was not immediately stamped out, as many British captains continued to kidnap slaves clandestinely, throwing them into the sea if they feared being caught by the Royal Navy. In 1827, the British government declared any participation in the slave trade an act of piracy and thereby punishable by death. The Slavery Abolition Act of 1833 finally eliminated the institution of slavery as a whole throughout the British Empire.

Slavery was abolished throughout the French colonies with the passage of the French constitution in 1795. Napoléon Bonaparte, however, absented the

Declaration of the Rights of Man from the constitution when he reprinted it in 1799, and he dispatched military troops to the French territories to reinstitute slavery. The colonies rose up in mass rebellion, which later resulted in the colony of Saint Domingue's independence and the formation of the republic of Haiti in 1804; however, many of the other rebellions were repressed and the people were re-enslaved. Slavery was again abolished in the French colonies in 1848.

The abolition of slavery swept through much of the world throughout the 19th century, finally reaching the United States in 1865. The abolition of slavery gradually gave way to other rights around the world. In 1870, the Fifteenth Amendment gave African-American men the right to vote in the United States, but it was not a guaranteed right until 1965. In South Africa, blacks were denied the right to vote until the end of apartheid in 1994.

Women's Rights Movement

The rights of women and slaves were closely intertwined topics during the Enlightenment, as both were the most clear "Other" in white, patriarchal society. In 1791, the French playwright and activist Olympe de Gouges wrote the Declaration of the Rights of Woman and the Female Citizen, in which she campaigned for equal rights for women. The Declaration mirrored the Declaration of the Rights of Man and Citizen, with the simple insertion of "woman" and "female citizen" to the phrasing. In the postscript, she cited the newly understood universality of rights:

> Woman, wake up; the tocsin of reason is being heard throughout the whole universe; discover your rights. The powerful empire of nature is no longer surrounded by prejudice, fanaticism, superstition, and lies . . . Enslaved man has multiplied his strength and needs recourse to yours to break his chains. Having become free, he has become unjust to his companion.[49]

Accused of being a counterrevolutionary and an "unnatural being (a 'woman-man')," de Gourges was executed on the guillotine in 1793.

In England, Mary Wollstonecraft published *Vindication of the Rights of Woman* in 1792, in which she argued for more comprehensive education for women. Women's minds, she averred, needed to be developed so that they could transcend their ornamental status and raise intelligent, responsible children, as well as become equal companions to their husbands. Though specifically addressing the rights of women in her era, Wollstonecraft also addressed the theories of such history-making philosophers as John Locke and Jean-Jacques Rousseau, while also evaluating the institution of marriage and women's status in society. Of women's education, she writes:

> It is acknowledged that they spend many of the first years of their lives in acquiring a smattering of accomplishments; meanwhile, strength of body and mind are sacrificed to libertine notions of beauty, to the desire of the establishing of themselves—the only way women can rise in the world—by marriage.[50]

The debate over women's rights waged on for more than a century before any real change took place. In 1848, the first call for women's rights in America was issued in the Declaration of Sentiments, in which Elizabeth Cady Stanton and others outlined the oppressive conditions in which women were living and demanded the right to vote. Frederick Douglass spoke at the first American women's rights convention not long after and linked the women's suffrage movement to that of abolition.[51]

Rights were won gradually over the course of several decades. New Zealand was the first country to grant equal voting rights to all women in 1893, while other countries such as England were granting certain women the right to vote in local elections. In 1918, Great Britain granted voting rights to all women over the age of 30 and men over the age of 21. Women gained the right to vote in the United States in 1920 and in England in 1928. Women's suffrage was not adopted in France until 1944.

Labor Movements

Major changes in agriculture, transportation, and production forever altered the European economy and culture in the 18th and 19th centuries. This shift is now known as the Industrial Revolution, which originated in the United Kingdom and rippled outward to encompass Western Europe and North America. The Industrial Revolution placed new emphasis on machines and moved production away from manual labor. The shift from agriculture to manufacturing led to large-scale immigrations from rural areas into urban centers of industry, and the jobs created by the industrial movement required little if any skill, which made workers easily replaceable. This also made it possible for employers to pay exceedingly low wages while demanding higher productivity, as they could almost always find someone else who would be willing to work harder and longer for less money. Children were particularly vulnerable to exploitation.

In an effort to protect their rights, many workers organized to collectively demand better work conditions, hours, and pay. This often occurred in the form of a strike, during which all of the laborers would stop working and bring production to a standstill. In England, these organized workers became known as trade unions (labor unions, in America), which were banned in 1799. Between 1838 and 1850, the Chartist movement became the first major working-class movement, creating a charter of reforms that was signed by more than 3 million people, but was rejected by Parliament in 1842. The Chartist movement organized a strike the same year that stopped cotton production throughout Great Britain. In the United States, men and women began organizing their labor in the late 18th century, but the labor movement did not come to prominence until after the Civil War (1861–65). The National Labor Union, founded in 1866, was the first national labor federation in the United States, but it was dissolved in 1873. A number of other unions developed over the years, including the American Federation of Labor in 1881, as well as specific trade unions and women's unions. In 1965, worker's rights were addressed in the Civil Rights movement, leading to legal reform that banned discriminatory hiring practices and pay scales.

Today, increasing globalization has posed new challenges to labor movements and has led to the development of international labor unions.

National Independence Movements

At many points throughout history, a people's demand for greater rights and freedoms has not been met, and it becomes clear that freedom, equality, and self-fulfillment will not be attainable under their current government. In some cases, this has led an entire people, or at least a large majority, to revolt and demand independence from the governing body.

Human rights movements often reflect the struggles of minority groups against majority groups and political structures, and this becomes particularly complicated when the minority group is a country that has been colonized by a foreign government for the exploitation of its natural resources and people. By virtue of the fact that their homeland was subsumed and colonized by a foreign government, a colonized people's relationship with their colonizer is fundamentally based on trampled rights and an imbalance of power, leading many to demand secession and independence from the occupying power. Such was the case for the early Americans when it became clear to them that the British government did not see the American colonies as a land inhabited by its own people, but as a resource to be exploited (the obvious complication being the fact that the early Americans had very recently colonized land formerly inhabited by Native American Indians). Many countries have experienced national independence movements, which have often arisen out of discussions of rights.

Introduction

In 2010, the Democratic Republic of the Congo (former Zaire) celebrated the 50th anniversary of its independence. At the forefront of the 1960 Congolese independence movement was Patrice Lumumba, who resented the authoritarianism of the Catholic and Protestant missionaries in the Congo. He dedicated himself to the vision of an emancipated, multiethnic Congo, and he was profoundly influenced by the relationships he developed with such leading anticolonial activists as the Caribbean writer and philosopher Frantz Fanon, the Pan-Africanist and Ghanaian leader Kwame Nhkruma, and the Pan-Arab nationalist Gamal Abdel Nasser. Lumumba's later administration as Congo's first democratically elected prime minister was defined by his commitment to national and Pan-African unity, as well as national economic independence.[52]

Other independence movements have arisen in a similar fashion. Prior to its independence, Chechnya had suffered for centuries under oppressive Russian occupation. Under Joseph Stalin's regime, the entire Chechen population was uprooted and exiled from Chechnya. Poverty, exploitation, and discrimination that made it virtually impossible for the average Chechen citizen to advance in a career all combined to lead to nationwide demand for independence. With the impending fall of the Soviet Union in 1991, the Chechen independence movement was formed under the leadership of the ex–Soviet Union Air Force general Dzhokar Dudaev. Dudaev, himself, had been exiled from Chechnya with his family as a child and did not see his homeland for the first time until he was 13 years old.

While national independence movements often chronicle the uprising of an oppressed group and the successful overthrow of its oppressor, it would be a mistake to simplify or romanticize such events as an underdog success story. While independence movements are often sparked by a demand for the respect and protection of human rights, they continue to face human rights challenges of their own following the overthrow of their occupying governments. Their stories do not end with their successful uprising, and many continue to struggle with human rights issues today.

INTERNATIONAL LAW

International law has always existed in one form or another, as nation-states, kingdoms, and oter communities have always had to deal with neighbors, invaders, and expanding empires. However, today the increasing ease of global communications and transportation has put new pressure on a standardization of international definitions of human rights while balancing complex and often contradictory international laws.

HUMAN RIGHTS

Unlike domestic national laws, which are based on statutes and cases, international law can be difficult to grasp concretely, as there is no one governing body that creates the laws. Rather, international law relies on treaties, which are contracts between two or more states, as well as customary practices of states, certain fundamental legal principles, and the development of legal precedent. In other words, international law relies on the cooperation of states and their agreement that the rules of international law are legally binding, otherwise the laws are ineffectual.

Two world wars in the first half of the 20th century made the development of international law an urgent necessity. Following World War I (1914–18), the League of Nations was created in 1919 under the Treaty of Versailles to "promote international cooperation and to achieve peace and security."[53] The League of Nations was unable to prevent World War II (1939–45), and in 1945, the United Nations was established with the signing and ratification of the UN Charter by the majority of the 51 member states.

Regional supranational bodies have organized to address the issues unique to certain areas and nation-communities. Such bodies include the European Union, the East African Community, the Union of South American Nations, and the Andean Community of Nations.

International courts have also been established to enforce and standardize international law. The 1950 European Convention on Human Rights led to the 1959 creation of the European Court of Human Rights, which allows individuals or member states to file applications of human rights violations against other member states.

In 2002, the International Criminal Court (ICC) was created to prosecute individuals for war crimes and crimes against humanity. As of 2010, the ICC has opened investigations into northern Uganda, the Democratic Republic of the Congo, Darfur, the Central African Republic, and the Republic of Kenya. Fourteen people have been indicted thus far. The court has a membership of 111 states, and an additional 37 states have signed the Rome Statute (on which the ICC is based), but have not yet ratified it. To date, the United States has signed, but not ratified the treaty. The establishment of the ICC is not necessarily a new concept altogether, but arises from a tradition of establishing ad hoc post-conflict tribunals to prosecute war crimes.

Organizations of activists, legal scholars, journalists, and volunteers have emerged in support of international human rights. Some of the largest organizations today were developed in response to particular human rights situations. Human Rights Watch was originally established as Helsinki Watch in 1978 to track and record the Soviet Union's compliance with the Helsinki Accords, a set of terms ratified at the Helsinki Conference held in Helsinki,

Finland, from July 30 to August 1, 1975. Helsinki Watch expanded and became Human Rights Watch in 1988, and today it functions by researching and publicizing human rights violations around the world under the belief that spotlighting the countries and groups that perpetrate such abuses will put pressure on them to compensate victims and avoid future abuses. Amnesty International (AI) is another major organization and is considered the oldest in the field of international human rights. Founded in London in 1961, Amnesty International's stated mission is to research and organize action in response to human rights violations, prevent future violations, and ensure justice for victims. In 1977, AI was awarded the Nobel Peace Prize for its campaign against torture. In addition to courts, other channels for enforcing human rights exist. Individual states can enforce human rights through their foreign policies, such as through sanctions; international organizations can pressure violators by publicizing bad practices, launching investigations, and organizing joint sanctions against offenders; and individual states can adopt international human rights standards and adjust their domestic laws accordingly, as a number of central European countries have done in response to the Violence Against Women agreement.

The Universal Declaration of Human Rights, 1948

In 1941, in the midst of World War II, the U.S. president Franklin D. Roosevelt delivered his State of the Union Address, in which he outlined four essential freedoms to which all human beings are entitled: freedom of speech, freedom of assembly, freedom from fear, and freedom from want. Roosevelt's "Four Freedoms" were adopted by the United Allies (the countries that had allied against the Axis powers of Germany, Japan, and Italy). Following World War II and the horrors of Nazi Germany, which was, by far, the most vivid human rights catastrophe in modern history, the United Nations General Assembly opted to expand on the Four Freedoms. In 1948, the Canadian John Peters Humphrey was appointed director of the newly created Division of Human Rights within the United Nations Secretariat, and charged with the responsibility of drafting a declaration of universal, international human rights. Authors of the draft included Eleanor Roosevelt of the United States, who was also chairman of the committee and the wife of the late U.S. president Franklin D. Roosevelt; the French law professor and jurist René Cassin; the Chinese professor and playwright Peng-chu (P. C.) Chan; and the Lebanese philosopher and diplomat Charles Malik; among others.

The United Nations Charter had been the first attempt to establish universal rights regardless of sex, race, or religion, but a fully fleshed universal declaration was needed to specify and define individual rights. On

December 10, 1948, the United Nations officially adopted and proclaimed the Universal Declaration of Human Rights, which begins: "Whereas recognition of the inherent dignity and of the equal and inalienable rights of all members of the human family is the foundation of freedom, justice, and peace in the world. . ." The first article of the document states unwaveringly, "All human beings are born free and equal in dignity and rights. They are endowed with reason and conscience and should act towards one another in a spirit of brotherhood."[54] Thus the UN Declaration became the first document in history to acknowledge universal human rights with the direct aim of uniting all countries in the drive toward world peace and justice. It is important to note, however, that the declaration did not establish any legal obligations for the countries that signed.

The Declaration contains 30 articles, and René Cassin described the structure of the document as that of the portico of a Greek temple. The seven clauses of the preamble are the steps that lead to the entrance of the temple; the first two articles, which put forth the principles of dignity, liberty, equality, and brotherhood, serve as the foundation for four columns of rights: rights of individuals, rights of individuals in relation to others, spiritual, public, and political rights, and economic, social, and cultural rights. The pediment of the portico consists of the last three articles, which outline the contexts of rights in terms of limits, duties, and the social and political order in which the rights are to be placed.[55]

The actual drafting and adoption of the Declaration was no easy feat. The drafters spent long, grueling hours debating the arrangement and wording of every article, and, as Eleanor Roosevelt later revealed in her biography:

> Early in the meetings of the commission we discovered that while it would be possible to reach some kind of agreement on the Declaration, we were going to be in for a great deal of controversy with the Russian representatives, particularly Dr. Pavlov, who attempted at every opportunity to write a bit of Communist philosophy into the document.[56]

Once again, the notion of human rights came into direct conflict with the tenets of communism. Communist countries emphasized the role of the government in establishing economic and social rights and claimed that political and civic rights were meaningless when citizens did not have adequate food, health care, employment, social insurance, and education. The United States also favored the inclusion of economic and social rights, but did not agree that the government had an obligation to assure these rights. While the UN General Assembly adopted the Declaration by a vote of 48 in favor and 0 against, the five Soviet Bloc states abstained, along with Saudi Arabia, Yugoslavia, and the

Introduction

Union of South Africa. It would not be the last time that countries would disagree over the definition and implementation of human rights.

Vienna World Conference on Human Rights, 1993

Following the fall of the Soviet Union and the end of the cold war, 171 nations and 800 NGOs (nongovernmental organizations) convened in Vienna, Austria, in June 1993 for the Vienna World Conference on Human Rights. The aim of the conference was to reevaluate the state of human rights around the world and resolve disparities in different nations' approaches to human rights. The first world conference on human rights was held in Tehran (Teheran), Iran, in 1968, but the Vienna World Conference saw the largest turnout of any event on human rights previously.

Because the conference was designed to be inclusive and facilitate international discussion, one of the rules of the conference specified that no individual countries could be named when discussing human rights violations. This was particularly problematic with regard to the countries with ongoing human rights abuses, such as China, as well as those involved in armed conflict where human rights abuses were being perpetrated, such as Bosnia and Liberia.

What made the Vienna Conference and the resulting Vienna Declaration and Programme of Action unique was its use as a means of inaugurating a new era of human rights standardization and protection. Prior to the fall of the Soviet Union, human rights had been used as rhetorical fodder for the cold war, and differing notions of human rights were used to wage an ideological battle. The end of the cold war presented an opportunity to include former Soviet states in the process of reaffirming and modernizing the Universal Declaration of Human Rights.[57]

Bangkok Declaration, 1993

In March 1993, the representatives of several Asian countries, including Iran, Mongolia, China, Singapore, Myanmar, Malaysia, Korea, and Indonesia, among others, met to draft a unified declaration on human rights that would represent all Asian governments at the Vienna World Conference. The meeting resulted in the Bangkok Declaration, in which the governments of Asia acknowledged a universal element of human rights, but disputed the universal application of human rights. Individual governments, the document claimed, should be able to interpret human rights as fits their culture and political system. Wong Kan Seng, the Singaporean minister of foreign affairs, gave a speech titled "The Real World of Human Rights," in which he argued that "the international consensus on human rights is still fragile," and "the extent and exercise of rights . . . varies greatly from one culture or political community to another."[58] Several articles in the Bangkok Declaration caused controversy at the conference, including one that states the importance of "respect for national sovereignty and territorial integrity as well as non-interference in the internal affairs of States, and the non-use of human rights as an instrument of political pressure." Another article outlined the Asian states' agreement that "while human rights are universal in nature, they must be considered in the context of a dynamic and evolving process of international norm-setting, bearing in mind the significance of national and regional particularities and various historical, cultural, and religious backgrounds."[59] Ultimately, the document's fundamental argument is that the interpretation, exercise, and protection of human rights should be left to individual countries. Wong Kan Seng of Singapore saw a problem in a universal consensus of what and who should be considered in a discussion of human rights, insisting that homosexuality and pornography, for example, were not entitled to inclusion in the human rights discussion.[60] To this, U.S. secretary of state Warren Christopher responded, "We cannot let cultural relativism become the last refuge of oppression."[61]

Nonetheless, considering the use of human rights rhetoric in war, as well as the fact that the basis of the Vienna Conference was to take advantage of the fall of the Soviet Union to standardize human rights, the Bangkok Declaration presented a unique perspective on this standardization process. Who sets the standard? While the Vienna Conference, as well as the Universal Declaration of Human Rights, emphasized the fact that the standard is founded upon international agreement, this is clearly undermined if nearly one half of the participating member states of the conference do not agree to the standard. The quandary becomes one of state sovereignty and cultural relativism versus the inherent and self-evident value of human rights. Allowing states the right to interpret and enforce human rights as they see fit naturally destabilizes the very definition of human rights. They are rights to which every human being is entitled, not rights that apply only to citizens, Westerners, adults, or men. It should be noted, however, that the situation of human rights is not static, and discussions in international relations can and have produced a number of positive developments in human rights around the world.

KEY ISSUES
Innate Human Rights versus Cultural Relativism

Cultural relativism, the notion that an individual's actions cannot be judged based on a universal standard, but must be understood in terms of that person's cultural context, is one of the key obstacles in the way of enforcing universal human rights, and human rights disputes have frequently centered upon what is considered a human right and what is culturally acceptable. Some countries at the Vienna World Conference, such as those who participated in the drafting of the Bangkok Declaration, have openly stated a refusal to be subsumed within what they consider to be Western cultural values. Islamic countries that base their national laws on the teachings of the Quran, for example, frequently dispute gay rights and certain women's rights on the grounds that they are not in accordance with the Quran.

Cultural relativists who participate in scholarly discourse on human rights argue that imposing the norms established in the Universal Declaration of Human Rights is an expression of "moral chauvinism and ethnocentric bias."[62]

Indeed, is it fair to hold all nations to the same standard? Are indigenous cultures that practice painful rites of passage in violation of human rights? Should Third World nations that are struggling under massive debt and disease be required to provide their citizens with a certain amount of paid vacation, as is outlined in the Universal Declaration of Human Rights? Should a country that espouses a conservative religious perspective be required to provide access to birth control and abortion for its female citizens, or uphold gay rights? While some cultural relativists might argue that imposing universal human rights on Third World and other nations belies a "racist assumption of fundamental Western superiority and Oriental inferiority," the scholar Anne Elizabeth Mayer argues the opposite, stating that enforcing universal human rights in such countries rests "on the premise that peoples in the West and the East share a common humanity, which means that they are equally deserving of rights and freedoms."[63] To do otherwise, Mayer asserts, would be to assume that the rights enjoyed in the West are fundamentally irrelevant to other countries and we do not, therefore, share a common humanity.

It must be understood, however, that states that refuse to acknowledge certain rights as human rights are not arguing for cultural relativism. Rather, they are arguing for their conceptualizations of human rights, based on their cultural perspectives (what is sometimes referred to as "soft relativism."). This leads to a conflict of rights: Should the world respect those states' religious and cultural values, or should those values be undermined to protect minority groups within those states? Some international relations scholars believe that allowing a group to decide on its own understandings of a human rights principle is a less paternalistic and more productive means of promoting global human rights.

Conflicting Rights

Human rights discussions are unavoidably fraught with complications arising from conflicting rights. How does one protect certain rights when doing so violates the rights of someone else? This often occurs where religious and cultural values are concerned, and historically this has occurred when civil and political rights have conflicted with economic and social rights. The general consensus among North American and European governments and human rights groups that gays and lesbians are entitled to live free from discrimination comes into direct conflict with governments based on religious and cultural beliefs that regard homosexuality as a sin or taboo. This type of conflict is not limited to international discussions of human rights, but frequently occurs within individual countries as well. In 2010, France became the subject of heated rights debates when the French government banned the traditional head coverings worn by Muslim women. The French government explained that the ban was put in place in an effort to eliminate practices that undermine the equality between men and women, as well as to maintain a secularist republic. Those opposed to the ban, however, argue that it is a violation of religious freedom.

Other rights have similarly come into conflict throughout history. During the era of American slavery, discussions of how to address runaway slaves frequently centered upon the conflict between the slave's right to freedom (in the North) versus the slaveholder's right to his/her property (in the South). A war was necessary to resolve the conflict and establish the African-American slave's human right to freedom, which, once established, nullified the slaveholder's right to own slaves.

Who Creates Rights

Who arbitrates rights discussions? How are rights conflicts to be resolved when two individuals or two groups have separate views on the matter? In national rights conflicts, courts, such as the U.S. Supreme Court, act as the bodies that create or recognizes rights. In the case of international law, there is no single body that creates laws. Laws must, instead, be agreed upon by the involved parties. The protection of human rights relies on cooperation. But how are rights to be discussed when cooperation is not or cannot be achieved?

The American Civil War stands as a distinct example of what can happen when two groups are so deeply divided and equally passionate about an issue that the conflict cannot be arbitrated. What, then, are human rights? Are they based on the will of the majority? Are they valid only insofar as the larger, stronger group holds them to be true? Or are they inherently recognizable in human nature? These questions are not new; they have framed the human rights discussion for centuries.

How to Enforce Rights

While discussions about what constitutes human rights and whether or not they are universally valid are difficult enough to resolve, an equally complex challenge arises in the task of enforcing those rights. Many of the world's countries are struggling with crippling poverty and simply do not have the means to support an infrastructure that could enforce rights, such as law enforcement, public lawyers, and so on. In many cases, as Gary Haugen, CEO of International Justice Mission, notes, a country's legal system was originally designed by colonial powers to support the privileges of the elite, not the rights of the poor. As it often happens in the post-colonial era, that legal system is not dissolved; it is merely appropriated by the new governing elite.[64] Haugen argues that where governments are open to reform, international agencies should step in to provide assistance through collaborative casework, a model in which international human rights lawyers and law enforcement professionals work with local authorities to protect the rights of the people in the community.

Governments that are not open to reform, however, remain a challenge, which is where nongovernmental organizations (NGOs) such as Human Rights Watch and Amnesty International get involved. NGOs conduct independent research, publicize challenges facing human rights around the world, and highlight ways that others can help effect change, such as writing letters to government leaders, signing petitions, or donating money. Calling attention to human rights violations and mobilizing activists puts pressure on governments to cooperate with international efforts to protect human rights.

CONCLUSION

The human rights debate is far from resolved, and some of the governments that participate in human rights discussions are the very governments that are sanctioning ongoing human rights violations. Shirin Ebadi, an Iranian human rights lawyer who was awarded the Nobel Peace Prize in 2003, has outlined several obstacles that she sees as standing in the way of global progress on human rights, including cultural relativism, the poor performance and idealism of the UN Council on Human Rights, the misuse of the concept of human rights to further political agendas, and the lack of focus on economic rights.[65] The last point is of particular interest, as human rights discussions tend to be largely focused on civil and political rights. Ebadi believes that the lack of attention on economy rights is partly responsible for the growing rates of poverty around the world.

Additionally, some human rights discussions have included the question of group rights, such as rights to engage in cultural practices and traditions as well as speak an indigenous language.

Despite the overwhelming nature of human rights and the multitude of questions that accompany them, progress is possible and measurable. Statistical evidence has shown that standardizing the definition and enforcement of rights can lead to worldwide reform. This is most clearly visible in specific areas of human rights. In 2009, United Nations Children's Fund (UNICEF) celebrated the 20th anniversary of the Convention on the Rights of the Child, and research reveals that in the 20 years since the Convention, an unprecedented number of countries around the world have established special institutions and measures to promote children's rights, implemented legislation to promote the interests of children, made efforts to combat violence against children, and are working to protect forgotten or invisible children.[66] Measurable progress is what human rights activists, NGOs, and lawmakers are looking for, and while challenges will continue to emerge in all areas of human rights, measurable data and results-oriented research will make it possible to address and resolve those issues so that all people can enjoy their human rights.

[1] John Locke. *The Second Treatise of Government.* New York: Barnes & Noble, 2004, p. 3.

[2] ———. *Two Treatises of Government.* London: Whitmore and Fenn, 1821, p. 259.

[3] Lynn Hunt. *Inventing Human Rights.* New York: W.W. Norton, 2007, p. 216.

[4] Victor H. Matthews. *Old Testament Parallels: Laws and Stories from the Ancient Near East.* Mahwah, N.J.: Paulist Press, 1991, pp. 97–98.

[5] ———. *Old Testament Parallels: Laws and Stories from the Ancient Near East.* Mahwah, N.J.: Paulist Press, 1991, pp. 97–100.

[6] David Levinson. *Encyclopedia of Crime and Punishment.* Thousand Oaks, Calif.: Sage Publications, 2002, p. 22.

[7] *The Avalon Project.* "The Code of Hammurabi." L. W. King. Yale School of Law (2008). Available online. URL: http://avalon.law.yale.edu/ancient/hamframe.asp. Accessed on September 5, 2009.

[8] Jon E. Lewis. *A Documentary History of Human Rights: A Record of the Events, Documents and Speeches That Shaped Our World.* New York: Carroll and Graff, 2003, p. 7.

[9] Micheline R. Ishay. *The History of Human Rights: From Ancient Times to the Globalization Era.* Berkeley: University of California Press, 2004, p. 19.

[10] A. Guillaume. "'Constitution' of Medina." *The Life of Muhammad.* Available online. URL: http://www.constitution.org/cons/medina/con_medina.htm. Accessed September 23, 2009.

Introduction

[11] Plato. *Republic.* Indianapolis: Hackett, 2004, pp. 38–317.

[12] Gary Herbert. *A Philosophical History of Rights.* New Brunswick, N.J.: Transaction Publishers, 2002, p. 29.

[13] Aristotle. *Politics.* Charleston: BiblioBazaar, 2006, pp. 28–29.

[14] Cicero. *Cicero: Selected Works.* New York: Penguin Group, 1960, p. 7.

[15] Douay-Rheims Bible, Latin Vulgate Bible. *Epistle of Saint Paul to the Galatians,* Galatians 3:28. Available online. URL: http://www.drbo.org/cgi-bin/d?b=drb&bk=55&ch=3&l=28&f=s#x. Accessed on September 6, 2009.

[16] Richard A. Bauman. *Human Rights in Ancient Rome.* New York: Routledge, 2000, pp. 2–23.

[17] Gerald Murphy. "The Magna Carta (The Great Charter)." Available online. URL: http://www.constitution.org/eng/magnacar.htm. Accessed on September 24, 2009.

[18] Jack Donnelly. *Universal Human Rights in Theory and Practice.* Ithaca, N.Y.: Cornell University, 2003, p. 76.

[19] Gary Herbert. *A Philosophical History of Rights.* New Brunswick, N.J.: Transaction Publishers, 2002, p. 61.

[20] Michael A. Mullett. *Martin Luther.* New York: Routledge, 2004, p. 149.

[21] John Locke. *Two Treatises of Government.* London: Whitmore and Fenn, 1821, p. 189.

[22] ———. *Two Treatises of Government,* p. 192.

[23] ———. *Two Treatises of Government,* p. 189.

[24] ———. *Two Treatises of Government,* p. 188.

[25] Jean-Jacques Rousseau. *Philosophy and Theology: Rousseau's Social Contract.* New York: E.P. Dutton, 1913, p. 5

[26] ———. *Philosophy and Theology: Rousseau's Social Contract.* New York: E.P. Dutton, 1913, p. 214.

[27] Thomas Paine. *Common Sense.* Forgotten Books (2008), p. 1. Available online. URL: http://books.google.com/books/p/pub-4297897631756504?id=wVt7VxvFyegC&pg=PP1&dq=thomas+paine&ei=tU6mSuy2G5iwMrW36YII#v=onepage&q=&f=false. Accessed on September 8, 2009.

[28] ———. *Common Sense.* Available online. URL: http://www.ushistory.org/paine/commonsense/sense2.htm. Accessed on September 8, 2009.

[29] ———. *Common Sense.* Available online. URL: http://www.ushistory.org/paine/commonsense/sense2.htm. Accessed on September 8, 2009.

[30] A. J. Ayer. *Thomas Paine.* Chicago: University of Chicago Press, 1988, pp. 36–37.

[31] Thomas Paine. *Common Sense.* Forgotten Books (2008), p. 1. Available online. URL: http://books.google.com/books/p/pub-4297897631756504?id=wVt7VxvFyegC&pg=PP1&dq=thomas+paine&ei=tU6mSuy2G5iwMrW36YII#v=onepage&q=&f=false. Accessed on September 10, 2009.

[32] George Mason. *Virginia Declaration of Rights.* Avalon Project. Available online. URL: http://avalon.law.yale.edu/18th_century/virginia.asp. Accessed on September 9, 2009.

[33] ———. *Virginia Declaration of Rights*. Avalon Project. Available online. URL: http://avalon.law.yale.edu/18th_century/virginia.asp. Accessed on September 9, 2009.

[34] Lynn Hunt. *Inventing Human Rights*. New York: W.W. Norton & Company, 2007, p. 20.

[35] Thomas Jefferson. "Jefferson's 'Original Rough Draught' of the Declaration of Independence." *The Papers of Thomas Jefferson*. Available online. URL: http://www.princeton.edu/~tjpapers/declaration/declaration.html. Accessed on September 13, 2009.

[36] Lynn Hunt. *Inventing Human Rights*. New York: W.W. Norton, 2007, p. 26.

[37] ———. *Inventing Human Rights*, p. 127.

[38] Thomas Paine. *Rights of Man*. Mineola: Dover, 1999, pp. 65–66.

[39] Lynn Hunt. *Inventing Human Rights*. New York: W.W. Norton, 2007, p. 125.

[40] Edmund Burke. *Reflections on the Revolution in France*. London: J. Dodsley, 1790, p. 72.

[41] ———. *Reflections on the Revolution in France*, pp. 72–73.

[42] ———. *Reflections on the Revolution in France*, p. 74.

[43] ———. *Reflections on the Revolution in France*, p. 113.

[44] Thomas Paine. *Rights of Man*. London: Watts, 1909, p. 10.

[45] Jack Mahoney. *The Challenge of Human Rights: Origins, Development, and Significance*. Malden, U.K.: Blackwell, 2007, p. 36.

[46] Eyler Robert Coates, Sr. "Thomas Jefferson on Politics & Government: Race." Available online. URL: http://etext.virginia.edu/jefferson/quotations/jeff1290.htm. Accessed on September 19, 2009.

[47] ———. "Thomas Jefferson on Politics & Government: Race." Available online. URL: http://etext.virginia.edu/jefferson/quotations/jeff1290.htm. Accessed on September 19, 2009.

[48] Olaudah Equiano. *The Interesting Narrative of the Life of Olaudah Equiano, or Gustavus Vassa, the African, Written by Himself*. Whitefish: Kessinger Publishing, 2004, p. 3.

[49] Olympe de Gouges. "Declaration of the Rights of Woman and Female Citizen, 1791." Available online. URL: http://www.library.csi.cuny.edu/dept/americanstudies/lavender/decwom2.html. Accessed on September 20, 2009.

[50] Mary Wollstonecraft. *A Vindication of the Rights of Woman*. London: J. Johnson, 1796, p. 8.

[51] National Women's History Project. "Living the Legacy: Women's Rights Movement 1848–1998" (1997–2002). Available online. URL: http://www.legacy98.org/move-hist.html.

[52] Georges Nzongola-Ntalaja. *The Congo from Leopold to Kabila: A People's History*. New York: St. Martin's Press, 2002, p. 84.

[53] UN.org. "History of the UN" (2000). Available online. URL: http://www.un.org/aboutun/history.htm. Accessed July 1, 2010.

[54] United Nations General Assembly. "The Universal Declaration of Human Rights" (12/10/48). Available online. URL: http://www.un.org/en/documents/udhr/. Accessed on September 24, 2009.

[55] Mary Ann Glendon. "The Rule of Law in the Universal Declaration of Human Rights." *Northwestern University Journal of International Human Rights* 2 (April 2004). Available

online. URL: http://www.law.northwestern.edu/journals/jihr/v2/5/. Accessed on September 24, 2009.

[56] Jack Mahoney. *The Challenge of Human Rights: Origins, Development, and Significance.* Malden, U.K.: Blackwell, 2007, p. 48.

[57] ———. *The Challenge of Human Rights: Origin, Development, and Significance,* p. 57.

[58] Eva Brems. *Human Rights: Universality and Diversity.* The Hague: Kluwer Law International, 2001, pp. 59–60.

[59] Ferdinand de Varennes. *Asia-Pacific Human Rights Documents and Resources, Volume I.* The Hague: Martinus Nijhoff, 1998, pp. 88–89.

[60] ———. *Human Rights: Universality and Diversity.* The Hague: Kluwer Law International, 2001, p. 60.

[61] Elaine Sciolino. "U.S. Rejects Notion That Human Rights Vary with Culture." *New York Times* (6/15/93). Available online. URL: http://www.nytimes.com/1993/06/15/world/us-rejects-notion-that-human-rights-vary-with-culture.html.

[62] Ann Elizabeth Mayer. *Islam and Human Rights: Tradition and Politics.* Boulder, Colo.: Westview Press, 1991, p. 9.

[63] ———. *Islam and Human Rights: Tradition and Politics,* 1991, p. 9.

[64] Gary Haugen, and Victor Boutros. "And Justice for All: Enforcing Human Rights for the World's Poor." ForeignAffairs.com. (June 2010). Available online. URL: http://www.foreignaffairs.com/articles/66210/gary-haugen-and-victor-boutros/and-justice-for-all. Accessed on July 1, 2010.

[65] Shirin Ebadi. "Obstacles to the Progress of Human Rights in the World." OpenDemocracy (5/14/09). Available online. URL: http://www.opendemocracy.net/article/email/obstacles-to-the-progress-of-human-rights-in-the-world. Accessed on July 1, 2010.

[66] UNICEF. "Convention on the Rights of the Child: What We Have Achieved" (2009). Available online. URL: http://www.unicef.org/crc/index_30223.html. Accessed July 1, 2010.

2

Focus on the United States

The history of human rights in the United States reveals an evolution of social thought and a growing awareness among its people of their place in the global human family. As various events that challenged and affirmed human rights unfolded in the United States, the frame of reference broadened from one centered on a European cultural perspective to one that becomes increasingly inclusive of other points of view. The French philosopher Jacques Derrida refers to this process as a "decentering," or "the moment when European culture . . . had been dislocated, driven from its locus and forced to stop considering itself as the culture of reference."[1] Frame of reference is an important consideration when studying the history and development of human rights: Who is writing the history? Who is guiding the discussion of human rights? These are two questions the researcher must consider. The debates about what a right is and who is entitled to rights will never really end, and as the people of the United States continue to probe and evaluate rights and minority groups, more and more formerly disenfranchised groups will be included in the human family and their rights will be clarified.

HISTORY OF HUMAN RIGHTS IN THE UNITED STATES

Exploration and Colonization: Sixteenth to Eighteenth Centuries

When Christopher Columbus and his crew sailed into the Bahaman Islands on October 12, 1492, they were greeted by a group of Arawak, who were eager to trade and establish a dialogue with the newcomers. The Arawak called the island Guanahani, but Columbus renamed it San Salvador.[2] Columbus's first impression of these people set the stage for the next several hundred years of American colonization, as he wrote in his log: "They do not bear arms, and do not know them . . . They have no iron. Their spears are made of cane . . . They would make fine servants . . . With fifty men we could subjugate them all and make them do whatever we want."[3]

Columbus, like other seafaring European explorers of his time, was not looking to establish a dialogue; he was looking for gold and spices. Convinced that the inhabitants were not being forthcoming as to where gold was, he took several as prisoners on board the ship. The language of his log and other historical documents is ambiguous as to whether or not he took the Arawak by force. Columbus writes, "I endeavored to procure them . . ."[4] while another historical account on the Bahamian History Online Web site writes, "with the help of a few natives and the promise of gold and spices on bigger islands they sailed on to discover Cuba and Haiti."[5] At later points in Columbus's narrative, however, it becomes clear that the Arawak were kept on board against their wills. Columbus writes, "a large canoe being near the caravel Nina, one of the San Salvador natives leaped overboard and swam to her; (another had made his escape the night before) the canoe being reached by the fugitive, the natives rowed for land too swiftly to be overtaken . . . some of my men went ashore in pursuit of them."[6] Ultimately, Columbus did not question the ethics of forcibly taking people on board his ship as prisoners. His purpose from the beginning was to "collect" some of the local people to bring back to Spain, writing to the king and queen, "I intend at my return to carry home six of them to your Highness."[7]

As Columbus alighted on new shores, he renamed them in honor of the king and queen of Spain and took hostages as he went, with no apparent concern for the lives and families of those individuals.

In the years to follow, Spain colonized the islands of Cuba and Hispaniola (the island that is now Haiti and the Dominican Republic), enslaving the native population and enforcing cruel punishments for those who did not comply with colonial rule. A young priest, Bartolomé de Las Casas, documented the conquest of Cuba, writing of his arrival to the islands in 1508, "there were 60,000 people living on this island, including the Indians; so that from 1494 to 1508, over three million people had perished from war, slavery, and the mines."[8]

BRITISH COLONIES

When the colonial settlers took up residence in the new world in the early 17th century, they, too, had to grapple with an already established native population. It so happened that Jamestown, founded in 1607 in Virginia, was built on land that belonged to a tribe of Algonquin, led by Chief Powhatan. Powhatan, who had already seen the devastation, disease, and massacre that had resulted from previous European settlement attempts, nevertheless allowed the settlement on his land, possibly under the belief that the British colonials would fail and die as so many others before them had. Indeed, the settlement was shaky at best. Having landed too late to plant crops, in addition to establishing their site on a swamp, the future of the settlement was not promising. But the bounty of the New World was too glorious to abandon, and the settlers persisted. Sir Walter Cope wrote of Virginia in 1607, "in steed of mylke we fynde pearl. & golde in steed of honye."[9] Relations between the English and the Algonquin quickly deteriorated. Being well versed in dealing with the uprisings against British control in Ireland, Captain John Smith and Ralph Lane saw intimidation and threat as the most effective way to discipline the Indian tribes into acquiescence. One particularly terrorizing way of doing this was to kidnap tribal children and hold them hostage whenever the British approached a village.[10]

In the winter of 1610, otherwise known as the Starving Time, many British settlers deserted the settlement and beseeched Powhatan for food and shelter. Colonial governors considered such an act to be highly offensive to Christian civility, and the punishments for desertion to the Indian enemy were severe, and even included death by hanging, shooting, and breaking upon the wheel. When the governor Thomas West De la Warr demanded that Powhatan return the deserters, Powhatan refused, and war ensued. The military campaign was headed by George Percy, who described falling upon the Indian village and putting "some fiftene or sixtene to Sworde and Almost all the reste to flyghte." After burning the crops and houses, the English settlers captured the "Quene and her children" and took them out on boats, where they killed the children by "throweinge them overboard [and] shoteinge owtt their Braynes in the water." While Percy's chief lieutenant suggested that they burn the queen alive, Percy had her stabbed to death instead.[11]

Thus began the war between the British colonials and Powhatan's tribe, which finally came to a standstill when the settlers captured Powhatan's daughter, Matoaka (otherwise known as Pocahontas), and Powhatan ordered a truce.

Similar violence between the English settlers and the American Indians occurred elsewhere in the colonies, particularly as the British numbers increased. Tensions came to a head in 1675 with the uprising known as King Philip's War, which lasted no more than a year, but proved to be one of the costliest and deadliest wars in American history.

Much of the conflict between the English settlers and the Indians can be traced back to the ultimate aim of the European settlers: capital. Being in direct competition with the Native Americans for land, the European settlers had to devise a rationale for forcing the Natives off their land and claiming it for themselves. To this end, John Winthrop, governor of the Massachusetts Bay Colony, argued that God explicitly commanded Adam and Eve to subdue the land. The earth, according to Winthrop, was God's garden and it was man's responsibility to tend to it. The Native inhabitants had not subdued the land, meaning they had not cleared it. Thus, in answer to those who objected to the forcible seizure of land by the English, Winthrop wrote:

> That land which lies comon, & hath beene replenished or subdued, is free to any that possesse & improve it: ffor God hath given to the sonnes of men a double right to the earth; theire is a naturall right, & a civill right . . . As for the Natives in New England, they inclose noe Land, neither have any setled habitation, nor any tame Cattle to improve the Land by, & soe have noe other but a Naturall Right to those Countries. Soe if we leave them sufficient for their use, we may lawfully take the rest, there being more than enough for them & us.[12]

The rights of the Native Americans were weighed against the rights of the colonies and, viewing the situation from their own frame of reference, the English settlers naturally decided in their own favor.

SLAVERY

The right to subdue the land not only justified the English settlers' seizure of the land from the American Indians but also justified the kidnapping and enslavement of Africans for the purpose of working and tending the land. The first African slaves were brought to New England in 1619, although African enslavement had been in existence for more than 100 years prior. Approximately 1 million Africans had already been shipped to South America and the Caribbean.[13]

The Transatlantic Slave Trade was a three-part journey that began in Europe, where a ship was packed with trade goods and sailed to Africa, where those goods were exchanged for slaves. The next phase of the voyage was known as the Middle Passage, so named because it was the second of the three-part journey, in which the slave ship sailed from the coast of Africa to New England, where the slaves were traded for sugar and tobacco. The voyage ended back in Europe.

Quantity was the key, and, knowing that the more slaves they brought to America, the larger their profit would be, slave traders utilized literally every square inch of space below deck for their human cargo. The slave hold was a hot, cramped space where Africans were packed so tightly that they scarcely had room in which to turn around. While they may have been given buckets for waste, few could access the buckets and many were forced to lie in their own excrement. Olaudah Equiano writes of the Middle Passage:

> I was soon put down under the decks, and there I received such a salutation in my nostrils as I had never experienced in my life . . . The closeness of the place, and the heat of the climate, added to the number in the ship, which was so crowded that each had scarcely room to turn himself, almost suffocated us. This produced copious perspiration, so that the air soon became unfit for respiration, from a variety of loathsome smells, and brought on a sickness amongst the slaves, of which many died . . .[14]

Alexander Falconbridge, a doctor who traveled on several slave expeditions, remarked that "the deck, that is, the floor of their rooms, was so covered in blood and mucus which had proceeded from them in consequence of the flux, that it resembled a slaughterhouse."[15]

Reverend Robert Walsh served on board a ship that intercepted ships illegally transporting slaves after the abolition of the slave trade in 1807. Remarking on the conditions of the slave hold in one slave ship in 1829, Walsh writes of how the slave deck was "shut out from light or air, and this when the thermometer, exposed to the open sky, was standing in the shade on our deck, at 89 [degrees]." To Walsh's horror, several of his comrades remarked that it was one of the more humane ships they had seen. He writes, "the height sometimes between decks was only eighteen inches, so that the unfortunate beings could not turn round or even on their sides, the elevation being less than the breadth of their shoulders; and here they are usually chained to the decks by the neck and legs."[16]

Concrete numbers are difficult to ascertain, but most scholars suggest that between 10 and 20 million Africans were kidnapped and sold into slavery in the United States, and one in three died en route.[17]

INDENTURED SERVITUDE

Africans were not the only group to be exploited and forced to labor for the gains of the wealthy European upper classes. Many poor Europeans immigrated to the American colonies as servants, often booking a passage to America under the signed agreement that they would work as many years as it took to pay off their debt. The span of their indenture typically ran from five to seven years, but a master could extend the terms of the contract by claiming that the servant had not served adequately or had broken some other term of the agreement. The term of indenture could also extend to the servant's children. In 1773, a white Maryland woman was charged with

43

bastardy for becoming pregnant by a black man, and her punishment was to be sold as a servant for a term of seven years, while her infant daughter was sold as a servant until she reached the age of 31 years.[18]

In the early Colonial years, labor was needed to increase the size of the tobacco crop for export overseas. The land of pearl and gold was worthless without hands to tend and gather the harvest. Indentured servants were significantly less expensive than African slaves, so they were an attractive commodity to Colonial planters. Up to two-thirds of all European migrants to the colonies came as indentured servants.[19]

While many scholars throughout history have insisted that indentured servitude and slavery were similar, there were some essential and striking differences. First, a servant agreed to the terms of service stipulated in the contract (unless he or she was convicted of a crime and sold into servitude as punishment) while a slave could not. Second, the servant worked for a specified amount of time, after which he or she was released from bondage and (sometimes) given a bonus in the form of land, money, and corn, while the slave had no hope of release from bondage. Third, and most important, the white indentured servant was not the subject of a racist ideology. While classist ideologies made it possible for wealthy colonialists to rationalize unfair treatment of poor whites, the enslavement of Africans was justified under the belief that they were subhuman, ignorant, and naturally prone to vice.[20]

Nonetheless, many servants faced inhumane working conditions, corporal punishment, and malnourishment that often mirrored the conditions of slavery. Under Colonial law, indentured servants, once purchased, became the legal property of their master, who exercised complete control over every aspect of their lives, including their sexuality. Servants who married without their master's permission were charged with adultery and fornication, and children born from such a union were considered illegitimate.[21] Several states even had laws addressing female servants who became pregnant during their servitude. If a female servant became pregnant, her indenture could be prolonged to make up for her decreased productivity. Furthermore, as in slavery, it was within the master's rights to whip or beat a servant for any perceived infraction, and female servants often faced sexual abuse from which they had little legal protection.

Unlike slaves, servants could seek redress from their masters in court, though it was highly uncommon for servants to win such cases. Slaves, on the other hand, had no legal right to seek redress. But possibly the most notable legal difference between servants and slaves was the fact that in many states, any white person, regardless of social standing, could apprehend and kill any black person who was deemed to be off his or her plantation without authorization.

Many servants and slaves committed suicide, ran away, or revolted. Runaway slaves were often given harsher sentences than runaway servants. In some cases, slaves and servants organized revolts together, several of which were discovered and foiled, which often resulted in the execution of the conspirators. Several states even passed laws banning any fraternization between blacks and whites to prevent flight and uprisings.

American Independence: 1776

The topic of rights became an issue in the 1700s as resentment began to ferment between the Americans and the British government regarding taxes. The British government had been instituting various taxes prior to the 1760s, but many Colonial Americans managed to evade them. It was not until the Seven Years' War, also known as the French and Indian War, that tensions came to a head. By the end of the war, the British national debt had ballooned from 75 to 145 million pounds, and George Greenville, the chief minister to England's 25-year-old King George III, campaigned for more taxes on the colonies. Greenville saw it as being only fair that the Americans should help pay for the cost of keeping British troops in the colonies to defend them against the French.[22]

The Sugar Act of 1764 came at a time of economic depression among the colonies. While the indirect tax was actually a reduction, stricter enforcement made it more difficult to avoid paying the tax, as many had done with the Molasses Act of 1731. Quickly following the Sugar Act was the Currency Act, which banned paper money, thereby hindering trade and lowering property values. Many colonists protested the acts, but to little effect as the colonies had no representation in Parliament. In 1765, the Quartering Act inflamed anger among the colonists, who were now forced to provide barracks, food, and supplies to the British troops stationed in the colonies.

The Stamp Act of 1765 was the first direct tax on the colonies, the aim of which was to collect revenue. The act taxed every newspaper, pamphlet, almanac, legal documents, college diploma, and even dice and playing cards, and stamps were to be fixed to the documents to show that the tax had been paid.[23] Groups organized throughout the colonies to protest the Stamp Act. One group known as the Loyal Nine went so far as to march to the local stampmaster's home and burn his effigy. The crowd consisted of both wealthy and poor Bostonians, and when the aristocratic protesters left, the poorer Bostonians destroyed much of the stampmaster's property.[24]

The Stamp Act was repealed the following year as many colonists rightly voiced their objection to being taxed without being allowed any representation in Parliament. Britain, however, was not ready to completely give up the power struggle, and immediately following the repeal of the Stamp Act, Parliament passed the Declaratory Act, which allowed Parliament to place laws on the colonists as they saw fit. In 1767, the Townshend Act collected revenue for Britain by taxing lead, paint, glass, paper, and tea in the colonies.

In 1768, Samuel Adams drafted a statement attacking the British Parliament for continuing to tax the colonists while simultaneously refusing them representation in Parliament. The statement was approved by the Massachusetts House of Representatives, and the British governor of Massachusetts responded by dissolving the state legislature. Tensions mounted, requiring more British troops to be sent to the colonies to prevent riots, and in 1770, the Townshend Acts were reduced, leaving only the tax on tea. Despite the concessions, violence erupted in New York and Boston, resulting in the deaths of five Americans.

The infamous Boston Tea Party came as a result of the 1773 Tea Act, which allowed the British East India Company duty-free export of tea, thereby giving the British tea merchants an unfair advantage over American tea merchants. On December 16, 1773, a group of Boston men dressed up as Indians raided British trading ships and dumped all of the tea into the harbor. In response to the Boston Tea Party, Parliament passed the Coercive Acts, which banned the loading or unloading of ships in Boston Harbor, transferred court cases involving riot suppression to England, and placed the election of Massachusetts government officials under British control. Further, Parliament expanded the Quartering Act, which required colonists to house British soldiers in their own homes.

Rights, resistance, and liberty were the topics of discussion in the years leading up to the American Revolution, which not only highlighted the inequality between the colonies and Britain but also illuminated the problematic social stratification at home. While the upper classes of the colonies were decrying oppression under British rule, particularly in regard to their lack of representation in Parliament, slaves, Native Americans, servants, women, and the exceedingly large segments of the population of America who did not own property had no representation in American government. In 1775, Thomas Paine wrote an article entitled "African Slavery in America," which was the first article to be published in the United States advocating abolition.[25] In 1776, Paine wrote in *Common Sense*, ". . . we have every opportunity and every encouragement before us, to form the noblest, purest constitution on the face of the earth. We have it in our power to begin the world over again."[26]

Slavery and Abolition: 1780–1865

The Declaration of Independence was approved by Congress on July 4, 1776. The Bill of Rights was introduced in 1789 and effected in 1791. The freedoms and rights outlined in the Bill of Rights include freedom of speech, assembly, press, and petition; the right to bear arms; protection from quartering of troops (at no time may a person be forced to house a soldier); protection from unreasonable search and seizure; the right to due process and the right to avoid self-incrimination; the right to a trial by jury, speedy, public trial, and legal counsel; the prohibition of excessive bail and cruel and unusual punishment; the protection of rights not specifically enumerated in the Constitution; and the protection of the powers of state and people. But how can a nation discuss human rights without taking all human beings into consideration? The colonies were dominated by a ruling planter class that virtually determined the growth and future of America in the sway it held over the legislatures and county courts.[27] In Boston alone, the top 10 percent of taxpayers held a full two-thirds of Boston's taxable property in the mid-18th century, while the lowest 30 percent of taxpayers had no taxable property. Propertyless individuals included sailors, apprentices, journeymen (skilled wage laborers who traveled looking for work), women, servants, blacks, and Indians, none of whom had the right to vote.[28] In South Carolina, slaves constituted two-thirds of the population.[29] When one also considers that servants constituted nearly half of all immigrants coming into the United States at this time, one sees a very large majority of the population who had no say in their future. The planters, on the other hand, derived their enormous wealth through slave and servant labor. Thus, while the planters were decrying the violation of their rights by the British government, they had a personal stake in the suppression of the rights of others.[30] Even Thomas Jefferson, who disparaged slavery, oppression, and religious intolerance, did not believe that women or slaves had any place in politics.[31]

Individuals began to emerge to give voice to marginalized groups. Mary Wollstonecraft began to speak of women's rights in England, and abolitionists were vocal in condemning the slave trade as both inhuman and unchristian. The United States abolished its participation in the slave trade in 1808, following England's abolition of the slave trade in 1807, and all of the Northern states had passed various emancipation acts by 1804. In the South, however, slavery thrived, particularly with the introduction of the cotton gin and the need for labor to produce this staple crop.[32] The divide between the North and the South grew as the legal status of slaves became dependent on what side of the Mason-Dixon Line (a line surveyed in the 1760s by Charles Mason and Jeremiah Dixon that ran along the borders of Pennsylvania, Maryland, Delaware, and Virginia to demarcate the North from the South) they lived on. As the nation began to expand westward and map new states, debates arose as to whether such states should be slave or free states. In 1820, fierce quarrels eventually resulted in Missouri being admitted into statehood as a slave state, while Maine was admitted as a free state to strike a balance.[33]

In response to the South's problem of the Underground Railroad and slaves fleeing to the North, Senator James Murray Mason of Virginia drafted the Fugitive Slave Act (or Law) of 1850, which allowed the owner of a runaway slave to cross state lines into the North to retrieve him or her, and prosecuted anyone (Northern or Southern) caught harboring a fugitive slave or helping to transport a fugitive slave.[34] The Fugitive Slave Act unsettled many Northern states, which saw the act as Southern slavery encroaching on Northern ideals. This resentment was compounded by the *Dred Scott* case, which began in 1846 when a 50-year-old black slave named Dred Scott, along with his wife, Harriet, filed a suit against their owner, Irene Emerson, for their freedom. During his lifetime of enslavement, Scott had spent nearly nine years with his master, a military surgeon named John Emerson, in the North (Illinois and Wisconsin), where he was technically free, before returning to Missouri. Historians are unclear as to why Scott did not leave Emerson while he was in the North and waited until after Emerson's death to file the suit. Some speculate that Scott and his wife were angry over being hired out by Irene Emerson, or that they had offered to buy their freedom and were refused, or that Irene Emerson was planning to sell one or both of them.[35] In any event, the Scotts sued Emerson for their freedom in the St. Louis Circuit Court, but were dismissed. In 1850, however, a second court reversed the decision and ruled in favor of the Scotts. But two years into the Scotts' freedom, the Missouri Supreme Court reversed the previous decision and ruled in favor of Emerson, thus reenslaving the Scotts. The Dred Scott case was debated in court for 11 years, during which time the Missouri Compromise of 1820, an act of Congress that prohibited slavery in the Northern territories, was overruled. Dred and Harriet Scott finally obtained their freedom when Irene Emerson remarried in 1857 and her husband, an abolitionist, helped secure their freedom. Dred Scott died the following year of tuberculosis.[36]

Yet more painful narratives of slavery began to arise at this time. Harriet Beecher Stowe published *Uncle Tom's Cabin* in 1852, which highlighted the suffering of slaves and the need for Christian love and brotherhood to destroy the institution of slavery. A case of staggering heartbreak occurred in

1856 in Cincinnati, Ohio, with the escape and retrieval of Margaret Garner. A slave in Kentucky, Garner and her husband, Robert, four children, and her husband's parents fled from two plantations into Ohio, where they took refuge with Margaret's uncle and cousin, Joseph and Elijah Kite. Shortly after their arrival, the Garners' owners arrived at the house with federal marshals and a shootout ensued. When it became clear that the Garners could not escape, Margaret Garner grabbed a knife and cut the throat of her two-year-old daughter to keep her from being taken back into slavery. She attempted to cut the throats of her two older children and struck the head of her infant daughter with a coal shovel before she was seized and carried away.[37] During her court case, she was asked about two scars on the left side of her face, to which she responded curtly, "white man struck me," thereby illuminating a dark history of cruelty and abuse.[38]

The narratives that arose regarding slavery during this time struck an empathetic chord among many white Americans, but as the nation expanded westward, so, too, did slavery. Each new territory was debated and selected as either a free state or a slave state, which not only meant that the institution of slavery would continue to grow and thrive, but it would skew the economic balance in favor of the South, which had the benefit of free labor. Again, the issue of rights became the predominant topic of discussion, but in a very unique way, for the issue was not only a matter of *whose* rights were at stake, but *what* rights. For the antislavery faction, the argument rested on slaves' right to freedom. For the proslavery faction, the issue was a matter of slaveholders' right to their property.

Compromises had been attempted: It was initially decided that all Northern states would be free and all Southern states would be slave states. But pro-slavery campaigners demanded that the decision be left to the inhabitants of the new territories by way of a vote. Finally, with the Dred Scott decision, slavery could exist even in states where the inhabitants had voted against it.

When Abraham Lincoln won the presidential election in 1860, South Carolina declared secession and was followed by the other Southern states. War erupted shortly after Lincoln took office in 1861, and by its end in 1865 with the victory of the Union and the emancipation of the slaves, 620,000 soldiers were dead, making the Civil War the deadliest war in American history.[39]

President Lincoln issued the Emancipation Proclamation in 1863, three years into the Civil War, and declared free all of the slaves of the states that had seceded from the Union.[40] The document was not without its limitations, as it did not include slaves in the border states, and the proclamation itself did not end slavery, but it nevertheless marked a turning point in American history. Slavery was officially abolished in the United States on January 31, 1865, with the passage of the Thirteenth Amendment, which stated that, "neither slavery nor involuntary servitude, except as a punishment for crime whereof the party shall have been duly convicted, shall exist within the United States, or any place subject to their jurisdiction."[41] African Americans were thus freed, but it would be another hundred years before they would be accepted as full and equal citizens.

Women's Rights: 1840–1919

While abolition was being debated, other groups were also organizing to demand their rights. Women's rights became intricately interwoven with the rights of African Americans in 1837, when 200 women, black and white, convened in New York City for the first Antislavery Convention of American Women. Women had long played a key role in the campaign against slavery, and Sarah Grimké, a suffragist and abolitionist, outlined woman's responsibility toward the cause of abolitionism by stating, "it is not only the cause of the slave that we plead, but the cause of woman as a moral, responsible being . . . Men and women are created equal!" Women's abolitionist groups were largely attacked, especially when white and black women began associating freely and openly at such gatherings as the Antislavery Convention of American Women. They were not only spurned by proslavery factions but by several male abolitionist groups as well, a fact that was driven home in 1840 at the first worldwide abolitionist convention in London, where the American female delegates were refused seats. A young New Yorker named Elizabeth Cady Stanton was present at the convention with her new husband and was enraged by the humiliation of the women abolitionists. Taking up the cause for women's rights, Stanton became a key player in the women's suffrage movement and helped organize the first Women's Rights Convention in Seneca Falls, New York, in 1848, which also hosted the abolitionist and former slave Frederick Douglass as a speaker.[42]

With the aim of securing women's right to vote, women's rights campaigners employed various methods to make their views heard and enlisted the help of other major human rights reformers, such as Sojourner Truth and Frederick Douglass. In 1869, Elizabeth Cady Stanton and fellow suffragist Susan B. Anthony created the National Woman Suffrage Association, which was largely focused on petitioning individual states to pass laws allowing women the right to vote. The National Woman's Party was established in 1917 with the specific aim of passing a constitutional amendment that would give women the vote. This finally became possible with the United States's involvement in World War I, which President Woodrow Wilson defined as a war to make the world "safe for democracy."[43] Such high-minded pro-democracy rhetoric could not avoid the issue of women's enfranchisement, and in 1919 Congress passed the Nineteenth Amendment, giving women the right to vote.

Children's Rights: Nineteenth Century

The 19th and 20th centuries were an evolutionary time for rights. Women and African Americans were not the only segments of society being discussed; the rights of children, workers, and immigrants were also coming to the forefront of the national discussion. Child labor was a particularly hot-button issue, and in 1832 the New England Association of Farmers, Mechanics, and Other Workingmen released a statement condemning child labor, insisting that "children should not be allowed to labor in the factories from morning till night, without any time for healthy recreation and mental culture," as it "endangers their . . . well-being and health."[44]

The Industrial Revolution moved many workers from farms to factories in urban areas, and children were often employed as they were cheaper and less likely to strike.[45] Throughout the 19th century, states debated the ethics of child labor, but frequently ran into problems when attempts were made to pass legislation banning child labor. Massachusetts passed the first state child labor law in 1836, which mandated that factory-working children under the age of 15 attend school at least three months out of the year. In 1842, Massachusetts followed this with a law limiting children's work days to 10 hours a day.

Institutions for abused and neglected children began to appear with greater frequency in the early 1800s, and in 1853, appalled by the conditions facing children in urban areas, Charles Loring Brace founded the New York Children's Aid Society. While his initial aim was to take children off the streets, his overarching goal was to get children out of the squalor of urban slums and away from their abusive and/or neglectful parents altogether. In 1854, Brace founded the Orphan Trains, which relocated vast swaths of children (usually the children of Catholic immigrants and not true orphans) from congested cities to the rural West, where they were taken into the homes of Protestant farmers.[46]

But the problem of child labor and poor working and living conditions for children persisted. Child abuse was also a sensitive area, as few were willing to suggest that the state should be allowed to overrule parents' rights. It was not until the infamous case of Mary Ellen Wilson emerged in 1874 that public awareness of child abuse began to merge into discussions of state involvement in child protection. Mary Ellen Wilson was 10 years old when she was discovered by a Methodist mission worker named Etta Wheeler. Alerted by residents in a New York tenement that a child was being badly mistreated, Wheeler found young Mary Ellen Wilson dirty and thin, and covered in cuts and bruises, with a large gash over the left side of her face from being struck with a pair of scissors. Wheeler sought help for Wilson, but New York City authorities were reluctant to get involved, and Wheeler finally turned to Henry Bergh, the founder of the American Society for the Prevention of Cruelty to Animals (ASPCA). Bergh contacted the *New York Times* and brought nationwide publicity to the case, and, following Mary Ellen's testimony describing her years of abuse, Judge Lawrence immediately issued a *writ de homine replagiando*, bringing Wilson under court custody. Mary Ellen's adoptive mother, Mary Connolly, was found guilty of felonious assault and was sentenced to one year of hard labor, and today the case is credited as the first to highlight the rights of children.[47]

Worker's Rights: 1911

The rights of workers, and particularly working children, came into sharp relief in 1911 with the Triangle Shirtwaist Factory fire in New York City. On the afternoon of March 25, a fire broke out on the ninth floor of the factory, which produced women's garments, and within minutes 146 of the 500 employees were dead. The vast majority of the employees were teenage girls, most of whom were recent Italian or European Jewish immigrants. The stresses of life in a new country made them particularly vulnerable to exploitation, and few were willing to speak out against the long hours and low wages. When the fire broke out, the girls found the exit doors locked, as the managers were in the habit of locking the doors to prevent employees from stealing the material. The fire escape was woefully unstable and bent under the weight of the girls attempting to climb down to safety.[48] Those who waited for the fire department to help them to safety found that not only did the hoses only reach the seventh floor but the ladders only reached the sixth floor. Unable to escape the flames, many of the girls jumped out of windows and down elevator shafts, falling nine stories to their deaths. A United Press reporter, William Shepherd, recounted the sight of so many falling bodies: "Thud—dead; thud—dead; thud—dead; thud—dead; sixty-two thud—deads. I call them that because the sound and the thought of death came to me each time, at the same instant."[49]

The Triangle Shirtwaist Factory fire came only five years after the publication of Upton Sinclair's book *The Jungle*, which revealed the exploitation of immigrants and the inhumane working conditions of factories in Chicago.

Federal response to the book, however, resulted in the Pure Food and Drug Act rather than an imposition of regulations on work conditions.[50]

When the fire was finally put out, dozens of charred bodies were found inside the building, and the city organized a day of mourning. Witnesses and members of the community were baffled and outraged that the conditions of the factory had led to the horrific deaths of so many young women, some of whom were only 15 years old. The case resulted in a statewide overhaul of safety regulations and the passage of new safety legislation. One of the onlookers at the scene of the fire, Frances Perkins, later became secretary of labor under President Franklin Delano Roosevelt and an advocate for worker's rights.[51]

Civil Rights: 1960s

While the basic rights to life and liberty had come under greater protection by the beginning of the 20th century, social inequalities persisted and continued to present challenges to lawmakers regarding the definition of human rights. Until the 1960s, social inequalities were not only popularly supported but institutionally maintained, particularly for African Americans. From the time of emancipation, African Americans struggled under the Jim Crow laws, which mandated segregation in virtually every public setting, from trains and schools to drinking fountains. The Jim Crow era, named after a white minstrel show performer who blackened his face and performed a jig to the song "Jump Jim Crow," was a time of social anxiety that often resulted in extreme acts of violence, including lynchings and race riots. Between 1889 and 1930, more than 3,700 black men and women were lynched.[52]

The Civil Rights Act of 1875 granted equal rights to African Americans, mandating that "all persons . . . shall be entitled to full and equal enjoyment of the accommodations, advantages, facilities, and privileges of inns, public conveyances on land or water, theaters, and other places of amusement." The act was ruled unconstitutional by the Supreme Court in 1883, and Chief Justice Joseph Bradley explained that the Fourteenth Amendment protected citizens from the state's infringement on their rights, but could not protect against discrimination from private businesses and other citizens.[53]

A wave of discriminatory legislation followed the Supreme Court's ruling, particularly among Southern states, and lynchings reached their highest peak in 1890.[54] From this precarious period arose Booker T. Washington, a former slave who worked his way through school by laboring in salt and coal mines. Washington, unlike Frederick Douglass and Harvard scholar W. E. B. DuBois, did not press for civil rights or higher education for African Americans, but rather urged for vocational training that would allow African Americans to earn an income while providing a service for society.[55] In 1895, Washington delivered his contentious Atlanta Compromise speech, in which he defended segregation with the now-famous statement: "In all things that are purely social we can be separated as the fingers. Yet one as the hand in all things essential to mutual progress."[56] Such statements made Washington highly popular among the white community, and institutionalized racial discrimination soon came under the heading of "separate but equal." This was most keenly exemplified in the Louisiana Separate Car Act of 1890, which mandated that all railway companies provide equal but separate accommodations for white and black passengers.

In 1896, a group of African-American protesters challenged the act by electing Homer Plessy, a man who was one-eighth black and seven-eighths white, to take a seat in the car reserved for white passengers. Plessy was charged with violating the Separate Car law and later lost his case in the Louisiana courts.[57]

Many Southern legislatures proposed new qualifications for voting rights between 1890 and 1908, and many African-American men were barred from voting because they did not qualify. In response to this, the National Association for the Advancement of Colored People (NAACP) was established by W. E. B. DuBois and several other black and white protesters. In 1954, the NAACP successfully quashed the separate-but-equal guideline of segregation in the landmark *Brown v. Board of Education* case. Plaintiffs in the case argued that the segregation of black and white public school children naturally resulted in discrimination as schools for black children were markedly inferior and underfunded. The psychologists Kenneth and Mamie White were instrumental in revealing the self-hatred and distorted self-images segregation produced in black children through their "Doll Test," in which several black children between the ages of three and seven not only preferred white dolls over black dolls but attributed positive qualities to the white dolls and negative qualities to the black dolls. Even more telling, when the children were asked to draw pictures of themselves, most of them did so with a white or yellow crayon.[58]

The African-American Civil Rights movement took place between 1955 and 1968. African-American community leaders had disagreed for years on the best approach to civil rights, some arguing for gradual desegregation, others for direct action, some for peaceful disobedience, and others for violent resistance. Credited today as the foremost leader of the Civil Rights movement, Reverend Martin Luther King, Jr., advocated peaceful protest to effect immediate results. Operating under the philosophy of nonviolence, civil rights campaigners organized boycotts, sit-ins, marches, and freedom rides. Despite the peaceful nature of the protests, the campaigners' efforts were often met with violence, and several key civil rights leaders, including Martin Luther King, Jr., Malcolm X, and Medgar Evers, were assassinated. Nevertheless, the Civil Rights movement was successful in achieving desegregation, outlawing racial discrimination and protecting voting rights among African Americans. The Civil Rights Act of 1964 was the largest civil rights bill in American history. Title VII of the act focused on job discrimination and prohibited employers from discriminating against individuals on the basis of race, sex, religion, or national origin.

This period in American history not only saw a revision of race relations between blacks and whites but also a reconstitution of rights for many groups. In California, the Chicano movement inspired the 1968 East L.A. walkouts to protest inequality and discrimination in Los Angeles Unified School District high schools. Also in California, the Mexican-American farmworker César Chávez cofounded the National Farm Workers Association, which later became United Farm Workers, and campaigned for farmworkers' rights. Chávez's efforts had a nationwide ripple effect that inspired nationwide boycotts and campaigns in other states.

Another singular movement of this time was the feminist movement, or the Women's Liberation movement, which campaigned not only for equal rights for women in the workplace and higher education but also for reproductive rights. Following years of working with poor women in New York City's Lower East Side, Margaret Sanger cofounded the American Birth Control League and campaigned for women's rights to contraception to prevent unwanted pregnancies and the dangers of self-induced abortions.[59] In 1960, the birth control pill was approved by the Food and Drug Administration, and in 1963 Betty Friedan's groundbreaking book *The Feminine Mystique* helped catalyze the Women's Liberation movement by challenging American women to reevaluate their lives and futures. Men and women alike were urged to recognize and protest patriarchy's pervasive presence both in the home and beyond. Workplace discrimination was a major area of concern, as women routinely earned less than men for the same work. In 1963, women earned 59 cents for every dollar that men earned, and that same year the Equal Pay Act was passed, requiring employers to pay female employees the same wages as their male counterparts for the same work.[60]

A more controversial victory came for Women's Liberation campaigners in the 1973 *Roe v. Wade* decision, which legalized abortion nationwide. When a pregnant, single woman under the pseudonym Jane Roe challenged the constitutionality of the Texas criminal abortion laws, the courts determined that laws barring a woman from aborting a pregnancy violated the Fourteenth Amendment.[61]

CURRENT SITUATION
Rights of Ethnic Minorities

In the last 50 years, studies of ethnic relations and race in America have challenged the concept of race and redefined rights as they are understood today. Following the Civil Rights movement of the 1960s, the concept of color blindness took on new widespread popularity in an attempt to address the historical reality of racism. The concept of color blindness suggests that by refusing to acknowledge race altogether, it is possible to avoid being racist or discriminatory. But race scholars such as Howard Winant and Michael Omi agree that such an attempt has been misguided, as color blindness does not, in fact, erase ethnic difference, but rather encourages avoidance of the topic.[62] The notion of color blindness allows one to avoid acknowledging his or her own ethnic perspective, which may be that of white, middle-class man or woman.

The concept of color blindness has largely clouded the definition of racism, which has consequently blurred the definition of discrimination. Racism is not necessarily marked by overt hostility, which makes it difficult for some to recognize discrimination based on race. Simply neglecting to include people of ethnic origins other than white is discriminatory, which is why Affirmative Action took effect in the 1960s. Affirmative Action is a set of policies that ensure ethnic and gender inclusion by mandating the hiring or admission of a certain percentage of women and minorities. While supporters of Affirmative Action argue that it is a means of encouraging the increasing inclusion of women and minorities in business, education, and employment, opponents see it as encouraging preferential selection of potential employees and students on the basis of sex and race.[63] Other countries with histories of institutionalized discrimination, such as India's caste system, have implemented similar measures to ensure inclusion.

Women's Rights

In 1963, American women earned 59 cents for every dollar that their male counterparts earned. In 2009, women of all ethnicities earned an average of 80 cents for every dollar that their white male counterpart earned. The wage gap fluctuates depending on race: African-American women earned 68.9 cents per every dollar that a white male employee in the same position earned.[64] Furthermore, men with children tend to earn on average 2 percent more than men without children, while women with children earn 2.5 percent less than women without children.[65] While the wage gap has improved significantly since 1963 and continues to creep to a close, the process is slow and unstable. But the wage gap is not the only issue that has emerged in discussions of women's rights. Affordable child care, paid maternity leave (as well as paid paternity leave), flexible work hours, and discrimination against pregnant women in hiring practices are also issues that still need to be resolved.

Discussions of women's rights are not limited to discrimination in the workplace. Advances in reproductive technologies continue to make reproductive rights an immediate issue. Mifepristone (known in the United States as RU486), a pill that is capable of inducing abortion within the first two months of pregnancy, was developed in Switzerland and later became available in France, Great Britain, and Sweden, but was blocked in the United States by the George H. W. Bush administration in 1989. It was legalized in 2000 by the Clinton administration, to much controversy and debate.

Workers' Rights

Workers' rights, or labor rights, have come a long way since the 19th century. In 1955, the American Federation of Labor merged with the Congress of Industrial Organizations to become the AFL-CIO, which now acts as an umbrella for 56 unions in the United States. Today, workers have the right to unionize and demand better pay and working conditions when they feel they are being mistreated by their employers. This has dramatically shifted the balance of power so that unions are now capable of challenging major corporations, which not only benefits unionized workers but nonunionized workers as well. Today, because of the development of organized labor, all workers in the United States are legally entitled to a federally stipulated minimum wage, two-day weekends, a safe working environment, nondiscriminatory hiring practices, and overtime pay.

Labor unions have had a difficult struggle and have been the subject of controversy over the course of their development in the United States. In 1947, Congress overrode President Harry Truman's veto to pass the Taft-Hartley Act, which was enacted to monitor and control the power of labor unions, such as their ability to strike. It also banned the closed shop, which was a union security agreement that permitted employers to hire only union members.

While both union and nonunion workers enjoy far better working conditions today than they did a century ago, workers in several industrial sectors continue to struggle for better pay and working conditions. Migrant farmworkers, for example, have frequently had to endure harsh working conditions with low wages and other difficulties. In California, many farmworkers labor for hours in oppressive heat, which has caused many to sicken and even die from heatstroke. The plight of farmworkers came to national attention in the summer of 2008, when 17-year-old Maria Jiminez died from heatstroke in Merced County after picking grapes for nine hours in 95-degree heat. California had been the first state to enact heat-illness prevention standards in the nation, which required employers to provide water and shade to their employees, but the system was faulty and poorly enforced. Maria Jiminez was one of six farmworkers to die from heatstroke in California in the summer of 2008. Her death appears to have improved enforcement to a limited degree, as there were no deaths in 2009. Nevertheless, there were several hospitalizations.[66]

Children's Rights

The rights of children have made significant progress in the last century, particularly in terms of child labor and abuse. While it was common for children to work 12- to 18-hour days in factories and on farms, they are now protected from such exploitative practices. But children's rights are unique in that they must, by nature, go beyond basic rights to health and well-being to include future health and well-being. One of the rights of children as outlined by UNICEF is the right to be considered distinctly from adults, with unique needs and rights different from those of adults. Unlike adults, children are incapable of providing for themselves or protecting themselves from exploitation. Most important, because their minds and bodies are in a state of development, they are not capable of making sound decisions for themselves regarding things like employment, education, sex, and health. Therefore, while it is important and, indeed, immediately necessary to implement policies and measures that will protect children from exploitation, it is also equally important to implement policies that will protect children's rights to education and health care so that they can lead healthy, fulfilling lives as adults.

One area of children's rights that remains somewhat nebulous is the issue of corporal punishment (otherwise known as spanking, slapping, or whipping) and at where the line may be drawn between corporal punishment and abuse. Many countries have banned the use of corporal punishment altogether, while others have placed limitations on physical punishment, such as banning the use of implements like belts or paddles, or implementing age restrictions. In the United States, corporal punishment, including the use of implements, remains legal and left to the parents' discretion, and is considered to cross over into abuse only if it leaves a mark (bruise or cut) that does not heal after 24 hours.

The question of what constitutes abuse remains a contentious issue, as some fear that placing too many restrictions on how a parent may punish his or her child violates the parent's rights. Some activist groups are seeking to eliminate corporal punishment of children altogether, such as the Global Initiative to End Corporal Punishment of Children. As of 2010, 26 countries have banned corporal punishment of children, beginning with Sweden in 1979.[67] Measures have been introduced in the United States to place further restrictions or bans on physical punishment of children, but none to date have been successful.

Rights of the Disabled

Like the Civil Rights and Women's Liberation movements of the 1960s and '70s, the Disability Rights movement sought to define disabilities, people who live with disabilities, and the rights to which they are entitled. People with disabilities range from deafness, blindness, and paraplegia, to mental disorders such as schizophrenia and mental retardation. The rights outlined by the Disability Rights movement include civil rights, such as employment and education, as well as the right to self-determination, or the right to live a fulfilling, independent life. Previously, care of people with mental or physical disabilities was the responsibility of family members; otherwise disabled individuals would be institutionalized. The Disability Rights movement emphasized the humanity and individuality of people with disabilities and the happiness to which they are constitutionally entitled. Like the rights of women and ethnic minorities, disability rights have much to do with inclusion and full access to public programs and institutions, as well as freedom from discrimination.

Along with the Civil Rights and Women's Liberation movements, the Disability Rights movement began gaining ground in the 1960s under President John F. Kennedy, when he signed Public Law 88–164 in 1963, which mandated access to education for children with physical and mental disabilities. In 1968, the Architectural Barriers Act required all federally financed buildings to be accessible to people with disabilities.

The Disability Rights movement continued to expand throughout the 1970s and '80s and adopted the methods of the Civil Rights movement, including peaceful protests, sit-ins, and boycotts. In 1973, the Rehabilitation Act was passed, prohibiting federally funded programs from discriminating against people with disabilities.

The Americans with Disabilities Act (ADA) of 1990 broadened the Rehabilitation Act to prohibit any and all discrimination based on disability.

This includes employment and education, as well as public transportation and accommodation. In 1999, a Supreme Court case ruled that an employee could not be considered disabled if the disability could be corrected. Another ruling determined that a disability could only be classified as such if it inhibited more than one major life activity (walking, eating, breathing, standing, lifting, bending, focusing, speaking, etc.). Both rulings were later overturned by the 2008 passage of the ADA Amendments Act (ADAAA), which expanded the rights of the disabled as outlined in the ADA.

Immigrants

Immigrants, both documented and undocumented, have been the target of nationalistic discrimination and xenophobia since the United States was first colonized by the British. Throughout American history, immigrants have been excluded from many of the basic rights enjoyed by U.S.-born citizens, including the right to purchase property, access to education and employment (in certain sectors), and even the right to leave the country without being barred from reentry. Certain ethnic groups were banned from immigrating to the United States altogether. In 1882, the Chinese Exclusion Act barred all Chinese from entry into the United States, making them the first group to be excluded on the basis of race. Those already living in the country, such as those who had come during the gold rush, were prohibited from being able to become citizens, which meant that they could not go back to China to visit their families if they wanted to remain in the United States. The act was not overturned until 1943.[68]

The rights of both documented and undocumented immigrants became strangely intertwined in 2010 with the passage of SB 1070 in Arizona, a bill that requires individuals suspected of being in the country illegally to show proof of legal status. The bill has been widely criticized by lawmakers, religious figures, and even the U.S. president Barack Obama, for what many see as its racist underpinnings. The only way for authorities to identify a person as a suspected illegal immigrant is to do so on the basis of race, which expressly targets the Mexican-American community in Arizona for racial profiling. Several states and cities across the country have consequently proposed boycotts on all Arizona products, including tourism boycotts.

President Barack Obama and others have responded to the Arizona bill and identified it as a sign that the U.S. immigration system is "broken."[69] The debate on immigration reform is evenly split between those who believe stricter laws on immigration are in order, such as caps and requirements, and those who support more lenient laws. Amnesty for current undocumented immigrants in the United States is also a sensitive topic. As it stands, illegal immigration is dangerous for both the U.S. economy and undocumented immigrants themselves as they are vulnerable to exploitation by employers (substandard wages and unsafe working conditions) and lack access to health care and other public services.

Prisoners' Rights

More than 2 million people are currently incarcerated in U.S. prisons, the majority of which are ethnic minorities.[70] Though prisoners are denied certain rights by virtue of their incarceration (liberty, property, voting, etc.), they are still entitled to basic human rights such as adequate shelter, clothing, and food. In the United States, prisoners are protected by the Eighth Amendment, which prohibits cruel and unusual punishment, but organizations such as the American Civil Liberties Union (ACLU) argue that prisoners' rights are not being adequately protected. Living conditions, mental health care, medical health care, immigrant detention, juvenile detention, incarcerated women, and restriction of rights are some of the issues that the ACLU is addressing. Specific cases range from defending the rights of prisoners to read religious materials of their choosing, as well as lobbying for the prohibition of shackling pregnant female inmates while they are in labor. Broader issues include the prevalence of sexual assault and violence in prison and the rights of prisoners to be protected from rape and abuse. A 2007 report by Human Rights Watch found that, on average, one in 20 inmates in U.S. prisons reports being the victim of sexual violence. The report also found that the prevalence of sexual violence in prisons is largely due to inadequate supervision of inmates and failure to respond to reported sexual violence.[71] A 2010 report on juvenile detention facilities revealed more than twice as many sexual assaults: 12 percent of all juveniles are sexually assaulted while in detention. Even more shocking to researchers is the fact that while adult male inmates are more likely to report inmate-on-inmate sexual violence, 80 percent of juvenile assaults are committed by staff.[72] Adult female inmates who are sexually assaulted are also more likely to be assaulted by staff (female inmates are also more likely to have been sexually abused prior to incarceration).[73]

Human rights organizations continue to lobby for reform that will not only address living conditions and health care but also gender and age-specific needs.

Gay Rights

In October 2009, the U.S. president Barack Obama signed the Matthew Shepard and James Byrd, Jr. Hate Crimes Prevention Act, which extends the 1969 federal hate crime law to include acts of violence motivated by gender, sexual orientation, or gender identity. The act became the first federal law to extend legal protection to transgendered people. The act is named after two victims of hate crimes. In 1998, Matthew Shepard, a 21-year-old student at the University of Wyoming, was offered a ride home by two men who then robbed him, beat and tortured him, and then tied him to a fence. He was found alive 18 hours later, but died from his injuries. James Byrd, Jr., an African-American man living in Jasper, Texas, was tied to the back of a truck and dragged until he was decapitated. Neither of the victims' murderers were prosecuted under hate crime laws, due, in part, to the fact that the 1969 federal hate crime law was restricted to victims who were assaulted while engaging in a federally protected activity, such as voting or attending school.

Violence against lesbian, gay, bisexual, and transgender (LGBT) persons is an expression of a larger cultural ideology of intolerance, an ideology that cannot be effectively eliminated until LGBT persons enjoy the same rights as heterosexual persons. Gay rights advocate groups, such as the Courage Campaign, call for the elimination of the 1993 "Don't Ask, Don't Tell" policy, which prohibits gays and lesbians from revealing their sexual orientation while serving in the military. Some universities have responded to discrimination against gays in the military by refusing to allow military recruiters on campus, due to their own nondiscrimination policies, to which the Supreme Court responded in 2006 by ruling that universities that bar military recruiters may be denied federal funds.

One of the more contentious issues in the area of LGBT rights is that of same-sex marriage. As of 2010, same-sex marriage is legal in New Hampshire, Iowa, Massachusetts, Vermont, and Connecticut, but federal recognition of same-sex marriage is inhibited by the 1996 Defense of Marriage Act (DOMA), which defines marriage as being between a man and a woman. Human rights groups and gay rights advocacy groups support the repeal of DOMA, but opponents argue that legalizing gay marriage will require its inclusion in sex and health education in schools, as well as the possibility that it will jeopardize the tax exemption status of religious institutions that refuse to perform gay marriage. Much of the controversy came to nationwide attention in 2008 with the debate over California's Proposition 8, a ballot initiative that proposed an amendment to the state constitution that would define marriage as being exclusively between a man and a woman. Proposition 8 was passed, but gay rights advocates took the case to the U.S. District Court for the Northern District of California in *Perry v. Schwarzenegger.* In August 2010, the case was stayed, pending appeal, but is predicted to go to the U.S. Supreme Court.[74]

In August 2010, Proposition 8 was overturned by U.S. District Chief Judge Vaughn R. Walker, but the U.S. Court of Appeals for the Ninth Circuit indefinitely extended a stay on the case to prevent new same-sex marriages from being performed pending appeal. The case is expected to go to the U.S. Supreme Court.

In October 2010, U.S. District Judge Virginia Phillips of Riverside, California, issued an injunction against the "don't ask, don't tell" policy. The U.S. Justice Department responded in turn by filing papers requesting that Phillips grant a stay allowing the policy to remain in place pending appeal, or until the policy is repealed by Congress.

Pressing for Rights Internationally

In March 2003, the United States invaded Iraq in what was later termed Operation Iraqi Freedom. While the events precipitating the invasion largely focused on the al-Qaeda attack on the World Trade Center and the Pentagon on September 11, 2001, as well as military intelligence that suggested that Saddam Hussein was harboring weapons of mass destruction (WMD) in Iraq, the mission statement for the invasion of Iraq became an amalgamation of national defense and efforts to defend human rights in Iraq (and Afghanistan, which the United States military invaded in 2001). Afghanistan and Iraq had long been world renowned for their poor record of protecting human rights, and much of the information surrounding the two invasions focused on the liberation of oppressed peoples. But the U.S. military and the George W. Bush administration came under attack by human rights groups for their violent interrogation techniques, termed "enhanced interrogation techniques" by the Bush administration. Techniques included slapping, grabbing, shaking, exposure to extreme cold, forcing the prisoner to stand while handcuffed and shackled for 40 hours, sleep deprivation, and water-boarding, a technique in which a cloth is placed over the prisoner's face and water is poured on the face to simulate drowning. Despite repeated assurances from the Bush administration and the Central Intelligence Agency (CIA) that enhanced interrogation techniques do not amount to torture, Human Rights Watch has highlighted the fact that "the person believes that they are being killed, and as such, it really amounts to a mock execution, which is illegal under international law."[75] Many of the human rights violations in dispute have occurred at the U.S. detention facility in Guantánamo Bay, Cuba, where many detainees have been held since 2002. The youngest detainee, Canadian-born Omar Khadr, was only 15 when he was incarcerated at Guantánamo

Bay, where he was physically and emotionally abused by guards, sleep deprived, forced to stand for several hours, and shackled in extreme stress positions until he soiled himself. Before his transfer to Guantánamo Bay, Khadr was interrogated at the Bagram Airfield base in Afghanistan, where he claims his hands were tied above his head to a door frame for hours, he was splashed with cold water, and he was hooded and threatened with barking dogs.[76]

According to Human Rights Watch, "Guantánamo has undermined America's moral authority around the world."[77] Immediately following his inauguration, one of President Barack Obama's first executive orders was the closing of the Guantánamo Bay detention facility within one year. However, as of July 2010, 181 detainees still remain at Guantánamo Bay.[78]

Such blatant violations of human rights as those that have occurred at Guantánamo Bay and elsewhere cast a shadow over the United States's position in the world as a champion of rights, particularly in their stated mission to protect human rights in Iraq and Afghanistan.

CONCLUSION

The nature and definition of rights have been debated throughout American history as new cases have challenged state and federal laws determining who is entitled to rights, what rights are to be protected over others, and how to enforce rights. But as American society decides who is to be included in the protection of human rights, who, then, is to be excluded? The likeliest answer is noncitizens, but as issues of immigration reform and illegal immigration are debated, even that is coming under closer scrutiny. Does a division between human and civil rights exist? Those who campaigned for civil rights in the 1960s and '70s would argue no, as the social exclusion of an individual or group inherently affects their rights as human beings to reach their fullest potential and achieve their goals.

As U.S. lawmakers, scholars, religious authorities, and everyday citizens continue to unravel the tangled lines of ideology and law, we will continue to see a deeper exploration of rights and the human community.

---

[1] Jacques Derrida. *Writing and Difference*. Chicago: University of Chicago Press, 1978, p. 356.

[2] Bahamian History Online. "Personalities in Bahamian History: Christopher Columbus." Available online. URL: http://www.bahamasnationalarchives.bs/Bahamian_Educators/Bahamian_Educators_Columbus _Christopher.htm. Accessed on October 7, 2009.

[3] Howard Zinn. *A People's History of the United States, 1492–Present*. New York: HarperCollins, 1980, p. 1.

[4] The Franciscan Archive. "Excerpts from Christopher Columbus' Log, 1492 A.D." Available online. URL: http://www.franciscan-archive.org/columbus/opera/excerpts.html. Accessed on October 7, 2009.

[5] Bahamian History Online. "Personalities in Bahamian History: Christopher Columbus." Available online. URL: http://www.bahamasnationalarchives.bs/Bahamian_Educators/Bahamian_Educators_Columbus _Christopher.htm. Accessed on October 7, 2009.

[6] The Franciscan Archive. "Excerpts from Christopher Columbus' Log, 1492 A.D." Available online. URL: http://www.franciscan-archive.org/columbus/opera/excerpts.html. Accessed on October 7, 2009.

[7] ———. "Excerpts from Christopher Columbus' Log, 1492 A.D." Available online. URL: http://www.franciscan-archive.org/columbus/opera/excerpts.html. Accessed on October 7, 2009.

[8] Howard Zinn. *A People's History of the United States, 1492–Present.* New York: HarperCollins, 1980, p. 7.

[9] David E. Stannard. *American Holocaust: Conquest of the New World.* New York: Oxford University Press, 1992, p. 102.

[10] ———. *American Holocaust: Conquest of the New World,* p. 105.

[11] ———. *American Holocaust: Conquest of the New World,* pp. 105–106.

[12] John Winthrop. *Life and Letters of John Winthrop.* Boston: Ticknor and Fields, 1864, p. 312.

[13] Howard Zinn. *A People's History of the United States, 1492–Present.* New York: HarperCollins, 1980, pp. 23–27.

[14] Olaudah Equiano. *The Interesting Narrative of the Life of Olaudah Equiano, or Gustavus Vassa, the African, Written by Himself.* London: Olaudah Equiano, 1794, p. 51.

[15] Alexander Falconbridge. *An Account of the Slave Trade on the Coast of Africa.* London: J. Philips and George Yard, 1788, p. 25.

[16] Reverend Robert Walsh. "Aboard a Slave Ship, 1829." Eyewitness to History. Available online. URL: http://www.eyewitnesstohistory.com/slaveship.htm. Accessed October 11, 2009.

[17] Faye Z. Belgrave, and Kevin W. Allison. *African-American Psychology: from Africa to America.* Thousand Oaks, Calif.: Sage Publications, 2006, p. 330.

[18] Maryland State Archives. "Understanding Maryland Records: Indentured Servants." Available online. URL: http://www.msa.md.gov/msa/refserv/html/servant.html. Accessed on October 12, 2009.

[19] Edwin J. Perkins. *The Economy of Colonial America.* New York: Columbia University Press, 1988, pp. 91–92.

[20] Edward Long. *The History of Jamaica.* Vol. 2. London: T. Lowndes, 1774, pp. 351–448.

[21] Howard Zinn. *A People's History of the United States, 1492–Present.* New York: HarperCollins, 1980, p. 45.

[22] Gary B. Nash. *The Unknown American Revolution: the Unruly Birth of Democracy and the Struggle to Create America.* New York: Penguin Books, 2005, p. 46.

[23] ———. *The Unknown American Revolution: the Unruly Birth of Democracy and the Struggle to Create America*, p. 46.

[24] Howard Zinn. *A People's History of the United States, 1492–Present.* New York: HarperCollins, 1980, p. 66.

[25] William M. Van der Weyde. *The Life and Works of Thomas Paine.* New York: Thomas Paine National Historical Society, 1925, pp. 19–20.

[26] Thomas Paine. *Common Sense.* New York: Peter Eckler, 1918, p. 57.

[27] Ronald Schultz. "A Class Society? The Nature of Inequality in Early America." *Inequality in Early America.* Carla Gardina Pestana and Sharon V. Salinger, eds. Hanover, N.H.: University Press of New England, 1999, p. 212.

[28] Howard Zinn. *A People's History of the United States, 1492–Present.* New York: Harper-Collins, 1980, p. 65.

[29] South Carolina Information Highway. "Growth of South Carolina's Slave Population." Available online. URL: http://www.sciway.net/afam/slavery/population.html. Accessed October 16, 2009.

[30] Ronald Schultz. "A Class Society? The Nature of Inequality in Early America." *Inequality in Early America.* Carla Gardina Pestana and Sharon V. Salinger, eds. Hanover, N.H.: University Press of New England, 1999, p. 212.

[31] Albert Jay Nock. *Jefferson.* New York: Hill and Wang, 1966, p. 57.

[32] Ronald Schultz. "A Class Society? The Nature of Inequality in Early America." *Inequality in Early America.* Carla Gardina Pestana and Sharon V. Salinger, eds. Hanover, N.H.: University Press of New England, 1999, p. 213.

[33] Dred Scott Case Collection. "Dred Scott Chronology." Available online. URL: http://library.wustl.edu/vlib/dredscott/chronology.html. Accessed on October 17, 2009.

[34] Yale Law School. "Fugitive Slave Act 1850." The Avalon Project. Available online. URL: http://avalon.law.yale.edu/19th_century/fugitive.asp. Accessed on October 17, 2009.

[35] National Park Service, U.S. Department of the Interior. "The Dred Scott Case." Available online. URL: http://www.nps.gov/archive/jeff/dred_scott.html. Accessed on October.

[36] Dred Scott Case Collection. "Dred Scott Chronology." Available online. URL: http://library.wustl.edu/vlib/dredscott/chronology.html. Accessed on October 17, 2009.

[37] Nikki Marie Taylor. *Frontiers of Freedom: Cincinnati's Black Community, 1802–1868.* Athens: Ohio University Press, 2005, p. 159.

[38] Henry Howe. *Historical Collections of Ohio.* Columbus, Ohio: Henry Howe & Son, 1891, p. 105.

[39] David Brion Davis. *Inhuman Bondage: The Rise and Fall of Slavery in the New World.* New York: Oxford University Press, 2006, p. 300.

[40] National Archives & Records Administration. "Featured Documents: The Emancipation Proclamation." Available online. URL: http://www.archives.gov/exhibits/featured_documents/emancipation_proclamation/. Accessed on October 19, 2009.

[41] Cornell University, Division of Rare & Manuscript Collections. "'I Will be Heard!' Abolitionism in America." Available online. URL: http://rmc.library.cornell.edu/abolitionism/thirteenth.htm. Accessed on October 19, 2009.

[42] Lynne Olson. *Freedom's Daughters: The Unsung Heroines of the Civil Rights Movement 1830 to 1970.* New York: Scribner, 2001, pp. 28–30.

[43] Woodrow Wilson. Sixty-Fifth Congress, 1 Session, Senate Document No. 5. Available online. History Matters. "Making the World 'Safe for Democracy': Woodrow Wilson Asks for War." URL: http://historymatters.gmu.edu/d/4943/. Accessed on October 30, 2009.

[44] Child Labor Public Education Project. "Child Labor in U.S. History." Available online. URL: http://www.continuetolearn.uiowa.edu/laborctr/child_labor/about/us_history.html. Accessed on October 30, 2009.

[45] ———. "Child Labor in U.S. History." Available online. URL: http://www.continuetolearn. uiowa.edu/laborctr/child_labor/about/us_history.html. Accessed on October 30, 2009.

[46] John E. B. Myers. *Legal Issues in Child Abuse and Neglect Practice.* Thousand Oaks, Calif.: Sage Publications, 1998, p. 38.

[47] American Humane Association. "Mary Ellen Wilson: How One Girl's Plight Started the Child-Protection Movement." Available online. URL: http://www.americanhumane.org/about-us/who-we-are/history/mary-ellen.html. Accessed on October 30, 2009.

[48] Cornell University ILR School. "The Story of the Triangle Fire: Part 3." Available online. URL: http://www.ilr.cornell.edu/trianglefire/narrative3.html. Accessed October 31, 2009.

[49] Gregg Yaz. "Leap for Life, Leap of Death." Available online. URL: http://www.csun.edu/~ghy7463/mw2.html. Accessed on October 31, 2009.

[50] Travel and History. "Pure Food and Drug Act." Available online. URL: http://www.u-s-history.com/pages/h917.html. Accessed on October 31, 2009.

[51] Cornell University ILR School. "The Story of the Triangle Fire: Investigation, Trial, and Reform." Available online. URL: http://www.ilr.cornell.edu/trianglefire/narrative6.html. Accessed October 31, 2009.

[52] Ronald L. F. Davis. "Creating Jim Crow." The History of Jim Crow. Available online. URL: http://www.jimcrowhistory.org/history/creating2.htm. Accessed on October 31, 2009.

[53] ———. "Creating Jim Crow." The History of Jim Crow. Available online. URL: http://www.jimcrowhistory.org/history/creating2.htm. Accessed November 1, 2009.

[54] Abraham L. Davis, and Barbara Luck Graham. *The Supreme Court, Race, and Civil Rights.* Thousand Oaks, Calif.: Sage Publications, 1995, p. 21.

[55] Claudia M. Stolz. "Biography: Booker T. Washington." The History of Jim Crow. Available online. URL: http://www.jimcrowhistory.org/resources/biographies/Washington_BookerT. htm. Accessed on November 1, 2009.

[56] ———. "Biography: Booker T. Washington." The History of Jim Crow. Available online. URL: http://www.jimcrowhistory.org/resources/biographies/Washington_BookerT.htm. Accessed on November 1, 2009.

[57] Abraham L. Davis, and Barbara Luck Graham. *The Supreme Court, Race, and Civil Rights.* Thousand Oaks, Calif.: Sage Publications, 1995, p. 24.

[58] Library of Congress: Exhibitions. "'With an Even Hand': Brown v. Board at Fifty." Available online. URL: http://www.loc.gov/exhibits/brown/brown-brown.html. Accessed on November 1, 2009.

[59] Ellen Chesler. *Woman of Valor: Margaret Sanger and the Birth Control Movement in America.* New York: Simon & Schuster, 1992, p. 223.

[60] National Committee on Pay Equity. "The Wage Gap Over Time: In Real Dollars, Women See a Continuing Gap." Available online. URL: http://www.pay-equity.org/info-time.html. Accessed on November 1, 2009.

[61] Cornell University Law School. "Roe v. Wade (No. 70-18), 314 F.Supp. 1217, affirmed in part and reversed in part." Available online. URL: http://www.law.cornell.edu/supct/html/historics/USSC_CR_0410_0113_ZS.html. Accessed on November 2, 2009.

[62] Howard Winant. *The New Politics of Race: Globalism, Difference, Justice.* Minneapolis: University of Minnesota Press, 2004.

[63] Stanford Encyclopedia of Philosophy. "Affirmative Action." Available online. URL: http://plato.stanford.edu/entries/affirmative-action/. Accessed on November 2, 2009.

[64] Institute for Women's Policy Research. "The Gender Wage Gap: 2009" (March 2010). Available online. URL: http://www.iwpr.org/pdf/C350.pdf. Accessed on July 2, 2010.

[65] United States General Accounting Office. "Women's Earnings: Work Patterns Partially Explain Difference Between Men's and Women's Earnings" (October 2003). Available online. URL: http://www.gao.gov/new.items/d0435.pdf. Accessed July 2, 2010.

[66] Kevin O'Leary. "Fatal Sunshine: The Plight of California's Farm Workers." *Time,* (8/8/09). Available online. URL: http://www.time.com/time/nation/article/0,8599,1914961,00.html. Accessed on July 3, 2010.

[67] Global Initiative to End Corporal Punishment of Children. "States with Full Abolition" (May 2010). Available online. URL: http://www.endcorporalpunishment.org/pages/progress/prohib_states.html. Accessed on July 3, 2010.

[68] Tomas Almaguer. *Racial Fault Lines: The Historical Origins of White Supremacy in California.* Berkeley and Los Angeles: University of California Press, 1994.

[69] VOA News. "Obama Urges Congress: Reform Immigration Rules" (7/2/10). Available online. URL: http://www1.voanews.com/learningenglish/home/world/Obama-Urges-Congress-Reform-Immigration-Rules-97707819.html. Accessed on July 3, 2010.

[70] ACLU. "Conditions of Confinement" (2010). Available online. URL: http://www.aclu.org/prisoners-rights/conditions-confinement. Accessed on July 3, 2010.

[71] Human Rights Watch. "U.S. Federal Statistics Show Widespread Prison Rape" (12/15/07). Available online. URL: http://www.hrw.org/en/news/2007/12/15/us-federal-statistics-show-widespread-prison-rape. Accessed on July 3, 2010.

[72] National Public Radio. "Sexual Abuse Persists in Juvenile Detention Centers" (6/7/10). Available online. URL: http://www.npr.org/templates/story/story.php?storyId=127536419. Accessed on July 3, 2010.

[73] Human Rights Watch. "All Too Familiar: Sexual Abuse of Women in U.S. State Prisons" (December 1996). Available online. URL: http://www.hrw.org/reports/1996/Us1.htm#_1_2. Accessed on July 3, 2010.

[74] Jesse McKinley. "Both Sides in California's Gay Marriage Fight See a Long Court Battle Ahead." *The New York Times* (6/26/10). Available online. URL: http://www.nytimes.com/2010/06/27/us/27prop8.html?_r=1. Accessed on July 3, 2010.

[75] Brian Ross, and Richard Esposito. "CIA's Harsh Interrogation Techniques Described." ABC News (11/18/05). Available online. URL: http://abcnews.go.com/WNT/Investigation/story?id=1322866. Accessed on July 8, 2010.

[76] Audrey Macklin. "Memory Loss and Torture." Human Rights Watch (5/25/10). Available online. URL: http://www.hrw.org/en/news/2010/05/25/memory-loss-and-torture. Accessed on July 8, 2010.

[77] Human Rights Watch. "Mark Guantánamo's Seventh Year by Closing It" (1/9/09). Available online. URL: http://www.hrw.org/en/news/2009/01/09/us-mark-guantanamo-s-seventh-year-closing-it. Accessed on July 8, 2010.

[78] Carol Rosenberg. "Federal Judge Orders Guantánamo Detainee Freed." *Miami Herald* (7/8/10). Available online. URL: http://www.miamiherald.com/2010/07/08/1721792/federal-judge-orders-guantanamo.html. Accessed on July 8, 2010.

3

⁓

Global Perspectives

The following case studies share many similarities, despite their strikingly different cultures and histories. Authoritarian regimes, silenced opposition, discrimination against women and minorities, and the use of violence to force obedience are just a few of the characteristics that these case studies have in common. A closer look reveals how the current state of human rights in each country came to be. Most of the case studies share the common characteristic of being in possession of a prized natural resource that is in high demand throughout the world, such as oil, diamonds, or coltan (columbite-tantalite: a material used to make computers and mobile phones); three out of the four countries have experienced foreign occupation or foreign-backed coups to install governments more friendly to particular world powers, such as the United States, Britain, or Russia; each country has also experienced a political revolution within the last 50 years.

Despite their similarities, the countries in this chapter have different conceptions of, and approaches to, human rights. Religious beliefs, social customs, and cultural traditions have wide-ranging effects on the development and protection of human rights in a given region, and one problem that continually resurfaces in discussions of standards for international human rights is the issue of how to define human rights. At what point does a religious rite or cultural tradition become a human rights abuse? What if the victims of such abuses do not believe they are being abused? Where does the international community draw the line between human rights protection and imperialistic intrusion?

International human rights organizations agree that while some rights are more urgent, such as the right to life and freedom from bodily harm, others, while not as urgent, must also be recognized, such as the right to free speech, peaceful assembly, and protest. Some of the topics discussed in this chapter include (but are not limited to):

Civil Rights

Civil rights refer to a division of rights that allows an individual to fully participate in the civil and political functioning of a state. This includes voting rights, equal education and employment, right to due process and a fair trial, freedom from discrimination, as well as more basic individual rights, such as freedom of expression. Before human rights in a given country can be established and protected, the citizens of that country must be able to discuss them. An exploration of rights is not possible without the freedom to disagree. Article 19 of the Universal Declaration of Human Rights declares: "Everyone has the right to freedom of opinion and expression; this right includes freedom to hold opinions without interference and to seek, receive, and impart information and ideas through any media regardless of frontiers."[1] In some countries, a governmental body may exert tight controls not only on the dissemination of information by censoring journalists and taking control of the press, but it may also impose blockages to access of information in the form of internet firewalls and intercepted e-mails. In such countries, the act of holding a different opinion may be not only illegal, but dangerous. Sometimes—particularly in the case of journalists and academics—the simple act of seeking information is fraught with danger, and individuals may be punished for such crimes as undermining national security, or attempting to access and disseminate classified information.

According to the Committee to Protect Journalists, 136 reporters, journalists, and photographers were in prison worldwide as of December 1, 2009, which is up from 125 in 2008. China continues to lead the world as the top jailer of journalists, with 24 in prison in 2009, while Iran comes in close behind with 23 in prison.[2] A total of 70 journalists were killed worldwide in 2009, and 67 percent of those killed were covering political issues.[3]

Harsh punishments are not strictly reserved for journalists. Protestors and those expressing oppositional opinions are routinely imprisoned, tortured, exiled, and murdered around the world. In Iran, the riots following the June 2009 elections resulted in 4,000 detained protesters and several imprisoned opposition leaders.[4] In China, several individuals who requested to be able to protest at designated sites during the 2008 Olympics in Beijing were arrested and sentenced to reeducation in labor camps.[5]

Women's Rights

Women's rights have many overlaps with civil rights, such as the right to equal education and employment, and freedom from discrimination, but they also include issues more specific to women, such as reproductive rights, right to adequate maternal health care, and legal protection from sexual abuse (including marital rape). According to the organization Women's Rights Worldwide, women's rights include the right to equal education, to literacy, to vote, to choose one's partner, to leave one's partner, to choose whether or not to become pregnant, to choose a career, to enter into legal contracts, to own property, to hold public office, to have free and equal access to information, to leave their home as they wish, and to not be forced to perform or submit to sexual acts.[6] While these may appear to be basic rights, the fact is that many of these have only recently been addressed in developed nations. In England, for example, married women did not obtain the right to own property or enter into legal contracts until 1935. In the United States, women continue to earn approximately 30 percent less than men for the same work, and most struggle to obtain affordable child care and paid maternity leave.[7]

In many countries today, a woman's survival is not even certain. Pregnancy and childbirth is the leading cause of death of women of reproductive age around the world.[8] In Afghanistan and Sierra Leone, one out of every eight pregnant women dies in childbirth. In Niger, one in seven dies.[9] The problem lies in the fact that in order to protect a woman's right to safe and healthy pregnancy and childbirth, governments must first respect and protect a woman's basic human rights, such as the rights to life, equality, and education. Generally speaking, a woman's right to safe pregnancy and childbirth is dependent upon her right to access information on reproductive health, such as sexual health, contraceptive use, birth spacing, safe abortion, and pre- and post-natal care.[10] Access to information for women, however, remains elusive in many countries. Of the world's 800 million illiterate people, two-thirds are women. Only one in 10 women in Niger can read.[11]

In many countries around the world, women are the object of institutionalized physical and sexual violence. In the Democratic Republic of the Congo (DRC), women and girls are routinely raped by both invading rebel soldiers and soldiers in the Congolese army as a means of terrorizing villages and punishing individual families. Thus, women's rights range from issues of equality and civil participation, to issues of basic safety and survival.

Children's Rights

November 20, 2009, marked the 20th anniversary of the Convention on the Rights of the Child, the most widely ratified human rights treaty in history. The convention emphasized the four basic principles of children's rights: nondiscrimination; actions taken in the best interest of the child; the right to life, survival, and development; and respect for the views of the child in accordance with age and maturity.[12]

Since the convention, significant progress in children's rights has been made. The number of deaths of children under age five worldwide has dropped from 12.5 million a year in 1990 to 9 million annually in 2008. HIV treatment for children under 15 has risen significantly throughout the world, as has the use of mosquito nets to prevent malaria in children under five. In education, the number of truant children has dropped from 115 million in 2002 to 101 million in 2007, more children are completing primary school education, and more girls are attending school. Despite this progress, many challenges still remain. Approximately 1 billion children around the world are not receiving one or more services essential to survival and development, 148 million children are underweight, and 101 million children are not attending primary school. In 2008, 8.8 million children under age five died.[13]

Children remain the most vulnerable victims of war, oppression, violence, poverty, and disease. Of even greater concern to children's rights activists is the fact that several dozen children continue to be executed as criminals globally every year. Iran is the leading executioner of child offenders in the world, followed by Sudan, Saudi Arabia, Pakistan, and Yemen. Hundreds of children (an estimated 130 or more) remain on death row, awaiting execution. This phenomenon is not exclusive to developing countries. There were 70 juvenile offenders on death row in the United States in 2005, when the U.S. Supreme Court ruled the execution of juvenile offenders illegal because it violates the U.S. Constitution's ban on cruel and unusual punishment.[14] In many countries, children are also routinely conscripted as child soldiers.

Children's rights remain precarious throughout the world, even more so because children are not capable of demanding their rights. Thus, it is incumbent upon governments and activists to speak for children and protect their rights.

These are some of the basic issues covered in this chapter, and many others fall under the umbrellas of civil rights, women's rights, and children's rights. Because the issues addressed in this chapter are specific to the countries profiled, not all major human rights topics are addressed. Human rights groups, journalists, and lawmakers are actively engaged in discussions about several other major topics, such as lesbian/gay/bisexual/transgender (LGTB) rights, HIV/AIDS research, the rights of prisoners, and the rights of other socially marginalized groups.

DEMOCRATIC REPUBLIC OF THE CONGO

Located in Central Africa, the Democratic Republic of the Congo is the third-largest country in Africa and was home to almost 70 million people in 2009. The country was one of the centers of the transatlantic slave trade from the 15th through 18th centuries and under harsh colonial rule from 1908 to 1960. Belgium failed to prepare the Congo for independence—there were few trained administrators, doctors, or teachers in place when Belgium abruptly pulled out of the country in 1960—and the Congo has been racked by civil war, poverty, and disease ever since. Since the outbreak of the Second Congo War in 1998, an estimated 5.4 million people have died from direct violence or from displacement and disease.[15] Approximately 45,000 continue to die each month, and the Congolese war has now accounted for more deaths than any other conflict since World War II.[16] Forty percent of the soldiers in the Democratic Republic of the Congo are children who were kidnapped during the country's second civil war, some of whom were forced into sexual slavery.[17] While the civil war, termed by some as Africa's World War, officially ended in 2003, violence and hostilities continue and thousands continue to die each month.

Historical and Cultural Perspectives

The complex and multilayered culture of the Democratic Republic of the Congo is derived from a historical intermingling of hundreds of different ethnic groups that were further stratified by colonial rule and the influence of European culture and religion. Today, more than 250 languages are spoken in the Democratic Republic of the Congo, which have been grouped into five official languages: the Bantu languages of Kikongo, Lingala, and Tshiluba, as well as Kingwana, a dialect of Swahili, and French, the official language of business. Because of the Congo's use as a primary source country in the transatlantic slave trade, traces of Congolese culture and language can be found all over the world, such as in the Gullah community of South Carolina in the United States.

The origins of cruelty, violence, and terror in the Democratic Republic of the Congo of today can be found in the quick stroke of a pencil on Christmas Eve, 1884, when the Belgian king Leopold II made official claims on the region. Prior to this, the Congo was a thriving, ethnically diverse community of cattle herders, farmers, and metallurgists. The Congo Basin was settled in successive waves of migration from all over Africa, primarily of Bantu-speaking people from Nigeria. The movement of Bantu people into the Congo Basin pushed the previous Mbuti and Twa inhabitants into the grasslands, and as groups of people from other regions in Africa converged in the Congo Basin, the ethnic makeup of the inhabitants became increasingly diverse.[18]

By the 14th century, the Kongo kingdom was a highly structured, matrilineal state, in which women functioned as the heads of families or *kandas*, and sons inherited not only rank and social prestige but also material goods

75

from their mothers. By the time of the first contact with the Portuguese in the 15th century, the Kongo kingdom included 3 million subjects, six major provinces, and an army of 80,000 men.[19] Portuguese explorers arrived in the Congo in 1482 (ten years before Columbus's voyage) and found what they considered a rich supply of slaves for the Atlantic slave trade. A system of slavery existed in the kingdom prior to the arrival of the Europeans; most of the slaves were war captives. The kingdom's power initially increased with the arrival of the Portuguese in the late 15th century. Hoping to gain superior tools and weapons, many of the Kongo people became actively involved in trade—especially the slave trade—with the Portuguese. However, when the Portuguese began to exploit the practice as a major commercial enterprise, King Afonso sent a letter to Portugal's King João III, begging him to put an end to the slave trade, which was gradually eroding the Kongo population. By the 19th century, 5 million Congolese people had been captured and sold as slaves, which played a significant role in destabilizing the country.[20]

Internal division also fragmented the kingdom following a battle with the Portuguese military that left the Congolese king António (r. 1661–65) dead and quashed attempts at unification by Capuchin priests. By the middle of the 19th century, the Kongo kingdom had dissolved, making the area vulnerable to European colonization.[21]

Noting the potential for the acquisition of capital in the Congo, the Belgian king Leopold II organized an expedition to Africa in 1876 to either deceive or force African rulers to relinquish their land to King Leopold and his organization, Association du Congo. Leopold's interest in the Congo was a wholly personal one with no initial ties to Belgium. With the help of an explorer named Henry Morton Stanley, King Leopold legitimated his claim to the Congo by presenting it to the Berlin West African Conference as a humanitarian endeavor.[22]

The Berlin Conference was organized by the German chancellor Otto von Bismarck in November 1884 with the goal of officially partitioning the African continent into zones of colonial rule by Europe and the United States. France, Germany, Great Britain, and Portugal already controlled large areas of Africa at this time, but the goal of the conference was to come to an official consensus on which zones were controlled by whom.[23] It was at the Berlin Conference that Leopold presented his project, under the guise of wishing to protect the Congolese from the "Arab slavers."[24] Before Leopold could claim the Congo, he had to define the exact territory that constituted the Congo. Henry Morton Stanley's expedition had delineated the Congo as a thin, serpentine strip along the Congo River from Boma to Kisangani. But when Leopold drew up his map of the Congo to present to the Berlin Conference, he had effectively tripled the size of the country.[25]

Having taken out several loans to pay for the expeditions into the Congo, Leopold endeavored to earn back the money he had borrowed and more by turning the Congo into a virtual plantation in itself. Congolese land became "crown domain" or "private domain of the state," and Leopold sought to profit from its rich stores of rubber and ivory. To squeeze the most use out of the land, Leopold established a regime of cruelty and brutality. Institutionalized rape and mutilation were used to punish those who did not meet their daily quota of production. Between the time Leopold declared the Congo Free State under his authority in 1885, to 1908, when he was forced to relinquish personal control of the state, after international condemnation of human rights abuses, the Congolese population dropped severely. According to 1911 census data, the Congolese population dropped from 30 million to 8.5 million people. Ironically, King Leopold II never once set foot on Congolese soil.[26]

Journalists and other observers began to notice the arrival of ships from the Congo bearing vast quantities of ivory and rubber, but returning to the Congo with nothing more than guns and ammunition, which sparked suspicions of forced labor. Reports from missionaries began to surface detailing brutal atrocities at the hands of Leopold's agents. In 1903, Roger Casement, the British consul in Boma, wrote a report in which he described graphic cases of violence, including the use of the *chicotte*, a type of whip made from raw, dried hippopotamus hide, and the practice of chopping off the right hands of adults and children who did not fulfill their quota.[27]

In the late 1890s, a British journalist named Edward Dene Morel began to expose Leopold's cruel regime in the Congo, which had avoided any implication in the use of slave labor by having selected Congolese authorities to terrorize and punish their own people.[28] Leopold and his Belgian agents could not claim ignorance as to the cruelty and inhumanity of the colonial conquest, as the Congolese overseers routinely shipped the dried hands of their victims back to the Belgian commissioner as proof that they were enforcing the regime.[29]

In 1908, pressure from worldwide outrage compelled Leopold to sell control of the Congo to the Belgian state. Forced labor continued for the next 40 years under Belgian colonial rule, and in 1935 the government of Belgium set a minimum requirement of 60 days of compulsory labor per year for the state for every Congolese citizen in the cultivation of export crops and labor on public projects. Conscripted labor was euphemized under the title "collective obligations to the state."[30] The minimum requirement was increased to 120 days in 1942. In 1959, anticolonial riots in Kinshasa resulted in independence from Belgium the following year.[31]

The legacy of Leopold's regime and the later Belgian colonial government is still visible in the Congolese culture today, and many of the current human rights crises in the Democratic Republic of the Congo can be traced back to the unequal distribution of power that was fostered under colonial rule. To be clear, slavery as an institution is highly complex, and the complexity of the transatlantic slave trade is further complicated by the fact that a flourishing slave trade had already existed in many parts of Africa before Europeans began exporting slaves to the Americas. Under Leopold, however, this practice was nurtured and exploited on the Congo's own home soil, and remnants of the barbarity of Leopold's regime, such as punitive mutilation and sexual violence, constitute the major human rights issues in the Democratic Republic of the Congo. Congolese culture today, while distinct from Europe and maintaining a unique identity of its own, is inseparable from the legacy of slavery and colonial discourse.

Unique Circumstances of Human Rights in the Democratic Republic of the Congo

Just as Congolese culture today is steeped in 400 years of slavery and European colonization, the current circumstances of human rights in the Democratic Republic of the Congo (DRC) must be understood within the context of the struggle for independence and the subsequent conflicts that arose not only within the Congolese population but on an international scale as well. The transition from Belgian to African rule in the Congo was a shaky one that paved the way for the later political and economic instability that would plague the country for years. Before Belgium officially relinquished control over the Congo, it robbed the treasury and transferred the debt to the new Congolese government (a scenario that has similarly occurred in other countries where independence has been won from colonial rule, such as Haiti).[32] There were 29,000 Europeans living in the Congo in 1960, and Congolese resentment of the social hierarchy that privileged whites resulted in widespread riots and insurrection. Congolese troops mutinied against white commanders who insisted on maintaining the status quo, and violence and rape were carried out against many European civilians.[33]

In addition to a rocky economy, the Congo's relations with other nations also became troubled, especially as cold war fears began to loom heavily over the United States, which feared that the Congo would align with the Soviet Union and provide minerals and other resources to the country. Congo's first elected leader, Prime Minister Patrice Lumumba, added to the unease when he stated: "The Soviet Union has been the only great power which supported the Congolese people in their struggle from the beginning."[34] Unnerved by the possibility of the Congo supplying the Soviet Union with resources, President Dwight Eisenhower ordered the CIA to "eliminate him" in favor of the more U.S.-friendly Joseph-Désiré Mobutu.[35] Lumumba was forced out of office in a coup d'état in 1961 and executed by a firing squad. In an attempt to conceal the murder, Lumumba's body was dismembered and dissolved in acid.[36] Mobutu later went on to repress and execute political rivals, with much support from the United States as long as he and the Congo remained anticommunist.[37] In 1971, Mobutu renamed the country Zaïre and remained president for 32 years, during which time he exploited state resources for his own use and squandered billions of dollars. By the time of his death in 1997, he and his family had amassed a fortune and left the Congo 12 billion dollars in debt.[38]

The current human rights crises in the DRC can be grasped within the context of the poverty in which Mobutu left the Congo, and the later multinational African war that stemmed from the 1994 Rwandan genocide. As one of the most (if not the most) mineral-rich countries in the world, much of the violence in the Congo and its conflicts with neighboring countries can be traced back to the struggles of different groups to control rich mining zones. In 1994, the Rwandan genocide and the subsequent takeover by the Tutsi rebels sent more than 1 million Hutu fleeing into neighboring Zaïre to avoid repercussions. The Hutu soldiers who fled to Zaïre allied themselves with the Mobutu government.

The Tutsi-run Rwandan army, allied with the anti-Mobutu group the Alliance for Democratic Liberation (AFDL), invaded Zaïre, attacked the refugee camps, and seized the capital, Kinshasa, in 1997, ousting Mobutu, who fled and died later that year of prostate cancer. The rebel leader, Laurent Kabila, declared himself president and renamed the country the Democratic Republic of the Congo. Approximately 200,000 Hutu refugees went missing in the forests of the Congo at this time, fleeing the Rwandan army, and the United Nations released a report suspecting mass slaughter, among other human rights abuses.[39] When President Kabila attempted to distance himself from Rwanda by removing all Tutsi from government positions, the Rwandan army invaded the Congo with the backing of the Ugandan army. Kabila received help from Zimbabwe, Namibia, and Angola to fight off the Rwandan army; the war became one of the largest ones in African history.[40] Laurent Kabila was assassinated in January 2001.[41]

The abundance of minerals in the Democratic Republic of the Congo and the scramble to secure claim on mining zones has fueled ongoing violence between the combatants. Poverty, war, and political instability have all but obliterated Congolese infrastructure, which has made the enforcement of human rights difficult, if not impossible in some instances. Local police battalions are underfunded, and police officers and soldiers are underpaid and often go months without being paid at all. Furthermore, it is not uncommon for those individuals who are arrested for serious crimes, such as rape, to avoid punishment by paying off judges. Even lack of vehicles for local police officers, compounded by poor roads, complicates enforcement. As the head of one police battalion in the city of Buvavu complained to the *Christian Science Monitor* in 2009: "A 9-year-old girl was raped by a soldier the other day, but we couldn't get there."[42]

International Response

The toll of the Congolese war has been unparalleled, with countless civilian lives lost and devastated. In 1999, the Democratic Republic of the Congo and five regional states signed the Lusaka Ceasefire Agreement in Zambia, but fighting continued nevertheless, and the UN Security Council created the peacekeeping mission United Nations Organization Mission in the Democratic Republic of the Congo (MONUC) to monitor the Lusaka Agreement.[43] In 2001, the United Nations released its first report on the Congolese war, which specifically located the root of the violence in the competition for control over and access to Congo's minerals.[44] The report found that all of the parties to the conflict, including Congolese officials, rebels, and allies, have participated in some form of pillage of the Congo's natural resources. A 2002 report also listed 85 international businesses that have capitalized on the conflict in the Congo, 21 of which were Belgian.[45] Although the war was declared over in 2003, fighting has continued unabated in the east of the country.

MONUC has recently come under heavy criticism from Human Rights Watch, which accuses the UN organization of knowingly backing a Congolese military operation that has resulted in widespread human rights violations. MONUC partnered with the Congolese army in operation Kimia II in March 2009 in an attempt to disarm the Hutu Rwandan group Democratic Forces for the Liberation of Rwanda (FDLR). To the shock of many, the Congolese army attacked Congolese villages that it accused of supporting or collaborating with the FDLR. Between March and October 2009, the Congolese army attacked and killed 505 Congolese civilians—the very people that the army is meant to protect. In retaliation, the FDLR killed 630 civilians between January and September 2009.[46]

On November 1, 2009, the head of the UN Department of Peacekeeping Operations, Alain Le Roy, announced that MONUC would suspend its support of the 213th Brigade of the Congolese army, which operates in the Nyabiondo region, but the move has been criticized as being too little, too late. Human Rights Watch argues that suspending support to only one of the units responsible for attacks on civilians hardly addresses the pervasive problem of human rights violations within the Congolese army, and furthermore, while UN officials were aware that the Congolese army was committing war crimes, they waited until eight months into the operation to partially suspend support. In November 2009, Human Rights Watch urged MONUC to suspend all support to the Congolese army until abusive commanders are removed and the government implements measures to protect civilians.[47]

In January 2010, the newly elected DRC president, Joseph Kabila, demanded the withdrawal of all MONUC forces by the end of June 2010, citing their ineffectiveness in securing peace and the further harm they have contributed to by supporting army brigades accused of mass rape and murder. That following May, the UN Security Council adopted Resolution 1925, which renews the mission of MONUC, but under the new title of United Nations Organization Stabilization Mission in the Democratic Republic of the Congo (MONUSCO). Effective July 1, 2010, the new mandate provides a timed withdrawal of the military element of MONUSCO under certain conditions, but if the human rights situation worsens, troops may be redeployed.[48]

A number of nongovernmental organizations and human rights groups are also actively working for the protection of human rights in the Democratic Republic of the Congo. Dismayed by the lack of international response to the prevalence of rape in the DRC, the Washington-based group Women for Women International has launched its own campaign to combat sexual violence by educating Congolese men. By partnering with prominent male community leaders, Women for Women organizes meetings and training sessions to educate civilians, soldiers, police officers, teachers, businessmen, priests, and others about the destructive power of rape. Because the enforcement of human rights in the Democratic Republic of the Congo is so unstable, groups like Women for Women see the potential for social change by working directly with civilians and law enforcement officials alike.[49]

Current Debates and Priorities in the Democratic Republic of the Congo

Many concerns regarding the current situation in the Democratic Republic of the Congo focus on the safety of women and children, who are particularly susceptible to violence, hunger, and disease. Children have accounted for 47 percent of all deaths since the war's beginning in 1998, even though they account for only 19 percent of the total population. The total mortality rate for the nation is 57 percent higher than the average rate for sub-Saharan Africa.[50] The vast majority of deaths are due to preventable conditions, such as hunger and illness caused by the collapse of the country's infrastructure, disruption of humanitarian aid, and lack of health care.[51]

Of primary concern is the use of pillage and rape as a common war practice. Rape cases are rarely pursued seriously by Congolese authorities, and soldiers in the warring armies commit sexual violence at staggering rates.[52] In the North Kivu Province alone, more than 2,200 cases of rape were reported between January and June of 2008. This likely only speaks to a minority of cases, as most tend to go unreported.[53]

Soldiers use sexual violence as a means of terrorizing civilians and asserting control over a strategic area, and sometimes to punish the civilians for perceived support for the enemy. As alliances continually shift, civilians cannot always be sure who the enemy is. Furthermore, after so many years of war, many villagers have been left with nothing, particularly as the conflict has made it virtually impossible for farmers to produce crops. When pillaging a village that is already destitute, soldiers use systematized rape to punish the villagers for what is believed to be a lack of support.[54]

Women who have been sexually assaulted are often reluctant to speak of their abuse as the position of women in the Congo was precarious even before the war, and women who have been raped may risk being rejected by their families and husbands. In some cases, rape victims are explicitly ordered by their husbands and/or other members of their families not to speak of the attack, so as to protect the family from shame. One woman who was abducted and raped by soldiers told interviewers that her husband was not upset with her when she returned home; "He was just worried about the diseases the soldier might have." Like so many others, she was ordered by her husband not to tell anyone of her rape.[55]

Even more alarming is the brutality with which some of the rapes are committed. In some cases, a vicious sexual assault is also accompanied by genital mutilation and beatings. While teenage girls and young women appear to be the most common victims of rape, soldiers have also been known to rape elderly women, boys, children under the age of nine, and even infants.[56] A number of human rights organizations, such as Oxfam and Human Rights Watch, have also noted a recent increase in the number of adult male rape victims.[57] Many of the victims have been left with life-threatening injuries, such as vaginal fistulas. A fistula occurs when the wall between the vagina and the rectum or bladder is ruptured due to trauma. Throughout the rest of the world, vaginal fistulas typically result only from severe complications in childbirth, and the average doctor in a developed country may go his or her entire career without ever encountering such a case. In the Democratic Republic of the Congo, however, the Panzi Hospital in Bukavu performed 540 fistula repairs in 2005 alone, 80 percent of which were due to sexual violence.[58] Complications from fistulas can include permanent incontinence, miscarriage, and infertility.

Conclusion: Efforts to Reform and Protect Human Rights

While the international community continues to pressure the Congolese government to implement laws and practices that would afford greater protection to civilians caught between warring armies, the process is slow, and many humanitarian organizations highlight the fact that the mineral-rich land is fueling not only the African armies at war but also international companies as well. Coltan (columbite-tantalite), is a highly sought-after ore as it provides material used to make mobile phones and computers. Between 1999 and 2000, the demand for coltan increased significantly, and a kilo of average-grade coltan sold for $200. During this time, the Rwandan army was exporting approximately 100 tons of coltan a month, and the UN Panel of Experts on the Illegal Exploitation of Natural Resources and Other Forms of Wealth in the Democratic Republic of the Congo estimates that the Rwandan army made at least $250 million over the course of 18 months, which is more than enough money to finance Rwanda's continued presence in the Democratic Republic of the Congo.[59] The private sector, therefore, has contributed heavily to the ongoing conflict in the Democratic Republic of the Congo, and some countries have played a direct role in fueling the violence by trading arms for natural resources. Several large and well-known companies have been implicated as direct or passive facilitators of the violence, such as Citibank (for its relationship with the Rwandan Banque de Commerce, du Developpement et d'Industrie [BCDI], which is directly involved in the diamond trade), Sabena (the national airline of Belgium), and even the U.S. honorary consul in Bukavu, Ramnik O. Kotecha, who openly deals in coltan.[60]

In 2001, the UN Panel of Experts on the Illegal Exploitation of Natural Resources and Other Forms of Wealth in the Democratic Republic of the Congo investigated and reported on the trade in minerals in the Congo, detailing the way in which coltan, diamonds, and other minerals continue to fuel the war.

In January 2009, the Congolese militia leader Thomas Lubanga became the first person ever tried by the International Criminal Court (ICC) in The Hague since its establishment as the world's first war crimes tribunal in 1998. Lubanga was being tried for conscripting children under the age of

15 as soldiers, and human rights organizations have had mixed responses. While many welcome the attention brought to the use of child soldiers in the Democratic Republic of the Congo (which has more child soldiers than any other African country), several have criticized the limited scope of the charges brought against Lubanga, who is also well known for orchestrating mass killings, rapes, and tortures.[61] In October 2009, the International Criminal Court suspended Lubanga's trial to determine if such charges could also be brought against him.[62]

The larger question is whether or not international involvement truly has an impact on conflicts in the Democratic Republic of the Congo. In 2007, Human Rights Watch led an investigation into the use of child soldiers in the DRC following the arrest of Thomas Lubanga. Investigators determined that the arrest had already had a significant impact on military officials, who in the past had boasted of having conscripted children with impunity but were now denying that they had any children in their militias, which suggests a new awareness of the possibility of prosecution.[63]

While this does not speak to any sudden elimination of the use of child soldiers altogether—as child soldiers are certainly still being conscripted—it does suggest that increased international pressure on DRC government officials, media exposure of private companies involved in the conflict, and the international prosecution of war crimes can have the effect of easing the crisis in Central Africa.

CHINA

October 1, 2009, marked the 60th anniversary of the establishment of the People's Republic of China (PRC) in 1949, which had been declared by Chairman Mao Zedong atop the Tiananmen Gate Tower. The day before the ceremony, the Chinese People's Political Consultative Conference delivered to Mao a list of 20 slogans that it had drafted for the parading troops to shout. Of the 20, Mao chose five, one of which was "long live Chairman Mao!" The media coverage of the event portrayed a cheering crowd, shouting, "long live Chairman Mao!" and the struggle over the press as a tool of state propaganda began.[64]

As the second-largest exporter of goods and the second-largest economy in the world, China has proven itself to be a major world power. China's increasing role in global politics has also brought more attention to its human rights record. Suppression of free speech, heavy restrictions on the press, unflinching control over the private lives of Chinese citizens, and China's repressive policies in Tibet have prompted many outcries from international observers who criticize both China and other major world powers that are willing to overlook China's human rights abuses in the interest of continuing trade relations.

Historical and Cultural Perspectives

One of the oldest civilizations in the world, China's written history dates back several thousand years and is notable for its maintenance of essential cultural characteristics. Today, China is home to 56 ethnic groups, the largest of which is the Han. Prior to the establishment of the Republic of China, China was ruled by dynastic emperors, and Chinese society was a hierarchy of aristocracy and peasantry. Throughout Chinese history, the population was largely rural, a fact that remains true today.[65] A strange occurrence in the late 18th and early 19th centuries, however, foreshadowed later troubles. Between 1790 and 1840, the Chinese population doubled from some 150–200 million to more than 400 million people. A similar increase in population occurred in Europe as a result of industrialization and increased production, but no such increase in production took place in China. Thus, while Europe saw a population increase that was directly related to increasing urbanization, production, and improvements in medical science that greatly reduced the infant mortality rate, China's population increase actually led to a worsening of living conditions.[66]

Despite China's sudden and extreme rise in population, the Manchu Qing government was unwilling to adopt the new technological and social advancements that Western countries had adopted, and many within the general population became resentful and restless. One citizen, Sun Yat-sen, was particularly bitter and worked toward the reformation of Chinese society. Born to a tenant-peasant family in 1866, Sun studied in China until he was 13, and then relocated to Hawaii to live with his wealthy older brother and study English, science, and math. During this time, Sun became habituated to Western ideals, including modes of government, philosophy, science, and religion. Upon returning to China in 1883, he was disturbed by what he saw as a backward society, in which the people were burdened with heavy taxes and kept in ignorance under a primitive education system. Following the Sino-French war, Sun became active in underground political movements to overthrow the Qing dynasty. He traveled and studied in England, Japan, and Hong Kong before returning to Hawaii to establish the Revive China Society, which joined other Chinese protest groups to form the Chinese Revolutionary Alliance. Ten uprisings occurred between 1895 and 1911, finally ending in the successful Wuchang Uprising, which saw the overthrow of the Qing dynasty. Sun, who was in Denver, Colorado, at the time, became the first elected provisional president of the Republic of China.[67]

Sun founded the Chinese Nationalist Party (otherwise known as the Kuomintang, or KMT) in 1912; he based his concept of government on three principles: nationalism (the Chinese government should belong to the Chinese people), democracy (leaders should be elected by the people), and equalization (wealth should be evenly distributed).[68] However, after the fall of the Qing dynasty the central government could not control the huge country, and it was divided among a number of warlords. In the early 1920s, the KMT and the newly founded Chinese Communist Party cooperated with the goal of defeating the warlords and united China. Following Sun Yat-sen's death in 1925, leadership of the KMT passed on to Chiang Kai-shek, a militant nationalist who purged all Communists from the KMT, thereby ushering in the Chinese civil war.

Leading the Chinese Communist Party was Mao Zedong, who envisioned China's success in the dismantling of the Four Authorities: political authority, clan authority, theocratic authority, and the authority of the husband (over women).[69] In 1949, the Communist Revolution succeeded in installing Mao as chairman of the People's Republic of China.

The first course of action under the new Communist rule was the redistribution of land, taking it away from wealthy landowners and distributing it to peasants who had little or no land of their own. A gradual process of collectivization began with a mandate that peasants had to assist one another with their individual plots of land, which later progressed into pooling together their land and tools, and finally, by 1956, all farms were completely collectivized into farming communes.[70]

The erosion of individual rights began, more or less, with the Hundred Flowers Campaign in 1956, during which Mao encouraged intellectuals and academics to offer constructive criticism of the government's socialist policies. Millions of responses came from students and intellectuals, criticizing the government and pleading for reform, and Mao promptly halted the campaign. China scholars today still debate whether the campaign was a deliberate trap, or if it truly began as an attempt to invite the people's involvement in policy making and ended in humiliation for Mao and his government, but regardless of the original design of the campaign, it resulted in widespread persecution of those who had spoken out against the government. Approximately 550,000 individuals were labeled as rightists and publicly humiliated, dismissed from their jobs, imprisoned, sent to labor camps, or tortured.[71]

In 1958, the National People's Congress announced the plan for the Great Leap Forward, the goal of which was massive productive output. Government propaganda promised overnight success, claiming that within three years China would be a land of abundance and the Chinese people would be able to live lives of leisure.[72] Grain and steel production were the primary focus, and Mao's government encouraged peasants to build furnaces in their own backyards to create steel. Peasants were required to meet a quota, and they worked tirelessly, cutting down huge swaths of forest to fuel the furnaces that would produce steel that was to be used toward the modernization of agriculture. In reality, however, the backyard furnaces produced poor-quality metal that was ultimately useless, and the campaign was abandoned as a failure. At the same time that steel production was being heavily pushed, Mao was also instituting a full-force revolution of agricultural practices based on the theories of Russian scientists who, themselves, were unsuccessful in producing the massive quantities of crops they had promised. Peasants were required to adopt dangerously experimental agricultural methods, such as planting seeds close together, employing new (and ultimately useless) methods of fertilization, and breeding animals before they were ready.[73] The new methods resulted in agricultural devastation throughout the nation. While the peasants starved, they were still required to produce grain for the government, and those caught stealing grain were severely punished. Grain production collapsed, and roughly 16 to 30 million people starved to death.[74]

The Great Leap Forward was heavily criticized as a failure, and decollectivization was followed by the Cultural Revolution in 1966. Fearful of the threat of counterrevolution, Mao announced the need to obliterate the Four Olds: old habits, old customs, old culture, and old ideas. Chinese citizens were organized to denounce friends, family members, teachers, and neighbors, and those denounced were forced to walk in marches with their "mistakes" written on placards that were hung around their necks. The Red Guards were created to scour the country, destroying monuments to old religions and traditions.[75]

Throughout Mao's reign, tens of millions of people died and several hundred thousand were killed, imprisoned, or sent to reeducation camps for disagreeing with Mao's policies. Many within his own government were suspected of rightist activity and were sent to reeducation camps, such as Deng Xiaoping, who later assumed power and reversed many of Mao's policies in 1978.

Following Mao's death in 1975, China was in economic disarray. In 1978, Deng Xiaoping seized control of the Chinese government and instituted reforms that would bring China out of seclusion and onto the global stage. With the aim of instituting a type of market socialism, competition and private businesses were encouraged, but many scholars highlight the fact that the state maintains total control over the market, thereby turning state socialism into "state capitalism."[76] In the quest for production, peasant farmers have been exploited and have seen little to no wage increase while the country's overall economy has flourished and the cost of living has soared. Illegal land seizures by local officials have left farmers stranded, often with little to no compensation, and because peasant farmers cannot own the land that they tend, they have no say if the government decides to sell it for commercial development.[77]

Human rights groups have long been outspoken in their protests against China's human rights abuses, but the concept of human rights has been debated by the Chinese government and some China scholars, who have claimed that China simply has a different conceptualization of human rights. Chinese culture, they have argued, is one in which the well-being of the collective takes precedence over the rights of the individual.[78] Some scholars have posited that by privileging the rights of the collective, such as prioritizing economic development over the rights of individual peasant farmers, individual rights are consequently improved (a stronger economy means the individual will be more likely to enjoy a more fulfilling life); whereas by privileging the rights of the individual at the expense of the collective, greater numbers of human rights are violated. Economic rights, Chinese theorists have argued, are just as valid and necessary to individual happiness as freedoms of speech, press, and religion.[79]

Unique Circumstances of Human Rights in China

Reports of public opinion to government activity and policy in China show mixed responses. A 2008 survey by the Pew Research Center found that more than eight in 10 Chinese citizens are satisfied with the current state of their country as well as the economy on the whole. The same survey, however, found growing concern among the respondents over specific social and environmental issues. Nine in 10 respondents cited the gap between the rich and the poor as a major problem, and almost half reported it as a very big problem. Corruption among officials and business leaders was also cited as a problem by 78 percent of respondents. In other areas of life, respondents reported surprising satisfaction. The controversial one-child policy, which restricts families in urban centers to one child only, is widely approved, with 76 percent of respondents reporting a positive view of the policy.[80] The overwhelmingly positive public opinion of the government in China poses a unique challenge to Western human rights organizations: Are the people of China being oppressed if they are happy with their government and its policies? What about the minority that is not happy?

Global Perspectives

While the Chinese government (and, perhaps, Chinese culture, as it has been argued) has views of human rights that do not reconcile with Western values, it has come under heavy criticism by both the international community and Chinese citizens for its authoritarianism and severity in clamping down on dissidents, particularly where freedom of speech is concerned. Many human rights activists in China have faced severe penalties for their criticism. Most notably, in December 2008, the prominent government critic Liu Xiaobo was arrested for his involvement in the human rights manifesto known as Charter 08. After six months in prison, Liu was charged with "incitement to subvert state power."[81] Liu's arrest and imprisonment would not be the first time that the Chinese government has dealt severe punishment to protesters. Charter 08 came 19 years after the Tiananmen Square Massacre in Beijing, during which anywhere from several hundred to 3,000 protesters were killed. Led primarily by students and intellectuals, the protests were ignited by the death of the pro-democracy former secretary general Hu Yaobang on April 15, but they soon developed into large-scale protests of the authoritarianism of the government and demands for reform. The protests were unorganized and scattered, with several thousand students, intellectuals, and civilians marching at a time on Tiananmen Square to convene with the crowd that was already gathered and growing. An estimated 100,000 people gathered in Tiananmen Square over the course of a few days, and the protests lasted seven weeks, during which time protesters organized hunger strikes and drafted a list of demands for government and social reform.[82] The protests grew and spread across the country, picking up momentum in anticipation of the May 16th Sino-Soviet Summit, in which the Soviet president Mikhail Gorbachev was scheduled to meet with the Chinese leader Deng Xiaoping. On May 17, 2 million people marched in Beijing, including laborers, teachers, scientists, and former government officials. Eighteen provinces reported mass protests, including a crowd of 150,000 in Hebei, and 100,000 in Shanghai. On May 20, Premier Li Peng declared martial law in Beijing. Armed military troops and tanks were deployed to quell the protests, though government officials repeatedly assured the protesters that they would not use force or violence to disperse the peaceful protests. Despite those repeated assurances, on June 3 and 4, troops began firing on the unarmed crowd, and government officials announced that they would take whatever measures were necessary to take control of the "social chaos."[83] In the weeks that followed, government officials tracked down and punished protesters and those accused of organizing the protests. Precise numbers of those killed in the Tiananmen Square Massacre are unknown, but estimates suggest that anywhere from several hundred to several thousand unarmed protesters were killed.

The Chinese government came under worldwide condemnation for its handling of the Tiananmen Square protests, and it has since made efforts to improve the state of human rights in China. In March 2004, the Chinese government amended the nation's constitution to include the protection of human rights and private property. Critics in China and abroad noted, however, that China already has laws to protect basic rights, such as freedom of speech and assembly, but the government routinely censors the press and arrests dissidents anyway.[84] In a June 2005 speech, President Hu Jintao outlined the need for uniform government commitment to rule of law, equity, and justice to support the continued development of social harmony in China. Despite his call for reforms, Hu Jintao's speech reaffirmed governmental authoritarianism and warned against dissent: "Independent thinking of the general public, their newly-developed penchant for independent choices and thus the widening gap of ideas among different social strata will pose further challenges to China's policy makers . . . Negative and corruptive phenomena and more and more rampant crimes in the society will also jeopardize social stability and harmony."[85]

International Response

In February 2009, Secretary of State Hillary Clinton visited China, and when asked by reporters whether she would bring up the issue of human rights, Clinton responded, "We have to continue to press them. But our pressing on those issues can't interfere with the global economic crisis, the global climate change crisis, and the security crisis."[86] Amnesty International released a statement shortly afterward expressing shock and disappointment at Clinton's statement, insisting that the United States is the only country that can truly and effectively press China on its human rights record.[87] Human Rights Watch urged inclusiveness by arguing:

[F]reedom for the press, whistleblowers, and critics is essential to preventing environmental damage and defective products that threaten China and the world; labor rights abuses and the lack of rule of law destabilize China's economy, which is part of a global economy; and unconditional aid to highly abusive governments destabilizes international peace and security.[88]

In November 2009, President Barack Obama visited China, and many human rights groups were dismayed at his decision not to meet with the Dalai Lama, the religious and political leader of Tibet, in October. China has long been criticized for its severe policies in Tibet, which was an independent country prior to Chinese invasion in 1949. In the 60 years that China has occupied Tibet, the Chinese government has implemented policies to restrict the practice of Tibetan Buddhism and has instituted prison sentences for possession of a Tibetan flag or an image of the Dalai Lama.[89] In a letter to President Obama shortly before his trip to China, Human Rights Watch emphasized three key points to stress when discussing human rights: freedom of expression and information, rule of law, and Tibet and Xinjiang.[90] In a televised address to an audience of Chinese students, Obama, indeed, stressed the importance of freedom of expression, access to information, political participation, and freedom of worship. However, Obama's visit was not widely publicized in China, and his address to the students was censored.[91]

Censorship in China has come under increasing attack by the international community following a dispute that arose between the Internet search engine company Google Inc. and the Chinese government in 2010, when a large-scale computer attack in January was determined to be the result of government hacking aimed at obtaining personal data on human rights activists who use G-mail. Google responded by moving its Chinese site offshore to avoid censorship rules and redirecting users to its Hong Kong site. In June 2010, Google's chief legal officer, David Drummond, called for U.S. and E.U. governments to press China to lift Internet restrictions, which not only limit free speech but also limit trade. According to Drummond: "The censorship, of course, is for political purposes but it is also used as a way of keeping multinational companies disadvantaged in the market." In response to the criticism over its censorship policies, the Chinese government released a list of topics that it censors, including material that threatens to "damage state honor and interests" or "subverts state power."[92]

Current Debates and Priorities in China

Human rights organizations in China and abroad have identified a number of ongoing rights violations, including China's repressive regime in Tibet, corruption of government officials that undermines rule of law, and the use of secret "black jails," where inmates are held incommunicado for days or even months. But none of these topics can be adequately addressed in open dialogue without freedom of speech. The severity of China's censorship policies came to the world's attention most recently with the 2008 Olympic Games in Beijing. Internet censorship and heavy restrictions placed on foreign journalists brought into sharp relief the reality of the degraded condition of rights in China. During the Games, an enforced news blackout suppressed the spread of information regarding melamine-tainted infant formula, which sickened

91

300,000 infants and killed six.[93] In May 2010, a book jointly issued by the Chinese government, the World Health Organization, and the International Olympic Committee, titled *The Health Legacy of the 2008 Beijing Olympic Games: Successes and Recommendations,* made no mention of the tainted infant formula. The book was criticized by human rights reporters and health advocates for its declaration that "no major outbreak of food-borne disease occurred during the Beijing Olympics."[94]

Shortly before the Games began, the International Olympic Committee and the Chinese government opened the doors to dissent by setting up three protest zones and allowing Chinese citizens to apply to protest. Seventy-seven applications were filed, and the Chinese government not only rejected all 77 but also arrested many of the applicants. Among those arrested were two women in their 70s who were sentenced to reeducation in labor camps, both of whom were freed only when international observers publicized the arrests and demanded their release.[95]

In December 2009, China was named the world's worst jailer of journalists for the 11th year in a row, beating out Iran, Cuba, Burma, and Eritrea.[96] The majority of China's imprisoned journalists are online reporters, many of whom work with overseas publications and businesses. The reporter Shi Tao was arrested in 2004 after writing an e-mail about media restrictions surrounding the 15th anniversary of the Tiananmen Square Massacre. The e-mail was intercepted by the Chinese government, and the Internet service provider Yahoo! gave Chinese authorities Shi's information, which allowed them to trace his e-mail back to his computer. Shi was sentenced to 10 years on charges of "leaking state secrets."[97]

In a more recent case, the activist and writer Tan Zuoren was sentenced in February 2010 to a five-year prison term on charges of "inciting subversion of state power" for his investigation into the poor construction of schools that had collapsed in the 2008 Sichuan earthquake, killing thousands of children. Tan's lawyer was blocked from calling witnesses or showing evidence in Tan's defense, and reporters and journalists were barred from the courtroom.[98]

Beginning in 1995, the European Union and Chinese government have met twice a year to discuss human rights, and in June 2010 Human Rights Watch urged the European Union to set measurable benchmarks for human rights progress in China. Among the topics in need of discussion, according to Human Rights Watch, are Internet censorship and the imprisonment of the dissidents Liu Xiaobo and Tan Zuoren.[99] In 2010, the Norwegian Nobel Committee awarded Liu Xiaobo the Nobel Peace Prize for his nonviolent campaign for human rights in China. The Chinese government responded to the Nobel Committee with disapproval, claiming that Liu Xiaobo is a criminal who has been found guilty in a Chinese court and that the committee's decision has thus violated the mission of the Nobel Peace Prize.

Conclusion: Efforts to Reform and Protect Human Rights

The amorphous nature of the Internet as a free flow of information has made it impossible for government officials to exercise complete control over what is published and read. Today, despite restrictions and censorship, the blogosphere remains the freest space for speech in China. Journalists who write stories that their editors refuse to publish may post them online, where the story will be released into the blogosphere even if the original post is deleted.[100] Observers speculate that news outlets will need to expand as China's economy continues to thrive, forcing government officials to relax restrictions on the press.[101] Furthermore, as China continues to grow as a world power, with greater sway in global politics, the Chinese government will become increasingly answerable to other world powers, such as the United States. According to the *Washington Post*, statements such as that made by Secretary Clinton that human rights must not "interfere" with dialogues on the global economy and the environment have the dangerous side effect of suggesting that the United States, as one of the most powerful countries in the world, is willing to look the other way, even if only briefly to prioritize other foreign policy goals. A *Washington Post* editorial in February 2009 states that such messages will "demoralize thousands of democracy advocates in China."[102] Rather, human rights organizations urge the United States and other world powers to demonstrate their commitment to human rights by continuing to press for reforms in China and thereby give hope to the Chinese people that their rights will not be ignored.[103]

CHECHNYA

Located within the northern Caucasus Mountains, Europe's highest mountain range, Chechnya, a constituent republic of the Russian Federation, borders the country of Georgia to the south, the Russian autonomous republic Dagestan to the east, Ingushetia and North Ossetia to the west, and Stavropol to the north. An Islamic Caucasian nation with a long history of struggle against imperialist expansion, Chechnya is home to some 1 million people who are ethnically and linguistically distinct from their Russian neighbors. Chechnya is a member of the Russian Federation, despite ongoing tensions between the two. After several decades—indeed, centuries—of struggle against Russian rule, Chechnya declared independence in 1991, following the collapse of the Soviet Union. Russia's refusal to accept Chechnya's secession prevented full realization of independence, resulting in two Chechen wars and the deaths of tens, and possibly hundreds of thousands of civilians.

Historical and Cultural Perspectives

In 1722, the Russian tsar Peter the Great landed on the shore of the Caspian Sea and sent a group of soldiers inland. When the soldiers began making their way into the mountains, however, they were repelled by a group of armed Chechens. Previous contact between Russia and the Caucasus had been made in the 16th century under Tsar Ivan the Terrible, but the coming of Peter the Great marked the beginning of Russian imperial rule over the Caucasus. While the Chechens were able to ward off that first group of Russian soldiers, they were helpless against the might of Russian territorial expansion. A number of factors, such as religious belief, folk traditions, and intense family ties prevented Chechens from truly assimilating into Russian culture, and they were consequently considered the most rebellious group within the Russian empire.[104]

As in so many other colonial conquests, colonization was justified by characterizing the Chechens as savages in need of an outside, civilizing force. The 19th-century geographer Adolf Berzhe wrote:

The Chechens are, more than all the other mountain tribes, far from civilization and close to barbarism, the beastly ways of a half-wild people predominate in their lives, they have a highly developed propensity to plundering and murder and this rules out any chance of industry or peaceful occupations amongst them.[105]

Such racist sentiments persisted throughout the Caucasian War against the mountain tribes and justified the cruelty and ruthlessness of Russian forces. In 1819, in an attempt to frighten the Chechen fighters into submission, Russian troops massacred 300 families in the village of Dada-Yurt.[106]

The Caucasian War lasted from 1817 to 1864, during which time the Chechens fiercely resisted Russian expansion, occasionally with great success. One of the first and most successful Chechen resistance fighters was an illiterate shepherd from the village of Aldy, who called himself Sheik Mansour (which translates to "victor"). In 1785, Mansour led a holy war against Russia, and his army was largely, though temporarily, successful. After several successful battles, including one that all but annihilated the Russian troops, Mansour was caught and taken back to Russia for imprisonment in 1791.[107] The most successful resistance campaign came from the Dagestani imam Shamil, whose holy war against Russia was so successful that in 1843 he became the sole ruler of Dagestan and Chechnya. Shamil proved to be a ruthless leader, and his own brutal reign over the Chechens, whom he despised as "bandits," proved to be just as repressive, if not more so, than the Russians'. Indeed, Shamil realized that the only way to maintain power was to ally himself with the Russians, and Chechnya and Dagestan were assimilated into Tsarist Russia in 1859.[108]

In 1922, Chechnya became the Chechen Autonomous Oblast. In 1934, Chechnya was merged with neighboring Ingushetia to form an Autonomous Republic in the Soviet Union (ASSR).

Shortly before his death in 1924, the Russian revolutionary leader and founder of the Russian Communist Party Vladimir Lenin wrote a testament on Joseph Stalin, noting Stalin's rudeness, intolerance, and capriciousness, and urging his removal from the position of general secretary.[109] Following Lenin's death, however, his testament was suppressed, and his prediction of the fragmentation of the Communist Party under Stalin's leadership was realized when Stalin came to power. Stalin's renowned paranoia and self-aggrandizement led to the labeling of multitudes as "enemies" who were then arrested, "disappeared," tortured, deported, or executed. Stalin's fear of spies was profound, and arrests for espionage in the Soviet Union leapt from 10 percent in 1937 to 27 percent in 1938.[110] Foreigners and even Soviet citizens of other ethnicities were particularly vulnerable, and state-sanctioned xenophobia led to several mass deportation campaigns, among which were the Chechens and the Ingush.

With the outbreak of World War II and the approach of the German front toward the Caucasus, Stalin feared that the Chechens would conspire with the Germans to invade Russia, and he ordered the deportation of the entire Chechen population—498,870 people—to Siberia and Kazakhstan on charges of "mass collaboration" with the Germans. On February 23, 1944, all of the villages of Chechnya were sealed off and communications were cut. At 5 A.M., a red flare gun was fired into the air and the deportation began as men, women, and children were roused from their homes and loaded into train carriages.[111] In an effort to reduce the number of carriages needed, the Russian troops attempted to "compress" the cargo, packing as many individuals into one carriage as possible, without any toilets or means of washing, which resulted in a massive outbreak of typhus. Anyone who ventured more than five meters from the trains could be shot.[112] Those who were deemed "untransportable" were to be "liquidated" on the spot.[113] Thousands were killed before the deportation even began. In the village of Khaibakh, more than 700 "untransportable" Chechens, including children, pregnant women, the sick, and the elderly, were locked in a stable, which had been stuffed with straw, doused with kerosene, and set ablaze. Those who managed to break down the door were gunned down by waiting Russian soldiers. Several thousand Chechens died en route to Kazakhstan and Siberia, and historians estimate that more than 100,000 more died within the first three years after deportation.[114] In Russia, Chechnya was erased from history. Chechen became a prohibited language, and the term *Chechen* disappeared from Russian textbooks altogether. The entire Chechen population was in exile for 13 years and could not return until Stalin's death and Khrushchev's rehabilitation of Chechnya and Ingushetia in 1957.[115]

Unique Circumstances of Human Rights in Chechnya

While the Chechens were allowed to return to their homeland in the late 1950s, various problems persisted under Moscow's government. The Chechens grew to resent being treated as a subclass in their own country, where many found it next to impossible to get a higher education or advance in their professions. Despite the flourishing oil industry, Chechnya and neighboring Ingushetia remained the poorest regions in the Soviet Union, with high rates of poverty and unemployment.[116]

On November 25, 1990, the All-National Congress of the Chechen Nation (OKChN) was formed, with Major-General Dzhokar Dudayev as its president. Dudayev, himself, had experienced Russian racism firsthand when, as a young man, he applied to be a pilot at the Tambov Higher Military Aviation College and was rejected because he had identified his nationality as Chechen on the application. The following year, he reapplied and identified his nationality as Ossetian and was accepted.[117] A few months after the breakup of the Soviet Union in 1991, the OKChN, under Dudayev's leadership, seized the building of the Supreme Soviet and violently forced the sitting president Doku Zavgayev to sign an act of abdication. In October 1991, Dudayev was elected president of Chechnya, and as his first decree he declared Chechnya's independence. Soviet buildings were seized and monuments to prominent Russian figures were toppled as the Chechen people celebrated their reclamation of Chechnya.

In response to the declaration of independence, Moscow, under the leadership of President Boris Yeltsin, declared a state of emergency in Chechnya, but no action was taken until 1994. Although not recognized by any foreign government, Chechnya was de facto independent from 1991 to 1994. During that time, Chechnya's infrastructure collapsed as state employees such as hospital workers and teachers were not paid, and Dudayev became increasingly dictatorial. In 1993, Dudayev disbanded the parliament in favor of direct and undivided presidential rule.

In 1994, mounting resentment toward Dudayev's leadership inspired an opposition movement that found backing in the Russian Federation.

Dudayev suppressed all oppositional campaigns with violence and authoritarian strictures such as curfews and seizures of all administrative buildings. Finally, on December 26, 1994, a pro-Moscow Chechen government was declared and Russian troops laid siege to Grozny, the Chechen capital, on December 31. After several weeks of fighting, 25,000 civilians were dead, and in March Grozny officially came under Russian control.[118]

Russia's refusal to accept Chechen independence likely stemmed from several causes, one being the potential for Chechen independence to undermine Russia's territorial power, but another, more likely reason was the presence of a major oil pipeline that carries oil from fields in Baku and Chechnya toward Ukraine, as well as a major oil refinery in Grozny.[119] Chechnya's wealth of oil brought it to the attention of many world powers, including the United States.

Chechnya continued its resistance against Russian rule, and the First Chechen War, which lasted from 1994 to 1996, resulted in the deaths of tens of thousands of civilians and the displacement of more than 500,000 people. In April 1996, Dzhokar Dudayev was fatally wounded in a rocket attack.[120]

Following the end of the First Chechen War, Chechnya was once again thrown into economic devastation, during which time Wahhabism, a militant and fundamentalist Islamic reform movement that originated in Saudi Arabia, came on the rise. In 1999, several bombings of apartment buildings in Moscow were assumed to be the work of Chechen terrorists, though this has never been proven. In October 1999, Russian troops invaded Chechnya, initiating a 10-year counterterrorism campaign that would finally come to an end in April 2009. Widespread human rights abuses were committed by Russian military forces, including looting, arson, beatings, and murder. According to Holly Cartner, executive director of the Europe and Central Asia Division of Human Rights Watch, "Russian troops in Alkhan-Yurt are killing civilians and looting their property with what appears to be complete impunity. It's a shocking case of Russian force's intentional violation of international law."[121] The human rights violations were so astounding that the European Union and the rest of the G8 (the United States, Canada, and Japan) threatened to isolate Moscow if it did not cease its violent campaign.[122]

Chechen rebels responded in turn by taking a theater of 700 people in Moscow hostage in October 2002. Russian authorities took action against the rebels and hostages alike and gassed the entire building, killing 130 hostages. Survivors have since reported severe health problems, including several varieties of cancer and neurological problems, but the Russian government has insisted that the gas is not to blame for their health problems. Doctors who have treated such patients have anonymously confided to journalists that they have been ordered to rescind a diagnosis of poisoning and diagnose the patient instead as a "victim of crime and terrorism."[123]

In 2003, the former separatist-turned-pro-Moscow leader, Akhmad Kadyrov, was elected president of Chechnya by way of elections that did not meet the standards of the Organization for Security and Cooperation in Europe (OSCE). The following year, Kadyrov was assassinated when a land mine placed beneath his stage exploded during a parade in Grozny. His son, Ramzan Kadyrov, later assumed the presidency in 2007 with the support of Russian president Vladimir Putin. In 2009, Russia announced the end of its counterterrorism campaign and withdrew its troops from Chechnya.

Chechnya's devastated economy, high rates of poverty and unemployment, easy access to firearms, and resentment over centuries of repression under Russia's authoritarian rule has promoted widespread radicalism and violence within the Chechen culture. Rates of violence spiked following the announcement of Russia's withdrawal from Chechnya. In the 200 days following the announcement (April to November 2009), there were 48 bombings in Chechnya, compared to 28 in the 200 days preceding the announcement. Kadyrov has responded with equal brutality not only against the rebels but their families and whole *taips* (clans) as well.[124]

International Response

Russia's 1999 invasion of Chechnya was met with alarm and condemnation around the world. Particularly troubling to the international community was Russia's ultimatum to civilians in Grozny to flee the city or face certain death as presumed terrorists in an air and artillery bombardment. A Russian leaflet dropped over Grozny by Russian warplanes warned inhabitants: "There will be no more talks. All those who do not leave the city will be destroyed. The countdown has started."[125] The U.S. president Bill Clinton issued a warning to Russia, but the Russian president Boris Yeltsin rebuffed the warning, stating:

> It seems Mr. Clinton has forgotten Russia is a great power that possesses a nuclear arsenal. We aren't afraid at all of Clinton's anti-Russian position. I want to tell President Clinton that he alone cannot dictate how the world should live, work, and play. It is us who will dictate.[126]

In November 1999, George W. Bush stated that Russia had "overstepped their bounds."[127] But the relationship between the United States and Chechnya took a sharp turn following the September 11th attacks in 2001. In 1999, Condoleezza Rice, the future National Security Advisor for the Bush administration, declared that "not every Chechen is a terrorist and the

Chechens' legitimate aspirations for a political solution should be pursued by the Russian government."[128] Two years later, the United States changed its stance on Chechnya, and Colin Powell made the unequivocal statement: "Russia is fighting terrorists in Chechnya, there is no question about that, and we understand that." To date, however, there is little if any evidence of Chechen involvement with al-Qaeda.[129]

In October 2004, the European Court of Human Rights began to hear cases by Chechen civilians against the Russian government. The judges, one of whom was Russian, declared that Moscow had violated several international laws on human rights, such as the right to life.[130] During the international court trials, several applicants were harassed and some even went missing.[131]

Current Debates and Priorities in Chechnya

Since Russia's withdrawal from Chechnya, authority has shifted from Russian leadership to pro-Moscow Chechen leaders. The Chechen president Ramzan Kadyrov, a strong supporter of Vladimir Putin, has been accused by human rights groups of establishing a regime of terror and oppression. In his efforts to root out insurgents, Kadyrov has focused punitive responses on the suspected insurgents' families and *taips,* whom he has accused of being co-conspirators. Kadyrov has stated openly and unapologetically that the parents, relatives, and *taips* of insurgents will be held responsible for their actions, and relatives of insurgents can be arrested, detained, beaten, and tortured.[132] Punitive house-burning has become a common method of punishing the families of insurgents, and between the summer of 2008 and the spring of 2009, the Chechen Memorial Human Rights Center identified 25 cases of punitive house-burning. The house-burnings are often systematic. The perpetrators typically arrive at night and evacuate the residents from their home, at which point the house is doused in gasoline and then set on fire. The perpetrators then wait for an hour to be sure that the residents and their neighbors will not be able to put out the flames. Because the house-burnings are perpetrated by members of the Chechen Ministry of Internal Affairs, not one allegation of punitive house-burning has resulted in a criminal investigation.[133]

The safety of human rights defenders in Chechnya has also become a primary concern of international human rights groups. In July 2009, the prominent human rights activist Natalia Estemirova was abducted and later found dead from gunshot wounds. Estemirova was a leading human rights activist in Chechnya and a researcher for the Memorial Human Rights Center who had been documenting cases of human rights violations committed in

Chechnya since the Russian invasion in 1999. Less than one month later, activists for the human rights group Save the Generation, Zarema Sadulayeva and her husband, Alik Dzhabrailov, were abducted in Grozny and found dead the next day. In another case, the abduction of Khadzhi-Murat Yandiyev by Russian servicemen in February 2000 was caught on video, with the Russian colonel-general Alexander Baranov yelling, "Come on, come on, come on, do it, take him away, finish him off, shoot him, damn it . . ." Yandiyev was taken into custody and never seen again.[134]

Since the abduction and murder of Natalia Estemirova, several other members of Memorial Human Rights Center have received threats. When the Memorial chairman Oleg Orlov accused President Ramzan Kadyrov of orchestrating Estemirova's death, Kadyrov filed a civil suit against Orlov for defamation. Kadyrov is suing for 10 million rubles ($330,000) for damages to his "honor and dignity." While Orlov admits that he has no physical evidence of Kadyrov's guilt, he stated to reporters outside of a Moscow courthouse: "There is no doubt of the political guilt of Ramzan Kadyrov in the murder of Estemirova." Kadyrov's lawyer contended that Orlov's accusations were part of a Western effort to weaken Russia.[135]

Conclusion: Efforts to Reform and Protect Human Rights

To date, the European Court of Human Rights has issued 122 judgments on cases concerning human rights violations committed by Russia against Chechens in the 10-year conflict following Russia's 1999 invasion. The court has found Russia responsible for enforced disappearances, extrajudicial executions, and torture, and the court has ruled that the Russian government must pay monetary compensation to the victims, prosecute perpetrators, and adopt general measures such as changes in policy to ensure that such crimes will not occur in the future. While the Russian government has compensated the victims, it has not conducted any meaningful investigation of the abuses or held perpetrators responsible. Despite their monetary compensation, many Chechen families still do not know what happened to their missing relatives, or if they are even still alive. One Chechen plaintiff, whose 31-year-old brother, Musa Gaitayev, was kidnapped from his home in January 2003 and never heard from again, expressed his distress: ". . . we received the compensation but it means nothing to us. This was never about money. We simply want my brother back. Our mother needs her son back. Or at least to know what happened to him!" In 2008, the European Court found Russia responsible for the disappearance and presumed death of Musa Gaitayev, but his family still has not learned of his whereabouts, or the location of his body. Several other families have suffered the same fate.[136]

To date, no perpetrator has been prosecuted in Russia, even when they have been directly named in the European Court judgments. In some cases, Russian investigators have even refuted the European Court's judgments and have refused to prosecute perpetrators. In 40 of the cases, the Russian government withheld critical documents, and the European Court found Russia to be in violation of its obligation to furnish all necessary "facilities" to support the investigation.[137]

Human rights groups urge the Russian government to fully implement the European Court's rulings and to respect the rule of law. To do this, the Russian government must immediately stop intimidating victims who have submitted cases to the European Court, and it must hold fair trials for those named or suspected as perpetrators of human rights violations.[138]

IRAN

Bordering the Persian Gulf to the south, Azerbaijan and Armenia to the north, Iraq and Turkey to the west, and Afghanistan and Pakistan to the east, Iran stretches across 628,000 square miles that support a population of 71 million people.[139] The region was settled in 1000 B.C.E. by a branch of Indo-European peoples known as Aryans. The name "Iran" is a cognate of "Aryan," and in 1935 Reza Shah asked the global community to begin referring to the country (formerly known as Persia) by its indigenous name. An ancient country with more than 2,500 years of recorded history, Iran has a rich cultural heritage. The Iranian Revolution of 1978–79 is viewed by many as one of the most significant revolutions in modern history due to the role that religion has played in unifying the opposition to an oppressive government supported by the West. Today, Iran is a site of great controversy and is known for its ultra-conservative theocratic government and the anti-Western and anti-liberal policies of its Shiite leaders. In more recent years, the Iranian government's nuclear program has overshadowed many of the ongoing human rights violations that the Iranian people continue to suffer.

Historical and Cultural Perspectives

Many of the human rights violations that occur in Iran arise from the government's literal and sometimes arbitrary interpretation of Islamic texts and teachings. From the beginning, Islam was both a religious and political system. At the time of Muhammad (ca. 570–632), the founder of Islam, this new monotheistic religion helped unite the Arab cities of Mecca and Medina. The spread of Islam was achieved by waging war on neighboring tribes, which also had the effect of expanding Muslim-ruled territories.[140]

The Sunni/Shia split occurred after the death of Muhammad in 632. The Sunnis saw Abu Bakr as the successor to Muhammad, while the Shiites believed that Muhammad's cousin and son-in-law, Ali, was his true successor. While Sunnis and Shiites both believe in the basic theology of Islam, such as the Five Pillars, they differ structurally, namely in terms of how they view the imams, or Muslim spiritual leaders. According to the Iranian Studies and Comparative Literature professor Hamid Dabashi, as Shia Islam developed, "it maintained that a religious community, because of its sacred nature, had to be led by a divinely inspired and infallible Imam," who must necessarily be without sin.[141] Sunnis, on the other hand, do not accept the infallibility of the imams.

Prior to the Islamic conquest of Persia in 651, Iran was part of the Sassanian Empire, which at its height in the fifth and sixth centuries stretched across the modern Middle East, from Egypt and Saudi Arabia to Central Asia and Afghanistan. Even earlier, Persia witnessed the great Achaemenid Empire (also known as Persian Empire), founded by Cyrus the Great. He was followed by Darius the Great, who established an effective administrative system for the vast empire. The Sassanian Persian army was defeated by the invading Arab army in the Battle of al-Qâdisiya in 636, which is considered the decisive battle that allowed for the Islamic conquest of Persia. The Arab army achieved final victory over the Sassanian army in 641 at the Battle of Nihawand, and the Sassanian Empire came to an end in 651. Over the following centuries, Islam gradually replaced Persia's ancient religion Zoroastrianism, and the Islamic conversion of Iran is believed to have fully solidified in the ninth century.[142] Iran remained mostly Sunni until the 16th century, when Shia Islam became Iran's state religion with the founding of the Safavid Dynasty in 1501.[143]

A series of events led up to the Iranian Revolution in 1979, which brought Iran to worldwide attention. In 1951, Mohammad Mossadegh (d. 1967) was elected prime minister under the shah, Mohammad Reza Pahlavi. Mossadegh became unpopular with Britain and the United States when he nationalized Iranian oil, and by way of retaliation, Britain put an embargo on Iranian oil. In 1953, President Dwight D. Eisenhower authorized a coup d'état to depose Mossadegh, known as Operation AJAX. On August 19, 1953, Mossadegh was arrested, leaving sole rule to the shah, who became increasingly dictatorial but was nevertheless guaranteed American and British support, despite mounting reports of unlawful imprisonment and torture. In 1957, the shah established an internal security service known by the acronym SAVAK, which was largely responsible for brutally quashing oppositional groups through beatings, imprisonment, torture, death, and exile.[144] In 1963, Ayatollah Ruhollah Khomeini openly criticized the Iranian and U.S. governments, and he was imprisoned and later exiled. But Khomeini did not represent the whole of the opposition; nor was he the only person to speak out against the shah. By 1977, the shah's repressive policies, his brutal practice of silencing dissidents, and his economic failures resulted in an opposition that was widespread and diverse, ranging from conservative Muslim clerics to leftists, pro-democracy reformists, and Communists. In June 1977, Dr. Karim Sanjabi, Dr. Shahpour Bakhtiar, and Darioush Forouhar, three elderly intellectuals who were formerly associated with Mossadegh's administration, delivered an open letter to the shah that epitomized the general dissatisfaction of the middle class: "Plans made in the guise of reform or revolution have failed. Worst of all, human rights and individual freedoms are being disregarded. The principles of the Constitution and the Universal Declaration of Human Rights have been violated on an unprecedented scale." The letter concluded by demanding the shah's observance of the constitution, the release of imprisoned dissidents, respect for freedom of speech, and the establishment of a government based on majority representation.[145] Also in 1977, the U.S. president Jimmy Carter announced that countries that violated basic human rights would not receive American aid or arms. Many Iranians who suffered under the repressive regime of the shah saw this as a show of support for their rights. The U.S. government, however, was reluctant to pressure the shah, and there was no severance of U.S. aid or arms to Iran.[146]

By 1979, resentment toward the shah's repressive regime cumulated in massive nationwide demonstrations for freedom of speech, rule of law, and observance of the constitution. Much of the opposition united behind the exiled Ayatollah Khomeini, who represented both religious tradition and opposition to the manipulative Western governments, of which the shah was considered a puppet.[147] The demonstrations were held for more than a year; ultimately, the shah fled the country with his family, seeking refuge in the United States and paving the way for Ayatollah Khomeini's return from exile. Upon his return, Khomeini condemned the secular provisional government and began to consolidate the anti-shah forces behind him, gaining ground as soldiers defected to his side. Khomeini appointed his own prime minister, Mehdi Bazargan, and declared unequivocally that his government was God's government, and that "Revolt against God's government is a revolt against God. Revolt against God is blasphemy."[148] His supporters took over police stations, government buildings, and TV and radio stations, and the secular provisional government fell on February 11, less than two weeks after Khomeini's return. Iran officially became an Islamic republic in April 1979, and a theocratic constitution was created. That same year, a group of Iranian students seized the U.S. embassy, an act which is believed to have been inspired by Ayatollah Khomeini's words: "It is incumbent upon students in the secondary schools and universities and the theology schools to expand their attacks against America and Israel. Thus, America will be forced to return the criminal, the deposed Shah."[149] While Ayatollah Khomeini was not consulted on the embassy takeover, he later openly approved of the hostage taking. On November 4, 1979, the students stormed the U.S. embassy and took 66 Americans hostage. Six of the hostages escaped during the takeover, and another 14 were later released. The remaining 52 hostages were held for more than a year—444 days—and were released on January 20, 1981. In later statements made by the students, their reasons for seizing the U.S. embassy included long-standing anger over the 1953 U.S.-orchestrated coup that removed the democratically elected prime minister, Mossadegh, and reinstalled the shah and his repressive regime. The students also feared possible U.S. plans to reinstate the shah, and the purpose of their takeover of the embassy was to curtail such efforts by teaching "the American government and the CIA a lesson, so it will keep its hands off of other countries, and particularly Iran!"[150]

Unique Circumstances of Human Rights in Iran

Continued distrust of outsiders—the American government, in particular—as well as literal and rigid interpretations of Islamic theology have resulted in the development of a complex setting for discussions on human rights. According to the 1989 constitution of Iran, supreme authority lies with the leader and the guardian council, and thus all attempts to introduce social change are monitored by the religious elite who rule Iran. Following the death of Ayatollah Khomeini in 1986, Ali Khamenei became the supreme leader, and he continued to silence opposition and crush dissidents. Throughout the 1990s and 2000s, many dissidents and journalists were jailed, beaten, and murdered for criticizing the Iranian government. One such journalist is Akbar Ganji, who was arrested in 2001 after publishing a series of articles investigating the deaths of prominent dissidents and accusing the government of being responsible. Ganji was imprisoned for five years, during which time he claimed to have been beaten and then threatened if he told anyone.[151] In 1999, Ayatollah Khamenei went on television to defend the Special Clerical Court, which operates outside of the Iranian judicial system to punish dissenting clerics. At the time of his television appearance, the Special Clerical Court, which the former interior minister Abdullah Nuri described as "illegal," had just found the editor of a leading reformist newspaper guilty of publishing anti-Islamic articles.[152]

Global Perspectives

In 2005, Mahmoud Ahmadinejad, a former teacher and mayor of Iran's capital, Tehran, was elected president of Iran after a campaign that was backed by Iran's ruling factions. Highly religious, conservative, and anti-West, Ahmadinejad's election marked a renaissance for Iran's neoconservative forces.[153] International human rights groups noticed a marked deterioration of human rights following Ahmadinejad's election. Within two years of his taking office, executions in Iran increased by 300 percent. In 2005, the year of Ahmadinejad's election, 86 people were executed. In 2007, that number ballooned up to 317 people. Mahmoud Ahmadinejad has proved to be a controversial international figure. In recent years, his commitment to the continued development of Iran's nuclear program has drawn worldwide attention, particularly for his refusal to negotiate on the project and his insistence that peaceful nuclear development is Iran's "inalienable right."[154]

His anti-Israel remarks have resulted in worldwide outrage. In a 2005 speech, he made a statement suggesting that Israel should be "wiped off the map" and replaced with a Palestinian state, though the translation has been called into question. He later denied that he was making a threat against Israel, but stated that Israel's "Zionist regime" would collapse on its own.[155] At a 2009 UN speech, Ahmadinejad stated that Israel was founded on racist principles, a comment that resulted in a walkout by delegates from 30 countries.

Many Iranian civilians and international observers are questioning Ahmadinejad's most recent claim to power after his success in the 2009 presidential elections, which they claim was fraudulent. Ahmadinejad defeated his rival, Hossein Mousavi, with approximately 63 percent of the votes—similar to his 2005 victory with 62 percent of the votes. The difference this time was the actual *number* of votes. While Ahmadinejad received 17 million votes in 2005, he received 24 million in 2009. A study by Ali Ansari, a professor of the Institute of Iranian Studies at the University of St. Andrews and the London think tank Chatham House, found discrepancies in the increased voter turnout. Two provinces showed a turnout of more than 100 percent, and four others showed a turnout of more than 90 percent. Furthermore, the increased turnout would have had to have resulted from a massive number of undecided voters deciding in favor of Ahmadinejad, but the report shows no such correlation. According to the study: "In a third of all provinces, the official results would require that Ahmadinejad took not only all former conservative voters, and all former centrist voters, and all new voters, but up to 44 percent of former reformist voters, despite a decade of conflict between these two groups."[156]

At the announcement of Ahmadinejad's victory, hundreds of thousands of Iranians poured into the streets of Tehran in protest. The Iranian government has admitted to detaining 4,000 people in the protests following the elections, including civilians, human rights activists, journalists, and former governmental leaders who oppose Ahmadinejad's regime.[157] Media groups have placed the death toll at approximately 150.[158] Reports have also surfaced alleging torture, rape, and abuse of detained prisoners, though the Iranian government has repeatedly denied the allegations, despite hospital records that attest to injuries consistent with torture.[159] Ayatollah Ali Khamenei, whose word is final in such matters, declared the election results a "divine assessment" and urged Iranians to unite behind Ahmadinejad.[160]

International Response

In 2007, Ahmadinejad was invited to speak at Columbia University, where he was directly taken to task by the university's president, Lee Bollinger. In his opening statement, Bollinger called Ahmadinejad a "petty and cruel dictator," outlining several examples of the execution of children, the oppression of women, and the torture and imprisonment of homosexuals, academics, and journalists. Bollinger finished his statement with the scathing remarks: "Frankly, and in all candor, Mr. President, I doubt you will have the intellectual courage to answer these questions." The invitation was highly controversial, and many protested the speech. It nevertheless provided many students and faculty with the unprecedented opportunity to pose several questions to Mahmoud Ahmadinejad regarding his regime. While Ahmadinejad was largely indirect in many of his answers, one question regarding the oppression of gays and lesbians in Iran elicited a surprising response from Ahmadinejad: "In Iran, we don't have homosexuals like in your country. In Iran, we do not have this phenomenon. I don't know who has told you we have that." The response was met with eruptions of laughter throughout the audience.[161]

On July 25, 2009, protesters gathered in major cities across six continents to protest the Iranian elections in a demonstration that was organized by United for Iran and supported by such major human rights organizations as Amnesty International, Human Rights Watch, and Reporters Without Borders. The demonstration also called on Western governments to demand respect for human rights from the Iranian government.[162] The United States and many other countries have rejected Ahmadinejad's claim to victory in the elections, and to date protests continue to take place in the Iranian capital of Tehran.[163] Following the June riots, the Iranian government responded by not only detaining thousands of protesters but also by cutting off cell phones and text messaging in Tehran and blocking pro-Mousavi Web sites.[164] On December 27, protests once again resulted in excessive violence and police brutality as the Ashura religious commemorations—which mark the death of Ali, the first imam of the Shia—doubled as a day of mourning and outrage over the June election results. Tear gas was used to disperse the crowds, and 300 people were arrested while several others were killed. Seyed Ali Mousavi, Hossein Mousavi's nephew, was reportedly shot dead. International human rights groups are calling on the Iranian government to end the violence that continues to take lives, and to respect the International Covenant on Civil and Political Rights (one of many human rights treaties to which Iran is bound) that guarantees the right to assemble and protest peacefully.[165]

Current Debates and Priorities in Iran

Iran is second only to China in the number of executions it carries out each year.[166] In 2008, there were 350 executions—higher than 2007, which saw 317 people executed.[167] In the 50 days following the June 2009 elections, 115 people were executed for crimes connected to the protests.[168] Even more worrisome to international human rights groups, however, is the number of juvenile offenders that Iran executes annually. One of only five countries that continue to execute children, Iran executes more juvenile offenders each year than any other country. Between 2005 and 2008, 26 of the 32 executions of children throughout the world were in Iran, far outnumbering those of other countries, which included Sudan (2), Saudi Arabia (2), Pakistan (1), and Yemen (1). Iranian law allows judges to apply the death sentence to offenders who are of the age of majority, which is nine for girls and 15 for boys.[169] In 2008, the youngest victim was 16-year-old Mohammad Hassanzadeh, who was executed for a murder he allegedly committed at the age of 14.[170] In May 2009, 22-year-old Delara Derabi was secretly executed for a murder she allegedly committed at the age of 17, after a trial that was flawed by a lack of evidence and the court's refusal to accept evidence that would have exonerated her. Neither her lawyer nor her family were notified of her impending execution, despite the fact that Iranian law mandates that a prisoner's lawyer must be notified 48 hours prior to the execution.[171] The execution of juveniles is prohibited by international law. The Convention on the Rights of the Child (CRC) and the International Covenant on Civil and Political Rights (ICCPR), both of which Iran ratified, explicitly prohibit the execution of minors.[172] As of 2009, there were at least 130 children awaiting execution in Iranian prisons.[173]

Gays and lesbians convicted of committing "homosexual acts" may also face the death penalty if convicted. In November 2009, three young Iranian men were scheduled for execution for allegedly engaging in homosexual acts as children. According to article 111 of the Islamic Punishments or Penal

Code, *lavat* (sexual activity between men) is "punishable by death so long as both the active and passive partners are mature, of sound mind, and have acted of free will." *Tafkhiz* (nonpenetrative sexual activity between men) is punishable by 100 lashes for each partner, but after four convictions, the death penalty may be imposed. Sexual activity between women is also punishable by 100 lashes per partner, but women may be sentenced to death after three convictions.[174] U.S. human rights organizations have been criticized by gay/lesbian/bisexual/transgender (GLBT) rights groups for not placing more emphasis on the oppression of gays and lesbians in Iran.[175]

Human rights groups are also concerned with the Iranian government's efforts to silence opposition groups by detaining, interrogating, and convicting opposition leaders, often with little if any evidence against them. In November 2009, Ehsan Fattahian, a Kurdish activist who was a member of the banned Kurdish activism group Komeleh, was executed on charges of committing acts against national security that amounted to "war against God and the state." In the Islamic Penal Code, acts of war against God are punishable by death, permanent exile, or amputation of the right hand and left foot. In a letter from Fattahian from prison, he describes how he endured three months of "unbearable torture," relentless interrogations, and demands to make a false confession.[176] Other jailed oppositionists (both men and women) have described how they were raped by prison personnel as a form of torture. In several cases, hospital documents have been destroyed to conceal acts of torture.[177]

Several women's rights activists have been arrested in connection with the "Million Signatures Campaign," a campaign cofounded in 2006 by the Nobel Peace Prize winner Shirin Ebadi to collect 1 million Iranian women's signatures to end institutionalized discrimination of women in Iranian law. Peaceful gatherings have been violently disrupted by authorities, and many activists and street canvassers have been arrested on exaggerated charges, such as "acting against national security by participating in an illegal gathering," "violating national security," "publicity against the Islamic Republic," "disturbing public order," and "gathering and colluding to disturb national security."[178] Women's rights deteriorated significantly after the 1979 revolution, at which many of the rights previously afforded to Iranian women were revoked. Under Khomeini, women were forced to observe *hijab*, the practice of completely covering one's body except for the face and hands. Appearing in public without complete covering is now punishable by up to 75 lashes. Gangs of men wielding clubs and employed by the "Center to Fight the Undesired" roam the streets, prepared to beat women who are not observing *hijab*. Public areas are now largely sex-segregated, and because many girls' schools have had to close due to a lack of female teachers, the illiteracy rate among girls and women has increased. Furthermore, when Khomeini assumed power, he reduced the legal marriage age for women from 18 to 13. Today, the legal marriage age for girls is nine years.[179] As women's rights activists protest such degradations of women's rights, they continue to be harassed, arrested, and even beaten by authorities.

Conclusion: Efforts to Reform and Protect Human Rights

The Million Signatures Campaign is one example of efforts to change the state of human rights from inside Iran. Other Iranian activists, journalists, and academics are actively engaged in the struggle to bring greater respect and protection for human rights. The outrage that met the 2009 election results is, itself, symptomatic of nationwide dissatisfaction with the current state of Iran under Ahmadinejad's regime. In a letter to the UN General Assembly, Human Rights Watch called on member states to condemn the human rights violations in Iran. The number of political dissidents that have been arrested, tortured, and executed amounts to what Human Rights Watch calls a "massive ideological purge," and the organization calls on the United Nations and the international community as a whole to take a firm position regarding the state of human rights in Iran.[180]

[1] General Assembly, United Nations. "The Universal Declaration of Independence" (1948). Available online. URL: http://www.un.org/en/documents/udhr/. Accessed on January 3, 2010.

[2] Committee to Protect Journalists. "2009 Prison Census: 136 Journalists Jailed Worldwide" (December 2009). Available online. URL: http://www.cpj.org/imprisoned/2009.php. Accessed on January 3, 2010.

[3] Committee to Protect Journalists. "Journalists Killed in 2009/Motive Confirmed" (December 2009). Available online. URL: http://www.cpj.org/killed/2009/. Accessed on January 3, 2010.

[4] BBC News. "Iran Admits 4,000 June Detentions" (August 2009). Available online. URL: http://news.bbc.co.uk/2/hi/middle_east/8195586.stm. Accessed on January 3, 2010.

[5] Minky Worden. "What an Olympic Glow Can't Mask." Human Rights Watch (October 2009). Available online. URL: http://www.hrw.org/en/news/2009/10/23/what-olympic-glow-cant-mask. Accessed on January 4, 2010.

[6] Women's Rights Worldwide. "Working Against the Oppression of Women Around the World" (2007). Available online. URL: http://womensrightsworldwide.org/. Accessed on January 4, 2010.

[7] Women's International Center. "Women's History in America" (1995). Available online. URL: http://www.wic.org/misc/history.htm. Accessed on January 4, 2010.

[8] World Health Organization. "UN Human Rights Council Recognizes Maternal Mortality as Human Rights Concern" (June 2009). Available online. URL: http://www.who.int/pmnch/

media/membernews/2009/20090617_humanrightsresolution/en/index.html. Accessed on January 4, 2010.

[9] UNICEF. "State of the World's Children, Special Edition" (November 2009). Available online. URL: http://www.unicef.org/rightsite/sowc/pdfs/statistics/SOWC_Spec_Ed_CRC_TABLE%208.%20WOMEN_EN_111309.pdf. Accessed on January 4, 2010.

[10] World Health Organization. "UN Human Rights Council Recognizes Maternal Mortality as Human Rights Concern" (June 2009). Available online. URL: http://www.who.int/pmnch/media/membernews/2009/20090617_humanrightsresolution/en/index.html. Accessed on January 4, 2010.

[11] Women's Rights Worldwide. "Working Against the Oppression of Women Around the World" (2007). Available online. URL: http://womensrightsworldwide.org/. Accessed on January 4, 2010.

[12] UNICEF. "State of the World's Children, Special Edition: Executive Summary" (November 2009). Available online. URL: http://www.unicef.org/rightsite/sowc/pdfs/SOWC_SpecEd_CRC_ExecutiveSummary_ EN_091009.pdf. Accessed on January 4, 2010.

[13] ———. "State of the World's Children, Special Edition: Executive Summary" (November 2009). Available online. URL: http://www.unicef.org/rightsite/sowc/pdfs/SOWC_SpecEd_CRC_ExecutiveSummary_ EN_091009.pdf. Accessed on January 4, 2010.

[14] Human Rights Watch. "The Last Holdouts: Ending the Juvenile Death Penalty in Iran, Saudi Arabia, Sudan, Pakistan, and Yemen" (2008). Available online. URL: http://www.hrw.org/sites/default/files/reports/crd0908web_0.pdf. Accessed on January 4, 2010.

[15] Stephanie McCrummen. "Surveys Indicate Staggering Congo Death Toll." *Washington Post* (August 11, 2009). Available online. URL: http://www.washingtonpost.com/wp-dyn/content/article/2009/08/01/AR2009080101889.html. Accessed on November 10, 2009.

[16] Joe Bavier. "Congo War-Driven Crisis Kills 45,000 a Month: Study." *Reuters* (January 2008). Available online. URL: http://www.reuters.com/article/worldNews/idUSL2280201220080122. Accessed on November 10, 2009.

[17] *Foreign Policy.* "The List: The World's Worst Places to Be a Kid" (December 2007). Available online. URL: http://www.foreignpolicy.com/story/cms.php?story_id=4059. Accessed on November 10, 2009.

[18] Ch. Didier Gondola. *The History of Congo.* Westport, Conn.: Greenwood Press, 2002, p. 24.

[19] ———. *The History of Congo,* p. 28.

[20] Human Rights Watch. "DR Congo: Chronology" (August 2009). Available online. URL: http://www.hrw.org/en/news/2009/08/20/dr-congo-chronology-key-events. Accessed on November 11, 2009.

[21] Ch. Didier Gondola. *The History of Congo,* p. 35.

[22] Georges Nzongola-Ntalaja. *The Congo from Leopold to Kabila: A People's History.* New York: Zed Books, 2002, p. 18.

[23] Bruce Vandervort. *Wars of Imperial Conquest in Africa, 1830–1914.* Bloomington: Indiana University Press, 1998, p. 35.

[24] Mark Dummett. "King Leopold's Legacy of DR Congo Violence." BBC News (February 2004). Available online. URL: http://news.bbc.co.uk/2/hi/africa/3516965.stm. Accessed November 11, 2009.

[25] Georges Nzongola-Ntalaja. *The Congo from Leopold to Kabila: A People's History*, p. 17.

[26] ———. *The Congo from Leopold to Kabila: A People's History*, pp. 21–23.

[27] Kevin C. Dunn. *Imagining the Congo: the International Relations of Identity.* New York: Palgrave Macmillan, 2003, p. 52.

[28] Human Rights Watch. "DR Congo: Chronology" (August 2009). Available online. URL: http://www.hrw.org/en/news/2009/08/20/dr-congo-chronology-key-events. Accessed on November 12, 2009.

[29] Paul S. Reinsch. "Real Conditions in the Congo Free State." *The North American Review* 178 (1904), p. 220.

[30] Georges Nzongola-Ntalaja. *The Congo from Leopold to Kabila: A People's History*, p. 35.

[31] Human Rights Watch. "DR Congo: Chronology" (August 2009). Available online. URL: http://www.hrw.org/en/news/2009/08/20/dr-congo-chronology-key-events. Accessed on November 12, 2009.

[32] ———. "DR Congo: Chronology" (August 2009). Available online. URL: http://www.hrw.org/en/news/2009/08/20/dr-congo-chronology-key-events. Accessed on November 12, 2009.

[33] Robert B. Edgerton. *The Troubled Heart of Africa: A History of the Congo.* New York: St. Martin's Press, 2002, pp. 186–190.

[34] ———. *The Troubled Heart of Africa: A History of the Congo*, pp. 186–190.

[35] Martin Kettle. "President 'Ordered Murder' of Congo Leader." *The Guardian* (August 10, 2000). Available online. URL: http://www.guardian.co.uk/world/2000/aug/10/martinkettle. Accessed on November 13, 2009.

[36] Human Rights Watch. "DR Congo: Chronology" (August 2009). Available online. URL: http://www.hrw.org/en/news/2009/08/20/dr-congo-chronology-key-events. Accessed on November 13, 2009.

[37] Derek Ingram. "40 Years on—Lumumba Still Haunts the West." Gemini News Service (September 2000). Available online. URL: http://www.globalissues.org/article/262/40-years-on-lumumba-still-haunts-the-west. Accessed on November 13, 2009.

[38] Sofia Bouderbala. "DR Congo, IMF in Talks on Three-Year-Plan." ReliefWeb (December 2007). Available online. URL: http://www.reliefweb.int/rw/RWB.NSF/db900SID/LRON-7A2GZC?OpenDocument. Accessed on November 13, 2009.

[39] Human Rights Watch. "The War Within the War: Sexual Violence Against Women and Girls in Eastern Congo" (June 2002). Available online. URL: http://www.hrw.org/legacy/reports/2002/drc/Congo0602.pdf. Accessed on November 15, 2009.

[40] ———. "DR Congo: Chronology" (August 2009). Available online. URL: http://www.hrw.org/en/news/2009/08/20/dr-congo-chronology-key-events. Accessed on November 13, 2009.

[41] Global Issues. "Democratic Republic of the Congo" (2009). Available online. URL: http://www.globalissues.org/article/87/the-democratic-republic-of-congo. Accessed on November 13, 2009.

[42] Matthew Clark. "Congo: Confronting Rape as a Weapon of War." *The Christian Science Monitor* (8/4/09). Available online. URL: http://www.csmonitor.com/World/Africa/2009/0804/p17s01-woaf.html. Accessed on July 6, 2010.

111

[43] Human Rights Watch. "Democratic Republic of the Congo: Events of 2008." Available online. URL: http://www.hrw.org/en/node/79181. Accessed on November 14, 2009.

[44] ———. "DR Congo: Chronology" (August 2009). Available online. URL: http://www.hrw.org/en/news/2009/08/20/dr-congo-chronology-key-events. Accessed on November 14, 2009.

[45] Georges Nzongola-Ntalaja. "From Zaire to the Democratic Republic of the Congo." *Current African Issues*, no. 28. Nordiska Afrikainstitutet, 2004, p. 17.

[46] Human Rights Watch. "Eastern DR Congo: Surge in Army Atrocities: UN Peacekeeping Force Knowingly Supports Abusive Military Campaigns" (November 2009). Available online. URL: http://www.hrw.org/en/news/2009/11/02/eastern-dr-congo-surge-army-atrocities. Accessed on November 15, 2009.

[47] ———. "Eastern DR Congo: Surge in Army Atrocities: UN Peacekeeping Force Knowingly Supports Abusive Military Campaigns" (November 2009). Available online. URL: http://www.hrw.org/en/news/2009/11/02/eastern-dr-congo-surge-army-atrocities. Accessed on November 15, 2009.

[48] International Federation for Human Rights. "The Democratic Republic of the Congo: The Security Council Replaces the MONUC by MONUSCO and Puts Protection of Civilians and Rule of Law at the Forefront of the New Mandate" (5/31/10). Available online. URL: http://www.fidh.org/Democratic-Republic-of-Congo-The-Security-Council. Accessed on July 6, 2010.

[49] Matthew Clark. "Congo: Confronting Rape as a Weapon of War." *The Christian Science Monitor* (August 4, 2009). Available online. URL: http://www.csmonitor.com/World/Africa/2009/0804/p17s01-woaf.html. Accessed on July 6, 2010.

[50] Internal Displacement Monitoring Centre. "5.4 Million People Estimated to Have Died as a Result of DRC War, According to IRC" (January 2008). Available online. URL: http://www.internal-displacement.org/idmc/website/countries.nsf/(httpEnvelopes)/ 43A25C93D9E8FA30802570B8005A74D0?OpenDocument. Accessed on November 15, 2009.

[51] Global Issues. "The Democratic Republic of the Congo" (2009). Available online. URL: http://www.globalissues.org/article/87/the-democratic-republic-of-congo. Accessed on November 15, 2009.

[52] Human Rights Watch. "The War Within the War: Sexual Violence Against Women and Girls in Eastern Congo" (June 2002). Available online. URL: http://www.hrw.org/legacy/reports/2002/drc/Congo0602.pdf. Accessed on November 15, 2009.

[53] ———. "Democratic Republic of the Congo: Events of 2008." Available online. URL: http://www.hrw.org/en/node/79181. Accessed November 15, 2009.

[54] ———. "The War Within the War: Sexual Violence Against Women and Girls in Eastern Congo" (June 2002). Available online. URL: http://www.hrw.org/legacy/reports/2002/drc/Congo0602.pdf. Accessed November 19, 2009.

[55] ———. "The War Within the War: Sexual Violence Against Women and Girls in Eastern Congo" (June 2002). Available online. URL: http://www.hrw.org/legacy/reports/2002/drc/Congo0602.pdf. Accessed November 19, 2009.

[56] ———. "The War Within the War: Sexual Violence Against Women and Girls in Eastern Congo" (June 2002). Available online. URL: http://www.hrw.org/legacy/reports/2002/drc/Congo0602.pdf. Accessed November 19, 2009.

[57] Jeffrey Gettelman. "Symbol of Unhealed Congo: Male Rape Victims." *The New York Times* (August 4, 2009). Available online. URL: http://www.nytimes.com/2009/08/05/world/africa/05congo.html. Accessed on July 6, 2010.

[58] Juhie Bhatia. "DRC: Rape Epidemic Fuels Fistula Cases." Global Voices Online (July 2009). Available online. URL: http://globalvoicesonline.org/2009/07/29/drc-rape-epidemic-fuels-fistula-cases/. Accessed November 19, 2009.

[59] United Nations. "Report of the Panel of Experts on the Illegal Exploitation of Natural Resources and Other Forms of Wealth of the Democratic Republic of the Congo" (April 2001). Available online. URL: http://www.un.org/news/dh/latest/drcongo.htm. Accessed on November 19, 2009.

[60] Environmental News Service. "Report Names Culprits in Central Africa's Dirty War" (April 2001). Available online. URL: http://www.ens-newswire.com/ens/apr2001/2001-04-18-10.asp. Accessed on November 19, 2009.

[61] Peter Walker and Chris McGreal. "Congo Militia Leader 'Trained Child Soldiers to Kill.'" *Guardian* (January 2009). Available online. URL: http://www.guardian.co.uk/world/2009/jan/26/thomas-lubanga-international-criminal-court. Accessed on November 19, 2009.

[62] Human Rights Watch. "The International Criminal Court Trial of Thomas Lubanga" (January 2009). Available online. URL: http://www.hrw.org/en/news/2009/01/22/international-criminal-court-trial-thomas-lubanga#_Why_is_the. Accessed on November 19, 2009.

[63] ———. "The International Criminal Court Trial of Thomas Lubanga" (January 2009). Available online. URL: http://www.hrw.org/en/news/2009/01/22/international-criminal-court-trial-thomas-lubanga#_Why_is_the. Accessed on November 19, 2009.

[64] Zhao Yan. "Sixty Years: Pervasive Dictatorship Propaganda, Limited Press Freedom." HRIC: Human Rights in China (2009). Available online. URL: http://www.hrichina.org/public/contents/article?revision%5fid=172154&item%5fid=172151. Accessed on November 20, 2009.

[65] William Scott Morton and Charlton M. Lewis. *China: Its History and Culture*. Columbus, Ohio: McGraw-Hill, 2005, p. 7.

[66] John King Fairbank and Merle Goldman. *China: A New History*. President and Fellows of Harvard College, 1998, p. 168.

[67] Sun Yat Sen Nanyang Memorial Hall. "Dr. Sun and 1911 Revolution." Available online. URL: http://www.wanqingyuan.com.sg/english/onceupon/china.html. Accessed on November 21, 2009.

[68] Richard Hooker. "Modern China: Sun Yat-sen" (1996). Available online. URL: http://wsu.edu/~dee/MODCHINA/SUN.HTM. Accessed on November 22, 2009.

[69] ———. "Modern China: Mao Tse-tung" (1996). Available online. URL: http://wsu.edu/~dee/MODCHINA/MAO.HTM. Accessed on November 22, 2009.

[70] ———. "Modern China: Communist China" (1996). Available online. URL: http://wsu.edu/~dee/MODCHINA/COMM2.HTM. Accessed on November 22, 2009.

[71] HRIC. "Petitioning for Redress Over the Anti-Rightist Campaign" (November 2005). Available online. URL: http://hrichina.org/public/PDFs/CRF.2.2007/CRF-2007-2_Petitioning.pdf. Accessed on November 22, 2009.

[72] Jasper Becker. *Hungry Ghosts: Mao's Secret Famine*. New York: Henry Holt, 1998, p. 60.

[73] ———. *Hungry Ghosts: Mao's Secret Famine,* pp. 65–75.

[74] Dennis Tao Yang. "China's Agricultural Crisis and Famine of 1959–1961: A Survey and Comparison to Soviet Famines." *Comparative Economic Studies,* vol. 50 (2008). Available online. URL: http://www.palgrave-journals.com/ces/journal/v50/n1/full/ces20084a.html. Accessed November 22, 2009.

[75] Richard Hooker. "Modern China: Communist China" (1996). Available online. URL: http://wsu.edu/~dee/MODCHINA/COMM2.HTM. Accessed on November 22, 2009.

[76] John Gittings. *The Changing Face of China: From Mao to Market.* New York: Oxford University Press, 2006, p. 3.

[77] Joseph Kahn. "In China, a Warning on Illegal Land Grabs." *New York Times* (January 20, 2006). Available online. URL: http://www.nytimes.com/2006/01/20/world/asia/20iht-china.html. Accessed on November 23, 2009.

[78] People's Daily Online. "Building Harmonious Society Crucial for China's Progress: Hu" (June 27, 2005). Available online. URL: http://english.peopledaily.com.cn/200506/27/eng20050627_192495.html. Accessed on July 6, 2010.

[79] China View. "Human Rights Can Be Manifested Differently" (12/12/05). Available online. URL: http://news.xinhuanet.com/english/2005-12/12/content_3908887.htm. Accessed on July 6, 2010.

[80] Pew Research Center. "The Chinese Celebrate Their Roaring Economy, As They Struggle with Its Costs" (July 22, 2008). Available online. URL: http://pewglobal.org/2008/07/22/the-chinese-celebrate-their-roaring-economy-as-they-struggle-with-its-costs/. Accessed on July 6, 2010.

[81] Kenneth Roth. "Letter to President Obama Ahead of His Visit to China." Human Rights Watch (November 2009). Available online. URL: http://www.hrw.org/en/news/2009/11/09/letter-president-barack-obama-trip-china. Accessed on November 24, 2009.

[82] International Committee of the Fourth International. "Origins and Consequences of the 1989 Tiananmen Square Massacre." World Socialist Web Site (6/5/09). Available online. URL: http://www.wsws.org/articles/2009/jun2009/tien-j05.shtml. Accessed on July 7, 2010.

[83] BBC News. "1989: Massacre in Tiananmen Square" (6/4/89). Available online. URL: http://news.bbc.co.uk/onthisday/hi/dates/stories/june/4/newsid_2496000/2496277.stm. Accessed on July 7, 2010.

[84] Edward Cody. "China Amends Constitution to Guarantee Human Rights." *The Washington Post* (March 14, 2004). Available online. URL: http://www.washingtonpost.com/ac2/wp-dyn?pagename=article&contentId=A57447-2004Mar14. Accessed on July 7, 2010.

[85] People's Daily Online. "Building Harmonious Society Crucial for China's Progress: Hu" (June 27, 2005). Available online. URL: http://english.peopledaily.com.cn/200506/27/eng20050627_192495.html. Accessed on July 7, 2010.

[86] "Not So Obvious: Hillary Clinton's Silence on Chinese Human Rights." *Washington Post* (February 24, 2009). Available online. URL: http://www.washingtonpost.com/wp-dyn/content/article/2009/02/23/AR2009022302412.html. Accessed on November 23, 2009.

[87] Tania Branigan. "Clinton Seeks Consensus with China on Tackling Global Economic Woes." *Guardian* (February 21, 2009). Available online. URL: http://www.guardian.co.uk/world/2009/feb/21/hillary-clinton-china-economy-human-rights. Accessed on November 23, 2009.

[88] ———. "Clinton Seeks Consensus with China on Tackling Global Economic Woes." *Guardian* (February 21, 2009). Available online. URL: http://www.guardian.co.uk/world/2009/feb/21/hillary-clinton-china-economy-human-rights. Accessed on November 23, 2009.

[89] The Official Web Site of the Central Tibetan Administration. "Issues Facing Tibet Today" (2009). Available online. URL: http://www.tibet.net/en/index.php?id=7&rmenuid=8. Accessed on July 7, 2010.

[90] Kenneth Roth. "Letter to President Obama Ahead of His Visit to China." Human Rights Watch (November 2009). Available online. URL: http://www.hrw.org/en/news/2009/11/09/letter-president-barack-obama-trip-china. Accessed on November 23, 2009.

[91] BBC News. "Obama Presses China Over Rights" (November 2009). Available online. URL: http://news.bbc.co.uk/2/hi/8361471.stm. Accessed on November 23, 2009.

[92] Douglas Macmillan, and Pavel Alpeyev. "Google Says U.S., E.U. Should Pressure China on Web Censorship." *Businessweek* (6/10/10). Available online. URL: http://www.businessweek.com/news/2010-06-10/google-says-u-s-e-u-should-pressure-china-on-web-censorship.html. Accessed on July 7, 2010.

[93] Minky Worden. "What an Olympic Glow Can't Mask." Human Rights Watch (October 2009). Available online. URL: http://www.hrw.org/en/news/2009/10/23/what-olympic-glow-cant-mask. Accessed on November 24, 2009.

[94] Phelim Kine. "China's Public Health Whitewash." Human Rights Watch (6/23/10). Available online. URL: http://www.hrw.org/en/news/2010/06/23/chinas-public-health-whitewash-0. Accessed on July 7, 2010.

[95] Minky Worden. "What an Olympic Glow Can't Mask." Human Rights Watch (October 2009). Available online. URL: http://www.hrw.org/en/news/2009/10/23/what-olympic-glow-cant-mask. Accessed on November 24, 2009.

[96] Committee to Protect Journalists. "2009 Prison Census: 136 Journalists Jailed Worldwide" (December 2009). Available online. URL: http://www.cpj.org/imprisoned/2009.php. Accessed on January 3, 2010.

[97] World Association of Newspapers. "Press Freedom: Golden Pen of Freedom" (2007). Available online. URL: http://www.wan-press.org/article14366.html. Accessed on November 24, 2009.

[98] Amnesty International. "China: Free Human Rights Activist Jailed After Unfair Trial" (February 9, 2010). Available online. URL: http://www.amnestyusa.org/document.php?id=ENGPRE201002091533&lang=e. Accessed on July 7, 2010.

[99] Human Rights Watch. "EU Should Demand Concrete Progress in Rights Dialogue" (June 28, 2010). Available online. URL: http://www.hrw.org/en/news/2010/06/25/china-eu-should-demand-concrete-progress-rights-dialogue. Accessed on July 7, 2010.

[100] Carin Zissis. "Media Censorship in China." Council on Foreign Relations (March 2008). Available online. URL: http://www.cfr.org/publication/11515/. Accessed on November 24, 2009.

[101] ———. "Media Censorship in China." Council on Foreign Relations (March 2008). Available online. URL: http://www.cfr.org/publication/11515/. Accessed on November 24, 2009.

[102] "Not So Obvious: Hillary Clinton's Silence on Chinese Human Rights." *Washington Post* (February 2009). Available online. URL: http://www.washingtonpost.com/wp-dyn/content/article/2009/02/23/AR2009022302412.html. Accessed on November 24, 2009.

[103] Kenneth Roth. "Letter to President Obama Ahead of His Visit to China." Human Rights Watch (November 2009). Available online. URL: http://www.hrw.org/en/news/2009/11/09/letter-president-barack-obama-trip-china. Accessed on November 24, 2009.

[104] Carlotta Gall, and Thomas de Waal. *Chechnya: Calamity in the Caucus.* New York: New York University Press, 1998, p. 20.

[105] ———. *Chechnya: Calamity in the Caucus*, p. 30.

[106] ———. *Chechnya: Calamity in the Caucus*, p. 40.

[107] GlobalSecurity.org. "The Old Caucasian War as Seen by General Yermolov, Imam Shamil, and Joseph Dzhugashvili" (2009). Available online. URL: http://www.globalsecurity.org/military/library/news/2000/04/white/part02.htm. Accessed on December 9, 2009.

[108] Tracey C. German. *Russia's Chechen War.* New York: RoutledgeCurzon, 2003, p. 3.

[109] Vladimir Illyich Lenin. "Testament, 1922." Available online. URL: http://www.fordham.edu/halsall/mod/lenin-testament.html. Accessed on December 9, 2009.

[110] Jeffrey Burds. "The Soviet War Against 'Fifth Columnists': The Case of Chechnya, 1942–4." *Journal of Contemporary History* (2007), pp. 267–314. Available online. URL: http://www.history.neu.edu/fac/burds/Burds-FifthColumnists.pdf. Accessed on December 9, 2009.

[111] ———. "The Soviet War Against 'Fifth Columnists': The Case of Chechnya, 1942–4."

[112] Carlotta Gall and Thomas de Waal. *Chechnya: Calamity in the Caucus*, p. 61.

[113] ———. "The Soviet War Against 'Fifth Columnists': The Case of Chechnya, 1942–4."

[114] ———. "The Soviet War Against 'Fifth Columnists': The Case of Chechnya, 1942–4."

[115] Tracey C. German. *Russia's Chechen War*, p. 4.

[116] Carlotta Gall, and Thomas de Waal. *Chechnya: Calamity in the Caucus*, pp. 79–80.

[117] ———. *Chechnya: Calamity in the Caucus*, p. 84.

[118] Memorial: Protection of Human Rights. "Armed Conflict in Chechnya: Principal Stages and Important Events." Available online. URL: http://www.memo.ru/hr/hotpoints/chechen/checheng/czecz.htm. Accessed on December 15, 2009.

[119] Anup Shah. "Crisis in Chechnya." Global Issues (September 2004). Available online. URL: http://www.globalissues.org/article/100/crisis-in-chechnya. Accessed on December 15, 2009.

[120] Globalsecurity.org. "First Chechnya War, 1994–1996" (2009). Available online. URL: http://www.globalsecurity.org/military/world/war/chechnya1.htm. Accessed on December 15, 2009.

[121] Human Rights Watch. "Russian Troops Rampage in Chechnya Village" (12/10/99). Available online. URL: http://www.hrw.org/en/news/1999/12/10/russian-troops-rampage-chechnya-village. Accessed on December 15, 2009.

[122] Anup Shah. "Crisis in Chechnya." Global Issues (September 2004). Available online. URL: http://www.globalissues.org/article/100/crisis-in-chechnya. Accessed on December 15, 2009.

[123] Amy S. Clark. "4 Years Later, Moscow Hostages Suffering." CBS Evening News (October 2006). Available online. URL: http://www.cbsnews.com/stories/2006/10/21/eveningnews/main2112859.shtml. Accessed on December 16, 2009.

[124] The Jamestown Foundation. "Violence in Chechnya Has Spiked Since Counter-Terrorist Operation's End" (November 2009). Available online. URL: http://www.jamestown.org/single/?no_cache=1&tx_ttnews%5Bswords%5D=8fd5893941d69d0be3f378576261ae3e&tx_ttnews%5Bany_of_the_words%5D=ramzan%20kadyrov&tx_ttnews%5Btt_news%5D=35703&tx_ttnews%5Bback Pid%5D=7&cHash=96c1e556c3. Accessed on December 16, 2009.

[125] BBC News. "Russia Will Pay for Chechnya" (December 1999). Available online. URL: http://news.bbc.co.uk/2/hi/europe/553304.stm. Accessed on December 16, 2009.

[126] Charles Hutzler. "Yeltsin Wins Chinese Support on Chechnya." *Portsmouth Herald* (December 1999). Available online. URL: http://archive.seacoastonline.com/1999news/12_9_w1.htm. Accessed on December 16, 2009.

[127] BBC News. "World: America's Bush Condemns U.S. Isolationism" (November 1999). Available online. URL: http://news.bbc.co.uk/2/hi/americas/527105.stm. Accessed on December 16, 2009.

[128] Brian Glyn Williams. "Shattering the Al Qaeda–Chechen Myth: Part I." The Jamestown Foundation (October 2003). Available online. URL: http://www.jamestown.org/programs/ncw/single/?tx_ttnews%5Btt_news%5D=28249&tx_ttnews%5BbackPid%5D=185&no_cache=1. Accessed on December 16, 2009.

[129] ——. "Shattering the Al Qaeda–Chechen Myth: Part I."

[130] BBC News. "Russia 'Committed Chechnya Abuse'" (February 2005). Available online. URL: http://news.bbc.co.uk/2/hi/europe/4295249.stm. Accessed on December 16, 2009.

[131] Human Rights Watch. "Russian Federation/Chechnya: Human Rights Concerns for the 61st Session of the U.N. Commission on Human Rights" (2005). Available online. URL: http://www.hrw.org/legacy/english/docs/2005/03/10/russia10298.htm. Accessed on December 16, 2009.

[132] The Jamestown Foundation. "Violence in Chechnya Has Spiked Since Counter-Terrorist Operation's End" (November 2009). Available online. URL: http://www.jamestown.org/single/?no_cache=1&tx_ttnews%5Bswords%5D=8fd5893941d69d0be3f378576261ae3e&tx_ttnews%5Bany_of_the_words%5D=ramzan%20kadyrov&tx_ttnews%5Btt_news%5D=35703&tx_ttnews%5B backPid%5D=7&cHash=96c1e556c3. Accessed on December 17, 2009.

[133] Human Rights Watch. "What Your Children Do Will Touch Upon You: Punitive House-Burning in Chechnya" (2009). Available online. URL: http://www.hrw.org/sites/default/files/reports/chechnya0709web.pdf. Accessed on December 17, 2009.

[134] ——. "Russia: Complying with European Court Key to Halting Abuse" (September 2009). Available online. URL: http://www.hrw.org/en/news/2009/09/25/russia-complying-european-court-key-halting-abuse. Accessed on December 17, 2009.

[135] Associated Press. "Russian Activist in Court Over Chechen Lawsuit" (September 2009). Available online. URL: http://sify.com/news/russian-activist-in-court-over-chechen-lawsuit-news-international-jjzxupai hhc.html. Accessed on December 17, 2009.

[136] ——. "'Who Will Tell Me What Happened to My Son?': Russia's Implementation of European Court of Human Rights Judgments on Chechnya" (September 2009). Available online. URL: http://www.hrw.org/sites/default/files/reports/russia0909web_0.pdf. Accessed on December 26, 2009.

[137] ——. "'Who Will Tell Me What Happened to My Son?': Russia's Implementation of European Court of Human Rights Judgments on Chechnya."

[138] Amnesty International. "No Progress in Chechnya Without Accountability" (April 2009). Available online. URL: http://www.amnesty.org/en/news-and-updates/news/no-progress-chechnya-without-accountability-20090417. Accessed on December 26, 2009.

[139] World Bank. "Iran, Islamic Rep. at a Glance" (September 2008). Available online. URL: http://siteresources.worldbank.org/INTIRAN/Resources/AAG-IRAM09.pdf. Accessed on December 27, 2009.

[140] Nikki R. Keddie, and Yann Richard. *Modern Iran: Roots and Results of Revolution.* New Haven, Conn.: Yale University Press, 2003, p. 5.

[141] Hamid Dabashi. *Authority in Islam: From the Rise of Muhammad to the Establishment of Umayyads.* New Brunswick, N.J.: Transaction Publishers, 1989, p. 8.

[142] Encyclopedia Iranica. "Iran in the Islamic Period (651-1980s)." Available online. URL: http://www.iranica.com/newsite/index.isc?Article=http://www.iranica.com/newsite/articles/unicode/v13f3/v13f3001a.html. Accessed on December 28, 2009.

[143] Nikki R. Keddie, and Yann Richard. *Modern Iran: Roots and Results of Revolution,* p. 9.

[144] ———. *Modern Iran: Roots and Results of Revolution,* p. 134.

[145] Robert Graham. *Iran: The Illusion of Power.* London: Croom Helm, 1978, p. 208.

[146] Nikki R. Keddie, and Yann Richard. *Modern Iran: Roots and Results of Revolution,* p. 214.

[147] Fereydoun Hoveyda. *The Shah and the Ayatollah: Iranian Mythology and Islamic Revolution.* Westport, Conn.: Praeger, 2003, p. 1.

[148] Baqer Moin. *Khomeini: Life of the Ayatollah.* New York: I.B. Tauris, 1999, p. 204.

[149] Kenneth M. Pollack. *The Persian Puzzle: The Conflict Between Iran and America.* New York: Random House, 2004, p. 154.

[150] One student's explanation as told to a hostage during the takeover. Kenneth M. Pollack. *The Persian Puzzle: The Conflict Between Iran and America.* New York: Random House, 2004, p. 154.

[151] BBC News. "Iranian Dissident Freed from Jail" (March 2006). Available online. URL: http://news.bbc.co.uk/2/hi/middle_east/4819440.stm. Accessed on December 29, 2009.

[152] ———. "Profile: Ayatollah Ali Khamenei" (June 2009). Available online. URL: http://news.bbc.co.uk/2/hi/middle_east/3018932.stm. Accessed on December 29, 2009.

[153] Anoushiravan Ehteshami, and Mahjoob Zweiri. *Iran and the Rise of its Neoconservatives: Tehran's Silent Revolution.* New York: I.B. Tauris, 2007, p. 65.

[154] Times Online. "Iran's President Ahmadinejad Plays Nuclear Card to Rally His Fractured Nation" (December 2009). Available online. URL: http://www.timesonline.co.uk/tol/news/world/middle_east/article6955225.ece. Accessed on December 29, 2009.

[155] BBC News. "Profile: Mahmoud Ahmadinejad" (June 2009). Available online. URL: http://news.bbc.co.uk/2/hi/middle_east/4107270.stm. Accessed on December 29, 2009.

[156] ———. "Iran: Where Did All the Votes Come From?" (June 2009). Available online. URL: http://news.bbc.co.uk/2/hi/middle_east/8113885.stm. Accessed on December 29, 2009.

[157] ———. "Iran Admits 4,000 June Detentions" (August 2009). Available online. URL: http://news.bbc.co.uk/2/hi/middle_east/8195586.stm. Accessed on December 29, 2009.

[158] CNN. "Chaos Prevails as Protesters, Police Clash in Iranian Capital" (June 2009). Available online. URL: http://edition.cnn.com/2009/WORLD/meast/06/20/iran.election/index.html. Accessed on December 29, 2009.

[159] ———. "Iran Speaker Rejects Detainee Rape Claims" (August 2009). Available online. URL: http://edition.cnn.com/2009/WORLD/meast/08/12/iran.detainees.rape/index.html?section=cnn_latest. Accessed on December 29, 2009.

[160] Anna Johnson, and Brian Murphy, Associated Press. "Election Battles Turn into Street Fights in Iran." ABC News (June 2009). Available online. URL: http://abcnews.go.com/International/wirestory?id=7830630&page=1. Accessed on December 30, 2009.

[161] Russell Goldman. "Ahmadinejad: No Gays, No Oppression of Women in Iran." ABC News (September 2007). Available online. URL: http://abcnews.go.com/US/story?id=3642673&page=1. Accessed on December 30, 2009.

[162] CNN. "Global Protests Staged Over Post-Election Crackdown in Iran" (July 2009). Available online. URL: http://edition.cnn.com/2009/WORLD/meast/07/25/iran.world.protests/index.html#cnnSTCText. Accessed on December 30, 2009.

[163] Carolyn Thompson, Associated Press. "U.S. Rejects Victory Claim by Iran's Ahmadinejad." ABC News (June 2009). Available online. URL: http://abcnews.go.com/Politics/wirestory?id=7832558&page=1. Accessed on December 30, 2009.

[164] Anna Johnson, and Brian Murphy, Associated Press. "Election Battles Turn into Street Fights in Iran." ABC News (June 2009). Available online. URL: http://abcnews.go.com/International/wirestory?id=7830630&page=1. Accessed on December 30, 2009.

[165] Amnesty International. "Iran Must End Slide into Bloodshed" (December 2009). Available online. URL: http://www.amnesty.org/en/news-and-updates/news/iran-must-end-slide-bloodshed-20091228. Accessed on December 30, 2009.

[166] Human Rights Watch. "Kurdish Activist Executed" (November 2009). Available online. URL: http://www.hrw.org/en/news/2009/11/10/iran-halt-execution-kurdish-activist. Accessed on December 30, 2009.

[167] ———. "At Least 350 Executions in 2008 in Iran" (February 2009). Available online. URL: http://iranhr.net/spip.php?article958. Accessed on December 30, 2009.

[168] ———. "Letter to UN Member States: Condemn Human Rights Violations in Iran" (November 2009). Available online. URL: http://www.hrw.org/en/news/2009/11/11/letter-un-member-states-condemn-human-rights-violations-iran. Accessed on December 30, 2009.

[169] ———. "Iran: Rights Crisis Escalates: Faces and Cases from Ahmadinejad's Crackdown" (September 2008). Available online. URL: http://www.hrw.org/sites/default/files/reports/iran0908web_0.pdf. Accessed on December 30, 2009.

[170] Iran Human Rights. "At Least 350 Executions in 2008 in Iran" (February 2009). Available online. URL: http://iranhr.net/spip.php?article958. Accessed on December 30, 2009.

[171] Human Rights Watch. "Secret Execution of Juvenile Offender" (May 2009). Available online. URL: http://www.hrw.org/en/news/2009/05/01/iran-secret-execution-juvenile-offender. Accessed on December 30, 2009.

[172] ———. "Revoke Death Sentences for Juvenile Offenders" (November 2009). Available online. URL: http://www.hrw.org/en/news/2009/11/03/iran-revoke-death-sentences-juvenile-offenders. Accessed on December 30, 2009.

173 ———. "Secret Execution of Juvenile Offender" (May 2009). Available online. URL: http://www.hrw.org/en/news/2009/05/01/iran-secret-execution-juvenile-offender. Accessed on December 30, 2009.

174 ———. "Revoke Death Sentences for Juvenile Offenders" (November 2009). Available online. URL: http://www.hrw.org/en/news/2009/11/03/iran-revoke-death-sentences-juvenile-offenders. Accessed on December 30, 2009.

175 Richard Kim. "Iran and Gay Rights." *Nation* (July 2006). Available online. URL: http://www.thenation.com/blogs/notion/103342/iran_and_gay_rights. Accessed on December 30, 2009.

176 Human Rights Watch. "Kurdish Activist Executed" (November 2009). Available online. URL: http://www.hrw.org/en/news/2009/11/10/iran-halt-execution-kurdish-activist. Accessed on December 30, 2009.

177 Human Rights Watch. "Iran: Stop Covering Up Sexual Assaults in Prison" (November 2009). Available online. URL: http://www.hrw.org/en/news/2009/06/09/iran-stop-covering-sexual-assaults-prison. Accessed on March 14, 2011.

178 Human Rights First. "Human Rights Defenders in Iran: One Million Signatures Campaign Timeline" (2008). Available online. URL: http://www.humanrightsfirst.org/defenders/hrd_iran/hrd_iran_timeline.htm. Accessed on December 30, 2009.

179 Haideh Moghissi. *Women and Islam: Women's Movements in Muslim Societies.* New York: Routledge, 2005, p. 285.

180 Human Rights Watch. "Letter to UN Member States: Condemn Human Rights Violations in Iran" (November 2009). Available online. URL: http://www.hrw.org/en/news/2009/11/11/letter-un-member-states-condemn-human-rights-violations-iran. Accessed on December 30, 2009.

PART II

Primary Sources

4

United States Documents

Christopher Columbus, Log Book Excerpts (1492)

The following excerpts from Christopher Columbus's log book reveal much more than the historic meeting of Europe and America. They reveal the underlying drives that pushed European expansion westward, as well as the perspectives of those European explorers as they sailed into the Bahama archipelago and met the indigenous peoples of the islands. Columbus's primary aim was gold, and his log book attests to his vain search for the precious metal, but he also saw in the native population an opportunity to convert whole groups of people to the Christian faith.

It is important to note that these excerpts have been translated from Spanish into English, which may alter certain contexts and connotations. For example, one famous passage refers to Columbus's perception of the ease with which he and his crew could conquer and rule the island population. Howard Zinn's translation of this passage in A People's History of the United States: 1492–Present *reads: "With fifty men we could subjugate them all and make them do whatever we want." The translation below, however, reads: "I could conquer the whole of them with fifty men, and govern them as I please." Also important to note is the context in which such controversial passages appear.*

Christopher Columbus set sail on Friday, August 3, 1492.

Thursday, 11 October.

[Upon landing on the island of Guanahani and meeting the inhabitants] As I saw that they were very friendly to us, and perceived that they could be much more easily converted to our holy faith by gentle means than by force, I presented them with some red caps, and strings of beads to wear upon the neck, and many other trifles of small value, wherewith they were much delighted, and became wonderfully attached to us. Afterwards they came swimming to the boats, bringing parrots, balls of cotton thread, javelins, and

many other things which they exchanged for articles we gave them, such as glass beads, and hawk's bells; which trade was carried on with the utmost good will. But they seemed on the whole to me, to be a very poor people. They all go completely naked, even the women, though I saw but one girl. All whom I saw were young, not above thirty years of age, well made, with fine shapes and faces; their hair short, and coarse like that of a horse's tail, combed toward the forehead, except a small portion which they suffer to hang down behind, and never cut. Some paint themselves with black, which makes them appear like those of the Canaries, neither black nor white; others with white, others with red, and others with such colors as they can find. Some paint the face, and some the whole body; others only the eyes, and others the nose. Weapons they have none, nor are acquainted with them, for I showed them swords which they grasped by the blades, and cut themselves through ignorance. They have no iron, their javelins being without it, and nothing more than sticks, though some have fish-bones or other things at the ends. They are all of a good size and stature, and handsomely formed. I saw some with scars of wounds upon their bodies, and demanded by signs the meaning of them; they answered me in the same way, that there came people from the other islands in the neighborhood who endeavored to make prisoners of them, and they defended themselves. I thought then, and still believe, that these were from the continent. It appears to me, that the people are ingenious, and would be good servants and I am of opinion that they would very readily become Christians, as they appear to have no religion. They very quickly learn such words as are spoken to them. If it please our Lord, I intend at my return to carry home six of them to your Highnesses, that they may learn our language. I saw no beasts in the island, nor any sort of animals except parrots.

. . .

Saturday, 13 October.

At daybreak great multitudes of men came to the shore, all young and of fine shapes, very handsome; their hair not curled but straight and coarse like horse-hair, and all with foreheads and heads much broader than any people I had hitherto seen; their eyes were large and very beautiful; they were not black, but the color of the inhabitants of the Canaries, which is a very natural circumstance, they being in the same latitude with the island of Ferro in the Canaries. They were straight-limbed without exception, and not with prominent bellies but handsomely shaped. They came to the ship in canoes, made of a single trunk of a tree, wrought in a wonderful manner considering the country; some of them large enough to contain forty or forty-five men, others of different sizes down to those fitted to hold but a single person. They rowed with an oar like a baker's peel, and wonderfully swift. If they happen to upset, they all jump into the sea, and swim till they have righted their canoe and emptied it with the calabashes they carry with them. They came loaded with balls of cotton, parrots, javelins, and other things too numerous to mention; these they exchanged for whatever we chose to give them. I was very attentive to them, and strove to learn if they had any gold. Seeing some of them with little bits of this metal hanging at their noses, I gathered from them by signs that by going southward or steering round the island in that direction, there would be found a king who possessed large vessels of gold, and in great quantities. I endeavored to procure them to lead the way thither, but found they were unacquainted with the route. I determined to stay here till the evening of the next day, and then sail for the southwest; for according to what I could learn from them, there was land at the south as well as at the southwest and northwest and those from the northwest came many times and fought with them and proceeded on to the southwest in search of gold and precious stones. This is a large and level island, with trees extremely flourishing, and streams of water; there is a large lake in the middle of the island, but no mountains: the whole is completely covered with verdure and delightful to behold. The natives are an inoffensive people, and so desirous to possess any thing they saw with us, that they kept swimming off to the ships with whatever they could find, and readily bartered for any article we saw fit to give them in return, even such as broken platters and fragments of glass. I saw in this manner sixteen balls of cotton thread which weighed above twenty-five pounds, given for three Portuguese ceutis. This traffic I forbade, and suffered no one to take their cotton from them, unless I should order it to be procured for your Highnesses, if proper quantities could be met with. It grows in this island, but from my short stay here I could not satisfy myself fully concerning it; the gold, also, which they wear in their noses, is found here, but not to lose time, I am determined to proceed onward and ascertain whether I can reach Cipango. At night they all went on shore with their canoes.

. . .

Sunday, 14 October.

In the morning, I ordered the boats to be got ready, and coasted along the island toward the north-northeast to examine that part of it, we having landed first at the eastern part. Presently we discovered two or three villages, and the people all came down to the shore, calling out to us, and giving thanks to God. Some brought us water, and others victuals: others seeing that I was not disposed to land, plunged into the sea and swam out to us, and we perceived that they interrogated us if we had come from heaven. An old man came on board my boat; the others, both men and women cried with loud voices—"Come and see the men who have come from heavens. Bring them victuals and drink." There came many of both sexes, every one bringing something, giving thanks to God, prostrating themselves on the earth, and lifting up their hands to heaven. They called out to us loudly to come to land, but I was apprehensive on account of a reef of rocks, which surrounds the whole island, although within there is depth of water and room sufficient for all the ships of Christendom, with a very narrow entrance. There are some shoals withinside, but the water is as smooth as a pond. It was to view these parts that I set out in the morning, for I wished to give a complete relation to your Highnesses, as also to find where a fort might be built. I discovered a tongue of land which appeared like an island though it was not, but might be cut through and made so in two days; it contained six houses. I do not, however, see the necessity of fortifying the place, as the people here are simple in warlike matters, as your Highnesses will see by those seven which I have ordered to be taken and carried to Spain in order to learn our language and return, unless your Highnesses should choose to have them all transported to Castile, or held captive in the island. I could conquer the whole of them with fifty men, and govern them as I pleased. Near the islet I have mentioned were groves of trees, the most beautiful I have ever seen, with their foliage as verdant as we see in Castile in April and May. There were also many streams. After having taken a survey of these parts, I returned to the ship, and setting sail, discovered such a number of islands that I knew not which first to visit; the natives whom I had taken on board informed me by signs that there were so many of them that they could not be numbered; they repeated the names of more than a hundred. I determined to steer for the largest, which is about five leagues from San Salvador; the others were some at a greater, and some at a less distance from that island. They are all very level, without mountains, exceedingly fertile and populous, the inhabitants living at war with one another, although a simple race, and with delicate bodies.

. . .

Monday, 15 October.
Stood off and on during the night, determining not to come to anchor till morning, fearing to meet with shoals; continued our course in the morning; and as the island was found to be six or seven leagues distant, and the tide

was against us, it was noon when we arrived there. I found that part of it towards San Salvador extending from north to south five leagues, and the other side which we coasted along, ran from east to west more than ten leagues. From this island espying a still larger one to the west, I set sail in that direction and kept on till night without reaching the western extremity of the island, where I gave it the name of Santa Maria de la Concepcion. About sunset we anchored near the cape which terminates the island towards the west to enquire for gold, for the natives we had taken from San Salvador told me that the people here wore golden bracelets upon their arms and legs. I believed pretty confidently that they had invented this story in order to find means to escape from us, still I determined to pass none of these islands without taking possession, because being once taken, it would answer for all times. We anchored and remained till Tuesday, when at daybreak I went ashore with the boats armed. The people we found naked like those of San Salvador, and of the same disposition. They suffered us to traverse the island, and gave us what we asked of them. As the wind blew southeast upon the shore where the vessels lay, I determined not to remain, and set out for the ship. A large canoe being near the caravel Nina, one of the San Salvador natives leaped overboard and swam to her; (another had made his escape the night before,) the canoe being reached by the fugitive, the natives rowed for the land too swiftly to be overtaken; having landed, some of my men went ashore in pursuit of them, when they abandoned the canoe and fled with precipitation; the canoe which they had left was brought on board the Nina, where from another quarter had arrived a small canoe with a single man, who came to barter some cotton; some of the sailors finding him unwilling to go on board the vessel, jumped into the sea and took him. I was upon the quarter deck of my ship, and seeing the whole, sent for him, and gave him a red cap, put some glass beads upon his arms, and two hawk's bells upon his ears. I then ordered his canoe to be returned to him, and dispatched him back to land.

I now set sail for the other large island to the west and gave orders for the canoe which the Nina had in tow to be set adrift. I had refused to receive the cotton from the native whom I sent on shore, although he pressed it upon me. I looked out after him and saw upon his landing that the others all ran to meet him with much wonder. It appeared to them that we were honest people, and that the man who had escaped from us had done us some injury, for which we kept him in custody. It was in order to favor this notion that I ordered the canoe to be set adrift, and gave the man the presents above mentioned, that when your Highnesses send another expedition to these parts it may meet with a friendly reception. All I gave the man was not worth four maravedis. We set sail about ten o'clock, with the wind southeast and stood southerly for the island I mentioned above, which is a very large one, and where according to the account of the natives on board, there is much gold, the inhabitants wearing it in bracelets upon their arms, legs, and necks, as well as in their ears and at their noses. This island is nine leagues distant from Santa Maria in a westerly direction. This part of it extends from northwest, to southeast and appears to be twenty-eight leagues long, very level, without any mountains, like San Salvador and Santa Maria, having a good shore and not rocky, except a few ledges under water, which renders it necessary to anchor at some distance, although the water is very clear, and the bottom may be seen. Two shots of a lombarda from the land, the water is so deep that it cannot be sounded; this is the case in all these islands. They are all extremely verdant and fertile, with the air agreeable, and probably contain many things of which I am ignorant, not inclining to stay here, but visit other islands in search of gold. And considering the indications of it among the natives who wear it upon their arms and legs, and having ascertained that it is the true metal by showing them some pieces of it which I have with me, I cannot fail, with the help of our Lord, to find the place which produces it.

. . .

Source: The Franciscan Archive. "Excerpts From Christopher Columbus' Log, 1492 A.D." Available online. URL: http://www.franciscan-archive.org/columbus/opera/excerpts.html. Accessed January 8, 2010.

The Declaration of Independence, Congress's Draft (1776)

The following document is the Declaration of Independence in its full and original format, including edits and additions to Thomas Jefferson's rough draft. (The edits appear as crossed-out text and the additions appear in italic.) The events leading up to the Declaration (the Tea Act, the Sugar Act, the Currency Act, the Stamp Act, the Quartering Act, etc.) had made it clear among the colonists that King George III viewed the colonies as his own capitalistic venture, even if his aims came at the expense of his subjects.

The 18th century saw the peak of the European Enlightenment, when governmental authority, civic life, and rights were being questioned and discussed. The Declaration was revolutionary in its philosophical underpinnings, and the power of asserting one's autonomy rippled throughout the Western world. One of the more well known revolutions that followed the American example was the French Revolution in 1789, but smaller colonies also asserted their autonomy. In

1791, enslaved Africans in the French colony of Saint-Domingue rose up against their enslavers in what would later be known as the Haitian Revolution. By 1804, Haiti became the first republic ruled exclusively by descendants of Africans.

The power of declaring made itself heard and felt in the American Declaration of Independence, which went through several drafts. Thomas Jefferson wrote the first draft and presented it to Benjamin Franklin and John Adams, who made minor changes but generally approved of the document as a whole. Other members of Congress, however, were uneasy with certain passages, most notably the references to slavery and the slave trade. Almost an entire paragraph was deleted, which has led many historians and scholars to wonder how the outcome of the American Revolution might have been different had the passage remained in the document.

When in the Course of human Events it becomes necessary for one People to dissolve the Political Bands which have connected them with another, and to assume among the Powers of the Earth the separate & equal Station to which the Laws of Nature and of Nature's God entitle them, a decent Respect to the Opinions of Mankind requires that they should declare the causes which impel them to the Separation. We hold these Truths to be self-evident, that all Men are created equal, that they are endowed by their Creator with ~~inherent and~~ unalienable Rights, that among these are Life, Liberty, & the Pursuit of Happiness:—That to secure these Rights, Governments are instituted among Men, deriving their just Powers from the Consent of the governed; that whenever any Form of Government becomes destructive of these Ends, it is the Right of the People to alter or abolish it, & to institute new Government, laying it's Foundation on such Principles, & organizing it's Powers in such Form, as to them shall seem most likely to effect their Safety & Happiness. Prudence indeed will dictate that Governments long established should not be changed for light & transient Causes; and accordingly all Experience hath shown that Mankind are more disposed to suffer, while Evils are sufferable, than to right themselves by abolishing the Forms to which they are accustomed. But when a long Train of Abuses & Usurpations ~~begun at a distinguished period and~~ pursuing invariably the same Object, evinces a Design to reduce them under absolute Despotism, it is their Right, it is their Duty to throw off such Government, & to provide new Guards for their future Security. Such has been the patient Sufferance of these Colonies; & such is now the Necessity which constrains them to ~~expunge~~ *alter* their former Systems of Government. The History of the present King of Great-Britain is a History of ~~unremitting~~ *repeated* Injuries & Usurpations, ~~among which appears no~~

~~solitary fact to contradict the uniform tenor of the rest but all have~~ *all having* in direct Object the Establishment of an absolute Tyranny over these States. To prove this, let facts be submitted to a candid World ~~for the truth of which we pledge a faith yet unsullied by falsehood~~.

He has refused his Assent to Laws, the most wholesome & necessary for the public Good.

He has dissolved Representative Houses repeatedly, ~~& continually~~ for opposing with manly Firmness his Invasions on the Rights of the People.

He has refused for a long Time, after such Dissolutions, to cause others to be elected, whereby the Legislative Powers, incapable of Annihilation, have returned to the People at large for their exercise; the State remaining in the meantime exposed to all the Dangers of Invasion from without, & Convulsions within.

He has endeavored to prevent the Population of these states; for that Purpose obstructing the laws for Naturalization of Foreigners; refusing to pass others to encourage their Migrations hither, & raising the Conditions of new Appropriations of Lands.

He has made ~~our~~ Judges dependent on his Will alone, for the Tenure of their Offices, & the Amount & payment of their Salaries.

He has erected a Multitude of new Offices ~~by a self-assumed power~~ and sent hither Swarms of new Officers to harass our People and eat out their Substance.

He has kept among us in Times of Peace, Standing Armies, ~~and ships of war~~ without the consent of our Legislatures.

He has affected to render the Military independent of, & superior to the Civil power.

He has combined with others to subject us to a Jurisdiction foreign to our Constitution, & unacknowledged by our Laws; giving his Assent to their Acts of pretended Legislation:

For quartering large Bodies of Armed Troops among us:

For protecting them, by a mock-Trial, from Punishment for any Murders which they should commit on the Inhabitants of these States:

For cutting off our Trade with all Parts of the World:

For imposing Taxes on us without our consent:

For depriving us, *in many Cases,* of the Benefits of Trial by Jury:

For transporting us beyond Seas to be tried for pretended Offences:

For abolishing the free System of English Laws in a neighboring Province, establishing therein an arbitrary Government, and enlarging it's Boundaries, so as to render it at once an Example and fit Instrument for introducing the same absolute Rule into these ~~states~~ *Colonies:*

For taking away our Charters, abolishing our most valuable Laws, and altering fundamentally the Forms of our Governments:

For suspending our own Legislatures, & declaring themselves invested with Power to legislate for us in all Cases whatsoever.

He has abdicated Government here by ~~withdrawing his governors, and declaring us out of his allegiance & protection~~ *declaring us out of his Protection, and Waging war against us.* He has plundered our Seas, ravaged our Coasts, burnt our towns, & destroyed the Lives of our People.

He is, at this time Transporting large Armies of foreign Mercenaries to complete the works of Death, Desolation & Tyranny, already begun with circumstances of Cruelty and Perfidy *scarcely paralleled in the most barbarous Ages, & totally* unworthy the Head of a civilized Nation. He has constrained our fellow Citizens taken Captive on the high Seas to bear Arms against their Country, to become the Executioners of their Friends & Brethren, or to fall themselves by their Hands.

He has *excited domestic Insurrections amongst us, & has* endeavored to bring on the Inhabitants of our Frontiers, the merciless Indian Savages, whose known Rule of Warfare, is an undistinguished Destruction, of all Ages, Sexes, & Conditions ~~of existence. He has incited treasonable insurrections of our fellow citizens, with the allurements of forfeiture & confiscation of our property. He has waged cruel war against human nature itself, violating it's most sacred rights of life and liberty in the persons of a distant people who never offended him, captivating & carrying them into slavery in another hemisphere, or to incur miserable death in their transportation thither. This piratical warfare, the opprobium of INFIDEL powers, is the warfare of the CHRISTIAN king of Great Britain. Determined to keep open a market where MEN should be bought & sold, he has prostituted his negative for suppressing every legislative attempt to prohibit or to restrain this execrable commerce. And that this assemblage of horrors might want no fact of distinguished die, he is now exciting those very people to rise in arms among us, and to purchase that liberty of which he has deprived them, by murdering the people on whom he also obtruded them: thus paying off former crimes committed against the LIBERTIES of one people, with crimes which he urges them to commit against the LIVES of another.~~

In every stage of these Oppressions we have Petitioned for Redress in the most humble Terms: Our repeated Petitions have been answered only by repeated Injury. A Prince whose Character is thus marked by every act which may define a Tyrant, is unfit to be the Ruler of a *free* People ~~who mean to be free. Future ages will scarcely believe that the hardiness of one man adventured, within the short compass of twelve years only, to lay a~~

~~foundation so broad & so undisguised for tyranny over a people fostered & fixed in principles of freedom.~~

Nor have we been wanting in Attentions to our British Brethren. We have warned them from Time to Time of Attempts by their Legislature to extend a *an unwarrantable* jurisdiction over ~~these our states~~ *us*. We have reminded them of the Circumstances of our Emigration & Settlement here~~, no one of which could warrant so strange a pretension: that these were effected at the expense of our own blood & treasure, unassisted by the wealth or the strength of Great Britain: that in constituting indeed our several forms of government, we had adopted one common king, thereby laying a foundation for perpetual league & amity with them: but that submission to their parliament was no part of our constitution, nor ever in idea, if history may be credited: and~~. We have appealed to their native Justice and Magnanimity ~~as well as to~~, *and we have conjured them by* the Ties of our common Kindred to disavow these Usurpations, which ~~were likely to~~, *would inevitably* interrupt our Connection and Correspondence. They too have been deaf to the Voice of Justice & of Consanguinity ~~,and when occasions have been given them, by the regular course of their laws, of removing from their councils the disturbers of our harmony, they have, by their free election, re-established them in power. At this very time too they are permitting their chief magistrate to send over not only soldiers of our common blood, but Scotch & foreign mercenaries to invade & destroy us. These facts have given the last stab to agonizing affection, and manly spirit bids us to renounce forever these unfeeling brethren. We must endeavor to forget our former love for them, and hold them as we hold the rest of mankind, enemies in war, in peace friends. We might have been a free and a great people together; but a communication of grandeur & of freedom it seems is below their dignity. Be it so, since they will have it. The road to happiness & to glory is open to us too. We will tread it apart from them, and~~

We must therefore acquiesce in the Necessity which denounces our ~~eternal~~ Separation, *and hold them, as we hold the rest of Mankind, Enemies in War, in Peace, Friends!*

We, therefore, the Representatives of the UNITED STATES OF AMERICA in General Congress Assembled, *appealing to the Supreme Judge of the World for the Rectitude of our Intentions*, do, in the name, & by the Authority of the good People of these ~~states reject and renounce all allegiance and subjection to the kings of Great Britain and all others who may hearafter claim by, through or under them; we utterly dissolve all political connection which may heretofore have subsided between us and the people or parliament of Great Britain: and finally we do assert and~~

declare these colonies to be free and independent states. *Colonies, solemnly Publish and Declare, That these United Colonies are, and are of Right to be, Free and Independent States; that they are absolved from all Allegiance to the British Crown, and that all political Connection between them and the State of Great-Britain is and ought to be totally dissolved;* & *that as Free* & Independent States, they have full Power to levy War, conclude Peace, contract Alliances, establish Commerce & to do all other Acts & Things which Independent States may of right do. And for the support of this declaration, *with a firm Reliance on the Protection of divine Providence,* we mutually pledge to each other our lives, our Fortunes, & our sacred Honor.

Source: The Independence Hall Association, UShistory.org. "The Declaration of Independence: the Want, Will, and Hopes of the People." July 1995. Available online. URL: http://www.ushistory.org/declaration/document/congress.htm. Accessed January 8, 2010.

Sojourner Truth, "Ain't I a Woman?" (1851)

Sojourner Truth was born Isabella in 1797, in Ulster County, New York. Much of her childhood was spent being bought and sold by various slaveholders, and in 1826 she escaped with one of her children. In 1843, she adopted the name Sojourner Truth, and throughout the 1840s and '50s she was involved in the abolitionist movement as well as the women's rights movement. In 1851, she attended a women's rights convention in Akron, Ohio, to the dismay of many other attendants. It was here that she delivered the powerful and moving speech, "Ain't I a Woman?" and she reportedly returned to her seat amid "roars of applause." Sojourner Truth spent the rest of her life traveling and speaking for the rights of African Americans and women. She died in Battle Creek, Michigan, in 1883.

Well, children, where there is so much racket there must be something out of kilter. I think that 'twixt the negroes of the South and the women at the North, all talking about rights, the white men will be in a fix pretty soon. But what's all this here talking about?

That man over there says that women need to be helped into carriages, and lifted over ditches, and to have the best place everywhere. Nobody ever helps me into carriages, or over mud-puddles, or gives me any best place! And ain't I a woman? Look at me! Look at my arm! I have ploughed and planted, and gathered into barns, and no man could head me! And ain't I a woman? I could work as much and eat as much as a man—when I could get it—and bear the lash as well! And ain't I a woman? I have borne thirteen children, and seen most all sold off to slavery, and when I cried out with my mother's grief, none but Jesus heard me! And ain't I a woman?

Then they talk about this thing in the head; what's this they call it? [member of audience whispers, "intellect"] That's it, honey. What's that got to do with women's rights or negroes' rights? If my cup won't hold but a pint, and yours holds a quart, wouldn't you be mean not to let me have my little half measure full?

Then that little man in black there, he says women can't have as much rights as men, 'cause Christ wasn't a woman! Where did your Christ come from? Where did your Christ come from? From God and a woman! Man had nothing to do with Him.

If the first woman God ever made was strong enough to turn the world upside down all alone, these women together ought to be able to turn it back, and get it right side up again! And now they is asking to do it, the men better let them.

Obliged to you for hearing me, and now old Sojourner ain't got nothing more to say.

Source: Sojourner Truth. "Ain't I a Woman?" 1851. Available online. URL: http://www.feminist.com/resources/artspeech/genwom/sojour.htm. Accessed January 9, 2010.

Frederick Douglass, *Narrative of the Life of Frederick Douglass, an American Slave* (1855) (Excerpts)

Born Frederick Augustus Washington Bailey in Maryland around 1817 or 1818, Frederick Douglass would go on to become a world-famous writer, orator, and abolitionist. As a child, Douglass was sent to Baltimore, where, as a house servant, he learned how to read and write. In 1838, he escaped slavery and fled to New York City, where he married, changed his name to Frederick Douglass, and began campaigning for the abolition of slavery. He addressed large crowds throughout the 1840s and '50s, and in 1855 he published his memoirs. Still several years away from nationwide emancipation of the slaves, Douglass's autobiography served a greater purpose than merely providing entertainment. It explicitly highlighted the horrors of slavery and its inconsistence with Christian values. As a persuasive text, Douglass's memoirs not only detailed the suffering of slaves, but also revealed the corrosive power slavery had on slaveholders, whose Christian souls were helpless to maintain wholeness under the cruelty and inhumanity that were required of a slaveholder.

The following excerpts were taken from chapters I through VI of Douglass's Narrative, *detailing his early childhood from his birth on a plantation to his move to Baltimore.*

I was born in Tuckahoe, near Hillsborough, and about twelve miles from Easton, in Talbot County, Maryland. I have no accurate knowledge of my age, never having seen any authentic record containing it. By far the larger part of the slaves know as little of their ages as horses know of theirs, and it is the wish of most masters within my knowledge to keep their slaves thus ignorant. I do not remember to have ever met a slave who could tell of his birthday. They seldom come nearer to it than planting-time, harvest-time, cherry-time, spring-time, or fall-time. A want of information concerning my own was a source of unhappiness to me even during childhood. The white children could tell their ages. I could not tell why I ought to be deprived of the same privilege. I was not allowed to make any inquiries of my master concerning it. He deemed all such inquiries on the part of a slave improper and impertinent, and evidence of a restless spirit. The nearest estimate I can give makes me now between twenty-seven and twenty-eight years of age. I come to this, from hearing my master say, some time during 1835, I was about seventeen years old.

My mother was named Harriet Bailey. She was the daughter of Isaac and Betsey Bailey, both colored, and quite dark. My mother was of a darker complexion than either my grandmother or grandfather.

My father was a white man. He was admitted to be such by all I ever heard speak of my parentage. The opinion was also whispered that my master was my father; but of the correctness of this opinion, I know nothing; the means of knowing was withheld from me. My mother and I were separated when I was but an infant—before I knew her as my mother. It is a common custom, in the part of Maryland from which I ran away, to part children from their mothers at a very early age. Frequently, before the child has reached its twelfth month, its mother is taken from it, and hired out on some farm a considerable distance off, and the child is placed under the care of an old woman, too old for field labor. For what this separation is done, I do not know, unless it be to hinder the development of the child's affection toward its mother, and to blunt and destroy the natural affection of the mother for the child. This is the inevitable result.

I never saw my mother, to know her as such, more than four or five times in my life; and each of these times was very short in duration, and at night. She was hired by a Mr. Stewart, who lived about twelve miles from my home. She made her journeys to see me in the night, travelling the whole distance on foot, after the performance of her day's work. She was a field hand, and a whipping is the penalty of not being in the field at sunrise, unless a slave has special permission from his or her master to the contrary—a permission which they seldom get, and one that gives to him that gives it the proud name of being a kind master. I do not recollect of ever seeing my mother by the light of day. She was with me in the night. She would lie down with me, and get me to sleep, but long before I waked she was gone. Very little communication ever took place between us. Death soon ended what little we could have while she lived, and with it her hardships and suffering. She died when I was about seven years old, on one of my master's farms, near Lee's Mill. I was not allowed to be present during her illness, at her death, or burial. She was gone long before I knew any thing about it. Never having enjoyed, to any considerable extent, her soothing presence, her tender and watchful care, I received the tidings of her death with much the same emotions I should have probably felt at the death of a stranger.

. . .

I have had two masters. My first master's name was Anthony. I do not remember his first name. He was generally called Captain Anthony—a title which, I presume, he acquired by sailing a craft on the Chesapeake Bay. He was not considered a rich slaveholder. He owned two or three farms, and about thirty slaves. His farms and slaves were under the care of an overseer. The overseer's name was Plummer. Mr. Plummer was a miserable drunkard, a profane swearer, and a savage monster. He always went armed with a cowskin and a heavy cudgel. I have known him to cut and slash the women's heads so horribly, that even master would be enraged at his cruelty, and would threaten to whip him if he did not mind himself. Master, however, was not a humane slaveholder. It required extraordinary barbarity on the part of an overseer to affect him. He was a cruel man, hardened by a long life of slave-holding. He would at times seem to take great pleasure in whipping a slave. I have often been awakened at the dawn of day by the most heartrending shrieks of an own aunt of mine, whom he used to tie up to a joist, and whip upon her naked back till she was literally covered with blood. No words, no tears, no prayers, from his gory victim, seemed to move his iron heart from its bloody purpose. The louder she screamed, the harder he whipped; and where the blood ran fastest, there he whipped longest. He would whip her to make her scream, and whip her to make her hush; and not until overcome by fatigue, would he cease to swing the blood-clotted cowskin. I remember the first time I ever witnessed this horrible exhibition. I was quite a child, but I well remember it. I never shall forget it whilst

I remember any thing. It was the first of a long series of such outrages, of which I was doomed to be a witness and a participant. It struck me with awful force. It was the blood-stained gate, the entrance to the hell of slavery, through which I was about to pass. It was a most terrible spectacle. I wish I could commit to paper the feelings with which I beheld it.

This occurrence took place very soon after I went to live with my old master, and under the following circumstances. Aunt Hester went out one night,—where or for what I do not know,—and happened to be absent when my master desired her presence. He had ordered her not to go out evenings, and warned her that she must never let him catch her in company with a young man, who was paying attention to her belonging to Colonel Lloyd. The young man's name was Ned Roberts, generally called Lloyd's Ned. Why master was so careful of her, may be safely left to conjecture. She was a woman of noble form, and of graceful proportions, having very few equals, and fewer superiors, in personal appearance, among the colored or white women of our neighborhood.

Aunt Hester had not only disobeyed his orders in going out, but had been found in company with Lloyd's Ned; which circumstance, I found, from what he said while whipping her, was the chief offence. Had he been a man of pure morals himself, he might have been thought interested in protecting the innocence of my aunt; but those who knew him will not suspect him of any such virtue. Before he commenced whipping Aunt Hester, he took her into the kitchen, and stripped her from neck to waist, leaving her neck, shoulders, and back, entirely naked. He then told her to cross her hands, calling her at the same time a d----d b---h. After crossing her hands, he tied them with a strong rope, and led her to a stool under a large hook in the joist, put in for the purpose. He made her get upon the stool, and tied her hands to the hook. She now stood fair for his infernal purpose. Her arms were stretched up at their full length, so that she stood upon the ends of her toes. He then said to her, "Now, you d----d b---h, I'll learn you how to disobey my orders!" and after rolling up his sleeves, he commenced to lay on the heavy cowskin, and soon the warm, red blood (amid heart-rending shrieks from her, and horrid oaths from him) came dripping to the floor. I was so terrified and horror-stricken at the sight, that I hid myself in a closet, and dared not venture out till long after the bloody transaction was over. I expected it would be my turn next. It was all new to me. I had never seen any thing like it before. I had always lived with my grandmother on the outskirts of the plantation, where she was put to raise the children of the younger women. I had therefore been, until now, out of the way of the bloody scenes that often occurred on the plantation.

. . .

To describe the wealth of Colonel Lloyd would be almost equal to describing the riches of Job. He kept from ten to fifteen house-servants. He was said to own a thousand slaves, and I think this estimate quite within the truth. Colonel Lloyd owned so many that he did not know them when he saw them; nor did all the slaves of the out-farms know him. It is reported of him, that, while riding along the road one day, he met a colored man, and addressed him in the usual manner of speaking to colored people on the public highways of the south: "Well, boy, whom do you belong to?" "To Colonel Lloyd," replied the slave. "Well, does the colonel treat you well?" "No, sir," was the ready reply. "What, does he work you too hard?" "Yes, sir." "Well, don't he give you enough to eat?" "Yes, sir, he gives me enough, such as it is."

The colonel, after ascertaining where the slave belonged, rode on; the man also went on about his business, not dreaming that he had been conversing with his master. He thought, said, and heard nothing more of the matter, until two or three weeks afterwards. The poor man was then informed by his overseer that, for having found fault with his master, he was now to be sold to a Georgia trader. He was immediately chained and hand-cuffed; and thus, without a moment's warning, he was snatched away, and forever sundered, from his family and friends, by a hand more unrelenting than death. This is the penalty of telling the truth, of telling the simple truth, in answer to a series of plain questions.

It is partly in consequence of such facts, that slaves, when inquired of as to their condition and the character of their masters, almost universally say they are contented, and that their masters are kind. The slaveholders have been known to send in spies among their slaves, to ascertain their views and feelings in regard to their condition. The frequency of this has had the effect to establish among the slaves the maxim, that a still tongue makes a wise head. They suppress the truth rather than take the consequences of telling it, and in so doing prove themselves a part of the human family. If they have any thing to say of their masters, it is generally in their masters' favor, especially when speaking to an untried man. I have been frequently asked, when a slave, if I had a kind master, and do not remember ever to have given a negative answer; nor did I, in pursuing this course, consider myself as uttering what was absolutely false; for I always measured the kindness of my master by the standard of kindness set up among slaveholders around us.

· · ·

As to my own treatment while I lived on Colonel Lloyd's plantation, it was very similar to that of the other slave children. I was not old enough to work in the field, and there being little else than field work to do, I had a great deal of leisure time. The most I had to do was to drive up the cows at evening, keep the fowls out of the garden, keep the front yard clean, and run of errands for my old master's daughter, Mrs. Lucretia Auld. The most of my leisure time I spent in helping Master Daniel Lloyd in finding his birds, after he had shot them. My connection with Master Daniel was of some advantage to me. He became quite attached to me, and was a sort of protector of me. He would not allow the older boys to impose upon me, and would divide his cakes with me.

I was seldom whipped by my old master, and suffered little from any thing else than hunger and cold. I suffered much from hunger, but much more from cold. In hottest summer and coldest winter, I was kept almost naked—no shoes, no stockings, no jacket, no trousers, nothing on but a coarse tow linen shirt, reaching only to my knees. I had no bed. I must have perished with cold, but that, the coldest nights, I used to steal a bag which was used for carrying corn to the mill. I would crawl into this bag, and there sleep on the cold, damp, clay floor, with my head in and feet out. My feet have been so cracked with the frost, that the pen with which I am writing might be laid in the gashes.

We were not regularly allowanced. Our food was coarse corn meal boiled. This was called MUSH. It was put into a large wooden tray or trough, and set down upon the ground. The children were then called, like so many pigs, and like so many pigs they would come and devour the mush; some with oyster-shells, others with pieces of shingle, some with naked hands, and none with spoons. He that ate fastest got most; he that was strongest secured the best place; and few left the trough satisfied.

I was probably between seven and eight years old when I left Colonel Lloyd's plantation. I left it with joy. I shall never forget the ecstasy with which I received the intelligence that my old master (Anthony) had determined to let me go to Baltimore, to live with Mr. Hugh Auld, brother to my old master's son-in-law, Captain Thomas Auld. I received this information about three days before my departure. They were three of the happiest days I ever enjoyed. I spent the most part of all these three days in the creek, washing off the plantation scurf, and preparing myself for my departure.

. . .

Very soon after I went to live with Mr. and Mrs. Auld, she very kindly commenced to teach me the A, B, C. After I had learned this, she assisted me in learning to spell words of three or four letters. Just at this point of my progress, Mr. Auld found out what was going on, and at once forbade Mrs. Auld to instruct me further, telling her, among other things, that it was unlawful, as well as unsafe, to teach a slave to read. To use his own words, further, he said, "If you give a nigger an inch, he will take an ell. A nigger should know nothing but to obey his master—to do as he is told to do. Learning would spoil the best nigger in the world. Now," said he, "if you teach that nigger (speaking of myself) how to read, there would be no keeping him. It would forever unfit him to be a slave. He would at once become unmanageable, and of no value to his master. As to himself, it could do him no good, but a great deal of harm. It would make him discontented and unhappy." These words sank deep into my heart, stirred up sentiments within that lay slumbering, and called into existence an entirely new train of thought. It was a new and special revelation, explaining dark and mysterious things, with which my youthful understanding had struggled, but struggled in vain. I now understood what had been to me a most perplexing difficulty— to wit, the white man's power to enslave the black man. It was a grand achievement, and I prized it highly. From that moment, I understood the pathway from slavery to freedom. It was just what I wanted, and I got it at a time when I the least expected it. Whilst I was saddened by the thought of losing the aid of my kind mistress, I was gladdened by the invaluable instruction which, by the merest accident, I had gained from my master. Though conscious of the difficulty of learning without a teacher, I set out with high hope, and a fixed purpose, at whatever cost of trouble, to learn how to read. The very decided manner with which he spoke, and strove to impress his wife with the evil consequences of giving me instruction, served to convince me that he was deeply sensible of the truths he was uttering. It gave me the best assurance that I might rely with the utmost confidence on the results which, he said, would flow from teaching me to read. What he most dreaded, that I most desired. What he most loved, that I most hated. That which to him was a great evil, to be carefully shunned, was to me a great good, to be diligently sought; and the argument which he so warmly urged, against my learning to read, only served to inspire me with a desire and determination to learn. In learning to read, I owe almost as much to the bitter opposition of my master, as to the kindly aid of my mistress. I acknowledge the benefit of both.

I had resided but a short time in Baltimore before I observed a marked difference, in the treatment of slaves, from that which I had witnessed in the country. A city slave is almost a freeman, compared with a slave on the plantation. He is much better fed and clothed, and enjoys privileges altogether unknown to the slave on the plantation. There is a vestige of decency, a sense of shame, that does much to curb and check those outbreaks of atrocious cruelty so commonly enacted upon the plantation. He is a desperate slave-holder, who will shock the humanity of his non-slaveholding neighbors with the cries of his lacerated slave. Few are willing to incur the odium attaching to the reputation of being a cruel master; and above all things, they would not be known as not giving a slave enough to eat. Every city slaveholder is anxious to have it known of him, that he feeds his slaves well; and it is due to them to say, that most of them do give their slaves enough to eat. There are, however, some painful exceptions to this rule. Directly opposite to us, on Philpot Street, lived Mr. Thomas Hamilton. He owned two slaves. Their names were Henrietta and Mary. Henrietta was about twenty-two years of age, Mary was about fourteen; and of all the mangled and emaciated creatures I ever looked upon, these two were the most so. His heart must be harder than stone, that could look upon these unmoved. The head, neck, and shoulders of Mary were literally cut to pieces. I have frequently felt her head, and found it nearly covered with festering sores, caused by the lash of her cruel mistress. I do not know that her master ever whipped her, but I have been an eye-witness to the cruelty of Mrs. Hamilton. I used to be in Mr. Hamilton's house nearly every day. Mrs. Hamilton used to sit in a large chair in the middle of the room, with a heavy cowskin always by her side, and scarce an hour passed during the day but was marked by the blood of one of these slaves. The girls seldom passed her without her saying, "Move faster, you black gip!" at the same time giving them a blow with the cowskin over the head or shoulders, often drawing the blood. She would then say, "Take that, you black gip!" continuing, "If you don't move faster, I'll move you!" Added to the cruel lashings to which these slaves were subjected, they were kept nearly half-starved. They seldom knew what it was to eat a full meal. I have seen Mary contending with the pigs for the offal thrown into the street. So much was Mary kicked and cut to pieces, that she was oftener called "pecked" than by her name.

Source: Frederick Douglass. *Narrative of the Life of Frederick Douglass, an American Slave.* 1855. Available online. URL: http://sunsite.berkeley.edu/Literature/Douglass/. Accessed January 9, 2010.

Abraham Lincoln, The Emancipation Proclamation (1863)

The Emancipation Proclamation was issued on January 1, 1863, and while it did not officially end slavery altogether, it served as a major milestone on the path to abolition. While the proclamation was not all-inclusive, as it applied only to those states that had seceded from the Union, it nonetheless allowed freed slaves to serve in the Union Army and Navy, and by the war's end roughly 200,000 African-American men had fought.

The same year as the proclamation, President Lincoln ordered 20,000 acres of land in South Carolina to be confiscated and sold to freed slaves in 20-acre plots, which was later increased to 40 acres. In 1865, General William T. Sherman agreed to loan out army mules. Less than a year later, President Andrew Jackson reversed the order and returned the confiscated land to its original owners.

Whereas, on the twenty-second day of September, in the year of our Lord one thousand eight hundred and sixty-two, a proclamation was issued by the President of the United States, containing, among other things, the following, to wit:

"That on the first day of January, in the year of our Lord one thousand eight hundred and sixty-three, all persons held as slaves within any State or designated part of a State, the people whereof shall then be in rebellion against the United States, shall be then, thenceforward, and forever free; and the Executive Government of the United States, including the military and naval authority thereof, will recognize and maintain the freedom of such persons, and will do no act or acts to repress such persons, or any of them, in any efforts they may make for their actual freedom.

"That the Executive will, on the first day of January aforesaid, by proclamation, designate the States and parts of States, if any, in which the people thereof, respectively, shall then be in rebellion against the United States; and the fact that any State, or the people thereof, shall on that day be, in good faith, represented in the Congress of the United States by members chosen thereto at elections wherein a majority of the qualified voters of such State shall have participated, shall, in the absence of strong countervailing testimony, be deemed conclusive evidence that such State, and the people thereof, are not then in rebellion against the United States."

Now, therefore I, Abraham Lincoln, President of the United States, by virtue of the power in me vested as Commander-in-Chief, of the Army and Navy of the United States in time of actual armed rebellion against the authority and government of the United States, and as a fit and necessary war measure for suppressing said rebellion, do, on this first day of January, in the year of our Lord one thousand eight hundred and sixty-three, and in accordance with my purpose so to do publicly proclaimed for the full period of one hundred days, from the day first above mentioned, order and designate as the States and parts of States wherein the people thereof respectively, are this day in rebellion against the United States, the following, to wit:

Arkansas, Texas, Louisiana, (except the Parishes of St. Bernard, Plaquemines, Jefferson, St. John, St. Charles, St. James Ascension, Assumption, Terrebonne, Lafourche, St. Mary, St. Martin, and Orleans, including the City of New Orleans) Mississippi, Alabama, Florida, Georgia, South Carolina, North Carolina, and Virginia, (except the forty-eight counties designated as West Virginia, and also the counties of Berkley, Accomac, Northampton, Elizabeth City, York, Princess Ann, and Norfolk, including the cities of Norfolk and Portsmouth[)], and which excepted parts, are for the present, left precisely as if this proclamation were not issued.

And by virtue of the power, and for the purpose aforesaid, I do order and declare that all persons held as slaves within said designated States, and parts of States, are, and henceforward shall be free; and that the Executive government of the United States, including the military and naval authorities thereof, will recognize and maintain the freedom of said persons.

And I hereby enjoin upon the people so declared to be free to abstain from all violence, unless in necessary self-defence; and I recommend to them that, in all cases when allowed, they labor faithfully for reasonable wages.

And I further declare and make known, that such persons of suitable condition, will be received into the armed service of the United States to garrison forts, positions, stations, and other places, and to man vessels of all sorts in said service.

And upon this act, sincerely believed to be an act of justice, warranted by the Constitution, upon military necessity, I invoke the considerate judgment of mankind, and the gracious favor of Almighty God.

In witness whereof, I have hereunto set my hand and caused the seal of the United States to be affixed.

Done at the City of Washington, this first day of January, in the year of our Lord one thousand eight hundred and sixty-three, and of the Independence of the United States of America the eighty-seventh.

Source: U.S. National Archives and Records Administration. "Featured Documents: The Emancipation Proclamation." Available online. URL: http://www.archives.gov/exhibits/featured_documents/emancipation_proclamation/transcript.html. Accessed on July 23, 2010.

Clara Lemlich, "Life in the Shops" (1909)

Clara Lemlich was an executive board member of Local 25 of the Ladies' Waist and Dress Makers' Union. In 1909, she called for a strike and initiated a mass walkout of shirtwaist makers. Her description of the working conditions of women and girls in dressmakers' shops was published in The New

York Evening Journal in November 1909, only a year and a half before the Triangle Shirtwaist Factory Fire in New York City, which killed 146 employees in March 1911.

First let me tell you something about the way we work and what we are paid. There are two kinds of work—regular, that is salary work, and piecework. The regular work pays about $6 a week and the girls have to be at their machines at 7 o'clock in the morning and they stay at them until 8 o'clock at night, with just one-half hour for lunch in that time.

The shops. Well, there is just one row of machines that the daylight ever gets to—that is the front row, nearest the window. The girls at all the other rows of machines back in the shops have to work by gaslight, by day as well as by night. Oh, yes, the shops keep the work going at night, too.

The bosses in the shops are hardly what you would call educated men, and the girls to them are part of the machines they are running. They yell at the girls and they "call them down" even worse than I imagine the Negro slaves were in the South.

There are no dressing rooms for the girls in the shops. They have to hang up their hats and coats—such as they are—on hooks along the walls. Sometimes a girl has a new hat. It never is much to look at because it never costs more than 50 cents, that means that we have gone for weeks on two-cent lunches—dry cake and nothing else.

The shops are unsanitary—that's the word that is generally used, but there ought to be a worse one used. Whenever we tear or damage any of the goods we sew on, or whenever it is found damaged after we are through with it, whether we have done it or not, we are charged for the piece and sometimes for a whole yard of the material.

At the beginning of every slow season, $2 is deducted from our salaries. We have never been able to find out what this is for.

Source: Cornell University ILR School. "The Triangle Factory Fire: Life in the Shops." March 2, 2002. Available online. URL: http://www.ilr.cornell.edu/trianglefire/texts/stein_ootss/ootss_cl.html. Accessed on July 23, 2010.

Etta Wheeler, "The Story of Mary Ellen" (1913) (Excerpts)

In 1913, Etta Angell Wheeler, the social worker who was responsible for rescuing nine-year-old Mary Ellen Wilson from a bitterly abusive home, gave the keynote address at the American Humane Association's national conference. In her address, she describes how she first learned about Mary Ellen, her first encounter with the child, and the resistance she faced in seeking to remove

Mary Ellen from the home. Though Mary Ellen was nine years old when she was removed from the home of her adoptive parents, she had been so severely malnourished that she was only the size of a five-year-old. Mary Ellen was rescued with the help of Henry Bergh, president of the American Society for the Prevention of Cruelty to Animals.

Late in the year 1873 there was brought to me by a poor working woman, the story of a child whose sad case inspired the founding of the first "Society for the Prevention of Cruelty to Children." The woman was a quiet, reserved Scotch woman, truthful and careful of her words. The story was that during the two previous years, there had lived in the rear tenement, 349 West 41st St., a family of three persons, a man, a woman and a little girl, supposed to be five or six years old; that during these two years the child had been a close prisoner having been seen only once by the other tenants; that she was often cruelly whipped and very frequently left alone the entire day with the windows darkened, and she locked in an inner room; that the other occupants of the house had not known to whom to make complaint, the guardian of the house, who lived on the premises, refusing to listen.

A week before, this family had moved to the rear tenement 341, on the same street. Later in the day I went to 349 and heard a like story from others; then, hoping to see the child, I went to 341. The house was separated from the one in front by a narrow paved court, each of the three floors had two apartments, a living room and a bedroom in each. The living rooms were separated by a thin partition through which, during weeks to come, the cries of the child gave evidence of her unhappy life. The family I sought was on the top floor. Wondering what reason I could give for my intrusion, I knocked at the door. It was not opened. Wishing, if possible, to learn if the child was there, I knocked at the door of the adjoining apartment. A faint voice bade me "Herein." I saw a tidy room and in the dark bedroom a young German woman apparently very ill. While sitting by her bed for a short time she told me of coming with her young husband, not long before, to this land of strangers and strange speech; of her homesickness and failing health.

I asked her of her new neighbors. She had not seen them, there was a child, she had "heard it crying, perhaps it too was sick." Promising to come again, I returned to the other apartment where, after a time, the door was slightly opened and a woman's sharp voice asked my errand. I began telling her of her sick and lonely neighbor and talked on until, unconsciously, she had opened the door, so that I could step in. This I did and, being an unbidden guest, made a very brief call. I was there only long enough to see the child and gain my own impression of her condition. While still talking with the woman, I saw a pale, thin child, barefoot, in a thin, scanty dress so tattered that I could see she wore but one garment besides.

It was December and the weather bitterly cold. She was a tiny mite, the size of five years, though, as afterward appeared, she was then nine. From a pan set upon a low stool she stood washing dishes, struggling with a frying pan about as heavy as herself. Across the table lay a brutal whip of twisted leather strands and the child's meagre arms and legs bore many marks of its use. But the saddest part of her story was written on her face in its look of suppression and misery, the face of a child unloved, of a child that had seen only the fearsome side of life. These things I saw while seeming not to see, and I left without speaking to, or of, the child. I never saw her again until the day of her rescue, three months later, but I went away determined, with the help of a kind Providence, to rescue her from her miserable life.

. . .

I had more than once been tempted to apply to the "Society for the Prevention of Cruelty to Animals," but had lacked courage to do what seemed absurd. However, when on the following Tuesday, a niece said: "You are so troubled over that abused child, why not go to Mr. Bergh? She is a little animal, surely." I said at once, "I will go." Within an hour I was at the society's rooms. Mr. Bergh was in his office and listened to my recital most courteously but with a slight air of amusement that such an appeal should be made there. In the end he said: "The case interests me much, but very definite testimony is needed to warrant interference between a child and those claiming guardianship. Will you not send me a written statement that, at my leisure, I may judge the weight of the evidence and may also have time to consider if this society should interfere? I promise to consider the case carefully."

It was the first promise of help and I was glad. The next morning I sent a paper giving what I had seen and heard, which was little, and the much that had been told me by others, and what seemed to me their credibility as witnesses. Going later in the day to see the sick woman, I found in her room a young man with a large official looking book under his arm. Hearing a nurse speak my name as I entered, he said to me: "I was sent to take the census in this house. I have been in every room." I inferred at once that this was a detective for Mr. Bergh. When I left the house, the young man was waiting on the sidewalk to tell me he had seen the child and was then going to Mr. Bergh with his report of her pitiable condition.

The next morning, Thursday, Mr. Bergh called upon me to ask if I would go to the Court House, the child having been already sent for. He expressed pleasure that he need not ask me to go to a police court, Judge Lawrence of the Supreme Court having kindly taken the case. After we had waited a short time in the Judge's Court, two officers came in, one of whom had the little girl in his arms. She was wrapped in a carriage blanket and was without other clothing than the two ragged garments I had seen her in months before. Her body was bruised, her face disfigured, and the woman, as if to make testimony sure against herself, had the day before, struck the child with a pair of shears, cutting a gash through the left eye-brow and down the cheek, fortunately escaping the eye.

The child was sobbing bitterly when brought in but there was a touch of the ludicrous with it all. While one of the officers had held the infuriated woman, the other had taken away the terrified child. She was still shrieking as they drove away and they called a halt at the first candy shop, so that she came into court weeping and terrified but waving as a weapon of defense a huge stick of peppermint candy. Poor child! It was her one earthly possession. The investigation proceeded. The child's appearance was testimony enough, little of mine was needed, and, thus, on Thursday, April 9, 1874, her rescue was accomplished. This Mr. Bergh had effected within forty-eight hours after first hearing of the case. The next day the woman, who had so often forgotten her own suffering in pity and prayer for the child, died, happy that little Mary Ellen was free. Now, for the first time, we knew the child's name.

The prosecution of the woman who had so ill-treated her, followed soon. One witness was a representative of the institution from which the woman had taken the child, then less than two years old. No inquiry as to the child's welfare had been made by the institution during the intervening seven years. Record of her admission to this institution had been lost in a fire. The testimony of fellow tenants, and the damaging witness of the woman against herself, under cross-examination, secured her conviction and she was sentenced to the penitentiary for a year.

. . .

He [Judge Lawrence] consulted with Mr. Bergh and soon after put Mary Ellen at my disposal. I took her to my mother near Rochester, New York, to my mother whose heart and home were always open to the needy.

Here began a new life. The child was an interesting study, so long shut within four walls and now in a new world. Woods, fields, "green things growing," were all strange to her, she had not known them. She had to learn, as a baby does, to walk upon the ground, she had walked only upon floors, and her eye told her nothing of uneven surfaces. She was wholly untaught; knew nothing of right and wrong except as related to punishments; did not know of the Heavenly Father; had had no companionship with children or toys. But in this home there were other children and they taught her as children alone can teach each other. They taught her to play, to be unafraid, to know her rights and to claim them. She shared their happy, busy life from the making of mud pies up to charming birthday parties and was fast becoming a normal child.

I had taken her to my mother in June. In the autumn following my mother died. She had asked that, after her death, my sister, living nearby, should take Mary. This she did and under her care were passed years of home and school life, of learning all good household ways; of instruction in church and Sunday school, and in gaining the love of many and the esteem of all who knew her.

When twenty-four she was married to a worthy man and has proved a good home maker and a devoted wife and mother. To her children, two bright, dutiful daughters, it has been her joy to give a happy childhood in sharp contrast to her own. If the memory of her earliest years is sad, there is this comfort that the cry of her wrongs awoke the world to the need of organized relief for neglected and abused children.

Source: American Humane Association. "The Story of Mary Ellen: The Beginnings of a Worldwide Child-Saving Crusade." 2010. Available online. URL: http://www.americanhumane.org/about-us/who-we-are/history/etta-wheeler-account.html. Accessed on July 23, 2010.

The Civil Rights Act (1964) (Excerpts)

Before his assassination in 1963, President John F. Kennedy had urged Congress to consider civil rights legislation and similarly urged the nation in a televised address to work toward guaranteeing equal rights for all Americans. The Civil Rights Act was approved by the House in 1964 and signed into law by Kennedy's successor Lyndon B. Johnson. The act was revolutionary, as, up until its passage, questions remained as to whether discrimination could be considered a federal issue at all. If restaurant owners refused to allow people of color into their establishments, or employers refused to hire women, then would the government's intervention amount to an infringement on those individuals' rights? Not only was the issue controversial for its time, but even the question of who was entitled to equal rights was fiercely debated.

The provisions of the Civil Rights Act of 1964 prohibited segregation and discrimination in hiring and voting practices based on an individual's race, ethnic status, or sex, but the word sex *was almost excluded from the bill. Democratic senator Howard W. Smith from Virginia added the word* sex, *and was criticized for attempting to kill the bill, but Smith, a vocal segregationist, maintained that he was a firm supporter of the National Women's Party.*

The bill was eventually approved, and President Johnson signed the Civil Rights Act into law on July 2, 1964.

An Act

To enforce the constitutional right to vote, to confer jurisdiction upon the district courts of the United States to provide injunctive relief against discrimination in public accommodations, to authorize the Attorney General to institute suits to protect constitutional rights in public facilities and public education, to extend the Commission on Civil Rights, to prevent discrimination in federally assisted programs, to establish a Commission on Equal Employment Opportunity, and for other purposes.

Be it enacted by the Senate and House of Representatives of the United States of America in Congress assembled, That this Act may be cited as the "Civil Rights Act of 1964".

TITLE I—VOTING RIGHTS

SEC. 101. Section 2004 of the Revised Statutes (42 U.S.C. 1971), as amended by section 131 of the Civil Rights Act of 1957 (71 Stat. 637), and as further amended by section 601 of the Civil Rights Act of 1960 (74 Stat. 90), is further amended as follows:

(a) Insert "1" after "(a)" in subsection (a) and add at the end of subsection (a) the following new paragraphs:

"(2) No person acting under color of law shall—

"(A) in determining whether any individual is qualified under State law or laws to vote in any Federal election, apply any standard, practice, or procedure different from the standards, practices, or procedures applied under such law or laws to other individuals within the same county, parish, or similar political subdivision who have been found by State officials to be qualified to vote;

"(B) deny the right of any individual to vote in any Federal election because of an error or omission on any record or paper relating to any application, registration, or other act requisite to voting, if such error or omission is not material in determining whether such individual is qualified under State law to vote in such election; or

"(C) employ any literacy test as a qualification for voting in any Federal election unless (i) such test is administered to each individual and is conducted wholly in writing, and (ii) a certified copy of the test and of the answers given by the individual is furnished to him within twenty-five days of the submission of his request made within the period of time during which records and papers are required to be retained and preserved pursuant to title III of the Civil Rights Act of 1960 (42 U.S.C. 1974—74e; 74 Stat. 88): Provided, however, That the Attorney General may enter into agreements with appropriate State or local authorities that preparation, conduct, and maintenance of such tests in accordance with the provisions of applicable State or local law, including such special provisions as are necessary in the preparation, conduct, and maintenance of such tests for persons who are blind or otherwise physically handicapped, meet the purposes of this subparagraph and constitute compliance therewith.

. . .

TITLE II—INJUNCTIVE RELIEF AGAINST DISCRIMINATION IN PLACES OF PUBLIC ACCOMMODATION

SEC. 201. (a) All persons shall be entitled to the full and equal enjoyment of the goods, services, facilities, and privileges, advantages, and accommodations of any place of public accommodation, as defined in this section, without discrimination or segregation on the ground of race, color, religion, or national origin.

(b) Each of the following establishments which serves the public is a place of public accommodation within the meaning of this title if its operations affect commerce, or if discrimination or segregation by it is supported by State action:

(1) any inn, hotel, motel, or other establishment which provides lodging to transient guests, other than an establishment located within a building which contains not more than five rooms for rent or hire and which is actually occupied by the proprietor of such establishment as his residence;

(2) any restaurant, cafeteria, lunchroom, lunch counter, soda fountain, or other facility principally engaged in selling food for consumption on the premises, including, but not limited to, any such facility located on the premises of any retail establishment; or any gasoline station;

(3) any motion picture house, theater, concert hall, sports arena, stadium or other place of exhibition or entertainment; and

(4) any establishment (A)(i) which is physically located within the premises of any establishment otherwise covered by this subsec-

tion, or (ii) within the premises of which is physically located any such covered establishment, and (B) which holds itself out as serving patrons of such covered establishment.

. . .

TITLE III—DESEGREGATION OF PUBLIC FACILITIES

SEC. 301. (a) Whenever the Attorney General receives a complaint in writing signed by an individual to the effect that he is being deprived of or threatened with the loss of his right to the equal protection of the laws, on account of his race, color, religion, or national origin, by being denied equal utilization of any public facility which is owned, operated, or managed by or on behalf of any State or subdivision thereof, other than a public school or public college as defined in section 401 of title IV hereof, and the Attorney General believes the complaint is meritorious and certifies that the signer or signers of such complaint are unable, in his judgment, to initiate and maintain appropriate legal proceedings for relief and that the institution of an action will materially further the orderly progress of desegregation in public facilities, the Attorney General is authorized to institute for or in the name of the United States a civil action in any appropriate district court of the United States against such parties and for such relief as may be appropriate, and such court shall have and shall exercise jurisdiction of proceedings instituted pursuant to this section.

. . .

TITLE IV—DESEGREGATION OF PUBLIC EDUCATION
DEFINITIONS

SEC. 401. As used in this title—

(a) "Commissioner" means the Commissioner of Education.

(b) "Desegregation" means the assignment of students to public schools and within such schools without regard to their race, color, religion, or national origin, but "desegregation" shall not mean the assignment of students to public schools in order to overcome racial imbalance.

(c) "Public school" means any elementary or secondary educational institution, and "public college" means any institution of higher education or any technical or vocational school above the secondary school level, provided that such public school or public college is operated by a State, subdivision of a State, or governmental agency within a State, or operated wholly or predominantly from or through the use of governmental funds or property, or funds or property derived from a governmental source.

(d) "School board" means any agency or agencies which administer a system of one or more public schools and any other agency which is responsible for the assignment of students to or within such system.

. . .

TITLE VI—NONDISCRIMINATION IN FEDERALLY ASSISTED PROGRAMS

SEC. 601. No person in the United States shall, on the ground of race, color, or national origin, be excluded from participation in, be denied the benefits of, or be subjected to discrimination under any program or activity receiving Federal financial assistance.

. . .

DISCRIMINATION BECAUSE OF RACE, COLOR, RELIGION, SEX, OR NATIONAL ORIGIN

SEC. 703. (a) It shall be an unlawful employment practice for an employer—

(1) to fail or refuse to hire or to discharge any individual, or otherwise to discriminate against any individual with respect to his compensation, terms, conditions, or privileges of employment, because of such individual's race, color, religion, sex, or national origin; or

(2) to limit, segregate, or classify his employees in any way which would deprive or tend to deprive any individual of employment opportunities or otherwise adversely affect his status as an employee, because of such individual's race, color, religion, sex, or national origin.

(b) It shall be an unlawful employment practice for an employment agency to fail or refuse to refer for employment, or otherwise to discriminate against, any individual because of his race, color, religion, sex, or national origin, or to classify or refer for employment any individual on the basis of his race, color, religion, sex, or national origin.

(c) It shall be an unlawful employment practice for a labor organization—

(1) to exclude or to expel from its membership, or otherwise to discriminate against, any individual because of his race, color, religion, sex, or national origin;

(2) to limit, segregate, or classify its membership, or to classify or fail or refuse to refer for employment any individual, in any way which would deprive or tend to deprive any individual of employment opportunities, or would limit such employment opportunities or otherwise adversely affect his status as an employee or as an

applicant for employment, because of such individual's race, color, religion, sex, or national origin; or

(3) to cause or attempt to cause an employer to discriminate against an individual in violation of this section.

(d) It shall be an unlawful employment practice for any employer, labor organization, or joint labor-management committee controlling apprenticeship or other training or retraining, including on-the-job training programs to discriminate against any individual because of his race, color, religion, sex, or national origin in admission to, or employment in, any program established to provide apprenticeship or other training.

(e) Notwithstanding any other provision of this title, (1) it shall not be an unlawful employment practice for an employer to hire and employ employees, for an employment agency to classify, or refer for employment any individual, for a labor organization to classify its membership or to classify or refer for employment any individual, or for an employer, labor organization, or joint labor-management committee controlling apprenticeship or other training or retraining programs to admit or employ any individual in any such program, on the basis of his religion, sex, or national origin in those certain instances where religion, sex, or national origin is a bona fide occupational qualification reasonably necessary to the normal operation of that particular business or enterprise, and (2) it shall not be an unlawful employment practice for a school, college, university, or other educational institution or institution of learning to hire and employ employees of a particular religion if such school, college, university, or other educational institution or institution of learning is, in whole or in substantial part, owned, supported, controlled, or managed by a particular religion or by a particular religious corporation, association, or society, or if the curriculum of such school, college, university, or other educational institution or institution of learning is directed toward the propagation of a particular religion.

(f) As used in this title, the phrase "unlawful employment practice" shall not be deemed to include any action or measure taken by an employer, labor organization, joint labor-management committee, or employment agency with respect to an individual who is a member of the Communist Party of the United States or of any other organization required to register as a Communist-action or Communist-front organization by final order of the Subversive Activities Control Board pursuant to the Subversive Activities Control Act of 1950.

(g) Notwithstanding any other provision of this title, it shall not be an unlawful employment practice for an employer to fail or refuse to hire and employ any individual for any position, for an employer to discharge any individual from any position, or for an employment agency to fail or refuse to refer any individual for employment in any position, or for a labor organization to fail or refuse to refer any individual for employment in any position, if—

   (1) the occupancy of such position, or access to the premises in or upon which any part of the duties of such position is performed or is to be performed, is subject to any requirement imposed in the interest of the national security of the United States under any security program in effect pursuant to or administered under any statute of the United States or any Executive order of the President; and

   (2) such individual has not fulfilled or has ceased to fulfill that requirement.

(h) Notwithstanding any other provision of this title, it shall not be an unlawful employment practice for an employer to apply different standards of compensation, or different terms, conditions, or privileges of employment pursuant to a bona fide seniority or merit system, or a system which measures earnings by quantity or quality of production or to employees who work in different locations, provided that such differences are not the result of an intention to discriminate because of race, color, religion, sex, or national origin, nor shall it be an unlawful employment practice for an employer to give and to act upon the results of any professionally developed ability test provided that such test, its administration or action upon the results is not designed, intended or used to discriminate because of race, color, religion, sex or national origin. It shall not be an unlawful employment practice under this title for any employer to differentiate upon the basis of sex in determining the amount of the wages or compensation paid or to be paid to employees of such employer if such differentiation is authorized by the provisions of section 6(d) of the Fair Labor Standards Act of 1938, as amended (29 U.S.C. 206(d)).

(i) Nothing contained in this title shall apply to any business or enterprise on or near an Indian reservation with respect to any publicly announced employment practice of such business or enterprise under which a preferential treatment is given to any individual because he is an Indian living on or near a reservation.

(j) Nothing contained in this title shall be interpreted to require any employer, employment agency, labor organization, or joint labor-management committee subject to this title to grant preferential treatment to any individual or to any group because of the race, color, religion, sex, or national origin of such individual or group on account of an imbalance which may exist with respect to the total number or percentage of persons of any race, color, religion, sex, or national origin employed by any employer, referred or classified for employment by any employment agency or labor organization, admitted to membership or classified by any labor organization, or admitted to, or employed in, any apprenticeship or other training program, in comparison with the total number or percentage of persons of such race, color, religion, sex, or national origin in any community, State, section, or other area, or in the available work force in any community, State, section, or other area.

OTHER UNLAWFUL EMPLOYMENT PRACTICES

SEC. 704. (a) It shall be an unlawful employment practice for an employer to discriminate against any of his employees or applicants for employment, for an employment agency to discriminate against any individual, or for a labor organization to discriminate against any member thereof or applicant for membership, because he has opposed, any practice made an unlawful employment practice by this title, or because he has made a charge, testified, assisted, or participated in any manner in an investigation, proceeding, or hearing under this title.

Source: OurDocuments.gov. "Transcript of Civil Rights Act (1964)." Available online. URL: http://www.ourdocuments.gov/doc.php?flash=true&doc=97&page=transcript. Accessed November 29, 2010.

Hillary Rodham Clinton, "Women's Rights Are Human Rights" (1995)

In 1995, the first lady Hillary Rodham Clinton delivered a speech at the UN Fourth World Conference on Women in Beijing, China. In the speech, Clinton outlines many of the abuses suffered by women around the world, as well as how greater protections of women's rights naturally benefit their families, which, in turn, benefits society as a whole. More important, Clinton emphasizes the fact that women's rights should not be considered distinct or separate from human rights. In a punctuated and powerful series of statements, she addresses individual human rights crises experienced primarily, if not exclusively, by women around the world, including female infanticide, sexual slavery, rape as a tactic of war, bride burning, genital mutilation, domestic violence, and denied reproductive rights.

155

Thank you very much, Gertrude Mongella, for your dedicated work that has brought us to this point, distinguished delegates, and guests:

I would like to thank the Secretary General for inviting me to be part of this important United Nations Fourth World Conference on Women. This is truly a celebration, a celebration of the contributions women make in every aspect of life: in the home, on the job, in the community, as mothers, wives, sisters, daughters, learners, workers, citizens, and leaders.

It is also a coming together, much the way women come together every day in every country. We come together in fields and factories, in village markets and supermarkets, in living rooms and board rooms. Whether it is while playing with our children in the park, or washing clothes in a river, or taking a break at the office water cooler, we come together and talk about our aspirations and concern. And time and again, our talk turns to our children and our families. However different we may appear, there is far more that unites us than divides us. We share a common future, and we are here to find common ground so that we may help bring new dignity and respect to women and girls all over the world, and in so doing bring new strength and stability to families as well.

By gathering in Beijing, we are focusing world attention on issues that matter most in our lives—the lives of women and their families: access to education, health care, jobs and credit, the chance to enjoy basic legal and human rights and to participate fully in the political life of our countries.

There are some who question the reason for this conference. Let them listen to the voices of women in their homes, neighborhoods, and workplaces. There are some who wonder whether the lives of women and girls matter to economic and political progress around the globe. Let them look at the women gathered here and at Huairou—the homemakers and nurses, the teachers and lawyers, the policymakers and women who run their own businesses. It is conferences like this that compel governments and peoples everywhere to listen, look, and face the world's most pressing problems. Wasn't it after all—after the women's conference in Nairobi ten years ago that the world focused for the first time on the crisis of domestic violence?

Earlier today, I participated in a World Health Organization forum. In that forum, we talked about ways that government officials, NGOs, and individual citizens are working to address the health problems of women and girls. Tomorrow, I will attend a gathering of the United Nations Development Fund for Women. There, the discussion will focus on local—and highly successful—programs that give hard-working women access to credit so they can improve their own lives and the lives of their families.

What we are learning around the world is that if women are healthy and educated, their families will flourish. If women are free from violence, their families will flourish. If women have a chance to work and earn as full and equal partners in society, their families will flourish. And when families flourish, communities and nations do as well. That is why every woman, every man, every child, every family, and every nation on this planet does have a stake in the discussion that takes place here.

Over the past 25 years, I have worked persistently on issues relating to women, children, and families. Over the past two-and-a half years, I've had the opportunity to learn more about the challenges facing women in my own country and around the world.

I have met new mothers in Indonesia, who come together regularly in their village to discuss nutrition, family planning, and baby care. I have met working parents in Denmark who talk about the comfort they feel in knowing that their children can be cared for in safe, and nurturing after-school centers. I have met women in South Africa who helped lead the struggle to end apartheid and are now helping to build a new democracy. I have met with the leading women of the Western Hemisphere who are working every day to promote literacy and better health care for children in their countries. I have met women in India and Bangladesh who are taking out small loans to buy milk cows, or rickshaws, or thread in order to create a livelihood for themselves and their families. I have met the doctors and nurses in Belarus and Ukraine who are trying to keep children alive in the aftermath of Chernobyl.

The great challenge of this conference is to give voice to women everywhere whose experiences go unnoticed, whose words go unheard. Women comprise more than half the word's population, 70% of the world's poor, and two-thirds of those who are not taught to read and write. We are the primary caretakers for most of the world's children and elderly. Yet much of the work we do is not valued—not by economists, not by historians, not by popular culture, not by government leaders.

At this very moment, as we sit here, women around the world are giving birth, raising children, cooking meals, washing clothes, cleaning houses, planting crops, working on assembly lines, running companies, and running countries. Women also are dying from diseases that should have been prevented or treated. They are watching their children succumb to malnutrition caused by poverty and economic deprivation. They are being denied the right to go to school by their own fathers and brothers. They are being forced into prostitution, and they are being barred from the bank lending offices and banned from the ballot box.

Those of us who have the opportunity to be here have the responsibility to speak for those who could not. As an American, I want to speak for those women in my own country, women who are raising children on the minimum wage, women who can't afford health care or child care, women whose lives are threatened by violence, including violence in their own homes.

I want to speak up for mothers who are fighting for good schools, safe neighborhoods, clean air, and clean airwaves; for older women, some of them widows, who find that, after raising their families, their skills and life experiences are not valued in the marketplace; for women who are working all night as nurses, hotel clerks, or fast food chefs so that they can be at home during the day with their children; and for women everywhere who simply don't have time to do everything they are called upon to do each and every day.

Speaking to you today, I speak for them, just as each of us speaks for women around the world who are denied the chance to go to school, or see a doctor, or own property, or have a say about the direction of their lives, simply because they are women. The truth is that most women around the world work both inside and outside the home, usually by necessity.

We need to understand there is no one formula for how women should lead our lives. That is why we must respect the choices that each woman makes for herself and her family. Every woman deserves the chance to realize her own God-given potential. But we must recognize that women will never gain full dignity until their human rights are respected and protected.

Our goals for this conference, to strengthen families and societies by empowering women to take greater control over their own destinies, cannot be fully achieved unless all governments—here and around the world—accept their responsibility to protect and promote internationally recognized human rights. The—The international community has long acknowledged and recently reaffirmed at Vienna that both women and men are entitled to a range of protections and personal freedoms, from the right of personal security to the right to determine freely the number and spacing of the children they bear. No one—No one should be forced to remain silent for fear of religious or political persecution, arrest, abuse, or torture.

Tragically, women are most often the ones whose human rights are violated. Even now, in the late 20th century, the rape of women continues to be used as an instrument of armed conflict. Women and children make up a large majority of the world's refugees. And when women are excluded from the political process, they become even more vulnerable to abuse. I believe that now, on the eve of a new millennium, it is time to break the silence. It is time for us to say here in Beijing, and for the world to hear, that it is no longer acceptable to discuss women's rights as separate from human rights.

These abuses have continued because, for too long, the history of women has been a history of silence. Even today, there are those who are trying to silence our words. But the voices of this conference and of the women at Huairou must be heard loudly and clearly:

It is a violation of human rights when babies are denied food, or drowned, or suffocated, or their spines broken, simply because they are born girls.

It is a violation of human rights when women and girls are sold into the slavery of prostitution for human greed—and the kinds of reasons that are used to justify this practice should no longer be tolerated.

It is a violation of human rights when women are doused with gasoline, set on fire, and burned to death because their marriage dowries are deemed too small.

It is a violation of human rights when individual women are raped in their own communities and when thousands of women are subjected to rape as a tactic or prize of war.

It is a violation of human rights when a leading cause of death worldwide among women ages 14 to 44 is the violence they are subjected to in their own homes by their own relatives.

It is a violation of human rights when young girls are brutalized by the painful and degrading practice of genital mutilation.

It is a violation of human rights when women are denied the right to plan their own families, and that includes being forced to have abortions or being sterilized against their will.

If there is one message that echoes forth from this conference, let it be that human rights are women's rights and women's rights are human rights once and for all. Let us not forget that among those rights are the right to speak freely—and the right to be heard.

Women must enjoy the rights to participate fully in the social and political lives of their countries, if we want freedom and democracy to thrive and endure. It is indefensible that many women in nongovernmental organizations who wished to participate in this conference have not been able to attend—or have been prohibited from fully taking part.

Let me be clear. Freedom means the right of people to assemble, organize, and debate openly. It means respecting the views of those who may disagree with the views of their governments. It means not taking citizens away from their loved ones and jailing them, mistreating them, or denying them their freedom or dignity because of the peaceful expression of their ideas and opinions.

In my country, we recently celebrated the 75th anniversary of Women's Suffrage. It took 150 years after the signing of our Declaration of Independence for women to win the right to vote. It took 72 years of organized struggle, before that happened, on the part of many courageous women and men. It was one of America's most divisive philosophical wars. But it was a bloodless war. Suffrage was achieved without a shot being fired.

But we have also been reminded, in V-J Day observances last weekend, of the good that comes when men and women join together to combat the forces of tyranny and to build a better world. We have seen peace prevail in most places for a half century. We have avoided another world war. But we have not solved older, deeply-rooted problems that continue to diminish the potential of half the world's population.

Now it is the time to act on behalf of women everywhere. If we take bold steps to better the lives of women, we will be taking bold steps to better the lives of children and families too. Families rely on mothers and wives for emotional support and care. Families rely on women for labor in the home. And increasingly, everywhere, families rely on women for income needed to raise healthy children and care for other relatives.

As long as discrimination and inequities remain so commonplace everywhere in the world, as long as girls and women are valued less, fed less, fed last, overworked, underpaid, not schooled, subjected to violence in and outside their homes—the potential of the human family to create a peaceful, prosperous world will not be realized.

Let—Let this conference be our—and the world's—call to action. Let us heed that call so we can create a world in which every woman is treated with respect and dignity, every boy and girl is loved and cared for equally, and every family has the hope of a strong and stable future. That is the work before you. That is the work before all of us who have a vision of the world we want to see—for our children and our grandchildren.

The time is now. We must move beyond rhetoric. We must move beyond recognition of problems to working together, to have the commen efforts to build that common ground we hope to see.

God's blessing on you, your work, and all who will benefit from it.

Godspeed and thank you very much.

Source: American Rhetoric, Top 100 Speeches. "Hillary Rodham Clinton: Remarks to the UN 4th World Conference on Women Plenary Session." September 5, 1995. Available online. URL: http://www.americanrhetoric.com/speeches/hillaryclintonbeijingspeech.htm. Accessed on July 23, 2010.

Department of Justice, "Americans with Disabilities Act of 1990, as Amended" (2008) (Excerpt)

The rights of the disabled were recognized most clearly and profoundly in 1990, with the passage of the Americans with Disabilities Act (ADA). Prior to the passage of ADA, the Rehabilitation Act of 1973 was the foremost outline of the rights of the disabled, prohibiting discrimination on the basis of disability in federally funded programs or by employers who receive federal funds. The Americans with Disabilities Act, however, expands those protections to include protection from non-federally-funded employer discrimination, the right to access to public facilities (such as wheelchair access), the right to public accommodations, and the right to telecommunications services. In short, the Americans with Disabilities Act affords disabled individuals the same civil rights that nondisabled citizens enjoy. The following text is an excerpt from the opening of the Americans with Disabilities Act as it was amended in 2008 to broaden the definition of a disability, which was previously defined as an impairment that affected at least two major life activities (walking, breathing, talking, etc.). The 2008 amendment changed this so that only one major life activity need be impaired for an individual to be considered disabled.

TITLE 42—THE PUBLIC HEALTH AND WELFARE
CHAPTER 126—EQUAL OPPORTUNITY FOR INDIVIDUALS WITH DISABILITIES
Sec. 12101. Findings and purpose

(a) **Findings**

The Congress finds that

(1) physical or mental disabilities in no way diminish a person's right to fully participate in all aspects of society, yet many people with physical or mental disabilities have been precluded from doing so because of discrimination; others who have a record of a disability or are regarded as having a disability also have been subjected to discrimination;

(2) historically, society has tended to isolate and segregate individuals with disabilities, and, despite some improvements, such forms of discrimination against individuals with disabilities continue to be a serious and pervasive social problem;

(3) discrimination against individuals with disabilities persists in such critical areas as employment, housing, public accommodations, education, transportation, communication, recreation, institutionalization, health services, voting, and access to public services;

(4) unlike individuals who have experienced discrimination on the basis of race, color, sex, national origin, religion, or age, individuals who have experienced discrimination on the basis of disability have often had no legal recourse to redress such discrimination;

(5) individuals with disabilities continually encounter various forms of discrimination, including outright intentional exclusion, the discriminatory effects of architectural, transportation, and communication barriers, overprotective rules and policies, failure to make modifications to existing facilities and practices, exclusionary qualification standards and criteria, segregation, and relegation to lesser services, programs, activities, benefits, jobs, or other opportunities;

(6) census data, national polls, and other studies have documented that people with disabilities, as a group, occupy an inferior status in our society, and are severely disadvantaged socially, vocationally, economically, and educationally;

(7) the Nation's proper goals regarding individuals with disabilities are to assure equality of opportunity, full participation, independent living, and economic self-sufficiency for such individuals; and

(8) the continuing existence of unfair and unnecessary discrimination and prejudice denies people with disabilities the opportunity to compete on an equal basis and to pursue those opportunities for which our free society is justifiably famous, and costs the United States billions of dollars in unnecessary expenses resulting from dependency and nonproductivity.

(b) Purpose

It is the purpose of this chapter

(1) to provide a clear and comprehensive national mandate for the elimination of discrimination against individuals with disabilities;

(2) to provide clear, strong, consistent, enforceable standards addressing discrimination against individuals with disabilities;

(3) to ensure that the Federal Government plays a central role in enforcing the standards established in this chapter on behalf of individuals with disabilities; and

(4) to invoke the sweep of congressional authority, including the power to enforce the Fourteenth Amendment and to regulate commerce, in order to address the major areas of discrimination faced day-to-day by people with disabilities.

Sec. 12101 note: Findings and Purposes of ADA Amendments Act of 2008, Pub. L. 110-325, § 2, Sept. 25, 2008, 122 Stat. 3553, provided that:

(a) Findings

Congress finds that—

(1) in enacting the Americans with Disabilities Act of 1990 (ADA), Congress intended that the Act "provide a clear and comprehensive national mandate for the elimination of discrimination against individuals with disabilities" and provide broad coverage;

(2) in enacting the ADA, Congress recognized that physical and mental disabilities in no way diminish a person's right to fully participate in all aspects of society, but that people with physical or mental disabilities are frequently precluded from doing so because of prejudice, antiquated attitudes, or the failure to remove societal and institutional barriers;

(3) while Congress expected that the definition of disability under the ADA would be interpreted consistently with how courts had applied the definition of a handicapped individual under the Rehabilitation Act of 1973, that expectation has not been fulfilled;

(4) the holdings of the Supreme Court in *Sutton v. United Air Lines, Inc.*, 527 U.S. 471 (1999) and its companion cases have narrowed the broad scope of protection intended to be afforded by the ADA, thus eliminating protection for many individuals whom Congress intended to protect;

(5) the holding of the Supreme Court in *Toyota Motor Manufacturing, Kentucky, Inc. v. Williams*, 534 U.S. 184 (2002) further narrowed the broad scope of protection intended to be afforded by the ADA;

(6) as a result of these Supreme Court cases, lower courts have incorrectly found in individual cases that people with a range of substantially limiting impairments are not people with disabilities;

(7) in particular, the Supreme Court, in the case of *Toyota Motor Manufacturing, Kentucky, Inc. v. Williams*, 534 U.S. 184 (2002), interpreted the term "substantially limits" to require a greater degree of limitation than was intended by Congress; and

(8) Congress finds that the current Equal Employment Opportunity Commission ADA regulations defining the term "substantially limits" as "significantly restricted" are inconsistent with congressional intent, by expressing too high a standard.

(b) Purposes

The purposes of this Act are–

(1) to carry out the ADA's objectives of providing "a clear and comprehensive national mandate for the elimination of discrimination" and "clear, strong, consistent, enforceable standards addressing

discrimination" by reinstating a broad scope of protection to be available under the ADA;

(2) to reject the requirement enunciated by the Supreme Court in *Sutton v. United Air Lines, Inc.,* 527 U.S. 471 (1999) and its companion cases that whether an impairment substantially limits a major life activity is to be determined with reference to the ameliorative effects of mitigating measures;

(3) to reject the Supreme Court's reasoning in *Sutton v. United Air Lines, Inc.,* 527 U.S. 471 (1999) with regard to coverage under the third prong of the definition of disability and to reinstate the reasoning of the Supreme Court in *School Board of Nassau County v. Arline,* 480 U.S. 273 (1987) which set forth a broad view of the third prong of the definition of handicap under the Rehabilitation Act of 1973;

(4) to reject the standards enunciated by the Supreme Court in *Toyota Motor Manufacturing, Kentucky, Inc. v. Williams,* 534 U.S. 184 (2002), that the terms "substantially" and "major" in the definition of disability under the ADA "need to be interpreted strictly to create a demanding standard for qualifying as disabled," and that to be substantially limited in performing a major life activity under the ADA "an individual must have an impairment that prevents or severely restricts the individual from doing activities that are of central importance to most people's daily lives";

(5) to convey congressional intent that the standard created by the Supreme Court in the case of *Toyota Motor Manufacturing, Kentucky, Inc. v. Williams,* 534 U.S. 184 (2002) for "substantially limits", and applied by lower courts in numerous decisions, has created an inappropriately high level of limitation necessary to obtain coverage under the ADA, to convey that it is the intent of Congress that the primary object of attention in cases brought under the ADA should be whether entities covered under the ADA have complied with their obligations, and to convey that the question of whether an individual's impairment is a disability under the ADA should not demand extensive analysis; and

(6) to express Congress' expectation that the Equal Employment Opportunity Commission will revise that portion of its current regulations that defines the term "substantially limits" as "significantly restricted" to be consistent with this Act, including the amendments made by this Act.

Sec. 12102. Definition of disability

As used in this chapter:

(1) Disability

The term "disability" means, with respect to an individual

(A) a physical or mental impairment that substantially limits one or more major life activities of such individual;

(B) a record of such an impairment; or

(C) being regarded as having such an impairment (as described in paragraph (3)).

(2) Major Life Activities

(A) In general

For purposes of paragraph (1), major life activities include, but are not limited to, caring for oneself, performing manual tasks, seeing, hearing, eating, sleeping, walking, standing, lifting, bending, speaking, breathing, learning, reading, concentrating, thinking, communicating, and working.

(B) Major bodily functions

For purposes of paragraph (1), a major life activity also includes the operation of a major bodily function, including but not limited to, functions of the immune system, normal cell growth, digestive, bowel, bladder, neurological, brain, respiratory, circulatory, endocrine, and reproductive functions.

(3) Regarded as having such an impairment

For purposes of paragraph (1)(C):

(A) An individual meets the requirement of "being regarded as having such an impairment" if the individual establishes that he or she has been subjected to an action prohibited under this chapter because of an actual or perceived physical or mental impairment whether or not the impairment limits or is perceived to limit a major life activity.

(B) Paragraph (1)(C) shall not apply to impairments that are transitory and minor. A transitory impairment is an impairment with an actual or expected duration of 6 months or less.

(4) Rules of construction regarding the definition of disability

The definition of "disability" in paragraph (1) shall be construed in accordance with the following:

(A) The definition of disability in this chapter shall be construed in favor of broad coverage of individuals under this chapter, to the maximum extent permitted by the terms of this chapter.

(B) The term "substantially limits" shall be interpreted consistently with the findings and purposes of the ADA Amendments Act of 2008.

(C) An impairment that substantially limits one major life activity need not limit other major life activities in order to be considered a disability.

(D) An impairment that is episodic or in remission is a disability if it would substantially limit a major life activity when active.

(E)

   (i) The determination of whether an impairment substantially limits a major life activity shall be made without regard to the ameliorative effects of mitigating measures such as

      (I) medication, medical supplies, equipment, or appliances, low-vision devices (which do not include ordinary eyeglasses or contact lenses), prosthetics including limbs and devices, hearing aids and cochlear implants or other implantable hearing devices, mobility devices, or oxygen therapy equipment and supplies;

      (II) use of assistive technology;

      (III) reasonable accommodations or auxiliary aids or services; or

      (IV) learned behavioral or adaptive neurological modifications.

   (ii) The ameliorative effects of the mitigating measures of ordinary eyeglasses or contact lenses shall be considered in determining whether an impairment substantially limits a major life activity.

   (iii) As used in this subparagraph

      (I) the term "ordinary eyeglasses or contact lenses" means lenses that are intended to fully correct visual acuity or eliminate refractive error; and

      (II) the term "low-vision devices" means devices that magnify, enhance, or otherwise augment a visual image.

Sec. 12103. Additional definitions

As used in this chapter

(1) Auxiliary aids and services

The term "auxiliary aids and services" includes

(A) qualified interpreters or other effective methods of making aurally delivered materials available to individuals with hearing impairments;

(B) qualified readers, taped texts, or other effective methods of making visually delivered materials available to individuals with visual impairments;

(C) acquisition or modification of equipment or devices; and

(D) other similar services and actions.

(2) State

The term "State" means each of the several States, the District of Columbia, the Commonwealth of Puerto Rico, Guam, American Samoa, the Virgin Islands of the United States, the Trust Territory of the Pacific Islands, and the Commonwealth of the Northern Mariana Islands.

. . .

Source: Department of Justice. "Americans with Disabilities Act of 1990, as Amended." 2008. Available online. URL: http://www.ada.gov/pubs/adastatute08.htm. Accessed on July 23, 2010.

American Civil Liberties Union, Open Letter Concerning Suicidal Prisoners in St. Tammany Parish (2010)

St. Tammany Parish is the fastest-growing and most politically conservative parish in the New Orleans region of Louisiana. The following letter was sent to the parish sheriff, Jack Strain, and parish president, Kevin Davis, to address reports of suicidal prisoners being forcibly held in what are called "squirrel cages," metal cages that are approximately three feet long by three feet wide. Prisoners reported being held in the cages for a minimum of 72 hours, while some reported being held for up to a month. Requests to use the bathroom were often ignored, and prisoners were forced to urinate into milk cartons or soil themselves in the cage. They were further humiliated by being forced to wear degrading clothing while in the cages and put on display in the main part of the jail for other prisoners to see. The letter sent by the ACLU came shortly after Sheriff Jack Strain made troubling public comments in reference to the inmate population as a whole: "They performed like animals in our society and they need to be caged like animals."

Dear Mr. Davis and Sheriff Strain:

The ACLU Foundation of Louisiana has determined—after numerous interviews and review of St. Tammany Parish government documents—that suicidal people detained in St. Tammany Jail are regularly held in what staff refer to as "squirrel cages." The "squirrel cages" are metal cages approximately three feet wide and three feet in length. People deemed suicidal are typically held in the cages for at least 72 hours. The cages are used on all suicidal prisoners, including those who have only expressed symptoms of suicide but who have not behaved violently toward themselves or others.

According to several reports, many have been held for days, weeks, and even over a month in the metal cages. The "squirrel cages" are too small to allow prisoners to lie down, causing physical pain and affecting the person's ability to sleep. We have reports that suicidal prisoners placed in the squirrel cages are stripped of their clothes and some have been made to wear short bright orange shorts with "HOT STUFF" scrawled in marker across the rear end. We have also received numerous reports that the cages are also used to hold prisoners who are being punished. We understand that the cages have been frequently used to hold more than one prisoner at a time, and that staff often ignore prisoners' requests to use the bathroom, forcing people to urinate in discarded milk cartons. Some prisoners report seeing pools of urine under the "squirrel cages."

These conditions are clearly unconstitutional. According to the St. Tammany Parish Code they are also inhumane. St. Tammany Parish Code 4-121.10 states that dogs must be kept in cages at least 6′ wide × 6′ feet deep, with "sufficient space [. . .] to lie down." Sick prisoners in your care are afforded approximately one quarter of the space required for animals under the Parish Code. In addition to violating the parish standards for housing animals, the cages also violate national standards for housing suicidal prisoners. Both the National Institute of Corrections (NIC) and the National Commission on Correctional Health Care (NCCH) disfavor the use of isolation and caution against "exacerbating (prisoners') psychiatric symptoms." In St. Tammany Parish, the cages have left prisoners with acute physical and psychological pain, and prisoners are hesitant to report suicidal thoughts, out of fear that they will be placed in the cages.

You have both recently worked to ensure that St. Tammany Parish Jail receives $2 million for brick and mortar improvements. As a component of the scheduled improvements we urge you to ensure that a safe and humane environment is created for people on suicide watch in the St. Tammany Parish Jail. We appreciate that the housing and responding to mentally ill people can be difficult. However, jails all across the country house persons who are mentally ill. They accomplish this—and protect the safety of their communities—without placing human beings in 3' × 3' cages. We encourage you to investigate how other jails handle mentally ill people, as well as what national best practices are for responding to suicidal prisoners. St. Tammany is one of the wealthiest parishes in Louisiana; not only can you afford to treat your sick better than this, but the Constitution mandates that you do so.

We hope that you will take corrective action, both for the safety of the prisoners, as well as to avoid legal liability for what are clearly unconstitutional and inhumane conditions.

If you have any questions or concerns, please feel free to contact me.

Sincerely,

Marjorie Esman

Executive Director

Source: American Civil Liberties Union. "Open Letter Concerning Suicidal Prisoners in St. Tammany Parish," July 8, 2010. Available online. URL: http://www.laaclu.org/PDF_documents/Open_Letter_StTam_Cages_070810.pdf. Accessed July 23, 2010.

www.ltdanchoi.com, "Dan Choi's Defense Memo" (2010)

Lieutenant Dan Choi became a major figure in the LGBT rights movement and a catalyst for the repeal of the "Don't ask, don't tell" policy that prohibits gays and lesbians from serving openly in the military when he went on the Rachel Maddow show in 2009 and announced that he was gay. Despite being a West Point graduate and one of only a handful of soldiers in his class who speaks fluent Arabic, making him particularly valuable as someone who can communicate quickly and easily with the people of Iraq during the war in Iraq, the army immediately initiated proceedings to discharge him under the "Don't ask, don't tell" (DADT) policy. Choi was officially discharged in June 2010. He is one of 59 Arabic speakers and nine Farsi speakers to have been discharged from the military between 2004 and 2009 for being gay. In March and April 2010, Lt. Dan Choi and fellow activist Captain James Pietrangelo were arrested after protesting DADT outside the White House. The following defense memorandum highlights their activism strategy, citing numerous occasions in which President Barack Obama called upon LGBT activists to pressure the government to repeal DADT.

HUMAN RIGHTS

MEMORANDUM FROM DEFENSE COUNSEL
MARK GOLDSTONE, ESQ.
ANN WILCOX, ESQ.

TO: INTERESTED PARTIES
DATE: JUNE 29, 2010
RE: DC v. James E Pietrangelo II, 2010-CTF-4849, 2010-CDC-6973
DC v. Daniel W. Choi, 2010-CDC-4862, 2010-CDC-6972

SUMMARY OF THE CASES

Lt. Dan Choi and Cpt. James Pietrangelo II are each charged with two counts of Failure to Obey a Lawful Order, pursuant to DC Municipal Regulations (18 DCMR 2000.2 [1995]; these charges stem from arrests at the White House sidewalk, on two separate occasions, March 18, 2010 and April 20, 2010. They face a nonjury trial on both charges, on Wed., July 14, 2010, in Courtroom 120 of DC Superior Court. This Court is located at 500 Indiana Avenue, NW, in Washington, DC. These are relatively minor charges (the Defendants may only be fined, from $100 to $1000, and may not receive jail time for these infractions). However, the Defendants seek to use their trials to highlight the ongoing effects of the "Don't Ask, Don't Tell" law and policy of the U.S. Armed Forces toward gay and lesbian servicemembers. They seek to compel the testimony of President Barack Obama, who has, on several occasions as President and Commander in Chief (and previously as a Senator and Presidential Candidate) called on the LGBT community to "pressure" him to change the DADT law and policy, thus allowing gay servicemembers to serve their country openly and honorably.

The subpoena of the President is necessary for the defense to prove that Defendants were following and obeying lawful orders or directives by their President and Commander in Chief, and were therefore under an obligation and authority to act as they did in order to pressure him—in a non-violent, visible way—on this important public issue. In addition, these statements support the contention that Defendants were acting out of necessity, in order to prevent discrimination and greater harm to gay servicemembers now serving.

WHY DID WE SUBPOENA THE PRESIDENT?

Defendants in the above-captioned cases seek the testimony of Barack Obama, President of the United States and Commander in Chief of the US Armed Forces, to testify about statements made by him, regarding his support for public pressure to abolish the "Don't Ask, Don't Tell" law and official policy regarding gay and lesbian members of the US Armed Forces. In particular, statements made on June 1, 2009 (Remarks for Pride Month), June 29, 2009 (Remarks for Pride Reception), October 10, 2009 (Human Rights Campaign Dinner).

Below we highlight several, but not all, remarks that will be relied upon for the defense. These remarks are necessary for the defense in that they reflect that Defendants were following and obeying lawful orders or directives by their President and Commander in Chief, and therefore under an obligation and authority to act as they did in order to pressure him in a non-violent visible way, on this important public issue. President Barack Obama's testimony is also necessary for the defense to prove the defense of necessity (which may excuse "illegal" actions which were taken to prevent a greater harm).

> "I'm here with a simple message: I'm here with you in that fight. For even as we face extraordinary challenges as a nation, we cannot—and we will not—put aside issues of basic equality. Now, I've said this before, I'll repeat it again—it's not for me to tell you to be patient, any more than it was for others to counsel patience to African Americans petitioning for equal rights half a century ago. We are moving ahead on 'don't ask, don't tell.' We should not—We should not be punishing patriotic Americans who have stepped forward to serve this country. We should be celebrating their willingness to show such courage and selflessness on behalf of their fellow citizens, especially when we're fighting two wars. We cannot afford to cut from our ranks people with the critical skills we need to fight any more than we can afford—for our military's integrity—to force those willing to do so into careers encumbered and compromised by having to live a lie. So I'm working with the Pentagon, its leadership and the members of the House and the Senate on ending this policy. Legislation has been introduced in the House to make this happen. I will end Don't Ask, Don't Tell. That's my commitment to you."—"Now, I've said this before, I'll repeat it again—it's not for me to tell you to be patient, any more than it was for others to counsel patience to African Americans petitioning for equal rights half a century ago," he said. "And that's why it's so important that you continue to speak out, that you continue to set an example, that you continue to pressure leaders—including me—and to make the case all across America," Obama added.

> Office of the Press Secretary (2009, October 10). Remarks by the President at Human Rights Campaign Dinner. Retrieved from http://transcripts.cnn.com/ TRANSCRIPTS/0910/10/cnr.05.html

> "And finally, I want to say a word about "don't ask, don't tell." As I said before—I'll say it again—I believe "don't ask, don't tell" doesn't contribute

to our national security. (Applause.) In fact, I believe preventing patriotic Americans from serving their country weakens our national security. (Applause.) I know that every day that passes without a resolution is a deep disappointment to those men and women who continue to be discharged under this policy—patriots who often possess critical language skills and years of training and who've served this country well. But what I hope is that these cases underscore the urgency of reversing this policy not just because it's the right thing to do, but because it is essential for our national security."

Office of the Press Secretary (2009, June 29). Remarks by the President Pride Reception Retrieved from http://www.whitehouse.gov/the-press-office/ remarks-president-lgbt-pride-month-reception

"I want you to hold our government accountable," "I want you to hold me accountable."

As Prepared For Delivery (2008, September 17). Remarks of Senator Barack Obama retrieved from http://www.opednews.com/articles/Failure-to-prosecute-why-by-Don-Smith-090829-170.html

"As president, I will work with Congress and place the weight of my administration behind enactment of the Military Readiness Enhancement Act, which will make nondiscrimination the official policy of the U.S. military. I will task the Defense Department and the senior command structure in every branch of the armed forces with developing an action plan for the implementation of a full repeal of Don't Ask, Don't Tell. And I will direct my Secretaries of Defense and Homeland Security to develop procedures for taking re-accession requests from those qualified service members who were separated from the armed forces under Don't Ask, Don't Tell and still want to serve their country. The eradication of this policy will require more than just eliminating one statute. It will require the implementation of anti-harassment policies and protocols for dealing with abusive or discriminatory behavior as we transition our armed forces away from a policy of discrimination. The military must be our active partners in developing those policies and protocols. That work should have started long ago. It will start when I take office."

Prepared Remarks (2007, November 9). Statement by Senator Obama for President Retrieved from http://www.barackobama.com/people/lgbt/

"My Administration has partnered with the LGBT community to advance a wide range of initiatives. At the international level, I have joined efforts at the United Nations to decriminalize homosexuality around the world. Here at home, I continue to support measures to bring the full spectrum of equal rights to LGBT Americans. These measures include enhancing hate crimes laws, supporting civil unions and Federal rights for LGBT couples, outlawing discrimination in the workplace, ensuring adoption rights, and ending the existing "Don't Ask, Don't Tell" policy in a way that strengthens our Armed Forces and our national security"

> Office of the Press Secretary (2009, June 1). Lesbian, Gay, Bisexual, Transgender Pride Month, 2009 Declaration Retrieved from http://www.whitehouse.gov/ the_press_office/Presidential-Proclamation-LGBT-Pride-Month/

Source: www.ltdanchoi.com. "Dan Choi's Defense Memo." June 29, 2010. Available online. URL: http://www.ltdanchoi.com/pdf/dan-choi-defense-memo.pdf. Accessed July 23, 2010.

Arizona State Senate, "Senate Bill 1070" (2010) (Excerpts)

In early 2010, Arizona Senate Bill 1070 (sb1070) erupted amid a hailstorm of controversy. Sharing a border with Mexico, Arizona has the highest rate of illegal immigration from Mexico, as of 2010, and Arizona residents have complained of high crime rates and increased traffic accidents as being the direct results of the unusually high number of undocumented immigrants. State Senator Russell Pearce is the major sponsor of the bill, and he has incited further controversy by referring to undocumented immigrants as "invaders of the American sovereignty." Pearce has also voiced plans to construct a bill in the future to block the issuing of birth certificates to infants born in the United States whose parents are undocumented immigrants, children that he has publicly called "anchor babies."

The language of Senate Bill 1070 has been called confusing, and misconceptions about the bill have consequently proliferated. One such misconception is that the bill allows police to question suspected undocumented immigrants. In truth, this is already legal. SB1070 requires police to question a person's immigration status, and allows Arizona residents to sue local entities (such as city councils and police departments) who do not enforce federal immigration laws. While the bill explicitly states that perceived race does not constitute sufficient evidence to consider an individual a suspected undocumented immi-

grant, critics argue that there is no other way for a person to become suspect, and that racial profiling is inevitable.

Be it enacted by the Legislature of the State of Arizona:

Section 1. *Intent*

The legislature finds that there is a compelling interest in the cooperative enforcement of federal immigration laws throughout all of Arizona. The legislature declares that the intent of this act is to make attrition through enforcement the public policy of all state and local government agencies in Arizona. The provisions of this act are intended to work together to discourage and deter the unlawful entry and presence of aliens and economic activity by persons unlawfully present in the United States.

Sec. 2. Title 11, chapter 7, Arizona Revised Statutes, is amended by adding article 8, to read:

ARTICLE 8. ENFORCEMENT OF IMMIGRATION LAWS

11-1061. *Cooperation and assistance in enforcement of immigration laws: indemnification*

A. NO OFFICIAL OR AGENCY OF THIS STATE OR A COUNTY, CITY, TOWN OR OTHER POLITICAL SUBDIVISION OF THIS STATE MAY ADOPT A POLICY THAT LIMITS OR RESTRICTS THE ENFORCEMENT OF FEDERAL IMMIGRATION LAWS TO LESS THAN THE FULL EXTENT PERMITTED BY FEDERAL LAW.

B. FOR ANY LAWFUL CONTACT MADE BY A LAW ENFORCE-MENT OFFICIAL OR AGENCY OF THIS STATE OR A COUNTY, CITY, TOWN OR OTHER POLITICAL SUBDIVISION OF THIS STATE WHERE REASONABLE SUSPICION EXISTS THAT THE PERSON IS AN ALIEN WHO IS UNLAWFULLY PRESENT IN THE UNITED STATES, A REASONABLE ATTEMPT SHALL BE MADE, WHEN PRACTICABLE, TO DETERMINE THE IMMIGRATION STATUS OF THE PERSON. THE PERSON'S IMMIGRATION STA-TUS SHALL BE VERIFIED WITH THE FEDERAL GOVERNMENT PURSUANT TO 8 UNITED STATES CODE SECTION 1373(c).

C. IF AN ALIEN WHO IS UNLAWFULLY PRESENT IN THE UNITED STATES IS CONVICTED OF A VIOLATION OF STATE OR LOCAL LAW, ON DISCHARGE FROM IMPRISONMENT OR ASSESS-MENT OF ANY FINE THAT IS IMPOSED, THE ALIEN SHALL BE TRANSFERRED IMMEDIATELY TO THE CUSTODY OF THE

UNITED STATES IMMIGRATION AND CUSTOMS ENFORCE-
MENT OR THE UNITED STATES CUSTOMS AND BORDER
PROTECTION.

D. NOTWITHSTANDING ANY OTHER LAW, A LAW ENFORCE-
MENT AGENCY MAY SECURELY TRANSPORT AN ALIEN WHO
IS UNLAWFULLY PRESENT IN THE UNITED STATES AND WHO
IS IN THE AGENCY'S CUSTODY TO A FEDERAL FACILITY IN
THIS STATE OR TO ANY OTHER POINT OF TRANSFER INTO
FEDERAL CUSTODY THAT IS OUTSIDE THE JURISDICTION OF
THE LAW ENFORCEMENT AGENCY.

E. A LAW ENFORCEMENT OFFICER, WITHOUT A WARRANT, MAY
ARREST A PERSON IF THE OFFICER HAS PROBABLE CAUSE TO
BELIEVE THAT THE PERSON HAS COMMITTED ANY PUBLIC
OFFENSE THAT MAKES THE PERSON REMOVABLE FROM THE
UNITED STATES.

F. EXCEPT AS PROVIDED IN FEDERAL LAW, OFFICIALS OR AGEN-
CIES OF THIS STATE AND COUNTIES, CITIES, TOWNS AND
OTHER POLITICAL SUBDIVISIONS OF THIS STATE MAY NOT
BE PROHIBITED OR IN ANY WAY BE RESTRICTED FROM SEND-
ING, RECEIVING OR MAINTAINING INFORMATION RELAT-
ING TO THE IMMIGRATION STATUS OF ANY INDIVIDUAL OR
EXCHANGING THAT INFORMATION WITH ANY OTHER FED-
ERAL, STATE OR LOCAL GOVERNMENTAL ENTITY FOR THE
FOLLOWING OFFICIAL PURPOSES:

1. DETERMINING ELIGIBILITY FOR ANY PUBLIC BENEFIT,
SERVICE OR LICENSE PROVIDED BY ANY FEDERAL, STATE,
LOCAL OR OTHER POLITICAL SUBDIVISION OF THIS
STATE.

2. VERIFYING ANY CLAIM OF RESIDENCE OR DOMICILE IF
DETERMINATION OF RESIDENCE OR DOMICILE IS REQUIRED
UNDER THE LAWS OF THIS STATE OR A JUDICIAL ORDER
ISSUED PURSUANT TO A CIVIL OR CRIMINAL PROCEEDING
IN THIS STATE.

3. CONFIRMING THE IDENTITY OF ANY PERSON WHO IS
DETAINED.

4. IF THE PERSON IS AN ALIEN, DETERMINING WHETHER
THE PERSON IS IN COMPLIANCE WITH THE FEDERAL REG-
ISTRATION LAWS PRESCRIBED BY TITLE II, CHAPTER 7 OF
THE FEDERAL IMMIGRATION AND NATIONALITY ACT.

G. A PERSON MAY BRING AN ACTION IN SUPERIOR COURT TO CHALLENGE ANY OFFICIAL OR AGENCY OF THIS STATE OR A COUNTY, CITY, TOWN OR OTHER POLITICAL SUBDIVISION OF THIS STATE THAT ADOPTS OR IMPLEMENTS A POLICY THAT LIMITS OR RESTRICTS THE ENFORCEMENT OF FEDERAL IMMIGRATION LAWS TO LESS THAN THE FULL EXTENT PERMITTED BY FEDERAL LAW. IF THERE IS A JUDICIAL FINDING THAT AN ENTITY HAS VIOLATED THIS SECTION, THE COURT SHALL ORDER ANY OF THE FOLLOWING:

1. THAT THE PERSON WHO BROUGHT THE ACTION RECOVER COURT COSTS AND ATTORNEY FEES.

2. THAT THE ENTITY PAY A CIVIL PENALTY OF NOT LESS THAN ONE THOUSAND DOLLARS AND NOT MORE THAN FIVE THOUSAND DOLLARS FOR EACH DAY THAT THE POLICY HAS REMAINED IN EFFECT AFTER THE FILING OF AN ACTION PURSUANT TO THIS SUBSECTION.

H. A COURT SHALL COLLECT THE CIVIL PENALTY PRESCRIBED IN SUBSECTION G AND REMIT THE CIVIL PENALTY TO THE DEPARTMENT OF PUBLIC SAFETY FOR DEPOSIT IN THE GANG AND IMMIGRATION INTELLIGENCE TEAM ENFORCEMENT MISSION FUND ESTABLISHED BY SECTION 41-1724.

I. A LAW ENFORCEMENT OFFICER IS INDEMNIFIED BY THE LAW ENFORCEMENT OFFICER'S AGENCY AGAINST REASONABLE COSTS AND EXPENSES, INCLUDING ATTORNEY FEES, INCURRED BY THE OFFICER IN CONNECTION WITH ANY ACTION, SUIT OR PROCEEDING BROUGHT PURSUANT TO THIS SECTION TO WHICH THE OFFICER MAY BE A PARTY BY REASON OF THE OFFICER BEING OR HAVING BEEN A MEMBER OF THE LAW ENFORCEMENT AGENCY, EXCEPT IN RELATION TO MATTERS IN WHICH THE OFFICER IS ADJUDGED TO HAVE ACTED IN BAD FAITH.

J. THIS SECTION SHALL BE IMPLEMENTED IN A MANNER CONSISTENT WITH FEDERAL LAWS REGULATING IMMIGRATION, PROTECTING THE CIVIL RIGHTS OF ALL PERSONS AND RESPECTING THE PRIVILEGES AND IMMUNITIES OF UNITED STATES CITIZENS.

Sec. 3. Title 13, chapter 15. Arizona Revised Statutes, is amended by adding section 13-1509, to read:

13-1509. *Trespassing by illegal aliens; assessment; exception; classification*

A. IN ADDITION TO ANY VIOLATION OF FEDERAL LAW, A PERSON IS GUILTY OF TRESPASSING IF THE PERSON IS BOTH:
    1. PRESENT ON ANY PUBLIC OR PRIVATE LAND IN THIS STATE.
    2. IN VIOLATION OF 8 UNITED STATES CODE SECTION 1304(e) OR 1306(a).
B. IN THE ENFORCEMENT OF THIS SECTION, THE FINAL DETERMINATION OF AN ALIEN'S IMMIGRATION STATUS SHALL BE DETERMINED BY EITHER:
    1. A LAW ENFORCEMENT OFFICER WHO IS AUTHORIZED BY THE FEDERAL GOVERNMENT TO VERIFY OR ASCERTAIN AN ALIEN'S IMMIGRATION STATUS.
    2. A LAW ENFORCEMENT OFFICER OR AGENCY COMMUNICATING WITH THE UNITED STATES IMMIGRATION AND CUSTOMS ENFORCEMENT OR THE UNITED STATES BORDER PROTECTION PURSUANT TO 8 UNITED STATES CODE SECTION 1373(c).
C. A PERSON WHO IS SENTENCED PURSUANT TO THIS SECTION IS NOT ELIGIBLE FOR SUSPENSION OR COMMUTATION OF SENTENCE OR RELEASE ON ANY BASIS UNTIL THE SENTENCE IMPOSED IS SERVED.
D. IN ADDITION TO ANY OTHER PENALTY PRESCRIBED BY LAW, THE COURT SHALL ORDER THE PERSON TO PAY JAIL COSTS AND AN ADDITIONAL ASSESSMENT IN THE FOLLOWING AMOUNTS:
    1. AT LEAST FIVE HUNDRED DOLLARS FOR A FIRST VIOLATION.
    2. TWICE THE AMOUNT SPECIFIED IN PARAGRAPH 1 OF THIS SUBSECTION IF THE PERSON WAS PREVIOUSLY SUBJECT TO AN ASSESSMENT PURSUANT TO THIS SUBSECTION.
E. A COURT SHALL COLLECT THE ASSESSMENTS PRESCRIBED IN SUBSECTION D OF THIS SECTION AND REMIT THE ASSESSMENTS TO THE DEPARTMENT OF PUBLIC SAFETY, WHICH SHALL ESTABLISH A SPECIAL SUBACCOUNT FOR THE MONIES IN THE ACCOUNT ESTABLISHED FOR THE GANG AND IMMIGRATION INTELLIGENCE TEAM ENFORCEMENT MISSION APPROPRIATION. MONIES IN THE SPECIAL SUBACCOUNT ARE SUBJECT TO LEGISLATIVE APPROPRIATION FOR DISTRIBU-

TION FOR GANG AND IMMIGRATION ENFORCEMENT AND FOR COUNTY JAIL REIMBURSEMENT COSTS RELATING TO ILLEGAL IMMIGRATION.

F. THIS SECTION DOES NOT APPLY TO A PERSON WHO MAINTAINS AUTHORIZATION FROM THE FEDERAL GOVERNMENT TO REMAIN IN THE UNITED STATES.

. . .

E. NOTWITHSTANDING ANY OTHER LAW, A PEACE OFFICER MAY LAWFULLY STOP ANY PERSON WHO IS OPERATING A MOTOR VEHICLE IF THE OFFICER HAS REASONABLE SUSPICION TO BELIEVE THE PERSON IS IN VIOLATION OF ANY CIVIL TRAFFIC LAW AND THIS SECTION.

. . .

Source: Arizona State Senate. "Senate Bill 1070." 2010. Available online. URL: http://www.azleg.gov/legtext/49leg/2r/bills/sb1070s.pdf. Accessed on July 23, 2010

5

International Documents

The international documents in this chapter are divided into the following sections:

Universal Documents
The Democratic Republic of the Congo
China
Chechnya
Iran

UNIVERSAL DOCUMENTS

General Assembly of the United Nations, The Universal Declaration of Human Rights (1948)

The Universal Declaration of Human Rights was adopted by the United Nations General Assembly in December 1948. During World War II, the United States under President Franklin Delano Roosevelt promoted the Four Freedoms: freedom of speech, freedom of conscience, freedom from fear, and freedom from want. Following the horrors of Nazi Germany, the Four Freedoms became the basis for the Universal Declaration of Human Rights, which was drafted by the Canadian United Nations secretary-general, John Peters Humphrey, along with René Cassin of France, P. C. Chang of China, Charles Malik of Lebanon, and Eleanor Roosevelt of the United States. As of 2010, the Universal Declaration of Human Rights has been translated into 370 different languages, making it the most widely translated document in the world.

PREAMBLE

Whereas recognition of the inherent dignity and of the equal and inalienable rights of all members of the human family is the foundation of freedom, justice and peace in the world,

HUMAN RIGHTS

Whereas disregard and contempt for human rights have resulted in barbarous acts which have outraged the conscience of mankind, and the advent of a world in which human beings shall enjoy freedom of speech and belief and freedom from fear and want has been proclaimed as the highest aspiration of the common people,

Whereas it is essential, if man is not to be compelled to have recourse, as a last resort, to rebellion against tyranny and oppression, that human rights should be protected by the rule of law,

Whereas it is essential to promote the development of friendly relations between nations,

Whereas the peoples of the United Nations have in the Charter reaffirmed their faith in fundamental human rights, in the dignity and worth of the human person and in the equal rights of men and women and have determined to promote social progress and better standards of life in larger freedom,

Whereas Member States have pledged themselves to achieve, in cooperation with the United Nations, the promotion of universal respect for and observance of human rights and fundamental freedoms,

Whereas a common understanding of these rights and freedoms is of the greatest importance for the full realization of this pledge,

Now, Therefore THE GENERAL ASSEMBLY proclaims THIS UNIVERSAL DECLARATION OF HUMAN RIGHTS as a common standard of achievement for all peoples and all nations, to the end that every individual and every organ of society, keeping this Declaration constantly in mind, shall strive by teaching and education to promote respect for these rights and freedoms and by progressive measures, national and international, to secure their universal and effective recognition and observance, both among the peoples of Member States themselves and among the peoples of territories under their jurisdiction.

Article 1.

- All human beings are born free and equal in dignity and rights. They are endowed with reason and conscience and should act towards one another in a spirit of brotherhood.

Article 2.

- Everyone is entitled to all the rights and freedoms set forth in this Declaration, without distinction of any kind, such as race, colour, sex, language, religion, political or other opinion, national or social origin, property, birth or other status. Furthermore, no distinction shall be made on the basis of the political, jurisdictional or international status of the country or territory to which a person belongs, whether it be independent, trust, non-self-governing or under any other limitation of sovereignty.

Article 3.

- Everyone has the right to life, liberty and security of person.

Article 4.

- No one shall be held in slavery or servitude; slavery and the slave trade shall be prohibited in all their forms.

Article 5.

- No one shall be subjected to torture or to cruel, inhuman or degrading treatment or punishment.

Article 6.

- Everyone has the right to recognition everywhere as a person before the law.

Article 7.

- All are equal before the law and are entitled without any discrimination to equal protection of the law. All are entitled to equal protection against any discrimination in violation of this Declaration and against any incitement to such discrimination.

Article 8.

- Everyone has the right to an effective remedy by the competent national tribunals for acts violating the fundamental rights granted him by the constitution or by law.

Article 9.

- No one shall be subjected to arbitrary arrest, detention or exile.

Article 10.

Everyone is entitled in full equality to a fair and public hearing by an independent and impartial tribunal, in the determination of his rights and obligations and of any criminal charge against him.

Article 11.

- (1) Everyone charged with a penal offence has the right to be presumed innocent until proved guilty according to law in a public trial at which he has had all the guarantees necessary for his defence.

- (2) No one shall be held guilty of any penal offence on account of any act or omission which did not constitute a penal offence, under national or international law, at the time when it was committed. Nor shall a heavier penalty be imposed than the one that was applicable at the time the penal offence was committed.

Article 12.

- No one shall be subjected to arbitrary interference with his privacy, family, home or correspondence, nor to attacks upon his honour and reputation. Everyone has the right to the protection of the law against such interference or attacks.

Article 13.

- (1) Everyone has the right to freedom of movement and residence within the borders of each state.
- (2) Everyone has the right to leave any country, including his own, and to return to his country.

Article 14.

- (1) Everyone has the right to seek and to enjoy in other countries asylum from persecution.
- (2) This right may not be invoked in the case of prosecutions genuinely arising from non-political crimes or from acts contrary to the purposes and principles of the United Nations.

Article 15.

- (1) Everyone has the right to a nationality.
- (2) No one shall be arbitrarily deprived of his nationality nor denied the right to change his nationality.

Article 16.

- (1) Men and women of full age, without any limitation due to race, nationality or religion, have the right to marry and to found a family. They are entitled to equal rights as to marriage, during marriage and at its dissolution.
- (2) Marriage shall be entered into only with the free and full consent of the intending spouses.
- (3) The family is the natural and fundamental group unit of society and is entitled to protection by society and the State.

Article 17.

- (1) Everyone has the right to own property alone as well as in association with others.
- (2) No one shall be arbitrarily deprived of his property.

Article 18.

- Everyone has the right to freedom of thought, conscience and religion; this right includes freedom to change his religion or belief, and freedom, either alone or in community with others and in public or private, to manifest his religion or belief in teaching, practice, worship and observance.

Article 19.

- Everyone has the right to freedom of opinion and expression; this right includes freedom to hold opinions without interference and to seek, receive and impart information and ideas through any media and regardless of frontiers.

Article 20.

- (1) Everyone has the right to freedom of peaceful assembly and association.
- (2) No one may be compelled to belong to an association.

Article 21.

- (1) Everyone has the right to take part in the government of his country, directly or through freely chosen representatives.
- (2) Everyone has the right of equal access to public service in his country.
- (3) The will of the people shall be the basis of the authority of government; this will shall be expressed in periodic and genuine elections which shall be by universal and equal suffrage and shall be held by secret vote or by equivalent free voting procedures.

Article 22.

- Everyone, as a member of society, has the right to social security and is entitled to realization, through national effort and international co-operation and in accordance with the organization and resources of each State, of the economic, social and cultural rights indispensable for his dignity and the free development of his personality.

Article 23.

- (1) Everyone has the right to work, to free choice of employment, to just and favourable conditions of work and to protection against unemployment.
- (2) Everyone, without any discrimination, has the right to equal pay for equal work.
- (3) Everyone who works has the right to just and favourable remuneration ensuring for himself and his family an existence worthy of human dignity, and supplemented, if necessary, by other means of social protection.
- (4) Everyone has the right to form and to join trade unions for the protection of his interests.

Article 24.

- Everyone has the right to rest and leisure, including reasonable limitation of working hours and periodic holidays with pay.

Article 25.

- (1) Everyone has the right to a standard of living adequate for the health and well-being of himself and of his family, including food, clothing, housing and medical care and necessary social services, and the right to security in the event of unemployment, sickness, disability, widowhood, old age or other lack of livelihood in circumstances beyond his control.
- (2) Motherhood and childhood are entitled to special care and assistance. All children, whether born in or out of wedlock, shall enjoy the same social protection.

Article 26.

- (1) Everyone has the right to education. Education shall be free, at least in the elementary and fundamental stages. Elementary education shall be compulsory. Technical and professional education shall be made generally available and higher education shall be equally accessible to all on the basis of merit.
- (2) Education shall be directed to the full development of the human personality and to the strengthening of respect for human rights and fundamental freedoms. It shall promote understanding, tolerance and friendship among all nations, racial or religious groups, and shall further the activities of the United Nations for the maintenance of peace.
- (3) Parents have a prior right to choose the kind of education that shall be given to their children.

Article 27.

- (1) Everyone has the right freely to participate in the cultural life of the community, to enjoy the arts and to share in scientific advancement and its benefits.
- (2) Everyone has the right to the protection of the moral and material interests resulting from any scientific, literary or artistic production of which he is the author.

Article 28.

- Everyone is entitled to a social and international order in which the rights and freedoms set forth in this Declaration can be fully realized.

Article 29.

- (1) Everyone has duties to the community in which alone the free and full development of his personality is possible.
- (2) In the exercise of his rights and freedoms, everyone shall be subject only to such limitations as are determined by law solely for the purpose of securing due recognition and respect for the rights and freedoms of others and of meeting the just requirements of morality, public order and the general welfare in a democratic society.
- (3) These rights and freedoms may in no case be exercised contrary to the purposes and principles of the United Nations.

Article 30.

- Nothing in this Declaration may be interpreted as implying for any State, group or person any right to engage in any activity or to perform any act aimed at the destruction of any of the rights and freedoms set forth herein.

Source: General Assembly, United Nations. "The Universal Declaration of Independence." 1948. Available online. URL: http://www.un.org/en/documents/udhr/. Accessed January 11, 2010.

General Assembly, United Nations, Vienna Declaration and Programme of Action (1993) (Excerpt)

The World Conference on Human Rights was held in Vienna, Austria, in June 1993, the first human rights conference to be held following the cold war. With representatives from 171 nations, 800 nongovernmental organizations (NGOs), and 7,000 additional participants, the World Conference on Human Rights was the largest conference on human rights in history. One of the rules of the conference was that no countries or regions could be specifically named as violators of human rights, but this rule was not widely respected. The conference resulted in the drafting of the Vienna Declaration and Programme of Action, which was adopted by all 171 states. What makes this declaration unique is the fact that the document emphasizes the fact that human rights are interdependent, indivisible, and interrelated, meaning that no one set of rights can be prioritized at the expense of another, excluded, or downplayed.

1. The World Conference on Human Rights reaffirms the solemn commitment of all States to fulfill their obligations to promote universal respect for, and observance and protection of, all human rights and fundamental freedoms for all in accordance with the Charter of the United Nations, other instruments relating to human rights, and international law. The universal nature of these rights and freedoms is beyond question.

   In this framework, enhancement of international cooperation in the field of human rights is essential for the full achievement of the purposes of the United Nations.

   Human rights and fundamental freedoms are the birthright of all human beings; their protection and promotion is the first responsibility of Governments.

2. All peoples have the right of self-determination. By virtue of that right they freely determine their political status, and freely pursue their economic, social and cultural development.

   Taking into account the particular situation of peoples under colonial or other forms of alien domination or foreign occupation, the World Conference on Human Rights recognizes the right of peoples to take any legitimate action, in accordance with the Charter of the United Nations, to realize their inalienable right of self-determination. The World Conference on Human Rights considers the denial of the right of self-determination as a violation of human rights and underlines the importance of the effective realization of this right.

   In accordance with the Declaration on Principles of International Law concerning Friendly Relations and Cooperation Among States in accordance with the Charter of the United Nations, this shall not be construed as authorizing or encouraging any action which would dismember or impair, totally or in part, the territorial integrity or political unity of sovereign and independent States conducting themselves in compliance with the principle of equal rights and self-determination of peoples and thus possessed of a Government representing the whole people belonging to the territory without distinction of any kind.

3. Effective international measures to guarantee and monitor the implementation of human rights standards should be taken in respect of people under foreign occupation, and effective legal protection against the violation of their human rights should be provided, in accordance with human rights norms and international law, particularly the Geneva Convention relative to the Protection of Civilian Persons in Time of War, of 14 August 1949, and other applicable norms of humanitarian law.

4. The promotion and protection of all human rights and fundamental freedoms must be considered as a priority objective of the United Nations in accordance with its purposes and principles, in particular the purpose of international cooperation. In the framework of these purposes and principles, the promotion and protection of all human rights is a legitimate concern of the international community. The organs and specialized agencies related to human rights should therefore further enhance the coordination of their activities based on the consistent and objective application of international human rights instruments.

5. All human rights are universal, indivisible and interdependent and interrelated. The international community must treat human rights globally in a fair and equal manner, on the same footing, and with the same emphasis. While the significance of national and regional particularities and various historical, cultural and religious backgrounds must be borne in mind, it is the duty of States, regardless of their political, economic and cultural systems, to promote and protect all human rights and fundamental freedoms.

6. The efforts of the United Nations system towards the universal respect for, and observance of, human rights and fundamental freedoms for all, contribute to the stability and well-being necessary for peaceful and friendly relations among nations, and to improved conditions for peace and security as well as social and economic development, in conformity with the Charter of the United Nations.

7. The processes of promoting and protecting human rights should be conducted in conformity with the purposes and principles of the Charter of the United Nations, and international law.

8. Democracy, development and respect for human rights and fundamental freedoms are interdependent and mutually reinforcing. Democracy is based on the freely expressed will of the people to determine their own political, economic, social and cultural systems and their full participation in all aspects of their lives. In the context of the above, the promotion and protection of human rights and fundamental freedoms at the national and international levels should be universal and

conducted without conditions attached. The international community should support the strengthening and promoting of democracy, development and respect for human rights and fundamental freedoms in the entire world.

9. The World Conference on Human Rights reaffirms that least developed countries committed to the process of democratization and economic reforms, many of which are in Africa, should be supported by the international community in order to succeed in their transition to democracy and economic development.

10. The World Conference on Human Rights reaffirms the right to development, as established in the Declaration on the Right to Development, as a universal and inalienable right and an integral part of fundamental human rights.

As stated in the Declaration on the Right to Development, the human person is the central subject of development.

While development facilitates the enjoyment of all human rights, the lack of development may not be invoked to justify the abridgement of internationally recognized human rights.

States should cooperate with each other in ensuring development and eliminating obstacles to development. The international community should promote an effective international cooperation for the realization of the right to development and the elimination of obstacles to development.

Lasting progress towards the implementation of the right to development requires effective development policies at the national level, as well as equitable economic relations and a favourable economic environment at the international level.

11. The right to development should be fulfilled so as to meet equitably the developmental and environmental needs of present and future generations. The World Conference on Human Rights recognizes that illicit dumping of toxic and dangerous substances and waste potentially constitutes a serious threat to the human rights to life and health of everyone.

Consequently, the World Conference on Human Rights calls on all States to adopt and vigorously implement existing conventions relating to the dumping of toxic and dangerous products and waste and to cooperate in the prevention of illicit dumping.

Everyone has the right to enjoy the benefits of scientific progress and its applications. The World Conference on Human Rights notes that certain advances, notably in the biomedical and life sciences as well as in information technology, may have potentially adverse consequences for the integrity, dignity and human rights of the individual, and calls for international cooperation to ensure that human rights and dignity are fully respected in this area of universal concern.

12. The World Conference on Human Rights calls upon the international community to make all efforts to help alleviate the external debt burden of developing countries, in order to supplement the efforts of the Governments of such countries to attain the full realization of the economic, social and cultural rights of their people.

13. There is a need for States and international organizations, in cooperation with non-governmental organizations, to create favourable conditions at the national, regional and international levels to ensure the full and effective enjoyment of human rights. States should eliminate all violations of human rights and their causes, as well as obstacles to the enjoyment of these rights.

14. The existence of widespread extreme poverty inhibits the full and effective enjoyment of human rights; its immediate alleviation and eventual elimination must remain a high priority for the international community.

15. Respect for human rights and for fundamental freedoms without distinction of any kind is a fundamental rule of international human rights law. The speedy and comprehensive elimination of all forms of racism and racial discrimination, xenophobia and related intolerance is a priority task for the international community. Governments should take effective measures to prevent and combat them. Groups, institutions, intergovernmental and non-governmental organizations and individuals are urged to intensify their efforts in cooperating and coordinating their activities against these evils.

16. The World Conference on Human Rights welcomes the progress made in dismantling apartheid and calls upon the international community and the United Nations system to assist in this process.

The World Conference on Human Rights also deplores the continuing acts of violence aimed at undermining the quest for a peaceful dismantling of apartheid.

17. The acts, methods and practices of terrorism in all its forms and manifestations as well as linkage in some countries to drug trafficking are activities aimed at the destruction of human rights, fundamental freedoms and democracy, threatening territorial integrity, security of States and destabilizing legitimately constituted Governments. The international community should take the necessary steps to enhance cooperation to prevent and combat terrorism.

18. The human rights of women and of the girl-child are an inalienable, integral and indivisible part of universal human rights. The full and equal participation of women in political, civil, economic, social and cultural life, at the national, regional and international levels, and the eradication of all forms of discrimination on grounds of sex are priority objectives of the international community.

   Gender-based violence and all forms of sexual harassment and exploitation, including those resulting from cultural prejudice and international trafficking, are incompatible with the dignity and worth of the human person, and must be eliminated. This can be achieved by legal measures and through national action and international cooperation in such fields as economic and social development, education, safe maternity and health care, and social support.

   The human rights of women should form an integral part of the United Nations human rights activities, including the promotion of all human rights instruments relating to women.

   The World Conference on Human Rights urges Governments, institutions, intergovernmental and non-governmental organizations to intensify their efforts for the protection and promotion of human rights of women and the girl-child.

19. Considering the importance of the promotion and protection of the rights of persons belonging to minorities and the contribution of such promotion and protection to the political and social stability of the States in which such persons live,

   The World Conference on Human Rights reaffirms the obligation of States to ensure that persons belonging to minorities may exercise fully and effectively all human rights and fundamental freedoms without any discrimination and in full equality before the law in accordance with the Declaration on the Rights of Persons Belonging to National or Ethnic, Religious and Linguistic Minorities.

   The persons belonging to minorities have the right to enjoy their own culture, to profess and practise their own religion and to use their own language in private and in public, freely and without interference or any form of discrimination.

20. The World Conference on Human Rights recognizes the inherent dignity and the unique contribution of indigenous people to the development and plurality of society and strongly reaffirms the commitment of the international community to their economic, social and cultural well-being and their enjoyment of the fruits of sustainable development. States should ensure the full and free participation of indigenous

people in all aspects of society, in particular in matters of concern to them. Considering the importance of the promotion and protection of the rights of indigenous people, and the contribution of such promotion and protection to the political and social stability of the States in which such people live, States should, in accordance with international law, take concerted positive steps to ensure respect for all human rights and fundamental freedoms of indigenous people, on the basis of equality and non-discrimination, and recognize the value and diversity of their distinct identities, cultures and social organization.

21. The World Conference on Human Rights, welcoming the early ratification of the Convention on the Rights of the Child by a large number of States and noting the recognition of the human rights of children in the World Declaration on the Survival, Protection and Development of Children and Plan of Action adopted by the World Summit for Children, urges universal ratification of the Convention by 1995 and its effective implementation by States parties through the adoption of all the necessary legislative, administrative and other measures and the allocation to the maximum extent of the available resources. In all actions concerning children, non-discrimination and the best interest of the child should be primary considerations and the views of the child given due weight. National and international mechanisms and programmes should be strengthened for the defence and protection of children, in particular, the girl-child, abandoned children, street children, economically and sexually exploited children, including through child pornography, child prostitution or sale of organs, children victims of diseases including acquired immunodeficiency syndrome, refugee and displaced children, children in detention, children in armed conflict, as well as children victims of famine and drought and other emergencies. International cooperation and solidarity should be promoted to support the implementation of the Convention and the rights of the child should be a priority in the United Nations system-wide action on human rights.

The World Conference on Human Rights also stresses that the child for the full and harmonious development of his or her personality should grow up in a family environment which accordingly merits broader protection.

22. Special attention needs to be paid to ensuring non-discrimination, and the equal enjoyment of all human rights and fundamental freedoms by disabled persons, including their active participation in all aspects of society.

23. The World Conference on Human Rights reaffirms that everyone, without distinction of any kind, is entitled to the right to seek and to enjoy in other countries asylum from persecution, as well as the right to return to one's own country. In this respect it stresses the importance of the Universal Declaration of Human Rights, the 1951 Convention relating to the Status of Refugees, its 1967 Protocol and regional instruments. It expresses its appreciation to States that continue to admit and host large numbers of refugees in their territories, and to the Office of the United Nations High Commissioner for Refugees for its dedication to its task. It also expresses its appreciation to the United Nations Relief and Works Agency for Palestine Refugees in the Near East.

The World Conference on Human Rights recognizes that gross violations of human rights, including in armed conflicts, are among the multiple and complex factors leading to displacement of people.

The World Conference on Human Rights recognizes that, in view of the complexities of the global refugee crisis and in accordance with the Charter of the United Nations, relevant international instruments and international solidarity and in the spirit of burden-sharing, a comprehensive approach by the international community is needed in coordination and cooperation with the countries concerned and relevant organizations, bearing in mind the mandate of the United Nations High Commissioner for Refugees. This should include the development of strategies to address the root causes and effects of movements of refugees and other displaced persons, the strengthening of emergency preparedness and response mechanisms, the provision of effective protection and assistance, bearing in mind the special needs of women and children, as well as the achievement of durable solutions, primarily through the preferred solution of dignified and safe voluntary repatriation, including solutions such as those adopted by the international refugee conferences. The World Conference on Human Rights underlines the responsibilities of States, particularly as they relate to the countries of origin.

* * *

39. Underlining the importance of objective, responsible and impartial information about human rights and humanitarian issues, the World Conference on Human Rights encourages the increased involvement of the media, for whom freedom and protection should be guaranteed within the framework of national law.

Source: General Assembly, United Nations, Office of the United Nations High Commissioner for Human Rights. "Vienna Declaration and Programme of Action." 1993. Available online. URL: http://www.unhchr.ch/huridocda/ huridoca.nsf/(symbol)/A.CONF.157.23.En?OpenDocument. Accessed January 11, 2010.

Coalition to Stop the Use of Child Soldiers, "Voices of Young Soldiers" (2007)

The use of child soldiers occurs around the world, but is particularly promi-nent in Africa, where children are either abducted, forcibly conscripted under threat, or enlist voluntarily due to poverty and devastation in their communi-ties. Demobilization, Disarmament, and Reintegration (DDR) programs have been established around the world to help former child soldiers cope with the trauma of their military activities and reintegrate into society, but lack of funds prevents many DDR programs from obtaining necessary resources. The Coalition to Stop the Use of Child Soldiers provides information on the complex challenges of combating the use of child soldiers, including psycho-social and socioeconomic issues. The following text is a collection of accounts from former child soldiers from several different countries and regions on the abuse they suffered as child soldiers as well as the problems they have faced in rehabilitation.

AFRICA

Central Africa

"I feel so bad about the things that I did. It disturbs me so much that I inflicted death on other people. When I go home I must do some tradi-tional rites because I have killed. I must perform these rites and cleanse myself. I still dream about the boy from my village that I killed. I see him in my dreams, and he is talking to me, saying I killed him for nothing, and I am crying." A 16-year-old girl after demobilization from an armed group (Source: U.S. State Dept. TIP Report 2005)

Democratic Republic of the Congo

"When they came to my village, they asked my older brother whether he was ready to join the militia. He was just 17 and he said no; they shot him in the head. Then they asked me if I was ready to sign, so what could I do—I didn't want to die." A former child soldier taken when he was 13. (Source: BBC report.)

"They gave me a uniform and told me that now I was in the army. They even gave me a new name: 'Pisco' They said that they would come back and kill my parents if I didn't do as they said." Report of interview with a 17-year-old former child soldier in 2006

"Being new, I couldn't perform the very difficult exercises properly and so I was beaten every morning. Two of my friends in the camp died because of the beatings. The soldiers buried them in the latrines. I am still thinking of them". Former child soldier interviewed in 2002.

Liberia

"I am now 14. I was with the LURD for two years in 2003 and 2004. I had to tow ammunition and arms for them. They beat me. They did not feed me. I didn't participate in DD (sic) because I did not know it was an option for me." Esther, former member of Liberians United for Reconciliation and Development. (Source: Amnesty International—Liberia: A flawed process discriminates against women and girls, March 2008.)

Sudan

"I joined the SPLA when I was 13. I am from Bahr Al Ghazal. They demobilized me in 2001 and took me to Rumbek, but I was given no demobilization documents. Now, I am stuck here because my family was killed in a government attack and because the SPLA would re-recruit me. At times I wonder why I am not going back to SPLA, half of my friends have and they seem to be better off than me." Boy interviewed by Coalition staff, southern Sudan, February 2004.

Uganda

"Sometimes in the bush, the rebels would beat us without mercy whether you made a mistake or not. We would also be made to carry heavy loads on our heads for long distances and made to assemble out in the cold each day as early as 5am." Boy, aged 15, abducted by the LRA (Source: Coalition: Returning Home—Children's perspectives on reintegration. A case study of children abducted by the Lord's Resistance Army in Teso, eastern Uganda, February 2008).

"I feel pain from the rape, as if I have wounds inside, and I am afraid I have a disease. I would like to get tested but there is no one to help me. I was tested in the reception centre in Gulu, but I was never told the result. The doctor said that it is better not to know the result." Girl aged 17, abducted by the LRA. (Source: Coalition: Returning Home—Children's perspectives on reintegration. A case study of children abducted by the Lord's Resistance Army in Teso, eastern Uganda, February 2008.)

International Documents

Zimbabwe

"There was no one in charge of the dormitories and on a nightly basis we were raped. The men and youths would come into our dormitory in the dark, and they would just rape us—you would just have a man on top of you, and you could not even see who it was. If we cried afterwards, we were beaten with hosepipes. We were so scared that we did not report the rapes The youngest girl in our group was aged 11 and she was raped repeatedly in the base." 19-year-old girl describing her experience in the National Youth Service Training Program.

ASIA/PACIFIC

India

"He had to run away to a forest with his friend to join the underground. He was 14 when he first held a gun in his hands. He said he loves to go to school but for the poverty of his family he has to lift a gun. Now he is earning enough money with the help of the gun for himself and send money for his family also." Report of interview with 16-year-old boy, northeast India, 2004.

Indonesia, Nanggroe Aceh Darussalam province (Aceh)

"I know the work [monitoring the apparatus] is dangerous, and my parents had tried to stop me from getting involved. But I want to do something for the nanggroe therefore I was called for the fight. I am ready for all risks" Boy interviewed in March 2004: worked as an informant for the armed political group Free Aceh Movement, to spy on the Indonesian military when he was 17 years old.

Myanmar (Burma)

"They filled the forms and asked my age, and when I said 16 I was slapped and he said, 'You are 18. Answer 18'. He asked me again and I said, 'But that's my true age'. The sergeant asked, 'Then why did you enlist in the army?' I said, 'Against my will. I was captured.' He said, 'Okay, keep your mouth shut then,' and he filled in the form. I just wanted to go back home and I told them, but they refused. I said, 'Then please let me make one phone call,' but they refused that too." Maung Zaw Oo, describing the second time he was forced into the Tatmadaw Kyi (army) in 2005.

Nepal

"They (the army) took us to the barracks. They beat us both with their guns and boots. After 15 days my friend died from the beatings. They beat me repeatedly. Once I was beaten unconscious and taken to the hospital. When I regained consciousness I was taken back to the barracks and beaten again. I nearly died. I don't know why they beat me." Ram, recruited in 2004 by the Maoists when he was 14 years old describes his capture by the Royal Nepal Army one year later. (Source: Human Rights Watch, Children in the Ranks: The Maoists use of child soldiers in Nepal, February 2007.)

Sri Lanka
"I ran away (to join an armed group) to escape a marriage I didn't like". Girl soldier in Sri Lanka.

EUROPE

Chechen Republic of the Russian Federation
"Russia has turned us into cattle. It is driving our youth into the arms of whoever comes along first and says 'Go with us'." Mother in Chechnya.

LATIN AMERICA

Colombia
"They give you a gun and you have to kill the best friend you have. They do it to see if they can trust you. If you don't kill him, your friend will be ordered to kill you. I had to do it because otherwise I would have been killed. That's why I got out. I couldn't stand it any longer." 17-year-old boy, joined paramilitary group aged 7, when a street child.

"I joined the guerrilla to escape . . . I thought I'd get some money and could be independent." 17-year-old girl soldier with the Revolutionary Armed Forces of Colombia, interviewed in 2002.

MIDDLE EAST AND NORTH AFRICA

Iraq
"I joined the Mahdi army to fight the Americans. Last night I fired a rocket-propelled grenade against a tank." A 12-year-old boy in Najaf, 2004.

Israel/Occupied Palestinian Territories
"I was detained on 18 March 2003 . . . We are in a very small room with 11 people . . . We are allowed to use the bathroom only three times a day at

specific times. Once a week we are allowed to take a 30-minute recess. The prison guards force us into shabeh position: they tie our hands up and one leg and then we have to face the wall." 15-year-old boy arrested by Israeli forces, reporting on detention conditions in an Israeli settlement outside Ramallah, April 2003.

Source: Coalition to Stop the Use of Child Soldiers. "Voices of Young Soldiers." 2007. Available online. URL: http://www.child-soldiers.org/childsoldiers/voices-of-young-soldiers. Accessed July 24, 2010.

THE DEMOCRATIC REPUBLIC OF THE CONGO

Roger Casement, "The Casement Report" (1903), Excerpted

Investigating rumors of forced labor in the Belgian-run Congo Free State, the British consul Roger Casement traveled to the Congo to gather evidence for his report. His report, today known as the Casement Report, depicts in graphic detail the brutality of King Leopold II's Congo administration, including accounts of kidnapping, beatings, murder, and mutilation, in addition to the crushing weight of forced labor. The report is 40 pages in length and was published to worldwide shock in 1904, leading to Leopold's relinquishment of the Congo in 1908.

On the whole the Government workmen (Congolese natives) . . . struck me as being well cared for. . . . The chief difficulty in dealing with so large a staff [3,000 in number] arises from the want of a sufficiency of food supply in the surrounding country. . . . The natives of the districts are forced to provide a fixed quantity each week . . . which is levied by requisitions on all the surrounding villages . . . This, however necessary, is not a welcome task to the native suppliers who complain that their numbers are yearly decreasing, while the demands made upon them remain fixed, or tend even to increase. . . . The (official in charge) is forced to exercise continuous pressure on the local population, and within recent times that pressure has not always taken the form of mere requisition. Armed expeditions have been necessary and a more forcible method of levying supplies [e.g., goats, fowl, etc.] adopted than the law either contemplated or justifies. The result of an expedition, which took place towards the end of 1900, was that in fourteen small villages traversed seventeen persons disappeared. Sixteen of these whose names were given to me were killed by the soldiers, and their bodies recovered by their friends . . . Ten persons were tied up and taken away as prisoners, but were released on payment of sixteen goats by their friends.

. . .

Complaints as to the manner of exacting service are . . . frequent . . . If the local official has to go on a sudden journey men are summoned on the instant to paddle his canoe, and a refusal entails imprisonment or a beating. If the Government plantation or the kitchen garden require weeding, a soldier will be sent to call in the women from some of the neighboring towns . . . ; to the women suddenly forced to leave their household tasks and to tramp off, hoe in hand, baby on back, with possibly a hungry and angry husband at home, the task is not a welcome one.

I visited two large villages in the interior . . . wherein I found that fully half the population now consisted of refugees . . . I saw and questioned several groups of these people . . . They went on to declare, when asked why they had fled (their district), that they had endured such ill-treatment at the hands of the government soldiers in their own (district) that life had become intolerable; that nothing had remained for them at home but to be killed for failure to bring in a certain amount of rubber or to die from starvation or exposure in their attempts to satisfy the demands made upon them. . . . I subsequently found other (members of the tribe) who confirmed the truth of the statements made to me.

. . . on the 25th of July (1903) we reached Lukolela, where I spent two days. This district had, when I visited it in 1887, numbered fully 5,000 people; today the population is given, after a careful enumeration, at less than 600. The reasons given me for their decline in numbers were similar to those furnished elsewhere, namely, sleeping-sickness, general ill-health, insufficiency of food, and the methods employed to obtain labor from them by local officials and the exactions levied on them.

At other villages which I visited, I found the tax to consist of baskets, which the inhabitants had to make and deliver weekly as well as, always, a certain amount of foodstuffs. (The natives) were frequently flogged for delay or inability to complete the tally of these baskets, or the weekly supply of food. Several men, including a Chief of one town, showed broad weals across their buttocks, which were evidently recent. One, a lad of 15 or so, removing his cloth, showed several scars across his thighs, which he and others around him said had formed part of a weekly payment for a recent shortage in their supply of food.

. . . A careful investigation of the conditions of native life around (Lake Mantumba) confirmed the truth of the statements made to me—that the great decrease in population, the dirty and ill-kept towns, and the complete absence of goats, sheep, or fowls—once very plentiful in this country—were to be attributed above all else to the continued effort made during many years to compel the natives to work india-rubber. Large bodies of native troops had formerly been quartered in the district, and the punitive measures undertaken to this end had endured for a considerable period. During the course of these operations there had been much loss of life, accompanied, I fear, by a somewhat general mutilation of the dead, as proof that the soldiers had done their duty.

. . . Two cases (of mutilation) came to my actual notice while I was in the lake district. One, a young man, both of whose hands had been beaten off with the butt ends of rifles against a tree; the other a young lad of 11 or 12 years of age, whose right hand was cut off at the wrist. . . . In both these cases the Government soldiers had been accompanied by white officers whose names were given to me. Of six natives (one a girl, three little boys, one youth, and one old woman) who had been mutilated in this way during the rubber regime, all except one were dead at the date of my visit.

[A sentry in the employ of one of the concessionary private companies] said he had caught and was detaining as prisoners (eleven women) to compel their husbands to bring in the right amount of rubber required of them on the next market day. . . . When I asked what would become of these women if their husbands failed to bring in the right quantity of rubber . . . he said at once that then they would be kept there until their husbands had redeemed them.

Source: Joseph V. O'Brien. "Atrocities in the Congo: The Casement Report, 1903." Available online. URL: http://web.jjay.cuny.edu/~jobrien/reference/ob73.html. Accessed July 24, 2010.

Organization of African Unity (African Union), African Charter on Human and Peoples' Rights (1981) (Excerpt)

The African Charter on Human and Peoples' Rights, also known as the Banjul Charter, was drafted following the 1979 Assembly of Heads of State and Government as a singular document that would outline, protect, and promote human rights throughout Africa. In 1987, the African Commission on Human and Peoples' Rights was established in Banjul, Gambia, to oversee and interpret the charter, which is similar to other human rights documents, but unique in its recognition of peoples' rights and group rights, as well as duties that every individual has toward others, such as the duty to pay taxes and honor family. In 2004, the African Court on Human and Peoples' Rights was created to oversee the compliance of all African Union member states with the charter.

PREAMBLE

The African States members of the Organisation of African Unity, parties to the present Convention entitled "African Charter on Human and Peoples' Rights"

Recalling Decision 115 (XVI) of the Assembly of Heads of State and Government at its Sixteenth Ordinary Session held in Monrovia, Liberia, from 17 to 20 July 1979 on the preparation of "a preliminary draft on an African Charter on Human and Peoples' Rights, providing inter alia for the establishment of bodies to promote and protect human and peoples' rights";

Considering the Charter of the Organisation of African Unity, which stipulates that "freedom, equality, justice and dignity are essential objectives for the achievement of the legitimate aspirations of the African peoples";

Reaffirming the pledge they solemnly made in Article 2 of the said Charter to eradicate all forms of colonialism from Africa, to coordinate and intensify their cooperation and efforts to achieve a better life for the peoples of Africa and to promote international cooperation having due regard to the Charter of the United Nations and the Universal Declaration of Human Rights;

Taking into consideration the virtues of their historical tradition and the values of African civilization which should inspire and characterize their reflection on the concept of human and peoples' rights;

Recognizing on the one hand, that fundamental human rights stem from the attitudes of human beings, which justifies their international protection and on the other hand that the reality and respect of peoples' rights should necessarily guarantee human rights;

Considering that the enjoyment of rights and freedoms also implies the performance of duties on the part of everyone;

Convinced that it is henceforth essential to pay particular attention to the right to development and that civil and political rights cannot be dissociated from economic, social and cultural rights in their conception as well as universality and that the satisfaction of economic, social and cultural rights is a guarantee for the enjoyment of civil and political rights;

Conscious of their duty to achieve the total liberation of Africa, the peoples of which are still struggling for their dignity and genuine independence, and undertaking to eliminate colonialism, neo-colonialism, apartheid, zionism and to dismantle aggressive foreign military bases and all forms of discrimination, language, religion or political opinions;

Reaffirming their adherence to the principles of human and peoples' rights and freedoms contained in the declarations, conventions and other instruments adopted by the Organisation of African Unity, the Movement of Non-Aligned Countries and the United Nations;

Firmly convinced of their **duty** to promote and protect human and peoples' rights and freedoms and taking into account the importance traditionally attached to these rights and freedoms in Africa;

HAVE AGREED AS FOLLOWS:
PART 1
RIGHTS AND DUTIES
CHAPTER 1
HUMAN AND PEOPLES' RIGHTS

ARTICLE 1

The Member States of the Organisation of African Unity, parties to the present Charter shall recognise the rights, duties and freedoms enshrined in the Charter and shall undertake to adopt legislative or other measures to give effect to them.

ARTICLE 2

Every individual shall be entitled to the enjoyment of the rights and freedoms recognised and guaranteed in the present Charter without distinction of any kind such as race, ethnic group, colour, sex, language, religion, political or any other opinion, national and social origin, fortune, birth or any status.

ARTICLE 3

1. Every individual shall be equal before the law

2. Every individual shall be entitled to equal protection of the law

ARTICLE 4

Human beings are inviolable. Every human being shall be entitled to respect for his life and the integrity of his person. No one may be arbitrarily deprived of this right.

ARTICLE 5

Every individual shall have the right to the respect of the dignity inherent in a human being and to the recognition of his legal status. All forms of exploitation and degradation of man, particularly slavery, slave trade, torture, cruel, inhuman or degrading punishment and treatment shall be prohibited.

ARTICLE 6

Every individual shall have the right to liberty and to the security of his person. No one may be deprived of his freedom except for reasons and conditions previously laid down by law. In particular, no one may be arbitrarily arrested or detained.

ARTICLE 7

1. Every individual shall have the right to have his cause heard. This comprises:
   a) The right to an appeal to competent national organs against acts of violating his fundamental rights as recognized and guaranteed by conventions, laws, regulations and customs in force;
   b) The right to be presumed innocent until proved guilty by a competent court or tribunal;
   c) The right to defence, including the right to be defended by counsel of his choice;
   d) The right to be tried within a reasonable time by an impartial court or tribunal.
2. No one may be condemned for an act or omission which did not constitute a legally punishable offence at the time it was committed. No penalty may be inflicted for an offence for which no provision was made at the time it was committed. Punishment is personal and can be imposed only on the offender.

ARTICLE 8

Freedom of conscience, the profession and free practice of religion shall be guaranteed. No one may, subject to law and order, be submitted to measures restricting the exercise of these freedoms.

ARTICLE 9

1. Every individual shall have the right to receive information.
2. Every individual shall have the right to express and disseminate his opinions within the law.

ARTICLE 10

1. Every individual shall have the right to free association provided that he abides by the law.
2. Subject to the obligation of solidarity provided for in Article 29, no one may be compelled to join an association.

ARTICLE 11

Every individual shall have the right to assemble freely with others. The exercise of this right shall be subject only to necessary restrictions provided for by law, in particular those enacted in the interest of national security, the safety, health, ethics and rights and freedoms of others.

ARTICLE 12

1. Every individual shall have the right to freedom of movement and residence within the borders of a State provided he abides by the law.
2. Every individual shall have the right to leave any country including his own, and to return to his country.

    This right may only be subject to restrictions, provided for by law for the protection of national security, law and order, public health or morality.
3. Every individual shall have the right, when persecuted, to seek and obtain asylum in other countries in accordance with the law of those countries and international conventions.
4. A non-national legally admitted in a territory of a State Party to the present Charter, may only be expelled from it by virtue of a decision taken in accordance with the law.
5. The mass expulsion of non-nationals shall be prohibited. Mass expulsion shall be that which is aimed at national, racial, ethnic or religious groups.

ARTICLE 13

1. Every citizen shall have the right to participate freely in the government of his country, either directly or through freely chosen representatives in accordance with the provisions of the law.
2. Every citizen shall have the right of equal access to the public service of the country.

3. Every individual shall have the right of access to public property and services in strict equality of all persons before the law.

ARTICLE 14

The right to property shall be guaranteed. It may only be encroached upon in the interest of public need or in the general interest of the community and in accordance with the provisions of appropriate laws.

ARTICLE 15

Every individual shall have the right to work under equitable and satisfactory conditions, and shall receive equal pay for equal work.

ARTICLE 16

1. Every individual shall have the right to enjoy the best attainable state of physical and mental health.
2. State Parties to the present Charter shall take the necessary measures to protect the health of their people and to ensure that they receive medical attention when they are sick

ARTICLE 17

1. Every individual shall have the right to education
2. Every individual may freely take part in the cultural life of his community.
3. The promotion and protection of morals and traditional values recognized by the community shall be the duty of the State.

ARTICLE 18

1. The family shall be the natural unit and basis of society. It shall be protected by the State which shall take care of its physical health and moral.
2. The State shall have the duty to assist the family which is the custodian of morals and traditional values recognized by the community.
3. The State shall ensure the elimination of every discrimination against women and also ensure the protection of the rights of women and the child as stipulated in international declarations and conventions.
4. The aged and the disabled shall also have the right to special measures of protection in keeping with their physical or moral needs.

ARTICLE 19

All peoples shall be equal; they shall enjoy the same respect and shall have the same rights. Nothing shall justify the domination of a people by another.

ARTICLE 20

1. All peoples shall have the right to existence. They shall have the unquestionable and inalienable right to self-determination. They shall freely determine their political status and shall pursue their economic and social development according to the policy they have freely chosen.
2. Colonized or oppressed peoples shall have the right to free themselves from the bonds of domination by resorting to any means recognized by the international community.
3. All peoples shall have the right to the assistance of the State Parties to the present Charter in their liberation struggle against foreign domination, be it political, economic or cultural.

ARTICLE 21

1. All peoples shall freely dispose of their wealth and natural resources. This right shall be exercised in the exclusive interest of the people. In no case shall a people be deprived of it.
2. In case of spoilation, the dispossessed people shall have the right to the lawful recovery of its property as well as to an adequate compensation.
3. The free disposal of wealth and natural resources shall be exercised without prejudice to the obligation of promoting international economic cooperation based on mutual respect, equitable exchange and the principles of international law.
4. State Parties to the present Charter shall individually and collectively exercise the right to free disposal of their wealth and natural resources with a view to strengthening African Unity and solidarity.
5. State Parties to the present Charter shall undertake to eliminate all forms of foreign exploitation particularly that practised by international monopolies so as to enable their peoples to fully benefit from the advantages derived from their national resources.

ARTICLE 22

1. All peoples shall have the right to their economic, social and cultural development with due regard to their freedom and identity and in the equal enjoyment of the common heritage of mankind.
2. States shall have the duty, individually or collectively, to ensure the exercise of the right to development.

ARTICLE 23

1. All peoples shall have the right to national and international peace and security. The principles of solidarity and friendly relations implicitly

affirmed by the Charter of the United Nations and reaffirmed by that of the Organisation of African Unity shall govern relations between States.

2. For the purpose of strengthening peace, solidarity and friendly relations, State Parties to the present Charter shall ensure that:

   a) any individual enjoying the right of asylum under Article 12 of the present Charter shall not engage in subversive activities against his country of origin or any other State Party to the present Charter;

   b) their territories shall not be used as bases for subversive or terrorist activities against the people of any other State Party to the present Charter.

ARTICLE 24

All peoples shall have the right to a general satisfactory environment favourable to their development.

ARTICLE 25

State Parties to the present Charter shall have the duty to promote and ensure through teaching, education and publication, the respect of the rights and freedoms contained in the present Charter and to see to it that these freedoms and rights as well as corresponding obligations and duties are understood.

ARTICLE 26

State Parties to the present Charter shall have the duty to guarantee the independence of the Courts and shall allow the establishment and improvement of appropriate national institutions entrusted with the promotion and protection of the rights and freedoms guaranteed by the present Charter.

CHAPTER 11
DUTIES

ARTICLE 27

1. Every individual shall have duties towards his family and society, the State and other legally recognised communities and the international community.

2. The rights and freedoms of each individual shall be exercised with due regard to the rights of others, collective security, morality and common interest.

ARTICLE 28

Every individual shall have the duty to respect and consider his fellow beings without discrimination, and to maintain relations aimed at promoting, safeguarding and reinforcing mutual respect and tolerance.

ARTICLE 29

The individual shall also have the duty:

1. To preserve the harmonious development of the family and to work for the cohesion and respect of the family; to respect his parents at all times, to maintain them in case of need.

2. To serve his national community by placing his physical and intellectual abilities at its service;

3. Not to compromise the security of the State whose national or resident he is;

4. To preserve and strengthen social and national solidarity, particularly when the latter is strengthened;

5. To preserve and strengthen the national independence and the territorial integrity of his country and to contribute to his defence in accordance with the law;

6. To work to the best of his abilities and competence, and to pay taxes imposed by law in the interest of the society;

7. To preserve and strengthen positive African cultural values in his relations with other members of the society, in the spirit of tolerance, dialogue and consultation and, in general, to contribute to the promotion of the moral well being of society;

8. To contribute to the best of his abilities, at all times and at all levels, to the promotion and achievement of African unity.

Source: African Commission on Human and People's Rights. "African Charter on Human and People's Rights." 1981. Available online. URL: http://www.achpr.org/english/_info/charter_en.html. Accessed January 12, 2010.

Georgianne Nienaber, "Exclusive Interview: Congo Rebel Leader Accused of War Crimes Tells His Story" (2009)

In January 2009, the journalist Georgianne Nienaber traveled to Kivu to interview General Laurent Nkunda, a former Congolese rebel leader who was widely accused by NGOs of mass human rights violations, including rape, pillage, and the deliberate massacre of civilians. In this interview, Nienaber questions Nkunda about such charges, including one charge that he ordered his troops to destroy a refugee camp, all of which he adamantly denies. In 2002, the UN Human Rights Commissioner Mary Robinson called for Nkunda's arrest after two UN investigators were abducted and beaten by Nkunda's troops. Nkunda was the leader of the National Congress for the Defense of the People (CNDP) before he was arrested in Rwanda in January 2009, shortly after his interview with Nienaber. Nkunda speaks English, French, Swahili, and Kinyarwanda (a Bantu language), studied psychology at Kisangani University, and is an ordained Seventh-day Adventist minister. Following his seizure in Rwanda, he was replaced by General Bosco Ntaganda.

Question. Would you say that you have been portrayed in a negative way in Western media?
Nkunda. They cut my voice and they speak on my behalf. Journalists tell what they think will be sensational.

Q. Are you the man to provide the leadership to develop Congo?
N. I never talk about an individual when I talk about change or about leadership. I always talk about a spirit. Because a man cannot do, but a spirit can do. If you can find leadership, leadership can change Congo, but not a leader.

Q. There have been terrible stories about how women are treated in Congo, especially how there have been mass rapes.
N. You are in the area under CNDP control. Ask the women who have been raped.

I cannot believe that they are raped here and then going to be treated in Goma or Bukavu. But if you go to Goma or Bukavu [under FARDC control] you are going to see hospitals full of women raped. Go to Rumangabo and they will tell you that the area under CNDP control is the most secure area in Congo.

They say that we massacre Hutu tribes. The executive secretary of CNDP is a Hutu.

Q. Can you tell the world what happened at Kiwanja?
N. Kiwanja was liberated by the CNDP on the 28th of October, [2008]. We were in Kiwanja for one week without any killing, any rape, any looting. One week later the government [FARDC], along with Mai Mai, attacked Kiwanja and they occupied Kiwanja for 24 hours. My forces went back [withdrew] from Kiwanja. And in 24 hours, 74 people were killed.

And before we came back to Kiwanja the governor of Goma, in the morning, announced that in Kiwanja there were massacres. When I heard

208

on the radio that there were massacres in Kiwanja, I called my guys [soldiers] on the ground and said, "Where are you?" They said, "We are in Rutshuru." I said, "Who is doing this?" They said they did not know, that they were in Rutshuru.

So we went back to Kiwanja on the afternoon of the 29th, or the 27th. [Nkunda leans over to check dates with an adviser.] We went back 24 hours later and some people were killed in the crossfire. To that we can testify. Because the Mai Mai, they do not know how to shoot; they shoot where they want and when they were retreating they were shooting.

And we saw that even the Hutu community in Rutshuru wrote a letter about that and they gave it to [unclear] and said they were not killed by CNDP.

Q. Do you have a copy of that letter?
N. Yes, I do.

Q. May we have a copy?
N. You will have a copy.

The same scenario was prepared in Goma. When we were around Goma, my intelligence services told me that there was a plan to kill people in Goma that night so that they could blame the CNDP. That is why I told my guys to not enter Goma.

I was informed that there was a plan for FARDC [the government forces] to kill in the night. Those who were in charge of the killing never knew that we withdrew. But I told MONUC [UN mission in DRC] that I was going to withdraw from Goma for 12 kilometers.

On that night, 64 people were killed in Goma.

Q. The other charge against you is that you ordered the refugee camps destroyed.
N. Please understand. Yes, there were internally displaced people in Kiwanja. When I came, I went to the camp and I told the population there, there are no houses here. You are in the rain. Please go back to your homes. I will take charge of your security. Please go home.

On the following morning they said Nkunda forced people to leave. I am asking people to go to their HOMES! MONUC has been unable to take charge. So it is a crime because I am asking them to go to their homes?

One day I told the person responsible for OCHA; the one in charge of humanitarian affairs, if we do a study in the camps around Goma, in each week there are about a hundred people dying from different diseases.

In four years, CNDP has been accused of killing 100 people. But you are killing one hundred people each week in your camps.

Who is the criminal?

Q. Can you explain the military ethic of your soldiers?
N. Rape will be punished by firing squad. This is known. And two weeks ago [approximately December 21, 2008] two officers were executed for this.

Q. Who executed them?
N. Other soldiers of the same rank. They were second lieutenants and they were killed by second lieutenants.

These are strong measures, I know.

Q. Some people call this a war for minerals.
N. How can you fight for your own minerals? [Laughter] If this were about minerals, I would not be here.

You see minerals are being exploited by China, by Belgium, by South Africa. Petrol is under French control, uranium under American control, copper under Belgium, diamonds under Jewish, and gold under South African control.

Q. Have you met personally with Alan Doss [MONUC]?
N. No. We talk only on the phone.

The first time I talked to him was in January when we were in Goma during the peace talks. One day I told him, you are coming with your tanks to ask us to shut our mouths.

And so you ask me to not fight. I said to him bring other tanks and other aviation forces because we will fight until we will be free. You want me to be a slave, an economic slave to China, I will not accept this. I'll fight till I die, then my brothers will continue to fight, and my elders will fight and my son will fight.

Q. So does China's influence concern you now?
N. Yes of course because we are going now into economic slavery. If we accept this Chinese contract it is the end for Congolese.

Q. Have you heard President-elect Obama's statement about Congo, that this is just an ethnic conflict?
N. He has to raise his thinking about Congo. If I could meet him one day, I would tell him that it is not a matter of ethnic conflict, it is a matter of leadership.

The world is talking about a black person in power, but Americans didn't vote for a black man, they voted for an American showing the capacity to rule. But they are talking about a black person. No, no, it is not that. On his identity card it doesn't say 'black'. When the American people were voting, they voted for an American.

Q. What are your views about Human Rights Watch?
N. I will tell you, they are writing from the UK and from the US and they are not on the ground.

I even talked to Anneke van Woudenberg. She came to see me in Masisi but after leaving here and then writing their things I had to call her back and say, "Why? You were here, now what are you doing?" She always says that the information is from "reliable sources." But all these reliable sources are unidentified.

Q. General, is there anything you want to say to us that we didn't ask you about as a last question?
N. I can say that what Congo expects from the world is help to be free from the leadership it is currently under. Instead of bringing so many troops, we want to have well-trained and equipped soldiers in Congo. Instead of spending money on MONUC we want to have roads. Instead of bringing ex-pats from elsewhere, we want well-trained leaders for Congo. Help Congolese leaders to have a vision for the country that is good for the people.

Source: Georgianne Nienaber. "Exclusive Interview: Congo Rebel Leader Accused of War Crimes Tells His Story." *The Huffington Post.* January 9, 2009. Available online. URL: http://www.huffingtonpost.com/georgianne-nienaber/exclusive-interview-congo_b_156374.html. Accessed July 24, 2010.

Vital Voices, "Testimony of Chouchou Namegabe" (2009)

In May 2009, 31-year-old Chouchou Namegabe, founder of the South Kivu Women's Media Association, testified in front of the United States Foreign Relations Committee on the use of rape as a weapon of war in the Democratic Republic of the Congo for the hearing "Confronting Rape and Other Forms of Violence Against Women in Conflict Zones." Namegabe became a highly controversial figure in the DRC when she began broadcasting Congolese women's testimonies of being raped on her radio show in 2001. The day after her first airing, three women appeared at the radio station, asking to speak about their experiences. The women, who are anonymous, give graphic accounts of being abducted, sexually assaulted, mutilated, and left for dead. In interviews, Namegabe has explained that despite their anonymity, the women express relief at being able to talk about their experiences in a country that does not have a word for rape. Namegabe has won several journalism awards for her dangerous and vitally important work, and in the following testimony, she provides two graphic accounts from women she interviewed as well as an outline of concrete steps that the United States can and must take to help end the use of rape as a weapon of war in the Democratic Republic of the Congo.

Thank you for having this important hearing. The women of the eastern Democratic Republic of Congo (DRC) have waited a long time for American policy-makers to take an interest in this situation. I am grateful for the invitation to be here.

Rape and sexual violence is used as a weapon and tactic of war to destroy the community. The rapes are targeted and intentional, and are meant to remove the people from their mineral-rich land through fear, shame, violence, and the intentional spread of HIV throughout entire families and villages.

The South Kivu Women's Media Association is the voice of thousands of voiceless women. We use radio to give them the space to express what has happened to them, begin their healing and to seek justice. We have interviewed over 400 women in South Kivu, and their stories are terrifying. In fact, the word rape fails to truly describe what is happening, because it is not only rape that occurs, but atrocities also accompany the rapes. That is what makes the situation in the eastern Congo so different, and horrible. Of all the testimonies we recorded there are two that stay in my mind that I will share with you.

I met a woman who had 5 children. They took her into the forest with her 5 children, and kept them there for several days. As each day passed the rebels killed one of her children and forced her to eat her child's flesh. She begged to be killed but they refused and said "No, we can't give you a good death."

Last month, after the joint operation between the Congolese army and the Rwandese army to break down the FDLR1, in their running away the FDLR raped more women. Our journalists were told that after they raped the women, they put fuel in their vaginas and set them on fire, and then extinguished the fire. This was done not to kill them, but to let them suffer. There were many other horrible atrocities.

The women ask WHY? Why such atrocities? Why do they fight their war on women's bodies? It is because there is a plan to put fear into the community through the woman, because she is the heart of the community. When she is pushed down, the whole community follows.

We also ask, Why the silence of the developed countries? When a gorilla is killed in the mountains, there is an outcry, and people mobilize great resources to protect the animals. Yet more than five hundred thousand women have been raped, and there is silence. After all of this you will make memorials and say "Never Again." But we don't need commemorations; we want you to act now.

There are six actions that I request of you to help end this situation:

1. The first need of the women is security and peace. Rape is not peace! Rape is used just like a gun, to show the force of the rebel groups. We ask for your involvement to station the U.N. peace-keepers not only in the cities and towns to protect business, but also in rural areas where they can actually protect the women.

2. In the Congo, we believe that there will be security when the FDLR returns to Rwanda. I ask that the American government get involved politically, by pressuring the Rwandan government to accept their return and to begin dialogue with the rebels, so that they stop fighting their war in our country, and on women's bodies.

3. We need strong justice to end impunity on rape and sexual violence. We ask the U.S. to join us in pressuring the Congolese government to stop giving amnesty to rebels who use rape as their war strategy. The American and Congolese governments should request International Criminal Court arrest warrants for the Congolese and Rwandan rebel leaders. We also ask you to pressure the International Criminal Court to include rape and sexual violence in the charges filed against these war criminals. Finally, we ask for assistance to pursue the legal reforms needed in Congo to end impunity for rape and sexual violence in war. We need Zero Tolerance on rape and sexual violence—at all levels of the justice system.

4. We ask that the American government and U.S. multinational corporations contribute financially to the recovery and healing of the women and the communities, because your economy benefits from the minerals of the Congo. The women and families need medical and psychological services to heal from the trauma to their bodies and minds. There are also children born of rape who live as orphans, because the community has rejected them and sees them as "ticking bombs" who will grow up to become like the rebels. These women and children are left with nothing.

5. Another part of this recovery is to help Congo to strengthen the formal economy in the eastern provinces, and end the profitability of blood minerals. We ask that you work with the U.S. multinational corporations to develop ways to ensure that Congolese minerals imported to the U.S. are "conflict-free" and that the security, infrastructure and capacity and of the eastern provinces is built up through this investment. Economic recovery is part of the total recovery of the women and their communities.

6. Lastly, I would like for the U.S. to have an increased presence in the eastern Congo. Toward that end, I invite the American government and private sector to send a delegation to the East to see the reality on the ground and explore ways to improve security and promote the formal economy. Having a presence in the East would also allow the U.S. government to have a better sense of what is happening in the area and would help the U.S. to be a better advocate for women and families.

I'd like to conclude by expressing our hope for the future. There are many people and organizations in the eastern Congo working tirelessly for peace, justice, and healing. This good work can be more effective and help even more people, if we have the support we are requesting. We, the women of the Congo want to work with you, and we need your support to stand with dignity. Stand with us, and help us to heal our nation. Thank you for your attention.

Source: Vital Voices: Global Partnership. "Testimony of Chouchou Namegabe, Founder, South Kivu Women's Media Association, Democratic Republic of the Congo, to the United States Senate Foreign Relations Committee, Subcommittee on International Operations and Organizations, Human Rights, Democracy, and Global Women's Issues; and the Subcommittee on African Affairs, for the Hearing of 'Confronting Rape and Other Forms of Violence Against Women in Conflict Zones.'" May 13, 2009.

CHINA

Representatives of Asian States at the Vienna World Conference on Human Rights, The Bangkok Declaration (1993)

In March 1993, representatives from 34 different Asian states met in Bangkok to prepare a document that would summarize the Asian perspective on human rights for the Vienna World Conference on Human Rights. The

Bangkok Declaration was presented at the conference amid much controversy, as it explicitly refutes universal rights on the grounds that common ideals of universal rights as embraced by the United Nations are, in fact, Western ideals of human rights that do not correspond to Asian values. The Asian representatives defended the Declaration, arguing that efforts to push universal rights on Asian states constituted Western efforts to encroach on and upend Asian culture. While cultural relativism does not accord with notions of universal rights and most state leaders and human rights organizations have rejected the Bangkok Declaration as an attempt to justify dictatorial governments' strangleholds on their people, it has, nonetheless, brought up some very important questions, such as whether or not Asian values are being incorporated into universal rights charters. What are Asian values, and have Western leaders taken a culturally blind approach to the enforcement of rights in Asian countries? How are we to distinguish between cultural relativism and cultural sensitivity? Human rights groups and scholars continue to investigate and learn more about Asian history and culture to facilitate more inclusive discussions.

The Ministers and representatives of Asian States, meeting at Bangkok from 29 March to 2 April 1993, pursuant to General Assembly resolution 46/116 of 17 December 1991 in the context of preparations for the World Conference on Human rights,

Adopt this Declaration, to be known as "The Bangkok Declaration," which contains the aspirations and commitments of the Asian region:

BANGKOK DECLARATION

Emphasizing the significance of the World Conference on Human Rights, which provides an invaluable opportunity to review all aspects of human rights and ensure a just and balanced approach thereto,

Recognizing the contribution that can be made to the World Conference by Asian countries with their diverse and rich cultures and traditions,

Welcoming the increased attention being paid to human rights in the international community,

Reaffirming their commitment to principles contained in the Charter of the United Nations and the Universal Declaration on Human Rights,

HUMAN RIGHTS

Recalling that in the Charter of the United Nations the question of universal observance and promotion of human rights and fundamental freedoms has been rightly placed within the context of international cooperation,

Noting the progress made in the codification of human rights instruments, and in the establishment of international human rights mechanisms, while expressing concern that these mechanisms relate mainly to one category of rights,

Emphasizing that ratification of international human rights instruments, particularly the International Covenant on Civil and Political Rights and the International Covenant on Economic, Social and Cultural Rights, by all States should be further encouraged,

Reaffirming the principles of respect for national sovereignty, territorial integrity and non-interference in the internal affairs of States,

Stressing the universality, objectivity and non-selectivity of all human rights and the need to avoid the application of double standards in the implementation of human rights and its politicization,

Recognizing that the promotion of human rights should be encouraged by cooperation and consensus, and not through confrontation and the imposition of incompatible values,

Reiterating the interdependence and indivisibility of economic, social, cultural, civil and political rights, and the inherent interrelationship between development, democracy, universal enjoyment of all human rights, and social justice, which must be addressed in an integrated and balanced manner,

Recalling that the Declaration on the Right to Development has recognized the right to development as a universal and inalienable right and an integral part of fundamental human rights,

Emphasizing that endeavours to move towards the creation of uniform international human rights norms must go hand in hand with endeavours to work towards a just and fair world economic order,

Convinced that economic and social progress facilitates the growing trend towards democracy and the promotion and protection of human rights,

International Documents

Stressing the importance of education and training in human rights at the national, regional and international levels and the need for international cooperation aimed at overcoming the lack of public awareness of human rights,

1. *Reaffirm* their commitment to the principles contained in the Charter of the United Nations and the Universal Declaration on Human Rights as well as the full realization of all human rights throughout the world;
2. *Underline* the essential need to create favourable conditions for effective enjoyment of human rights at both the national and international levels;
3. *Stress* the urgent need to democratize the United Nations system, eliminate selectivity and improve procedures and mechanisms in order to strengthen international cooperation, based on principles of equality and mutual respect, and ensure a positive, balanced and non-confrontational approach in addressing and realizing all aspects of human rights;
4. *Discourage* any attempt to use human rights as a conditionality for extending development assistance;
5. *Emphasize* the principles of respect for national sovereignty and territorial integrity as well as non-interference in the internal affairs of States, and the non-use of human rights as an instrument of political pressure;
6. *Reiterate* that all countries, large and small, have the right to determine their political systems, control and freely utilize their resources, and freely pursue their economic, social and cultural development;
7. *Stress* the universality, objectivity and non-selectivity of all human rights and the need to avoid the application of double standards in the implementation of human rights and its politicization, and that no violation of human rights can be justified;
8. *Recognize* that while human rights are universal in nature, they must be considered in the context of a dynamic and evolving process of international norm-setting, bearing in mind the significance of national and regional particularities and various historical, cultural and religious backgrounds;
9. *Recognize further* that States have the primary responsibility for the promotion and protection of human rights through appropriate infrastructure and mechanisms, and also recognize that remedies must be sought and provided primarily through such mechanisms and procedures;

10. *Reaffirm* the interdependence and indivisibility of economic, social, cultural, civil and political rights, and the need to give equal emphasis to all categories of human rights;

11. *Emphasize* the importance of guaranteeing the human rights and fundamental freedoms of vulnerable groups such as ethnic, national, racial, religious and linguistic minorities, migrant workers, disabled persons, indigenous peoples, refugees and displaced persons;

12. *Reiterate* that self-determination is a principle of international law and a universal right recognized by the United Nations for peoples under alien or colonial domination and foreign occupation, by virtue of which they can freely determine their political status and freely pursue their economic, social and cultural development, and that its denial constitutes a grave violation of human rights;

13. *Stress* that the right to self-determination is applicable to peoples under alien or colonial domination and foreign occupation, and should not be used to undermine the territorial integrity, national sovereignty and political independence of States;

14. *Express concern* over all forms of violation of human rights, including manifestations of racial discrimination, racism, apartheid, colonialism, foreign aggression and occupation, and the establishment of illegal settlements in occupied territories, as well as the recent resurgence of neo-nazism, xenophobia and ethnic cleansing;

15. *Underline* the need for taking effective international measures in order to guarantee and monitor the implementation of human rights standards and effective and legal protection of people under foreign occupation;

16. *Strongly affirm* their support for the legitimate struggle of the Palestinian people to restore their national and inalienable rights to self-determination and independence, and demand an immediate end to the grave violations of human rights in the Palestinian, Syrian Golan and other occupied Arab territories including Jerusalem;

17. *Reaffirm* the right to development, as established in the Declaration on the Right to Development, as a universal and inalienable right and an integral part of fundamental human rights, which must be realized through international cooperation, respect for fundamental human rights, the establishment of a monitoring mechanism and the creation of essential international conditions for the realization of such right;

18. *Recognize* that the main obstacles to the realization of the right to development lie at the international macroeconomic level, as

reflected in the widening gap between the North and the South, the rich and the poor;

19. *Affirm* that poverty is one of the major obstacles hindering the full enjoyment of human rights;

20. *Affirm also* the need to develop the right of humankind regarding a clean, safe and healthy environment;

21. *Note* that terrorism, in all its forms and manifestations, as distinguished from the legitimate struggle of peoples under colonial or alien domination and foreign occupation, has emerged as one of the most dangerous threats to the enjoyment of human rights and democracy, threatening the territorial integrity and security of States and destabilizing legitimately constituted governments, and that it must be unequivocally condemned by the international community;

22. *Reaffirm* their strong commitment to the promotion and protection of the rights of women through the guarantee of equal participation in the political, social, economic and cultural concerns of society, and the eradication of all forms of discrimination and of gender-based violence against women;

23. *Recognize* the rights of the child to enjoy special protection and to be afforded the opportunities and facilities to develop physically, mentally, morally, spiritually and socially in a healthy and normal manner and in conditions of freedom and dignity;

24. *Welcome* the important role played by national institutions in the genuine and constructive promotion of human rights, and believe that the conceptualization and eventual establishment of such institutions are best left for the States to decide;

25. *Acknowledge* the importance of cooperation and dialogue between governments and non-governmental organizations on the basis of shared values as well as mutual respect and understanding in the promotion of human rights, and encourage the non-governmental organizations in consultative status with the Economic and Social Council to contribute positively to this process in accordance with Council resolution 1296 (XLIV);

26. *Reiterate* the need to explore the possibilities of establishing regional arrangements for the promotion and protection of human rights in Asia;

27. *Reiterate further* the need to explore ways to generate international cooperation and financial support for education and training in the field of human rights at the national level and for the establishment

of national infrastructures to promote and protect human rights if requested by States;

28. *Emphasize* the necessity to rationalize the United Nations human rights mechanism in order to enhance its effectiveness and efficiency and the need to ensure avoidance of the duplication of work that exists between the treaty bodies, the Sub-Commission on Prevention of Discrimination and Protection of Minorities and the Commission on Human Rights, as well as the need to avoid the multiplicity of parallel mechanisms;

29. *Stress* the importance of strengthening the United Nations Centre for Human Rights with the necessary resources to enable it to provide a wide range of advisory services and technical assistance programmes in the promotion of human rights to requesting States in a timely and effective manner, as well as to enable it to finance adequately other activities in the field of human rights authorized by competent bodies;

30. *Call for* increased representation of the developing countries in the Centre for Human Rights.

Source: Representatives of Asian States, Vienna World Conference on Human Rights. "The Bangkok Declaration." 1993. Available online. URL: http://law.hku.hk/lawgovtsociety/Bangkok%20Declaration.htm. Accessed January 11, 2010.

"Charter 08" (2008) (Excerpt)

Inspired by Charter 77, in which more than 200 Czech and Slovak intellectuals convened in 1977 in Czechoslovakia to work toward respect for human and civil rights, Charter 08 calls for an end to China's authoritarian governmental rule and the ushering in of a more transparent and inclusive democratic system. Charter 08 was signed by more than 2,000 Chinese citizens, ranging from dissidents and opponents of the Chinese government, to those within the government. Chinese government officials responded by detaining several of the charter's drafters. Two days before the charter was announced, 20 police officers entered the home of Zhang Zuhua, one of the primary drafters, and confiscated books, notebooks, Zhang's passport, and all of the computers in the household. Later, Zhang found that his family's bank accounts (even those of his wife's parents) had been emptied.

On the same day that Zhang's house was ransacked by police officers, China's most prominent dissident and literary critic, Liu Xiaobo, was taken into police custody. He was later indicted on charges of "incitement to subvert state power." In December 2009, Liu was sentenced to 11 years in prison. Human rights organizations around the world, including several Nobel Peace Prize winners and several prominent writers associated with PEN, have called for the Chinese president Hu Jintao to release Liu.

II. OUR FUNDAMENTAL CONCEPTS

At this historical juncture of the future destiny of China, it is necessary to rethink the last 100 years of modernization and reaffirm the following concepts:

Freedom: Freedom is at the core of universal values. The rights of speech, publication, belief, assembly, association, movement, and to demonstrate are all the concrete realizations of freedom. If freedom is not flourishing, then there is no modern civilization of which to speak.

Human Rights: Human rights are not bestowed by the state, but are rights that each person is born with and enjoys. To ensure/guarantee human rights must be the foundation of the first objective of government and lawful public authority, and is also the inherent demand of "putting people first." The past political calamities of China are all closely related to the disregard of human rights by the ruling authorities.

Equality: Each individual, regardless of social status, occupation, gender, economic situation, ethnic group, skin color, religion, or political belief, is equal in human dignity and freedom. The principle of equality before the law and a citizen's society must be implemented; the principle of equality of economic, cultural, and political rights must be implemented.

Republicanism: Republicanism is "governing together; living peacefully together," that is, the decentralization of power and balancing of interests, that is comprised of diverse interests, different social groups, pluralistic culture and groups seeking religious belief, on the foundation of equal participation, peaceful competition, public discussion, and peaceful handling of public affairs.

Democracy: The most basic meaning is that sovereignty resides in the people and the people elect government. Democracy has the following basic characteristics: (1) the legitimacy of government comes from the people, the source of government power is the people; (2) government must be chosen by the people; (3) citizens enjoy the right to vote, important civil servants and officials of all levels should be produced through elections at fixed times; (4) the decisions of the majority must be respected while protecting the basic rights of the minority. In a word, democracy will become the modern tool for making government one "from the people, by the people, and for the people."

Constitutionalism: Constitutionalism is the principle of protecting basic constitutionally-guaranteed freedoms and rights of citizens through law and a rule of law, delimiting the boundaries of government power and actions, and providing corresponding systemic capacity.

In China, the era of imperial power has long passed and will not return; in the world, authoritarian systems are approaching the dusk of their endings. The only fundamental way out for China: citizens should become the true masters of the nation, throw off the consciousness of reliance on a wise ruler or honest and upright official, make widely public civic consciousness of the centrality of rights and the responsibility of participation, and practice freedom, democracy, and respect for law.

III. OUR BASIC STANDPOINT

In line with a responsible and constructive citizens' spirit towards the country's political system, civil rights and various aspects of social development, we put forward the following specific standpoints:

1. **Amend the Constitution:** Based on the aforementioned values and concepts, amend the Constitution, abolishing the provisions in the current Constitution that are not in conformity with the principle that sovereignty resides in the people so that the Constitution can truly become a document for guaranteeing human rights and [appropriate use of] public power. The Constitution should be the implementable supreme law that any individual, group or party shall not violate, and lay the legal foundation for the democratization of China.

2. **Separation and balance of power:** A modern government that separates, checks and keeps balance among powers guarantees the separation of legislative, judicial, and administrative power. The principle of governing by laws and being a responsible Government shall be established. Over-expansion of executive power shall be prevented; the Government shall be responsible to the taxpayers; the separation, checking and keeping balance of powers between the central and

local governments shall be set up; the central power authority shall be clearly defined and mandated by the Constitution, and the local governments shall be fully autonomous.

3. **Democratize the lawmaking process:** All levels of the legislative bodies shall be directly elected. Maintain the principles of fairness and justice in making law, and democratize the lawmaking process.

4. **Independence of the judiciary:** The judiciary shall be nonpartisan, free from any interference. Ensure judicial independence, and guarantee judicial fairness. Establish a Constitutional Court and a system of judicial review; maintain the authority of the Constitution. Abolish as soon as possible the Party's Committees of Political and Legislative affairs at all levels that seriously endanger the country's rule of law. Avoid using public tools for private objectives.

5. **Public institutions should be used for the public:** Realize the nationalization of the armed forces. The military shall be loyal to the Constitution and to the country. The political party organizations in the armed forces should be withdrawn. The level of military professionalism should be raised. All civil servants including the police shall remain politically neutral. Discrimination in employment of civil servants based on party preference should be eliminated and equal employment without any party preference should be adopted.

6. **Protect human rights:** Protection of human rights should be effectively implemented and human dignity should be safeguarded. A Commission on Human Rights shall be established that is responsible to the highest level of authority representing public opinion. [This Commission] will prevent government abuse of public power and violation of human rights, and especially protect the personal freedom of citizens. All persons should be free from unlawful arrest, detention, summons, interrogation, and punishment. The system of Reeducation-Through-Labor should be abolished.

7. **Election of public officials:** The democratic electoral system should be fully implemented, with the realization of the equal voting right of one person one vote. Direct election of all levels of administrative heads should be institutionalized step by step. Free competition in the elections on a regular basis and citizen participation in the election of public officials are inalienable basic human rights.

8. **Urban and rural equality:** The current urban-rural household registration system should be repealed. The equal rights for all citizens

guaranteed by the Constitution should be implemented. The freedom of movement for citizens should be protected.

9. **Freedom of association:** Citizens' right to freedom of association shall be safeguarded. The current system for registration and examination before approval for civil society organizations should be changed to a registration and recording system. The ban on freely organizing political parties should be lifted. All activities of parties should be regulated by the Constitution and law. One-party monopolization of ruling privileges should be abolished. The principle of freedom of activities of political parties and fair competition should be established. The normalization of party politics and a rule by law should be realized.

10. **Freedom of assembly:** Peaceful assembly, protest, demonstration and freedom of expression are fundamental rights guaranteed by the Constitution. They should not be subject to unlawful interference and unconstitutional restrictions by the ruling party and the government.

11. **Freedom of expression:** The freedom of speech, freedom of the press and academic freedom should be implemented. Citizens' right to know and to monitor supervise should be protected. A press and publication law should be promulgated. The ban on freely publishing newspapers should be lifted. The current provision of "inciting subversion of state power" in the Criminal Law should be repealed and criminal punishment for speech should be eliminated.

12. **Freedom of religion:** Freedom of religion and freedom of belief should be protected. Religion and politics should be separated. Religious activities should be free from government interference. All administrative regulations, administrative rules and local regulations and rules that restrict or deprive citizens' freedom of religion should be reviewed and repealed. Management of religious activities by administrative legislature should be prohibited. The current prior approval system in which religious groups (including places of worship) must be registered before obtaining legal status should be abolished, and instead, a new record-keeping system for religious groups and their worship places should replace the current one.

13. **Citizen Education:** Abolish political education and examinations that are deeply ideological and serve one-party rule. Promote citizen education that encompasses universal values and civil rights, establishes civil consciousness, and promotes the civil virtue of serving society.

14. **Property Protection:** Establish and protect private property rights, implement a free and open market economy, protect the freedom of entrepreneurship, and eliminate administrative monopoly; set up a state-owned property management committee that is responsible to the highest legislative agency, initiate property rights reforms legally and orderly, make clear the property rights of owners and obligors, initiate a new land movement, advance land privatization, and strictly protect citizens', in particular, farmers', land rights.

15. **Fiscal Reforms:** Firmly establish democracy in finance and protect taxpayers' rights. Build a public finance system and operational mechanisms in which powers and obligations are clear, and create a reasonable and effective division of power in finance among all levels of government; implement major reforms in the tax system to reduce the tax rate, simplify the tax system, and achieve tax equity. The administrative departments should not be allowed to increase tax or create new tax arbitrarily without a social public choice and resolutions of the legislative agencies. Pass reforms on property rights, introduce diverse market subjects and competition mechanisms, lower the market-entry threshold in banking, and create conditions for the development of privately-owned banking to energize the financial system.

16. **Social Security:** Build a social security system that covers all of the citizens, and provide them with fundamental protections for education, medical care, elderly care and employment.

17. **Environmental Protection:** Protect the ecological environment, promote sustainable development, and take up responsibility to future generations and humanity; enforce the respective responsibilities of the state and government officials of all levels; perform the function of participation and supervision by civil organizations on environmental protection.

18. **Federal Republic:** Participate in and maintain regional peace and development with an equal and fair attitude, and create an image of a responsible great country. Protect the free systems of Hong Kong and Macao. Under the precondition of freedom and democracy, seek a settlement resolution on cross-strait relations by way of equal negotiation and cooperative interaction. Explore possible ways and an institutional design to promote the mutual prospects of all ethnicities with great wisdom, and to establish China's federal republic under the structure of democracy and constitutionalism.

19. **Transitional Justice:** Rehabilitate the reputation of and give state compensation to the victims who suffered political persecution

during past political movements as well as their families; release all political prisoners, prisoners of conscience, and people who are convicted because of their beliefs; establish a truth commission to restore historical truth, to pursue accountability and to fulfill justice; seek a settlement of the society on this foundation.

Source: Various. "Charter 08." 2008. Human Rights in China (HRIC). Available online. URL: http://www.hrichina. org/public/contents/press?revision_id=85750&item_id=85717. Accessed January 11, 2010.

Mary Dejevsky, "Tiananmen Square Remembered: An Eye-Witness Account" (2009) (Excerpts)

June 2009 marked the 20th anniversary of the Tiananmen Square Massacre, which the journalist Mary Dejevsky witnessed as a foreign correspondent in Beijing. The following is an account in Dejevsky's own words about the city's political climate shortly before the massacre, the events of the military attack on the students, and Chinese politics since the massacre. Dejevsky also includes her personal views on the events at Tiananmen Square—namely that the uprising itself was disorganized and doomed to ineffectuality from the beginning, which is why the government should not have considered the uprising a threat in the first place. According to Dejevsky, the government's rash overreaction points to the fundamental weakness of the Chinese government in 1989.

The Beijing I had landed in could not have been more different from the one I had left only a couple of days before. Saturday afternoon had been sunny, cheerful and joyously anarchic. The vast expanse of Tiananmen Square thronged with activity, as it had done for a good month. Here was an alternative city, of tent-houses, tent-cafes, tent-streets. At one time there had been informal first-aid stations where hunger-strikers, with their white head-bands, were ministered to by concerned fellow-students. There was spontaneous music-making and earnest philosophising. Tannoys relayed the fierce oratory of youthful idealism; rival quotations from Mao Zedong and Deng Xiaoping were parsed for hidden meaning.

On my return, the weather was dismal; and the closer to the city outskirts we came, the more agitated my taxi driver grew. The whole of the centre was out of bounds, barricaded by troops; tanks and armoured personnel carriers guarded bridges and intersections. Elsewhere all was emptiness and quiet, where bustle, noise and life had been before.

. . .

International Documents

In the foreign community that evening there was near-panic. Those relatively unfazed by the military assault had their resolve shattered when troops fired, apparently in error, and glanced one of their residential compounds. The mass exodus to the airport I had seen was the response. And the sense of menace was reinforced by ghosts crowding in from the past. Westerners and their "decadence" had been targeted during Mao Zedong's Cultural Revolution in the 1960s. But it was knowledge of the violent Boxer uprising of 1898–1901 against foreign ownership and influence that cast the longer shadow. The market reforms instituted by Deng Xiaoping, were still at an early stage; they had brought not only higher living standards, but resentment, too—resentment that a paranoid regime could be tempted to divert on to foreigners.

The authorities had no need to extend their crackdown. The regime had planned its assault, applied massive force, and annihilated this challenge to its rule in a matter of hours. In so doing, it effectively eradicated open dissent for at least a generation.

With the benefit of hindsight, it is easy to conclude that the student protests of 20 years ago were doomed; easy, too, to chart how the movement progressively sowed the seeds of its own downfall. Its young leaders were arrogant, increasingly demagogic, and poorly organised. Their calls for democracy in China were not only unrealistic, but in many ways derivative and naïve. It is remarkable that the protest grew to the point where it was seen as a serious threat to Communist Party rule.

That it did so reflects an extraordinary, and completely unforeseeable convergence of circumstances: historical precedents that spooked the authorities; weak leadership at the top of the Chinese Communist Party and government, and a series of unrelated events that no contingency planners could ever have foreseen.

The protests began with the death in April that year of Hu Yaobang, a former head of the Chinese Communist Party who had been purged from the leadership as too reform-minded—the very trait which earned him a following among students and intellectuals. After his death, more than 50,000 mainly young people marched to Tiananmen Square in his memory, to protest at what they saw as the disgracefully low-key funeral organised by the state.

Demonstrations continued into May, when they merged with ceremonies to mark the 70th anniversary of the May Fourth Movement—an expression of intellectual discontent that swept China as students returned from Europe at the end of the First World War. From that anniversary, it was a mere matter of days before the Soviet President, Mikhail Gorbachev, was due for a full state visit to China.

This was no routine visit. For Gorbachev and his reformist allies in the Soviet leadership, it was intended to consolidate his uncertain authority at home, while also marking the reconciliation of international communism after the Sino-Soviet split of the early 1970s. That was the significance of the visit at state and party level.

But China's rebellious students sensed that there was an opportunity for them, too. Gorbachev was presiding over an unprecedented thaw in political, intellectual and economic life in the Soviet Union. Non-communists were being encouraged to participate in state bodies, and censorship was in retreat. Many of the students who had flocked to Hu Yaobang's funeral and then celebrated the May Fourth Movement declared a hunger strike and vowed to stay in Tiananmen Square until the Communist Party granted political reforms. They hailed Gorbachev as their ally.

The Soviet President received an ecstatic reception; on the second day of Gorbachev's visit, 1 million people massed in Tiananmen Square. The Chinese authorities understood that the enthusiasm on the streets for Gorbachev was simultaneously a protest against them and whole cities were paralysed. But they could do nothing about it without risking even greater disorder, even bloodshed, in the presence of a foreign leader. They held back. And in so doing, they exposed a truth common to every revolution. At some undefined point, fear had changed sides.

Ridiculing all official appeals to leave the streets, student activists were dispatching envoys across the country, fomenting protests in universities and trying to muster support for their cause in factories and farms. Their efforts to recruit workers and peasants to their revolution were not especially successful, but as police left their posts in Beijing to join the marchers, red signals were routinely ignored, and groups of euphoric students on flatbed trucks took over the capital's streets by night, the spectre was raised of a breakdown of all law and order.

Such fears were not irrational. Beijing with no police or public transport and as many as 2 million people milling, unmarshalled, on the streets was a frightening and at times intimidating place to be. But, as contradictory editorials appeared in official newspapers, it was apparent that the regime was as paralysed as the country's major cities.

With Gorbachev gone, Prime Minister Li Peng acted. After failing to agree any compromise with the student leaders, Li declared martial law. It was the evening of 19 May. The protesters on Tiananmen Square had been alerted by loudspeaker to stand by for a special announcement. Li's declaration was relayed across the silent encampment.

The tension was palpable, and followed by confusion among the students about what to do; but the confusion was not only theirs. Around midnight, the Communist Party leader, Zhao Ziyang, came into the square in person with the offer of a last-minute compromise. His intervention failed; the protest continued. He did not appear in public again; three weeks later he was removed.

It might have been expected that the imposition of martial law in a country with a monopoly party in power would be instantaneous and definite. At the outset, though, it seemed half-hearted; the dawn to dusk curfew was enforced patchily. Few troops were initially to be seen, though reports of night-time advances into the city outskirts multiplied. Residents constructed elaborate barricades to impede the advance.

The Tiananmen Square camp thinned out, but remained stubbornly, squalidly, in place. As the days passed, it was noticeable how much more khaki there was about town; khaki jeeps, khaki uniforms, groups of khaki clad officers in restaurants. But nothing actually happened.

Then early one morning, I opened the curtains of my room to see scores of pitifully young soldiers encamped on the grass verge of the dual carriageway below. They had backpacks, but appeared unarmed. Half an hour later they were picked up in fleets of buses and gone. As late as the afternoon before the night-time assault, martial law had an unreal, ephemeral character. The thundering tank assault on Tiananmen Square shattered that consoling illusion.

To this day there is still no accepted death toll. The Chinese authorities insist that fewer than 250 people died; others cite figures into several thousand. Certainly, some—perhaps many—escaped, including the two charismatic student leaders, Wang Dan and Chai Ling, who were smuggled out of the country. An unknown number may also have fled into the protection of friends and family, picking up their pre-rebel lives where they left off. Tiananmen Square was written out of China's official history as soon as it happened, the numbers are in such doubt not only because the dead cannot speak, but because the living are still reluctant to admit they were there.

Twenty years on, a whole generation of Chinese has watched the country be changed—and changed radically—from the top down, while still waiting for the chance to influence politics from the bottom up. Nor were the international consequences of Tiananmen Square long-lasting. The Western world's cold shoulder and the upsurge of resistance in Hong Kong to being reincorporated into China had little effect. Like it or not, China's potential economic might handed its rulers a free moral pass, and still does.

It's not uncommon now to hear Tiananmen Square described as an "incident." Perhaps that is how this military assault by a frightened one-party regime on its rising intellectual elite is slipping into history. But this is a travesty. To belittle what happened at Tiananmen Square is to ignore something everyone needs to know about China.

HUMAN RIGHTS

Consortium, "Letter from the Consortium for Liu Xiaobo to NPC Chairman Wu Bangguo" (2010)

In March 2010, more than 100 prominent writers, human rights activists, and scholars signed a letter calling for the release of the literary critic Liu Xiaobo, who was sentenced to 11 years in prison in December 2009 for subversion of state power. Liu was one of the primary drafters and signatories of Charter 08, and he has since received the 2010 Nobel Peace Prize. The letter calling for Liu's release condemns the Chinese government's actions and emphasizes the right to freedom of expression as it is guaranteed by the Chinese constitution and international law. The letter was signed by a number of prominent individuals from around the world, including the South African Nobel laureate in literature Nadine Gordimer, the executive director of Human Rights Watch Kenneth Roth, and the award-winning author Salman Rushdie.

Dear Chairman Wu Bangguo,

Dear Deputies to the National People's Congress,

We, the undersigned scholars, writers, lawyers, and human rights advocates, write to ask you to intervene to protect literary critic and former professor Liu Xiaobo who was sentenced to 11 years in prison on December 25, 2009, for "incitement to subvert state power and overthrow the socialist system" (Article 105 of the Criminal Law of the People's Republic of China).

Liu's "crime" was writing and circulating six articles on the internet which criticized communist party rule and "colluding with others to draft and concoct 'Charter 08,'" a petition calling for greater respect for the rule of law and human rights in China. Charter 08 was released on December 10, 2008, a date celebrated worldwide as Human Rights Day. Dr. Liu was arrested two days earlier.

We believe that Dr. Liu was arrested solely for exercising his right to freedom of expression, as guaranteed under China's constitution and by international law. We believe further that the crime of incitement to subvert state power as currently defined in Chinese law violates international human rights standards.

Dr. Liu's activities have always been peaceful and in accordance with the law. In recent years, his reputation has grown as his essays on current affairs in China and his principled defense of human rights and democracy circulated widely. Dr. Liu has consistently opposed recourse to violence. In his articles, he has lauded amendments to the Chinese constitution that stipulate respect for human rights and property rights. He has written strongly in favor of the development of a free civil society in China.

230

The National People's Congress is the highest organ of state power of the People's Republic of China. It supervises enforcement of the constitution (Article 62). Therefore, it is your duty as delegates to ensure that the basic rights of the Chinese citizens that you represent are guaranteed. By pressing for the release of Dr. Liu you will honor yourselves and demonstrate that China is serious about its intention to achieve a rule of law.

For the international community to take seriously China's oft-stated commitment to respect human rights and the rule of law, and for China's own citizens to trust the judicial system to redress legitimate grievances, it is urgent that China's National People's Congress ensure that no one is sent to prison simply for the peaceful expression of his or her views.

It is equally urgent that judicial authorities throughout China cease to use China's anti-subversion law to prosecute peaceful critics such as Dr. Liu. He should be released immediately without conditions.

Source: Human Rights Watch. "Letter From the Consortium for Liu Xiaobo to NPC Chairman Wu Bangguo." March 9, 2010. Available online. URL: http://www.hrw.org/en/news/2010/03/09/letter-consortium-liu-xiaobo-npc-chairman-wu-bangguo. Accessed July 24, 2010.

CHECHNYA

Council of Europe, Convention for the Protection of Human Rights and Fundamental Freedoms (1950) (Excerpt)

The Convention for the Protection of Human Rights and Fundamental Free-doms, also known informally as the European Convention on Human Rights, was drafted in 1950 by the Council of Europe, and all Council of Europe member states are party to the convention. The convention founded the European Court of Human Rights, an international body that hears complaints from individuals whose rights have been violated by their own governments, or even foreign governments. In recent years, several cases have been brought by individual Chechens against the Russian government for damages they suffered during Russia's counterterrorist campaign in Chechnya.

Unlike other human rights documents, the convention is unique for its protocols, which member states may or may not accept. For example, Protocol 6 restricts the death penalty, while Protocol 13 prohibits the death penalty altogether. All of the Council of Europe members have signed and ratified Protocol 6 except for Russia, which has signed but not yet ratified the protocol.

The Governments signatory hereto, being Members of the Council of Europe,

HUMAN RIGHTS

Considering the Universal Declaration of Human Rights proclaimed by the General Assembly of the United Nations on 10 December 1948;

Considering that this Declaration aims at securing the universal and effective recognition and observance of the Rights therein declared;

Considering that the aim of the Council of Europe is the achievement of greater unity between its Members and that one of the methods by which the aim is to be pursued is the maintenance and further realization of Human Rights and Fundamental Freedoms;

Reaffirming their profound belief in those Fundamental Freedoms which are the foundation of justice and peace in the world and are best maintained on the one hand by an effective political democracy and on the other by a common understanding and observance of the Human Rights upon which they depend;

Being resolved, as the Governments of European countries which are like-minded and have a common heritage of political traditions, ideals, freedom and the rule of law to take the first steps for the collective enforcement of certain of the Rights stated in the Universal Declaration;

Have agreed as follows:

Article 1

The High Contracting Parties shall secure to everyone within their jurisdiction the rights and freedoms defined in Section I of this Convention.

SECTION I

Article 2

1. Everyone's right to life shall be protected by law. No one shall be deprived of his life intentionally save in the execution of a sentence of a court following his conviction of a crime for which this penalty is provided by law.
2. Deprivation of life shall not be regarded as inflicted in contravention of this article when it results from the use of force which is no more than absolutely necessary:
   (a) in defence of any person from unlawful violence;
   (b) in order to effect a lawful arrest or to prevent escape of a person lawfully detained;

(c) in action lawfully taken for the purpose of quelling a riot or insurrection.

Article 3

No one shall be subjected to torture or to inhuman or degrading treatment or punishment.

Article 4

1. No one shall be held in slavery or servitude.
2. No one shall be required to perform forced or compulsory labour.
3. For the purpose of this article the term forced or compulsory labour' shall not include:
   (a) any work required to be done in the ordinary course of detention imposed according to the provisions of Article 5 of this Convention or during conditional release from such detention;
   (b) any service of a military character or, in case of conscientious objectors in countries where they are recognized, service exacted instead of compulsory military service;
   (c) any service exacted in case of an emergency or calamity threatening the life or well-being of the community;
   (d) any work or service which forms part of normal civic obligations.

Article 5

1. Everyone has the right to liberty and security of person.

   No one shall be deprived of his liberty save in the following cases and in accordance with a procedure prescribed by law:
   (a) the lawful detention of a person after conviction by a competent court;
   (b) the lawful arrest or detention of a person for non-compliance with the lawful order of a court or in order to secure the fulfillment of any obligation prescribed by law;
   (c) the lawful arrest or detention of a person effected for the purpose of bringing him before the competent legal authority of reasonable suspicion of having committed and offence or when it is reasonably considered necessary to prevent his committing an offence or fleeing after having done so;
   (d) the detention of a minor by lawful order for the purpose of educational supervision or his lawful detention for the purpose of bringing him before the competent legal authority;

(e) the lawful detention of persons for the prevention of the spreading of infectious diseases, of persons of unsound mind, alcoholics or drug addicts, or vagrants;

(f) the lawful arrest or detention of a person to prevent his effecting an unauthorized entry into the country or of a person against whom action is being taken with a view to deportation or extradition.

2. Everyone who is arrested shall be informed promptly, in a language which he understands, of the reasons for his arrest and the charge against him.

3. Everyone arrested or detained in accordance with the provisions of paragraph 1(c) of this article shall be brought promptly before a judge or other officer authorized by law to exercise judicial power and shall be entitled to trial within a reasonable time or to release pending trial. Release may be conditioned by guarantees to appear for trial.

4. Everyone who is deprived of his liberty by arrest or detention shall be entitled to take proceedings by which the lawfulness of his detention shall be decided speedily by a court and his release ordered if the detention is not lawful.

5. Everyone who has been the victim of arrest or detention in contravention of the provisions of this article shall have an enforceable right to compensation.

Article 6

1. In the determination of his civil rights and obligations or of any criminal charge against him, everyone is entitled to a fair and public hearing within a reasonable time by an independent and impartial tribunal established by law. Judgment shall be pronounced publicly by the press and public may be excluded from all or part of the trial in the interest of morals, public order or national security in a democratic society, where the interests of juveniles or the protection of the private life of the parties so require, or the extent strictly necessary in the opinion of the court in special circumstances where publicity would prejudice the interests of justice.

2. Everyone charged with a criminal offence shall be presumed innocent until proved guilty according to law.

3. Everyone charged with a criminal offence has the following minimum rights:

(a) to be informed promptly, in a language which he understands and in detail, of the nature and cause of the accusation against him;

(b) to have adequate time and the facilities for the preparation of his defence;

(c) to defend himself in person or through legal assistance of his own choosing or, if he has not sufficient means to pay for legal assistance, to be given it free when the interests of justice so require;

(d) to examine or have examined witnesses against him and to obtain the attendance and examination of witnesses on his behalf under the same conditions as witnesses against him;

(e) to have the free assistance of an interpreter if he cannot understand or speak the language used in court.

Article 7

1. No one shall be held guilty of any criminal offence on account of any act or omission which did not constitute a criminal offence under national or international law at the time when it was committed. Nor shall a heavier penalty be imposed than the one that was applicable at the time the criminal offence was committed.

2. This article shall not prejudice the trial and punishment of any person for any act or omission which, at the time when it was committed, was criminal according the general principles of law recognized by civilized nations.

Article 8

1. Everyone has the right to respect for his private and family life, his home and his correspondence.

2. There shall be no interference by a public authority with the exercise of this right except such as is in accordance with the law and is necessary in a democratic society in the interests of national security, public safety or the economic well-being of the country, for the prevention of disorder or crime, for the protection of health or morals, or for the protection of the rights and freedoms of others.

Article 9

1. Everyone has the right to freedom of thought, conscience and religion; this right includes freedom to change his religion or belief, and freedom, either alone or in community with others and in public or private, to manifest his religion or belief, in worship, teaching, practice and observance.

2. Freedom to manifest one's religion or beliefs shall be subject only to such limitations as are prescribed by law and are necessary in a democratic society in the interests of public safety, for the protection of public order, health or morals, or the protection of the rights and freedoms of others.

Article 10

1. Everyone has the right to freedom of expression. This right shall include freedom to hold opinions and to receive and impart information and ideas without interference by public authority and regardless of frontiers. This article shall not prevent States from requiring the licensing of broadcasting, television or cinema enterprises.

2. The exercise of these freedoms, since it carries with it duties and responsibilities, may be subject to such formalities, conditions, restrictions or penalties as are prescribed by law and are necessary in a democratic society, in the interests of national security, territorial integrity or public safety, for the prevention of disorder or crime, for the protection of health or morals, for the protection of the reputation or the rights of others, for preventing the disclosure of information received in confidence, or for maintaining the authority and impartiality of the judiciary.

Article 11

1. Everyone has the right to freedom of peaceful assembly and to freedom of association with others, including the right to form and to join trade unions for the protection of his interests.

2. No restrictions shall be placed on the exercise of these rights other than such as are prescribed by law and are necessary in a democratic society in the interests of national security or public safety, for the prevention of disorder or crime, for the protection of health or morals or for the protection of the rights and freedoms of others. This article shall not prevent the imposition of lawful restrictions on the exercise of these rights by members of the armed forces, of the police or of the administration of the State.

Article 12

Men and women of marriageable age have the right to marry and to found a family, according to the national laws governing the exercise of this right.

Article 13

Everyone whose rights and freedoms as set forth in this Convention are violated shall have an effective remedy before a national authority notwithstanding that the violation has been committed by persons acting in an official capacity.

Article 14

The enjoyment of the rights and freedoms set forth in this Convention shall be secured without discrimination on any ground such as sex, race, colour, language, religion, political or other opinion, national or social origin, association with a national minority, property, birth or other status.

Article 15

1. In time of war or other public emergency threatening the life of the nation any High Contracting Party may take measures derogating from its obligations under this Convention to the extent strictly required by the exigencies of the situation, provided that such measures are not inconsistent with its other obligations under international law.
2. No derogation from Article 2, except in respect of deaths resulting from lawful acts of war, or from Articles 3, 4 (paragraph 1) and 7 shall be made under this provision.
3. Any High Contracting Party availing itself of this right of derogation shall keep the Secretary-General of the Council of Europe fully informed of the measures which it has taken and the reasons therefore. It shall also inform the Secretary-General of the Council of Europe when such measures have ceased to operate and the provisions of the Convention are again being fully executed.

Article 16

Nothing in Articles 10, 11, and 14 shall be regarded as preventing the High Contracting Parties from imposing restrictions on the political activity of aliens.

Article 17

Nothing in this Convention may be interpreted as implying for any State, group or person any right to engage in any activity or perform any act aimed at the destruction on any of the rights and freedoms set forth herein or at their limitation to a greater extent than is provided for in the Convention.

Article 18

The restrictions permitted under this Convention to the said rights and freedoms shall not be applied for any purpose other than those for which they have been prescribed.

Source: Council of Europe. "The European Convention on Human Rights." 1950. Hellenic Resources Institute. Available online. URL: http://www.hri.org/docs/ECHR50.html. Accessed January 13, 2010.

BBC News, "School Siege: Eyewitness Accounts" (2006)

On September 1, 2004, 32 Chechen and Ingush rebels stormed a school in Beslan, Chechnya, and took more than 1,000 people hostage in the school gym, which they wired with homemade explosives. The group acted under the direction of the Chechen warlord Shamil Basayev, and upon taking the school hostage, the gunmen issued a demand to Russian authorities to end their military activity in Chechnya. Russian troops surrounded the school and fought a bloody battle with the Chechen rebels, using grenades and other explosives. The shoot-out lasted for three days, and 331 children and adults were killed in the siege. Only one of the Chechen gunmen survived and was sentenced to life in prison in a Russian court. But during the trial, the version of events presented by the Russian government conflicted with eyewitness accounts, including some claims that there were more than 32 gunmen and that several escaped. Furthermore, the Russian military claims that the shoot-out began when the Chechens' explosives went off in the school, but physical evidence from the scene as well as accounts from the hostages contradict this claim. One weapons and explosives expert found that the explosions that initiated the gun battle did not, in fact, come from the rebels' homemade explosives, but came from the outside, which also correlates with many eyewitness accounts claiming that the first explosions did not come from the rebels' explosives. The following accounts come from students, parents, Russian soldiers, and civilians who aided in the rescue.

Unnamed officer in special unit of Federal Security Service (FSB) in Russia TV interview

"We heard a powerful explosion, and the snipers who had been posted to keep an eye on things said the gym had blown up. Shooting began straight away . . .

"The hostages started running in our direction . . . We could hear the characteristic crack of bullets over our heads—they were firing from the direction of the school . . .

"I saw children with gunshot wounds being dragged. There were about 12 children who started running out. About four of our lads immediately, without waiting for orders, formed a human shield, and kept the windows [of the school] in their sights . . .

"All the entrances were barricaded from inside with desks, chairs and all sorts of rubbish they could gather . . . So we had to go in through the canteen window.

"When we went in, we had nowhere to tread on the floor—there were too many hostages, women and children . . .

"A gunman sprang out from a small utility room—it was a dead end, so he tried to break out. He shot one of our men at point-blank range and immediately threw a powerful grenade among the hostages. He was immediately killed by another of our men, who was injured by the fragments of that same grenade. It also killed several hostages.

"There was a dark corridor in front of us, and they were firing from there all the time. We stood a bit to the side, so as not to be hit. I shouted, 'Throw a grenade in there!' but the lads said, 'How can we? There are children in there!'" . . .

"There were so many grenades being thrown at us, so much firing—what could we do, with all the children there? We could not throw grenades there or do anything. So that's how it was."

Marina Kozyreva, mother of schoolgirl Diana, spent the whole time in the school gym and was later interviewed by Kommersant newspaper
"Throughout the three days that we were held hostage we were virtually on top of each other. There were about 1,100 of us crammed in there.

"Periodically gunmen came in and for a joke ordered all of us to stand up or sit down. It went on like that all day long. They put a huge explosive device in the middle—about 50cm by 50cm—controlled by a trigger mechanism. One of the terrorists kept squeezing it with his foot. When they got tired they put a pile of books on the button.

"The children behaved very calmly—much more so than the adults. The adults were talking to each other and because of that the gunmen shot many of them. They were all prepared for death, especially on the second and third days, because the gunmen were saying nobody would be able to enter the school and also that people outside didn't give a damn about them. 'They don't even want to give you water or food,' they said. They said nobody had contacted them and nobody had requested anything from them.

"Sometimes they took the boys' clothes, soaked them in a bucket used for the floor mop, then threw the clothes at us, saying 'drink that!'"

Marat Khamayev, 15, also spoke to Kommersant

"Initially we were escorted to the toilet together, then they stopped doing that, and only took the little kids. All the time the explosives were hanging above us—they used adhesive tape to fix it there.

"Before the assault the bandits started arguing with each other about something. I've spent a long time in Chechnya, I know the Chechen language, and they weren't speaking Chechen—they were just speaking a strange language like Arabic, and also Ingush.

"One of the gunmen was reading the Koran constantly, and I counted exactly 23 gunmen altogether. The leader was on the roof the whole time with a sniper's rifle. We realised that, because the others went to him for advice.

"The older pupils were forced to carry desks to barricade the windows. When the assault started one of the bandits shouted, 'I'll save you'. Everybody ran towards him and then he blew himself up, killing many people.

"The whole time they never let anybody sleep—if somebody dozed off they would shake him awake again, saying 'no sleeping!' The explosion took place under the roof—there was no external explosion . . . When the assault came I pulled two girls out with me."

Diana Gadzhinova, 14-year-old girl hostage,
speaking to Izvestiya newspaper

"It took us all by surprise. We were told there would be talks and we were ordered to lie face down [in the gym] . . . Then there was an explosion in the yard. Then there was shooting . . . [My sister and I] stayed where we were, lying on the floor. But suddenly there was another explosion above us and part of the ceiling fell in. People were screaming, there was panic.

"I looked up and saw some children lying on the floor covered in blood and not moving. There was a dead lady lying beside me. Torn-off arms and legs were lying everywhere. There were bombs hanging on the rope they'd strung up between the basketball hoops, across the gym. And now these bombs began going off, one after the other, coming closer and closer to us. Anyone who could get up ran screaming to the windows and the back entrance corridor. Alina and I were near a window [both sisters managed to escape unscathed]."

Irina, girl hostage

"I woke up under the debris and all was covered in sand—my ears, nose and eyes—and I could not see anything. Then we were taken to the dining room. There we were given water, then explosions started. And then we jumped out of the window and we were taken to the hospital."

Survivor Santa Zangiyeva, 15, spoke to Izvestiya

"There was this thin tall man of about 35, a typical Chechen, his right hand bandaged. He was the angriest of our captors, he was threatening us all the time and firing into the ceiling. It was so stuffy I was unwell, I fainted several times, so my mum asked him to take me to the corridor for a while to take a breath of air. To my surprise he agreed. In the corridor I was nearly sick, my legs gave way, and sat on a rucksack lying by the wall. But he said: 'Don't sit on this one, there are mines in it, sit on that one instead' . . .

"I asked him, 'Will you at least let the children go?' He said: 'No—why? Your Russian troops in Chechnya catch children just like you and cut their heads off. I had a daughter, about your age, and they killed her,' he said."

Moskovskaya Gazeta interviewed Oleg Tideyev, whose son escaped from the besieged school

"I saw a wounded gunman fall out of the [school] window during the fighting. Militiamen were evacuating children nearby. When they saw the gunman, they tore him to bits within seconds. I did not even have time to realise what was happening. I'll be honest: not even for a second did I think—I am witnessing the killing of a human being. It felt like a venomous snake was being trampled . . .

"They were scum. Professional, well-trained scum. Their actions were highly skilful, their shooting was first-class—you could not raise your head . . . The only thing they did badly was booby-trapping the building. It was not a good idea to let the hostages assemble explosive devices."

Kommersant interviewed Anzor, a rescuer who helped in the smaller of the school's gyms

"We broke in, and saw piles of men and women, and children too. The children were naked from the waist up. There was nowhere for us to tread, but we had to go in, so we did.

"I pulled four people out. Many people were thrown to the corners by the blast, or maybe they crawled there themselves. Few were alive. We had to find those who were still alive, but how? I made two mistakes myself. When I pulled one young girl out, there was another explosion. Just before that, two girls shouted and waved to us from a window, one was about seven, the other a bit older. I waved back to show I'd come for them right now, and they laughed they were so happy! Then there was an explosion, and I never saw these girls again. I'll keep looking for them in the school . . ."

Source: BBC News. "School Siege: Eyewitness Accounts." September 7, 2004. Available online. URL: http://news. bbc.co.uk/2/hi/europe/3627406.stm. Accessed July 24, 2010.

European Court of Human Rights, "Chamber Judgments in Six Applications against Russia" (2005) (Excerpts)

The following excerpts come from the European Court of Human Rights' judgments regarding applications put forth by six individuals claiming human rights violations by Russia. All of the applicants were harmed during the Russian counterterrorist campaign in Chechnya, and the excerpts provided below focus specifically on the case of Magomed Khashiyev and Rosa Akayeva, both of whom accused the Russian government of murdering their relatives. The court found in favor of Khashiyev and Akayeva, and specifies which articles of the European Convention on Human Rights were violated.

In the case of Khashiyev and Akayeva

- by six votes to one that the Government's preliminary objection was unfounded;
- unanimously that there had been a **violation of Article 2** (right to life) of the European Convention on Human Rights in respect of the applicants' relatives' deaths;
- unanimously that there had been **a violation of Article 2** of the Convention in that the authorities had failed to carry out an adequate and effective investigation into the circumstances of the applicants' relatives' deaths;
- unanimously that there had been **no violation of Article 3** (prohibition of torture) in respect of the failure to protect the applicants' relatives from torture;
- unanimously that there had been a **violation of Article 3** in respect of the failure to carry out an adequate and effective investigation into the allegations of torture;
- by five votes to two that there had been a **violation of Article 13** (right to an effective remedy).

Under Article 41 of the Convention (just satisfaction) the Court unanimously awarded 15,000 euros (EUR) to the first applicant and EUR 20,000 to the second applicant in respect of non-pecuniary damage, and EUR 10,927 in respect of costs and expenses.

. . .

1. SUMMARY OF THE FACTS

Magomed Khashiyev and Rosa Akayeva, who were born in 1942 and 1955 respectively, were at the material time residents of Grozny, Chechnya. They complained about extra-judicial executions of their relatives by Russian Army personnel in Grozny at the end of January 2000. The bodies of Mr Khashiyev's brother and sister and two of his sister's sons and Ms Akayeva's brother were found with numerous gunshot wounds. A criminal investigation, opened in May 2000, was suspended and reopened several times, but those responsible were never identified. In 2003 a civil court in Ingushetia ordered the Ministry of Defense to pay damages to Mr Khashiyev in relation to the killing of his relatives by unidentified military personnel.

. . .

3. SUMMARY OF THE JUDGMENTS

Complaints

Mr Khashiyev and Ms Akayeva alleged that their relatives had been tortured and murdered by members of the Russian Army, that the investigation into their deaths had been ineffective and that they had had no access to effective remedies at national level. They relied on Article 2 (right to life), Article 3 (prohibition of torture and inhuman or degrading treatment) and Article 13 (right to an effective remedy) of the European Convention on Human Rights.

. . .

Decision of the Court

The Government's preliminary objection in all three cases (exhaustion of domestic remedies)

The Government submitted that Russian law provided two avenues of recourse for the victims of illegal and criminal acts attributable to the State or its agents, namely civil procedure and criminal remedies.

As regards a civil action, two possibilities had been advanced: an application to the Supreme Court or filing a complaint with other courts. However, at the date of the admissibility decisions in these three cases, no example had been produced of the Supreme Court or other courts being able, in the absence of results from the criminal investigation, to consider the merits of a claim relating to alleged serious criminal actions.

In the course of the proceedings Mr Khashiyev had brought an action before a district court. However, despite a positive outcome in the form of a financial award, without the benefit of the conclusions of a criminal investigation, this action was incapable of leading to findings as to the perpetrators of assaults or their responsibility.

The applicants had accordingly not been obliged to pursue the civil remedies, and the preliminary objection was in that respect unfounded.

As to criminal law remedies, the objection raised issues concerning the effectiveness of the criminal investigation and was joined by the Court to the merits.

Alleged violation of Article 2 of the Convention

The applicants in all three cases alleged failure on the part of the State to protect the right to life in breach of Article 2. They also submitted that the authorities had failed to carry out an effective and adequate investigation.

A. The alleged failure to protect life

The Court set out its case-law in this area and notably the following general principles. First, in assessing evidence as to the violation of Article 2, the relevant standard of proof was "beyond reasonable doubt." The Court recalled, however, that strong presumptions of fact arose in respect of injuries and death occurring during detention. In such circumstances the burden of proof lay with the authorities to provide a satisfactory and convincing explanation. It then noted that, where potentially lethal force was used in pursuit of a permitted aim, the force used had to be strictly proportionate to the achievement of that aim. Operations involving potential use of lethal force had to be planned and controlled by the authorities so as to minimise the risk to life. Authorities had to take all feasible precautions in the choice of means and methods with a view to avoiding and, in any event, minimising incidental loss of civilian life.

Case of Khashiyev and Akayeva

The Court first noted that, in reply to its request, the Government had submitted only about two-thirds of the criminal investigation file. The rest was, in the Government's view, irrelevant. It was inherent in proceedings related to cases of this nature that in certain instances solely the respondent Government had access to information capable of corroborating or refuting the applicant's allegations. A failure on the

Government's part to submit such information without a satisfactory explanation could give rise to the drawing of inferences as to the well-founded character of such allegations.

On the basis of the material in its possession the Court found it established that the applicants' relatives had been killed by military personnel. No other plausible explanation as to the circumstances of the deaths had been forthcoming, nor had any justification been relied on in respect of the use of lethal force by the State agents. There had been accordingly a violation of Article 2 of the Convention.

. . .

B. The alleged inadequacy of the investigation

The Court recalled its case-law in this area and notably the need, in cases involving state agents or bodies, to ensure their accountability for deaths occurring under their responsibility. The obligations under Article 2 could not be satisfied merely by awarding damages. The investigation had to be timely, effective and not to be dependent for its progress on the initiative of the survivors or the next of kin.

Case of Khashiyev and Akayeva

An investigation had been carried out into the killings of the applicants' relatives. However, it had been flawed by serious failures once it commenced, which it had done only after a considerable delay. In particular, the investigation did not seem to have pursued the possible involvement of a certain military unit directly mentioned by several witnesses.

The Government pointed out that the applicants could have appealed the results of the investigation. The Court was not persuaded that such appeal would have been able to remedy its defects, even if the applicants had been properly informed of the proceedings and had been involved in it. The applicants must therefore be regarded as having complied with the requirement to exhaust the relevant criminal-law remedies.

The Court accordingly found that the authorities had failed to carry out an effective criminal investigation into the circumstances surrounding the deaths of the applicants' relatives. There had therefore been a violation of Article 2 also in this respect.

. . .

Alleged violation of Article 3 of the Convention
Case of Khashiyev and Akayeva

The Court was unable to find that beyond all reasonable doubt the applicants' relatives had been subjected to treatment contrary to Article 3 of the Convention.

On the other hand, having regard to the lack of a thorough and effective investigation into credible allegations of torture, the Court held that there has been a violation of the procedural requirements of Article 3.

Source: European Court of Human Rights. "Chamber Judgments in Six Applications Against Russia." 2005. Available online. URL: http://www.echr.coe.int/Eng/Press/2005/Feb/ChamberJudgmentsChechencases2422005. htm. Accessed January 13, 2010.

IRAN

Ayatollah Ruhollah Khomeini, Speech Number Sixteen (1964)

A stalwart political dissident and highly charismatic speaker, Ayatollah Ruhollah Khomeini garnered a massive political following during his outspoken denunciation of the shah's regime. The following speech was delivered in response to the 1964 Capitulation Bill, in which the shah and the Iranian parliament granted immunity to American military personnel in Iran in exchange for a loan of $200 million. American soldiers charged with crimes in Iran would be tried in a U.S. military court. Additionally, the $200 million loan carried an interest rate of $100 million. The agreement was not made public, and media outlets were barred from publishing or broadcasting any information on the bill. Khomeini publicized and condemned the agreement in a speech that later led to his arrest and exile.

I cannot express the sorrow I feel in my heart. My heart is heavy. Since the day I heard of the latest developments affecting Iran, I have barely slept. I am profoundly disturbed. With sorrowful heart, I count the days until death shall come and deliver me (the audience weeps). Iran no longer has a festival to celebrate; they have turned our festival into mourning. They have turned it into mourning and have lit up the city; they have turned it into mourning and are dancing together with joy. They have sold us, they have sold our independence, and still they light up the city and dance.

If I were in their place, I would forbid all these lights; I would tell the people to raise black flags over the bazaars and houses, to hang black awnings.

246

International Documents

Our honour has been trampled underfoot; the dignity of Iran has been destroyed. The dignity of the Iranian army has been trampled underfoot!

They have taken a law to the Parliament according to which first of all we are to accede to the Vienna Convention, and secondly we have to add a provision that all American military advisers, together with their families, technical and administrative officials, and servants—in short, anyone in any way connected to them—are to enjoy legal immunity with respect to any crime they may commit in Iran! If some American's servant, some American's cook, assassinates your *marja'-i taqlid* in the middle of the bazaar, or runs over him, the Iranian police do not have the right to apprehend him! Iranian courts do not have the right to judge him! The dossier must be sent to America so that our masters there can decide what is to be done!

The previous government approved this measure without telling anyone, and now the present government just recently introduced a bill in the Senate and settled the whole matter in a single session without breathing a word to anyone. A few days ago, the bill was taken to the lower house of the Parliament and there were discussions, with a few deputies voicing their opposition, but the bill was passed anyhow. They passed it without any shame, and the government shamelessly defended this scandalous measure. They have reduced the Iranian people to a level lower than that of an American dog. If someone runs over a dog belonging to an American, he will be prosecuted. Even if the Shah himself were to run over a dog belonging to an American, he would be prosecuted. But if an American cook runs over the Shah, or the *marja'* of Iran, or the highest official, no one will have the right to object.

Why?

Because they wanted a loan from America and America demanded this in return! This is apparently the case. A few days after this measure was approved, they requested a $200 million loan from America and America agreed to the request. It was stipulated that the sum of $200 million would be paid to the Iranian government over a period of five years, and that $300 million would be paid back to America over a period of ten years. Do you realise what this means? In return for this loan, America is to receive $100 million—or 800 million tumans—in interest! But in addition to this, Iran has sold itself to obtain these dollars! The government has sold our independence, reduced us to the level of a colony, and made the Muslim nation of Iran appear more lowly than savages in the eyes of the world! They have done this for the sake of a $200 million dollar loan for which they have to pay back $300 dollars!

What are we to do in the face of this disaster?

What are our clergymen to do? Where shall they turn to for help?

To what country should they present their appeal?

HUMAN RIGHTS

Other countries imagine that it is the Iranian nation that has abased itself in this way. They do not know that it is the Iranian government, the Iranian Parliament—this Parliament which has nothing to do with the Iranian people. This is a Parliament elected at bayonet point, what does such a Parliament have to do with the people. The Iranian nation did not elect these deputies. Many of the high-ranking *'ulama* and *maraji'* ordered a boycott of the elections, and the people obeyed them and did not vote. But then came the power of the bayonet, and these deputies were seated in the Parliament.

. . .

It is a dangerous situation. It is clear that there are things kept under cover that we know nothing about. In the Parliament they have said that they have to be kept secret! It is evident that they are dreaming up further plans for us. What else can they do that is worse than this? What are they planning? What will this loan inflict on this nation? Should this impoverished nation now pay $100 million in interest to America over the next ten years and at the same time should you sell us for this? What use to you are the American soldiers and military advisers? If this country is occupied by America, then what is all this noise you make about progress? If these advisers are to be your servants, then why do you treat them like something superior to masters, superior to a Shah? If they are servants, why not treat them as such? If they are your employees, then why not treat them as any other government treats its employees? If our country is now occupied by the US then tell us outright and throw us out of this country! What do they intend to do? What does this government have to say to us? What has this Parliament done to us? This illegal, unlawful Parliament; this Parliament that the *maraji'-I taqlid* have declared illegitimate with their edicts and decrees; this Parliament which not one of its representatives has been chosen by the people; this Parliament which makes such empty claims about independence and revolution saying: "We have undergone a White Revolution!" Where is this "White Revolution?" They have made these people suffer!

God knows that I am aware of what is happening (and my awareness causes me pain), I know what is happening in the remote villages and provincial towns, in this our own impoverished city of Qum (the audience weeps). I am aware of the hunger of our people and the depressed state of our agrarian economy.

Do something for this country, for this nation, instead of piling up debts and enslaving yourself. Of course, taking the dollars means that someone has to become a slave; you want to use the dollars and we have to become

248

the slaves! If an American runs over me with his car, no one will have the right to say anything to him! So you use the dollars; this is the issue.

. . .

O presidents and kings of the Muslim peoples! O Shah of Iran! Look at yourselves, look at us. Are we to be trampled underfoot by the boots of the Americans simply because we are a weak nation? Because we have no dollars? America is worse than Britain, Britain is worse than America and the Soviet Union is worse than both of them. Each one is worse than the other, each one is more abominable than the other. But today we are concerned with this malicious entity which is America. Let the American President know that in the eyes of the Iranian nation, he is the most repulsive member of the human race today because of the injustice he has imposed on our Muslim nation. Today, the Qur'an has become his enemy, the Iranian nation has become his enemy. Let the American government know that its name has been ruined and disgraced in Iran.

. . .

This is high treason! O God, they have committed treason against this country. O God, this government has committed treason against this country, against Islam, against the Qur'an. All the members of both houses who gave their agreement to this affair are traitors. Those old men in the Senate are traitors, and all those in the lower house who voted in favour of this affair are traitors. They are not our representatives. The whole world must know that they are not the representatives of Iran! Or, suppose they are, now I dismiss them. They are dismissed from their posts and all the bills they have passed up until now are invalid.

From the very beginning of the constitutional period in Iran according to the text of the law, according to Article 2 of the Supplementary Constitutional Law, no law is valid unless the *mujtahids* (Islamic jurisprudents) exercise a supervisory role in the Parliament. Which *mujtahid* is supervising the Parliament now? They have to destroy the influence of the clergymen! If there were five clerics in this Parliament, if there were only one clergyman in this Parliament, he would punch them in the mouth! He would not allow this bill to be enacted.

. . .

We do not recognise this as a law. We do not recognise this Parliament as a true Parliament. We do not recognise this government as a true government. They are traitors, traitors to the people of Iran!

O God, remedy the affairs of the Muslims (the audience replies with "Amen").

O God, bestow majesty on this sacred religion of Islam!

O God, destroy those individuals who are traitors to this land, who are traitors to Islam and to the Qur'an.

Source: IRIB World Service. "Khomeini's Speech 16." 1964. Available online. URL: http://www2.irib.ir/ worldservice/imam/speech/16.htm. Accessed July 24, 2010.

Mahboubeh Hosseinzadeh, "All Women Are Victims, Not Just Those in Prison" (2007)

Mahboubeh Hosseinzadeh and Nahid Keshavarz were arrested in April 2007 and charged with undermining national security for collecting signatures for the One Million Signatures Campaign, which seeks to end legal discrimination against women in Iran. Hosseinzadeh wrote the following article from Evin Prison shortly before she and Keshavarz were released on bail. Nahid Keshavarz is a sociologist and writer, and Mahboubeh Hosseinzadeh is a journalist and a member of the Iran Civil Society Organizations Training and Research Center. Both were told that the demands of the One Million Signatures Campaign for equal rights to inheritance for women, the elimination of polygamy, equal financial compensation for injury or death, and equal value of testimony of women and men were in violation of the tenets of Islam.

"Our husbands are lying in enclosed graves and we are in open graves. We too ceased to live the very day that we killed our husbands." These are the words of a woman who spends her nights on the three story bed across from me. Her nights are filled with nightmares about the death of her husband—a husband she stabbed to death.

This is Evin prison—the women's ward. Nahid and I do not fully comprehend which national security we have undermined, nonetheless with this charge we spend our days in limbo in the midst of these women. Ten of the 16 women with whom we have shared a cell for over a week, are here on charges of murdering their husbands. These women, having lost faith in a legal system that offers no hope and no protection, weave their days to the darkness of the night that lingers behind the tall walls of Evin. If our laws had the capacity to defend women charged with murder, they would not be here now, spending their time idly in waiting for the day that would swallow them—a term used by female inmates to describe execution day.

HUMAN RIGHTS

And I laugh. He does not even have the courage to speak his name and to defend his opinion. A few other judges visiting the prison become excited. One speaks of Mehrangiz Kar and her effort to defend women's rights. My heart aches and I feel a sadness as vast as all the days that Mehrangiz Kar, Shirin Ebadi and other women like them have spent in Evin prison, on charges of having defended women's human rights. One of the judges pulls me to a corner to ask how I am being treated by the other inmates. Are we bothered here, he inquires. I recall the smoke-filled cells of Ward One of Evin Prison (the punishment ward, as it is infamously referred to) and the immense feeling of insecurity we felt during our time there. I remember having stood at the foot of the stairs in Ward One, when several inmates began beating a woman, pushing her down the stairs. Several female inmates beat this woman, to an inch of her life, while others held her hands so that she could not escape. I watched frightened and stunned. Injured and fearful, she gazed at the eyes of on lookers for help, but there was no libera-tor or even prison guard present to provide her with a reprieve.

I wanted to tell the man about a girl, who wailing, in this very ward, smashed the television set in her cell to the ground. I wanted to speak about a girl whose scar-filled arms, a testament to repeated attempts at suicide, shattered the glass of a window with her head. And this time, the prison guard was present, only to faint at the sight of this violence . . .

But instead I only told the judge that he should visit Ward One of Evin prison. To date, no reporter has managed to visit this Ward, and no reports about the condition of prisoners in this section of Evin have been prepared. Of course, according to the women in Ward One, no judge has ever visited this section of Evin prison either. The doors to this section remain perpetu-ally closed—and even judges do not bear witness to the atrocities that take place there.

My dear mother, my sister and her small child have come to visit me. Nahid had a chance to speak with my mother as well, and heard her lament about the worries of my aging father. My nephew Soheil is a year and a half. He places his small hands on the window of the cabinet that divides us, and laughs out loud. My sister cries. Her tears are warranted. She is spending her last days with her child. After 4 months of uncertainty, with the unrelent-ing assistance and support of her lawyer, she has finally managed to get her husband to agree to a divorce, on condition that she give up all her rights, even rights to her child—this very small child, whose laughter and play had interrupted the silence of my mother's home over the past four months. My sister worries for her child, and I feel more powerless than before when faced with her tears. She is only 23 years old. "I too am one of the victims of

HUMAN RIGHTS

And I laugh. He does not even have the courage to speak his name and to defend his opinion. A few other judges visiting the prison become excited. One speaks of Mehrangiz Kar and her effort to defend women's rights. My heart aches and I feel a sadness as vast as all the days that Mehrangiz Kar, Shirin Ebadi and other women like them have spent in Evin prison, on charges of having defended women's human rights. One of the judges pulls me to a corner to ask how I am being treated by the other inmates. Are we bothered here, he inquires. I recall the smoke-filled cells of Ward One of Evin Prison (the punishment ward, as it is infamously referred to) and the immense feeling of insecurity we felt during our time there. I remember having stood at the foot of the stairs in Ward One, when several inmates began beating a woman, pushing her down the stairs. Several female inmates beat this woman, to an inch of her life, while others held her hands so that she could not escape. I watched frightened and stunned. Injured and fearful, she gazed at the eyes of on lookers for help, but there was no liberator or even prison guard present to provide her with a reprieve.

I wanted to tell the man about a girl, who wailing, in this very ward, smashed the television set in her cell to the ground. I wanted to speak about a girl whose scar-filled arms, a testament to repeated attempts at suicide, shattered the glass of a window with her head. And this time, the prison guard was present, only to faint at the sight of this violence . . .

But instead I only told the judge that he should visit Ward One of Evin prison. To date, no reporter has managed to visit this Ward, and no reports about the condition of prisoners in this section of Evin have been prepared. Of course, according to the women in Ward One, no judge has ever visited this section of Evin prison either. The doors to this section remain perpetually closed—and even judges do not bear witness to the atrocities that take place there.

My dear mother, my sister and her small child have come to visit me. Nahid had a chance to speak with my mother as well, and heard her lament about the worries of my aging father. My nephew Soheil is a year and a half. He places his small hands on the window of the cabinet that divides us, and laughs out loud. My sister cries. Her tears are warranted. She is spending her last days with her child. After 4 months of uncertainty, with the unrelenting assistance and support of her lawyer, she has finally managed to get her husband to agree to a divorce, on condition that she give up all her rights, even rights to her child—this very small child, whose laughter and play had interrupted the silence of my mother's home over the past four months. My sister worries for her child, and I feel more powerless than before when faced with her tears. She is only 23 years old. "I too am one of the victims of these laws," explains my sister. "From today onward, I will start collecting signatures in support of the Campaign. I will collect so many signatures, so that these laws finally change."

The female inmate who has now started to record her own experiences in a small diary, pulls me aside and asks: "can I help you in collecting signatures for the Campaign?" She wants me to use whatever means possible to get her a signature form, so that women who are condemned to spend their days at Evin prison, too can have the opportunity to create change for others. So that with their individual signatures they can bring hope to other women. And this reminds me of the last question asked by my interrogator before I was brought here "your demands in the Campaign, including banning of polygamy, equal rights to blood money and testimony, are in contradiction to the foundations of Islamic jurisprudence and the foundations of the Islamic Regime. Given these facts, will you continue to ask for changes in the laws?" In response to this question, I wrote: "Yes! I know that our demands are not in contradiction to Islam." And today, after this experience, I am more determined than ever and I write: "I ask for changes to these discriminatory laws. I ask them in an effort to honor the dignity of all the women in my country."

Source: Mahboubeh Hosseinzadeh. "All Women Are Victims, Not Just Those in Prison." 2007. Iran Human Rights Library. Available online. URL: http://www.iranrights.org/english/document-282.php. Accessed January 13, 2010

Ehsan Fattahian, "A Letter from Political Prisoner Ehsan Fattahian, Two Days before His Execution" (2009)

The Kurdish activist Ehsan Fattahian was arrested in July 2008 and charged with committing acts against national security and waging war against God and the state, known as Moharebeh in Shari'a law. Fattahian admitted to being a member of the banned Kurdish opposition group Komeleh, but denied any involvement in any acts of violence. During the closed court proceedings, no evidence was brought forth to prove that Fattahian had committed any act of violence, according to Fattahian's lawyer. Nevertheless, he was convicted and sentenced to death. Ehsan Fattahian was executed by hanging at Sanandaj Central Prison on the morning of November 11, 2009. Two days before his execution, he sent a letter from prison, detailing his torture, trial, and conviction, and insisting upon his innocence. His family was not allowed to visit him before his execution.

> *Last ray of sun at sunset/*
> *is the path that I want to write on/*

HUMAN RIGHTS

The sound of leaves under my feet/
say to me: Let yourself fall/
and only then you find the path to freedom./

I have never been afraid of death, even now that I feel it closest to me. I can sense it and I'm familiar with it, for it is an old acquaintance of this land and this people. I'm not writing about death but about justifications for death, now that they have translated it to restoring justice and freedom, can one be afraid of future and destiny? "We" who have been sentenced to death by "them," were working to find a small opening to a better world, free of injustice, are "they" also aware of what they are working towards?

I started life in city of Kermanshah, the city that my country people consider grand, the birthplace of civilization in our country. I soon noticed descrimination and oppression and I felt it in the depth of my existence, this cruelty, and the "why" of this cruelty and trying to resolve it made me come up with thousands of thoughts. But alas, they had blocked all the roads to justice and made the atmosphere so repressive that I didn't find any way to change things inside, and I migrated to another resort: "I became the pishmarg of Koomaleh," the temptation to find myself and the identity that I was deprived of made me go in that direction. Although leaving my birthplace was difficult but it never made me cut ties with my childhood hometown. Every now and then I would go back to my first home to revisit my old memories, and one of these times "they" made my visit sour, arrested and imprisoned me. From that first moment and from the hospitality (!!) of my jailers I realized that the tragic destiny of my numerous compeers also awaits me: torture, file building, closed and seriously influenced court, an unjust and politically charged verdict, and finally death . . .

Let me say it more casually: after getting arrested in town of Kamyaran on 29/4/87 and after a few hours of being a "guest" at the information office of that town, while handcuffs and a blindfold took away my right to see and move, a person who introduced himself as a deputy of the prosecutor started asking a series of unrelated questions that were full of false accusations (I should point out that any judicial questioning outside of courtroom is prohibited in the law). This was the first of my numerous interrogation sessions. The same night I was moved to the information office of Kurdestan province in city of Sanandaj, and I experienced the real party there: a dirty cell with an unpleasant toilet with blankets that had probably not seen water in decades! From that moment my nights and days passed in the interrogation offices and lower hallway under extreme torture and beatings and this lasted three months. In these three months my interrogators, probably in pursuit of a promotion or some small raise, came up with strange and false accusations against me, which they better than anyone knew how far from reality they were. They tried very hard to prove that I was involved with an armed attempt to overthrow the regime. The only charges they could pursue was being a part of "Koomaleh" and advertising against the regime. The first "shobe" of Islamic republic court in Sanandaj found me guilty of these charges and gave me 10 years sentence in exile in Ramhormoz prison. The government's political and bureaucratic structure always suffers from being centralized, but in this case they tried to de-centralize the judiciary and gave the powers to re-investigate (appeal?) the crimes of political prisoners, even as high as death penalties, to the appeal courts in Kurdestan province. In this case the prosecutor Mr. Kamyaran appealed the verdict by the first court and the Kurdestan appeals court changed my verdict from 10 years in prison to death sentence, against the Islamic republic laws. According to section 258 of "Dadrasi Keyfari" law, an appeals court can increase the initial verdict only in the case that the initial verdict was less than minimum punishment for the crime. In my case, the crime was "Moharebeh" (animosity with God), which has the minimum punishment of one-year sentence, and my verdict was a 10-year sentence in exile, clearly above the minimum. Compare my sentence to the minimum sentence for this crime to understand the unlawful and political nature of my death sentence. Although I also have to mention that shortly before changing the verdict they transferred me from the main prison in Sanandaj to the interrogation office of the Information Department and requested that I do a video interview confessing to crimes I have not committed, and say things that I do not believe in. In spite of a lot of pressure I did not agree to do the video confession and they told me bluntly that they will change my verdict to death sentence, which they shortly did, and demonstrated how the courts follow forces outside of judiciary department. So should they be blamed??

A judge has been sworn to stay fair in every situation, at all times and towards every person and look at the world from the legal perspective. Which judge in this doomed land can claim to [have] not broken this [oath] and has stayed fair and just? In my opinion the number of such judges is less than fingers on one hand. When the whole judicial system of Iran with the suggestion of an interrogator (with no knowledge of legal matters), arrests, tries, imprisons and executes people, can we really blame the few judges of a province which is always repressed and discriminated against? Yes, this house is ruined from its foundations . . .

This is in spite of the fact that in my last visit with my prosecutor he admitted that the death sentence is unlawful, but for the second time they gave me the notice for carrying out the execution. Needless to say that this insistence on carrying a death sentence under any circumstance is the result of pressure from security and political forces from outside of the judiciary department. Said people look at life and death of political prisoners only from the point of view of their paychecks and political needs, nothing else matters to them other than their own goals, even if it is about the most fundamental right of other human beings, their right to live. Forget international laws, they completely disregard even their own laws and procedures.

But my last words: If in the minds of these rulers and oppressors my death will get rid of the "problem" called Kurdestan [the province], I should say, what an illusion. Neither my death nor the death of thousands like me will be remedy to this incurable pain and perhaps would even fuel this fire. Without a doubt, every death points to a new life.

Ehsan Fattahian

Sanandaj Central prison

17/8/1388

Source: Ehsan Fattahian. "A Letter From Political Prisoner Ehsan Fattahian, Two Days Before His Execution." 2009. Iran Human Rights Library. Available online. URL: http://www.iranrights.org/english/document-797.php. Accessed January 13, 2010.

PART III

Research Tools

6

How to Research Human Rights

The topic of human rights is wide-ranging and spans several disciplines and schools of thought. In addition to the various approaches one can take to understanding human rights, there are a number of different topics that are classified under the rubric of human rights. Civil rights, women's rights, children's rights, torture, arms, press freedom, GLBT rights, immigration, and health all have a place under the umbrella of human rights. If you are researching one particular area of human rights, such as women's rights or press freedom, you will have a relatively easy time finding groups, Web sites, books, and other resources devoted exclusively to your topic. But if you are taking a broad approach to the topic of human rights as a whole, then it will help to understand the various perspectives and angles from which human rights scholars and writers approach the issue.

HOW TO APPROACH HUMAN RIGHTS

One of the most basic, fundamental questions in the historical discussion of rights is: Who determines rights? Are they inherent in all people, or are they created and subject to change according to time and place?

More often than not, those who determine what constitutes a right and who is entitled to rights are those who have the most prominent voices on the global and historical stage. In 1947, the newly created United Nations Educational, Scientific and Cultural Organization (UNESCO) adopted a resolution to draft a document called *History of the Scientific and Cultural Development of Mankind.* According to the then executive secretary of the Preparatory Commission Julian Huxley, "The chief task before the Humanities today would seem to be to help in constructing a history of the development of the human mind, notably in its highest cultural achievement."

The work resulted in the publication of a six-volume *History* in 1968 that was translated into English, French, Greek, Spanish, Slovene, and Serbo-Croat. The *History* came under heavy criticism, however, for a number of shortcomings. Its Eurocentric perspective was particularly troubling to many readers and scholars around the world. Only 27 pages of volume II were devoted to China, and 30 were devoted to India. Of the 1,200 pages of text in volume V, only 3.5 percent were devoted to Latin America, and 1.5 percent to the entire continent of Africa. Of the 100-page section in volume V concerned with music, 74 pages were devoted to Europe, 16 to Asia and North Africa, and none to the rest of the African continent. Furthermore, when the document did chart the histories of certain countries, it did so from a predominantly Western vantage point, especially where Islam and Muslim countries were concerned. Even Europe, itself, was covered from a largely Western European perspective, with few mentions of Eastern European countries and their contributions to the sciences and humanities. In 1979, it was decided at the 20th session of the UNESCO General Conference to revise the work.

While UNESCO's first drafting of a *History of the Scientific and Cultural Development of Mankind* and its narrow cultural vision would not appear to have any relation to the issue of human rights, it reveals the critical problem of how a governing body (like the United Nations) can determine rights when it recognizes only certain peoples as world players and participants in the global exchange. This became apparent in a dispute that arose during the revision regarding the significance of the Haitian Revolution. The Barbadian poet and professor Kamau Brathwaite was on the UNESCO board of directors and collaborated on the project as a representative of the Caribbean, and when he protested the lack of space devoted to the Haitian Revolution and Caribbean slavery, the chairman Charles Morazé reportedly responded that while slavery was an unspeakable tragedy, it was "but a painful footnote on the page of history."

What does this event mean in terms of human rights? While the chairman conceded to the fact that the institution of slavery was deplorable, his remark suggests that slavery was a peripheral event in a larger world history—a history that belongs to certain players. Whose history is he referring to? This complication in UNESCO's second drafting of a *History of the Scientific and Cultural Development of Mankind* mirrors the challenge that has faced discussions of human rights throughout history. Who are the players whose rights are being discussed? Is it the rights of the slave to his own body, or the rights of the master to his property? Haiti is actually a shining example of just such a quandary. In 1804, Haiti won its independence from France and became the first nation to arise out of a slave revolt. Suffering from the economic loss of a slave colony, in 1825 the French government demanded that the newly independent Haitians compensate France by paying 150 million francs (today $21 billion) as the price of their freedom, otherwise they would not be recognized as participants in the world market. Warships were stationed just outside the Haitian capital, and an emissary demanded that Haiti agree to the terms or face reenslavement. The Haitians reluctantly agreed, and in 1883 they made their final payment to France, but not before Haiti's economy and infrastructure were devastated by poverty. Following a recent string of dictators who literally stole millions of dollars worth of aid money, Haiti is now struggling to survive under a $1.2 billion debt that is paid in annual installments of $50–80 million, twice the health budget, three times the education budget, and four times the agricultural budget. Debt constitutes more than one-third of Haiti's GDP. At the dawn of the 21st century, approximately 120 years after it paid off the last installment of its debt to France, Haiti has asked for the money back: $21 billion, with interest. The French government has refused, and a spokesman for France's Foreign Ministry, Hervé Ladsous, remarked, "This case has been closed since 1885." With the help of U.S. and French lawyers, Haiti is preparing a legal brief to demand $22 billion dollars in restitution for an act of "gunboat diplomacy."

For France, the issue of slavery and Haiti's debt is in the past, but for Haiti, this is still a very pressing and urgent issue, as this 120-year-old debt is largely responsible for Haiti's present-day poverty. In the 19th century, the global community made its position clear on the debate between whose rights took precedence: France's right to its property overruled Haiti's right to freedom from slavery. Today, many organizations and individual human rights activists are campaigning to have Haiti's debt canceled as illegitimate, but the question of a right to restitution still lingers. Racked by poverty due to an unreasonable sum of money demanded of it 120 years ago, does Haiti have a right to demand that same unreasonable sum of money back from France, even though it would likely devastate France's economy in turn? Is there a middle ground that would satisfy both nations and allow both to prosper? If not, whose rights will take precedence?

When researching human rights, it is important to determine who is speaking and why. It is equally important to take note of who is not speaking. Historical documents, such as the U.S. Declaration of Independence and the French Declaration for the Rights of Man and Citizen often aim for universality, but it was taken for granted at the time of their drafting that equality and human rights did not include slaves or women.

A CHANGING WORLD STAGE

Much work has been done since to universalize the aims of human rights groups and specify to whom they are referring and why. Nevertheless, understanding human rights is a continuing process and the field of human rights scholarship and activism continues to expand to adapt to new developments on the global stage. Rising worldwide Internet use, for example, has prompted discussions of Internet censorship and whether U.S.-based companies such as Yahoo! and Google should accommodate authoritarian governments like China that seek to limit information flow. For the first time in human history, people from all over the world can access information and communicate freely and immediately, without intermediaries, making cyberspace the first truly universal space for human interaction. So when one country imposes censors on all incoming and outgoing information for Internet users within its borders, it affects the entire global community. In recent years, the Internet giant Yahoo! has come under heavy criticism for providing information on Chinese dissidents to the government, the most famous case involving Shi Tao, who was sentenced to 10 years in prison for an e-mail he sent to a human rights group in New York. But representatives of Yahoo! have defended the company's actions on the grounds that governments are not required to inform service providers why they wish to obtain information on users, and the company does not wish to interfere with government investigations, particularly if they involve serious crimes, like murders or kidnappings. Other Internet service providers have also been criticized for tapping into the Chinese market and accommodating the regime's policies. In 2006, Google launched Google.cn, agreeing to censor Web sites that are forbidden in China. In 2005, Microsoft shut down a Chinese blog on its MSN Spaces site. Human rights groups and activists around the world have criticized such companies for stressing profits over human rights, but what responsibilities do major corporations have to protecting human rights? Should they be expected to decide who is correct in the debate over universal human rights? The Chinese government maintains that its Internet censorship practices are critical to maintaining national security, and U.S. attempts to undermine such practices are tantamount to imposing "information imperialism" on China. If a company has the opportunity to enter a new market and raise its profits, should it also assume the responsibility of being the arbiter in human rights debates? In January 2010, Google issued a threat to pull out of China if the government did not lift its Internet censorship policies. The threat came after the company discovered a "highly sophisticated" cyber attack that hacked into its system to access the e-mail accounts of major Chinese human rights activists. A spokesman for the Chinese Foreign Affairs Ministry has said only that "Chinese laws prohibit any form of cyber attacks including hacking."

UNDERSTANDING THE BASICS: DEFINITIONS

Forming a solid grasp on the major players and topics of human rights is a good way to start answering the tougher questions, such as whether or not companies should abstain from operating in countries with poor human rights records. Some of the major topics in human rights discussions today include:

- *Press Freedom:* the freedom to publish and disseminate information on any topic, as well as the freedom to access information. In 1823, Thomas Jefferson wrote: "The only security of all is in a free press. The force of public opinion cannot be resisted when permitted freely to be expressed. The agitation it produces must be submitted to." In many countries around the world, journalists, news organizations, and other media outlets are suppressed and censored. Without a free press, human rights discussions are severely hampered and government actions cannot be questioned, making press freedom (and freedom of speech in general) a major priority among human rights organizations.

- *Torture:* the act of inflicting extreme pain or forcing the body to endure prolonged stress, often with the aim of eliciting a confession and/or names and information. Torture can also be used as a means of punishment or intimidation. Torture can be state-sponsored, as is the case in repressive regimes such as Iran and China, or it can be used by violent rebel or militia groups, as is the case in the Democratic Republic of the Congo. Torture is expressly forbidden by Article 5 of the Universal Declaration of Human Rights, but it still remains in practice as a method of punishment and coercion in many countries. In recent years, the United States military's extreme interrogation practices against suspected terrorists during the war in Iraq, which included waterboarding, prolonged sleep deprivation, and sensory bombardment (loud noise, bright lights), have been called into question as to whether or not they constituted torture.

- *Women's Rights:* rights to self-determination, education, employment, equal pay, equal value of testimony in court, divorce, and to choose whether or not to marry and get pregnant. In even the most developed of countries, women often do not enjoy full equality with men. In the United States, women continue to earn a third less than men for the same work. In some regions, however, the situation for women is much more extreme. In several countries, women's status precludes

263

education, employment, and access to women's health services, such as birth control and maternal health care. In 1979, the United Nations General Assembly adopted the Convention on the Elimination of All Forms of Discrimination Against Women (CEDAW), which summarizes governments' responsibilities to eradicate discrimination against women and has been ratified by 186 countries. As of 2010, the only countries that have not ratified the treaty are the United States, Iran, Sudan, Somalia, Palau, Tonga, and Nauru.

- *Children's Rights:* rights to safe and healthy growth and development, education, housing, health care, and protection of the best interests of the child in all situations, which includes the right to be raised in a loving family, whatever form that takes. In many regions of the world, particularly in impoverished areas, children must work to earn incomes for the family. This is also true for certain communities within the United States. In many war-torn regions of the world, children are routinely kidnapped and conscripted as child soldiers, where they are abused, raped, and malnourished. Children's rights organizations work on such issues as child labor, education, health, child homelessness, child soldiers, and violence against children.

- *Health:* a broad spectrum that includes the rights to clean drinking water, access to health care and medical services, and disease prevention and treatment. Some of the leading priorities among human rights organizations are child and maternal health care and HIV/AIDS. More than two-thirds of all people living with HIV (human immunodeficiency virus) are in sub-Saharan Africa, where poverty, malnutrition, and lack of medical care intensify the effects and spread of the disease. Among developing countries, 9.5 million people are in immediate need of AIDS medication, but only 4 million are receiving treatment. Human rights groups focus on government responsibilities to provide medical care to people with HIV/AIDS and to prevent the spread of the disease, as well as to protect the rights of people living with HIV/AIDS. On January 4, 2010, the Obama administration lifted a travel ban on people with HIV/AIDS coming into the United States, a travel ban that has been in place since the 1980s and has been widely criticized by human rights groups as discriminatory.

- *Gay/Lesbian/Transgender/Bisexual (GLTB) Rights:* equal rights to employment, education, voting, and access to public services and institutions as heterosexual people, as well as the right to live free from violence and discrimination. Like women's and children's rights, GLTB rights are wide ranging and face different challenges in different regions of the world—some more urgent and severe than others. In rigidly conservative countries where homophobia is prevalent, many gay and lesbian individuals live in daily fear for their lives, particularly where hate crimes against gays and lesbians are not addressed by law enforcement. In some countries, such as Iran, homosexuality is a crime and punishable by death. In other countries, current campaigns in GLTB rights organizations include the right to marry, the right to adopt, and the right to medical care for adults (and in some cases, children) who wish to pursue a sex-change procedure.

- *Immigrants and Refugees:* rights to asylum from violence or imminent violence in one's home country, access to medical attention and health care, safe and sanitary living conditions, and protection from exploitation. Migrant workers in many parts of the world report having to endure long hours, dangerous working conditions, confiscated passports, and unpaid wages. In some countries, migrants suffer under repressive and often discriminatory policies, as is the case in several Thai provinces, where migrants are required to be confined to their homes or workplaces at night and are not allowed to travel within the province. In the United States, illegal immigrants and refugees who have not filed the necessary paperwork to stay in the country face indefinite detention. Migrant rights groups campaign for greater protections for such individuals.

- *Arms:* refers to campaigns to ban the use of certain weapons that pose a particular threat to civilians during wartime, such as landmines and cluster munitions. Cluster munitions, also known as cluster bombs, are explosive weapons that release a cluster of bomblets that increase the area of destruction. They can be land-launched or air-dropped, and because their purpose is to scatter bomblets over as wide an area as possible, they can cause untold damage, especially when targeted on civilian-populated areas. Furthermore, undetonated bomblets can lay dormant for years, posing a risk to civilians long after a war has ended. In 2008, the Convention on Cluster Munitions was adopted in Dublin, Ireland, and has been ratified by 24 states. The 1997 Mine Ban Treaty, which seeks the elimination of all antipersonnel mines (meaning they are designed to injure or kill people) has been endorsed by 158 countries, including all of the United States' military allies, but the United States has yet to sign the treaty.

- *Terrorism:* acts of violence targeted primarily at civilian noncombatants with the aim of instilling fear. Human rights organizations focus on the protection of civilians, pressing governments to find and apprehend terrorists in their home countries, as well as monitoring counterterror-ist campaigns, which can be equally devastating to civilian populations, as was the case in Russia's second invasion of Chechnya. Continued counterterrorist efforts in Chechnya have led to several dozen state-sanctioned house-burnings to punish the families of terrorists. In Saudi Arabia, counterterrorist campaigns have led to the indefinite detention of 9,000 people since 2003. Probably the most well known and contro-versial counterterrorism campaign among developed nations today is the U.S. invasion of Iraq in 2003, which critics say has used extreme methods to locate and apprehend suspected terrorists.

SOURCES

With a firm grasp of the major issues and participants in human rights discussions, you can now begin to sort through which sources will be most beneficial to your research.

Primary Documents

Primary documents include any original source material, such as first-person narratives, autobiographies, interviews, diaries, letters, census data, and sta-tistics. Primary documents include any material that you, as a researcher and writer, will use to build and defend your argument. In discussions of human rights, primary documents are particularly helpful, especially first-person nar-ratives and statistics. Statistics and other numerical data provide a general and logical overview of the facts of an issue, such as the number of people affected, the areas and communities in which an issue is concentrated, and international response, such as aid and supplies. In the case of human rights, however, one cannot separate numerical facts from the human element of such tragedies as war, terrorism, torture, and repression. In this respect, first-person accounts such as interviews, autobiographies, and letters provide a more empathetic means of connecting with the issue. This is not to suggest that human rights must be argued purely through an appeal to emotion, but rather that one must be careful not to ignore the human reality of rights and oppression. Providing statistical facts regarding how many people were killed in the Russian invasion of the Chechen capital of Grozny, for example, may not be as informative as a personal account of what it was like to experience such an invasion firsthand. Help your readers understand the human cost of human rights abuses.

One thing to be aware of when researching primary documents, however, is that more often than not you are reading a translation. Most translations are generally very faithful to the original document, but certain connotations may be altered or inferred. In a letter from Ehsan Fattahian, a death row inmate in an Iranian prison, for example, he describes his experiences during the first three months following his arrest, which include beatings, torture, and constant interrogations in which he is pressured to make false confessions. Different translations of the letter into English, however, describe these experiences differently. On the Human Rights in Iran Web site, this section is translated: "From that moment my days and nights passed in the interrogation offices and lower hallway under extreme torture and beatings and this lasted three months." On the Human Rights Watch Web site, this section is translated: "From then on, every night and day I was taken to the interrogation rooms in the lower hallway and faced beatings and unbearable torture, which continued endlessly for three months." And on the Web site Uruknet.info, the letter makes no mention of torture at all, reading only: "This was the beginning of three months of going up and down the hall from my cell to the interrogation room, always being beaten along the way." Which translation is one to believe? Because it is not always possible to translate on your own, read several different translations to get an idea of the main point of the document. In the example of Fattahian's letter, two translations mention torture while one does not; therefore, it is reasonable to assume that the original document did mention torture. You may also want to simply lean toward sources that are well known and have a track record of impartiality. Human Rights Watch is a well-known global human rights organization that would be held accountable for any misleading information published on its Web site, so one may be inclined to trust information on that Web site over a lesser-known publication or newsletter.

Secondary Documents

Secondary documents include sources that refer to or examine primary sources, such as essays, biographies, newspaper articles, documentaries, and summaries of numerical data. For the topic of human rights, secondary sources are prolific and helpful, especially if you are new to the subject and looking for guidance into a broader understanding of the issue.

PRINT

Print resources may include newspapers, books, journals, and essays, much of which can actually be found online. To start off with the most recent status of human rights in a given region, you may want to start with some news reports. Newspaper articles abound with discussions of human rights issues, and you can be certain that you are reading the most up-to-date status of an issue or country, which is important because human rights are not static but in a constant process of change. Many newspapers archive their articles, which means you may be asked to subscribe to the newspaper online in order to read them. If you are a college student, your institution will likely already have a subscription that you can access through their databases. If you are a high school student, you can ask your librarian if your school subscribes to any major newspapers. Generally, though, if you are looking for recent information on a particular country or topic in human rights, entering the terms into an online search engine will invariably bring back a plethora of news articles, some of which may have been published only moments ago.

To obtain a broader perspective of the subject, you may want to look up books that have been written on your research topic. Depending on the specific topic you are researching, you may want to start by reading one or two books on the issue, which will usually provide a historical account of the conflict and why it persists today, before you look up any recent news articles. On the other hand, you may find it helpful to find out what is going on now within the region or topic of your research, and then work backward to find out how it all started. For example, if you wish to research conflict diamonds in Africa, it may be more fruitful to start with a look at the current state of diamond mining in Africa and then work backward to get a better understanding of how today's situation came to be. If your research is broader, however, or focused on human rights in a region as a whole, you may be better off to start with a historical account. If you are new to the topic, a book will not only provide historical data but also analyses and explanations that are meant to guide you to a more thorough understanding of the issue. One thing to bear in mind when you are researching books that have been written on your topic is that you are reading one author's account, which may be slanted, however subtly, in favor of his or her opinion on the issue. It is a good idea to read several books to get a complete understanding of an issue and the numerous opinions and perspectives from which to approach it. More likely than not, though, you do not have time to read six or seven complete books, so you may want to focus your attention on specific chapters, such as introductory overviews and historical accounts.

WEB

Much of your research can be done on the Internet, as many newspapers archive their articles on the Internet, and, in some cases, you can even read whole books online. You may, in fact, want to begin your research by simply typing your topic into a search engine and seeing what crops up. If you are researching a specific issue in human rights, such as women's rights or health care, you may find it helpful to look up message boards to see what people are discussing. Activist Web sites can also be very helpful and informative.

How to Research Human Rights

An often-disputed source of information is Wikipedia.org. Because anyone can enter or change information in a Wikipedia entry, you must be very careful to check facts and figures against other sources. Wikipedia can, however, be a very useful way to access other sources by checking the works cited, which are often accessible online. This can be especially handy if there is a particular fact or figure that you are looking for. If the Wikipedia entry refers to this area that you are researching, you can check the document that the author(s) cited. This will also enable you to put the fact or figure into context and cite a more credible source on your paper.

Some of the most helpful online resources are human rights organization Web sites such as Human Rights Watch and Amnesty International, both of which are on the forefront of new developments in human rights issues and often suggest certain measures by which to solve specific crises. Such Web sites also tend to divide up information into neat and easily navigable categories, such as region, country, and topic. If there is a specific event that you want to learn more about, you can also type the search terms (such as the country and the date) into the search box and browse through the Web site's archives.

Human rights organizations can be divided into the categories of international and local, both of which can be very helpful to your research. If you are looking for information on a specific region, country, or topic, you may want to look for human rights groups that deal specifically with that area of research. If you want more information on human rights in China, for example, running a Web search will bring up a number of organizations devoted specifically to human rights in China (HRIC). Similarly, if you want information on a specific topic such as conflict diamonds or child homelessness, a Web search will provide a number of organizations and publications on just such an issue.

WEB SOURCE RELIABILITY

Due to the open and anonymous nature of the Internet, it can be difficult to determine whether or not your sources are trustworthy. This can be particularly frustrating when data pertaining to a research question is hard to come by and you are inclined to simply use what little information you have been able to find. When incorporating data into your paper, consider whether or not your instructor would agree that the source is reliable. Generally, information from major organizations, research institutes, universities, and governmental bodies is likely to be accurate, but be sure you know who is writing the data. Occasionally, you might find an online source that is credited to a university, but this does not mean that the university supports the data.

269

Search through the Web site (find a button for "Home" or "Main Menu") and find out who gathered and published the information. You may find that the source is actually a student project, which is not a reliable source of information. This does not mean that you cannot use the information you find there; it simply means you must verify what you decide to use by finding a more reliable source. Check the works cited and find out if the writer retrieved his or her information from a more trustworthy organization or Web site.

When perusing Web sites for information, there are a couple of different ways to determine whether or not the site is a reliable source. When a site claims to be part of an organization, you should check the domain name to be sure. Domain names are easy-to-remember URL addresses that indicate authorship and ownership, and as such they must be purchased and registered. While this does not automatically make them concretely reliable sources, it does make them more reliable than other Web sites that do not have domain names, which are more likely to be personal or student projects. Web sites with domain names (URLs that end in .com, .net, or .org) are public and thus more accountable Web sites. It is also helpful to ascertain the language of the Web site. Is the language emotionally charged and inflammatory? Does it make large-scale generalizations about groups of people (i.e. "all Chinese citizens want an uncensored Internet")? The topic of human rights is an emotionally charged subject, but it is important to exercise a certain level of neutrality regarding facts and figures while avoiding assumptions and snap judgments, which often cloud the real situation and preclude making real progress in human rights. Most major human rights organizations understand that dialogues about human rights are not black and white, and groups that are perceived to be oppressive cannot simply be judged and dismissed as such. Ongoing human rights discussions require a level of open-mindedness about an individual's, group's, or government's capacity to change its way of thinking about rights and to implement new policies, so reliable sources are likely to be those that use more neutral language (when appropriate) and present ways in which human rights situations can be improved.

Another way to ascertain a source's reliability is to determine authorship of an article or report. Does the organization take full responsibility for all of the information that appears on its Web site? If not, then you should fact-check the information. Is the Web site more blog-oriented? If so, then the information that you retrieve from such a Web site is unlikely to be centralized and verified by a primary authority, which means you will have to check the information against other sources.

To avoid wasting time and energy on fact-checking everything you read, your best bet is to avoid Web sites that are run as blogs or discussion forums. Try to restrict your sources to books, news articles, peer-reviewed journals, and the Web sites of well-known public organizations, all of which must go through some level of peer-review prior to publication. The Web sites maintained by Human Rights Watch (hrw.org) and Amnesty International (amnesty.org), for example, consist entirely of articles and reports that the organizations take full responsibility for, which means that the information has already been fact-checked, peer-reviewed, and verified for you.

Also be sure to check when the Web site was last updated. Human rights information changes minute-to-minute, so an accurate and reliable human rights Web site will be updated often and regularly.

Avoiding Plagiarism

Plagiarism is defined as any form of using another individual's or group's work without giving proper credit to them. This often occurs unintentionally when students are not sure how to cite sources properly, particularly as much of the information surrounding human rights is public, such as historical and political facts. Certain information should always be cited, though. You should always cite your sources when presenting numerical data, such as population figures, financial transactions, and other facts and rates. Similarly, quotes and statements should always be cited, as well as any information that is not necessarily public or common knowledge. For example, if you are writing about the Democratic Republic of the Congo and you wish to include information on President Dwight Eisenhower's role in the American-orchestrated coup that ousted Patrice Lamumba, you must cite your sources, as such information is not common knowledge and may be challenged by your readers. Information is rarely self-evident, so it is important to back up your claims with verifiable data from legitimate sources.

CONCLUSION

The issue of human rights is a broad topic that covers a wide range of subtopics, which, at first glance, might seem overwhelming. Developing a strategy for your research based on some of the steps outlined in this chapter will help you focus your energy and attention and avoid feeling bogged down in details. As you conduct your research, you may find it helpful to work up an outline and write down some of the issues, names, dates, and events that you wish to research in more depth. By making a list of topics you would like to cover in your research (especially if you are writing a paper on human rights), you can keep your thoughts organized and then go back and cross out topics that are not particularly relevant, or for which you simply will not have time. Due to the abundance of information on human rights, you are not likely to have a difficult time developing a well-researched position on the topic of your choice.

7

Facts and Figures

UNIVERSAL
1.1 Worldwide Distribution of People Suffering from Hunger

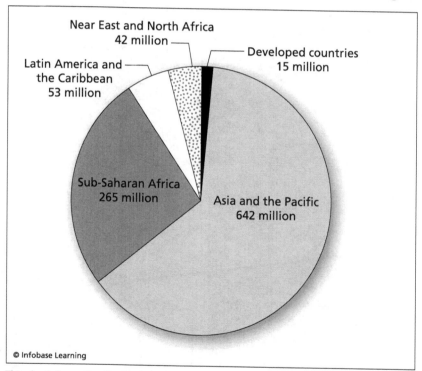

This chart shows the distribution of hungry people throughout the world, by region. In this chart, hunger is defined as malnourishment due to lack of calories and protein.

Source: World Hunger Education Service. "World Hunger Facts 2009." Hunger Notes, 2010. Available online. URL: http://www.worldhunger.org/articles/Learn/world%20hunger%20 facts%202002.htm. Accessed March 4, 2010

1.2 United Nations Human Development Index Map

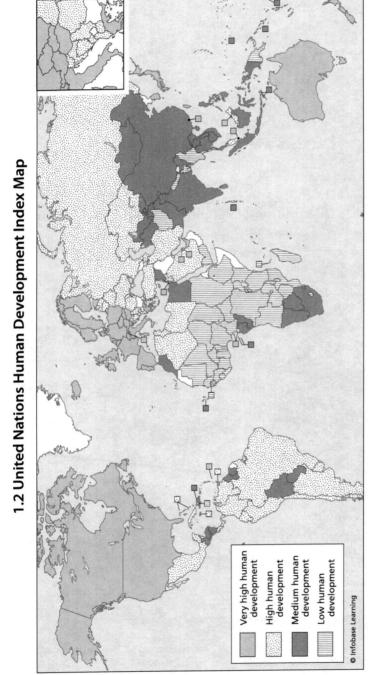

© Infobase Learning

Very high human development

High human development

Medium human development

Low human development

This map offers a graphic image of the Human Development Index (HDI) rankings around the world by region and country, based on the 2010 Human Development Report data. The Human Development Index is measured by several criteria, including life expectancy at birth, literacy, and per capita income.

Source: United Nations Development Programme (UNDP), Human Development Report 2010. "International Human Development Indicators." Available online. URL: http://hdr.undp.org/en/statistics/. Accessed May 19, 2010.

1.3 Ten Leading Causes of Death in Women by Country Income Group

Low-Income Countries

Rank	Cause	Deaths (000s)	%
1	Lower respiratory infections	1,397	11.4
2	Ischaemic heart disease	1,061	87
3	Diarrhoeal diseases	851	7.0
4	Stroke	745	6.1
5	HIV/AIDS	742	6.1
6	Maternal conditions	442	3.6
7	Neonatal infections**	426	3.5
8	Prematurity and low birth weight	405	3.3
9	Maleria	404	3.3
10	COPD*	404	3.3

High-Income Countries

Rank	Cause	Deaths (000s)	%
1	Ischaemic heart disease	650	15.80
2	Stroke	459	11.2
3	Alzheimer and other dementias	195	4.7
4	Lower respiratory infections	165	4.0
5	Breast cancer	163	4.0
6	Trachea, bronchus and lung cancers	159	3.9
7	Colon and rectum cancers	130	3.2
8	COPD*	126	3.1
9	Diabetes mellitus	123	3.0
10	Hypertensive heart disease	91	202

*Chronic obstructive pulmonary disease
**Includes severe neonatal infections and non-infectious causes arising in the perinatal period.

This table shows the disparity in causes of death among women depending on whether they live in a high- or low-income country.

Source: World Heath Organization. "Women and Health: Today's Evidence, Tomorrow's Agenda." 2009. Available online. URL: http://whqlibdoc.who.int/publications/2009/9789241563857_eng.pdf. Accessed March 26, 2010.

1.4 Worldwide Statistics on Journalists Killed Since 1992

Beats Covered by Journalists

Business	4%
Corruption	21%
Crime	14%
Culture	8%
Human Rights	14%
Politics	38%
Sports	3%
War	35%

Job

Broadcast reporter	22%
Camera Operator	10%
Columnist / Commentator	9%
Editor	16%
Photographer	7%
Internet reporter/writer	1%
Print reporter/writer	32%
Producer	6%
Publisher/Owner	4%
Technician	2%

Type of Death

Crossfire/Combat	18%
Dangerous Assignment	10%
Murder	72%

Impunity

Complete impunity	89%
Partial justice	7%
Full justice	4%

This table represents a statistical breakdown of journalists killed since 1992 by topic (beats), job, type of death, and whether or not the killer was identified and prosecuted.

Source: Committee to Protect Journalists. "Journalists Killed Since 1992." 2010. Available online. URL: http://www.cpj.org/killed/. Accessed July 26, 2010.

UNITED STATES

2.1 U.S. Child Victims of Abuse by Maltreatment Type and Age, 2007

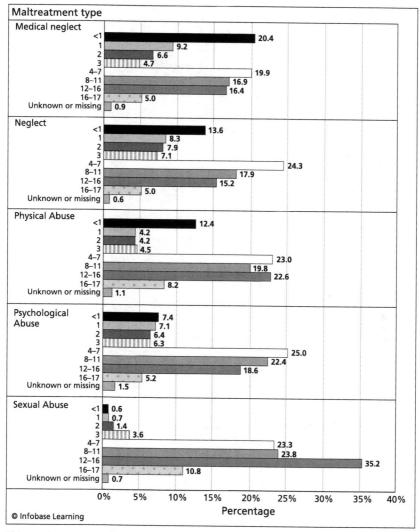

This graph represents the occurrence of child abuse by the age of the victim and the type of abuse.

Source: U.S. Department of Health and Human Services, Administration for Children and Families, Children's Bureau. "Child Maltreatment, 2007." 2009. Available online. URL: http://www.acf.hhs.gov/programs/ch/pubs/cmo7/cmo7.pdf. Accessed March 29, 2010.

2.2a Total U.S. Population by Race/Ethnicity, 2008

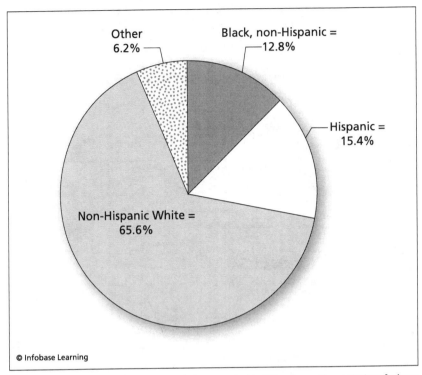

Other
6.2%

Black, non-Hispanic =
12.8%

Hispanic =
15.4%

Non-Hispanic White =
65.6%

© Infobase Learning

More than 2 million people are currently incarcerated in U.S. prisons, the majority of whom are ethnic minorities. These two graphs show the total U.S. population by race/ethnicity in 2008 (2.2a) in comparison with the prison population by race/ethnicity during the same year (2.2b).

Source: The National Databook. "The 2010 Statistical Abstract." U.S. Census Bureau. Available online. URL: http://www.census.gov/compendia/statab/cats/population.html. Accessed July 27, 2010.

2.2b U.S. Prison Population by Race/Ethnicity, 2008

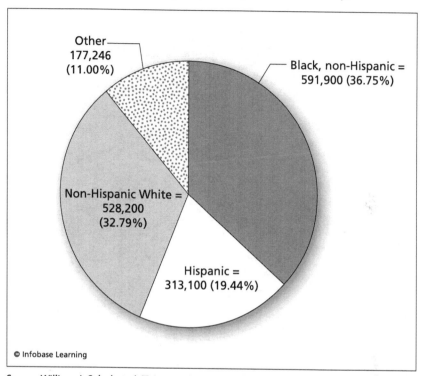

Other
177,246
(11.00%)

Black, non-Hispanic =
591,900 (36.75%)

Non-Hispanic White =
528,200
(32.79%)

Hispanic =
313,100 (19.44%)

© Infobase Learning

Source: William J. Sabol et al. "Prisoners in 2008." *Bulletin,* Bureau of Justice Statistics, U.S. Department of Justice, December 2009, p. 2.

2.3 Growth in the Rate of Imprisonment in the United States

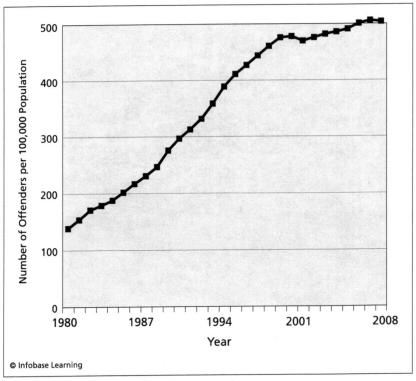

© Infobase Learning

In 1980, some 139 out of every 100,000 Americans in the U.S. population were sentenced inmates incarcerated in state and federal prisons in the United States. By 2008, the rate of imprisonment had more than tripled to just over 500 out of every 100,000 Americans in the U.S. population.

Source: Bureau of Justice Statisics. "Corrections: Key Facts at a Glance." Available online. URL: http://bjs.ojp.usdoj.gov/content/glance/incrt.cfm. Last updated December 8, 2009.

2.4 State Employment Nondiscrimination Laws

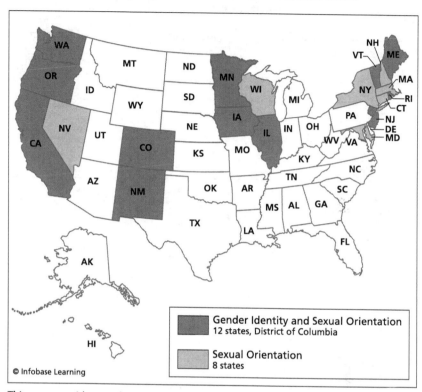

Gender Identity and Sexual Orientation
12 states, District of Columbia

Sexual Orientation
8 states

© Infobase Learning

This map provides a color-coded guide highlighting states that have laws prohibiting employment discrimination based on gender identity and sexual orientation as of January 1, 2009.

Source: Human Rights Campaign Foundation. "The State of the Workplace." February 12, 2009. Available online. URL: http://www.hrc.org/about_us/7061.htm. Accessed July 26, 2010.

2.5 Victims of Forced Labor in the United States by Country of Origin, 2004

Reported Country of Origin of Victims of Forced Labor	Number of Cases	Estimated Number of Individuals
Mexico	25	ca 1,500
United States	20	ca71
China	11	ca 10,000
Thailand	9	ca 150
India	9	ca 70
Bangladesh	8	ca 200
Russia	8	ca 100
Vietnam	6	ca 250
Honduras	5	ca 70
Philippines	5	ca 200
Korea	4	ca 6
Guatemala	3	ca 5
Indonesia	3	4
Cambodia	2	30
Cameroon	2	3
Estonia	2	15
Ghana	2	2
Kenya	2	2
Malaysia	2	8
Zambia	2	2
Albania	1	1
Brazil	1	1
Czech Republic	1	10
Ecuador	1	1
Ethiopia	1	3
Guyana	1	1
Haiti	1	1
Hungary	1	13
Jamaica	1	2
Kyrgyzstan	1	1

Reported Country of Origin of Victims of Forced Labor	Number of Cases	Estimated Number of Individuals
Latvia	1	5
Micronesia	1	2
Nigeria	1	2
Peru	1	8
Romania	1	10
Tonga	1	4
Ukraine	1	27
Uzbekistan	1	1
Yugoslavia	1	1

Specific Nationality Not Reported

Asia	6	ca 10,000
Southeast Asia	4	ca 30
"Hispanic"	2	ca 70
Eastern European	1	1

This table shows the breakdown of victims of forced labor according to country of origin. The number of cases and the number of individuals affected vary. While the majority of cases of forced labor were of people from Mexico, the cases with the largest numbers of individuals affected were those of Chinese origin.

Source: Free the Slaves and Human Rights Center, University of California, Berkeley. "Hidden Slaves: Forced Slavery in the United States." 2004. Available online. URL: http://digital commons.ilr.cornell.edu/cgi/viewcontent.cgi?article=1007&context=forced labor. Accessed July 26, 2010.

2.6 Economic Sectors Where Forced Labor Is Most Commonly Employed, 2004

Economic and Demographic Sectors	Frequency of cases (not individuals)	Percent
Prostitution	58	46.4
Domestic service	34	27.2
Agriculture	13	10.4
Sweatshop-factory	6	4.8
Service-food-care	5	3.8

Economic and Demographic Sectors	Frequency of cases (not individuals)	Percent
Sexual exploitation of children	4	3.1
Entertainment	4	3.1
Main-order bride	1	.8
TOTAL	**125**	**100.0**
No economic sector reported	6	
Total (all cases)	131	

This table reveals the industries and economic sectors where victims of forced labor are most commonly exploited. Almost half of all victims of forced labor end up in prostitution, while the second-most common area of work for victims of forced labor is domestic service.

Source: Free the Slaves and Human Rights Center, University of California, Berkeley. "Hidden Slaves: Forced Slavery in the United States." 2004. Available online. URL: http://digital commons.ilr.cornell.edu/cgi/viewcontent.cgi?article=1007&context=forced labor. Accessed July 26, 2010.

DEMOCRATIC REPUBLIC OF THE CONGO
3.1 Displacement Statistics in the Democratic Republic of the Congo, 2010

Residing in Democratic Republic of the Congo [1]

Refugees [2]	185,809
Asylum Seekers [3]	643
Returned Refugees [4]	44,296
Internally Displaced Persons (IDPs) [5]	2,052,677
Returned IDPs [6]	78,859
Stateless Persons [7]	0
Various [8]	11
Total Population of Concern	**2,362,295**

Originating from Democratic Republic of the Congo [1]

Refugees [2]	455,852
Asylum Seekers [3]	31,126
Returned Refugees [4]	44,296
Internally Displaced Persons [5]	2,052,677
Returned IDPs [6]	78,859
Various [8]	11
Total Population of Concern	**2,662,821**

1. Country or territory of asylum or residence. In the absence of government estimates, UNHCR has estimated the refugee population in most industrialized countries based on 10 years of asylum-seekers recognition.

2. Persons recognized as refugees under the 1951 UN Convention/1967 Protocol, the 1969 OAU Convention, in accordance with the UNHCR Statute, persons granted a complementary form of protection and those granted temporary protection. It also includes persons in a refugee-like situation whose status has not yet been verified.

3. Persons whose application for asylum or refugee status is pending at any stage in the procedure.

4. Refugees who have returned to their place of origin during the calendar year. *Source:* Country of origin and asylum.

5. Persons who are displaced within their country and to whom UNHCR extends protection and/or assistance. It also includes persons who are in an IDP-like situation.

6. IDPs protected/assisted by UNHCR who have returned to their place of origin during the calendar year.

7. Refers to persons who are not considered nationals by any country under the operation of its laws.

8. Persons of concern to UNHCR not included in the previous columns but to whom UNHCR extends protection and/or assistance.

9. The category of people in a refugee-like situation is descriptive in nature and includes groups of people who are outside their country of origin and who face protection risks similar to those of refugees, but for whom refugee status has, for practical or other reasons, not been ascertained.

This table shows the numbers of individuals who have been displaced in the Democratic Republic of the Congo as of January 2010.

Source: United Nations High Commissioner for Refugees (UNHCR). "2010 UNHCR Country Operations Profile—Democratic Republic of the Congo." January 2010. Available online. URL: http://www.unhcr.org/cgi-bin/texis/vtx/page?page=49e45c366#. Accessed July 26, 2010.

3.2 Statistics of Sexual Violence in the Democratic Republic of the Congo, 2007/2008

Number of rapes reported in 2008	15,996
Number of rapes reported in North Kivu province in 2008	4,820
Rape victims under the age of 18	65%
Rape victims under the age of 10	10%
Percentage of rape victims who have access to health centers	50%
Rapes committed by the Congolese National Army in the first six months of 2007	54%
Cases of rape that were heard before the military court for low-ranking soldiers in North Kivu in 2008	34
Convictions of rape cases heard before the military court in North Kivu in 2008	10

This table represents the statistical figures for sexual violence in the Democratic Republic of the Congo in 2007 and 2008. Concrete numbers are difficult to ascertain, as rape is widely underreported in the DRC, and some numbers represent estimates.

Source: Human Rights Watch. "Soldiers Who Rape, Commanders Who Condone: Sexual Violence and Military Reform in the Democratic Republic of the Congo." July 2009. Available online. URL: http://www.hrw.org/en/node/84366/section/7. Accessed July 26, 2010.

CHINA
3.3 Multi-Country Poll on Internet Access as a Human Right, 2010

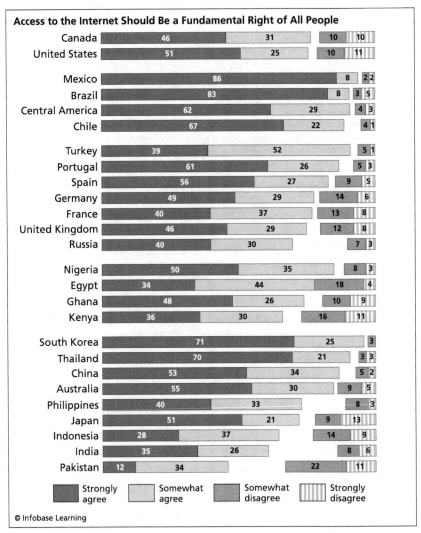

Access to the Internet Should Be a Fundamental Right of All People

Country	Strongly agree	Somewhat agree	Somewhat disagree	Strongly disagree
Canada	46	31	10	10
United States	51	25	10	11
Mexico	86	8	2	2
Brazil	83	8	3	5
Central America	62	29	4	3
Chile	67	22	4	1
Turkey	39	52	5	1
Portugal	61	26	5	3
Spain	56	27	9	5
Germany	49	29	14	6
France	40	37	13	8
United Kingdom	46	29	12	8
Russia	40	30	7	3
Nigeria	50	35	8	3
Egypt	34	44	18	4
Ghana	48	26	10	9
Kenya	36	30	16	11
South Korea	71	25	3	
Thailand	70	21	3	3
China	53	34	5	2
Australia	55	30	9	5
Philippines	40	33	8	3
Japan	51	21	9	13
Indonesia	28	37	14	9
India	35	26	8	6
Pakistan	12	34	22	11

© Infobase Learning

This table represents the results of a worldwide BBC poll on Internet access as a human right. Note that more Chinese respondents strongly agree that Internet access is a fundamental human right than U.S., Canadian, or British respondents.

Source: BBC News. "Internet Access is a 'Fundamental Right.'" March 3, 2010. Available online. URL: http://news/bbc/co/uk/2/shared/bsp/hi/pdfs/08_03_10_BBC_internet_poll.pdf. Accessed March 29, 2010.

3.4 Issues Facing China as Rated by Chinese Respondents, 2008

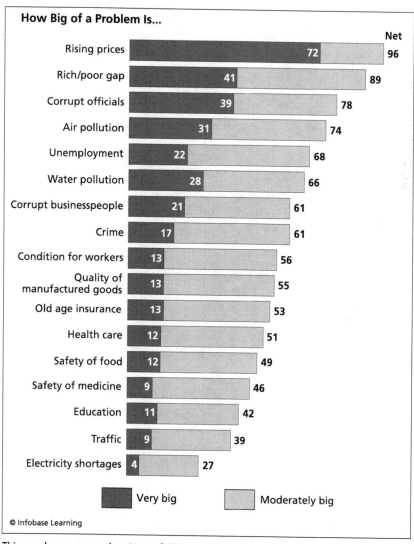

How Big of a Problem Is...

Issue	Very big	Net
Rising prices	72	96
Rich/poor gap	41	89
Corrupt officials	39	78
Air pollution	31	74
Unemployment	22	68
Water pollution	28	66
Corrupt businesspeople	21	61
Crime	17	61
Condition for workers	13	56
Quality of manufactured goods	13	55
Old age insurance	13	53
Health care	12	51
Safety of food	12	49
Safety of medicine	9	46
Education	11	42
Traffic	9	39
Electricity shortages	4	27

Very big   Moderately big

© Infobase Learning

This graph represents the views of Chinese citizens regarding major issues in China and how urgent the situations are.

Source: Pew Research Center. "The Chinese Celebrate Their Roaring Economy, As They Struggle with Its Costs." July 22, 2008. Available online. URL:http://pewglobal.org/2008/07/22/the-chinese-celebrate-their-roaring-economy-as-they-struggle-with-its-costs/. Accessed July 26, 2010.

CHECHNYA
3.5 Survey of Displaced Persons in Chechnya, 2004

	Chechnya (16–20 Feb 2004)	Ingushetia (26–30 Jan 2004)
Displacement history (n)	256	283
1994	48%	37%
1999	41%	54%
Displaced more than once	92%	82%
Wish to return home	86%	86%
Reason for not going home		
lack of shelter	78%	46%
insecurity	10%	49%
Living Circumstances		
Poor shelter against weather	4%	38%
Unable to keep warm	18%	40%
Poor toilet facilities	73%	90%
Insufficient food	50%	41%
Dependence on outside assistance	95%	94%
Insecurity		
Present		
Fears for personal safety	67%	38%
Loss of family member in past 2 months	7%	9%
loss due to violence	39%	19%
Past experiences		
Arrests/disappearances		
Family	53%	50%
Friend/neighbour	80%	62%
Attack on house/village	70%	73%
Cross-fire	62%	60%
Ariel bombardments	81%	78%
Mortar fire	72%	69%
Destruction of property	79%	81%
Witnessed killings	23%	24%
Detention	10%	10%
Kidnapping	7%	7%
Loss of someone close	89%	83%
Family	54%	37%
Neighbour	69%	63%
Loss of property	97%	88%

	Chechnya (16–20 C 2004)	Ingushetia (26–30 Jan 2004)
Loss of possessions	99%	95%
Health Status		
Frequent physical complaints in past 6 months	46%	53%
Poor access to medical services	54%	47%
Poor access to medicines	62%	55%

This table organizes information obtained from displaced individuals from Chechnya and Ingushetia due to the Russian counterterrorism campaign in Chechnya.

Source: de Jong, Kaz, Saskia van der Kam, Nathan Ford, Sally Hargreaves, Richard van Oosten, Debbie Cunningham, Gerry Boots, and Elodie Andrault. "The Trauma of Ongoing War in Chechnya: Quantitative Assessment of Living Conditions, and Psychosocial and General Health Status Among War Displaced in Chechnya and Ingushetia." Médecines Sans Frontihres. August 2004. Available online. URL: http://www.doctorswithoutborders.org/publications/reports/2004/chechnya_report_9-9-04.pdf. Accessed March 26, 2010.

3.6 Abductions and Disappearances in Chechnya by Year, 2004–2008

Year	Abductions	Disappearances of Abducted persons
2004	450	203
2005	325	126
2006	187	63
2007	25	Unknown
2008	100	Unknown

This table represents a breakdown of abductions and disappearances in Chechnya between 2004 and 2008, according to estimates by Memorial Human Rights Center. The Chechen president Ramzan Kadyrov assumed the presidency in 2007, which may explain to some extent why abductions and disappearances appear to have dropped off so suddenly that year.

Source: Human Rights Watch. "What Your Children Do Will Touch Upon You." July 2, 2009. Available online. URL: http://www.hrw.org/en/reports/2009/07/02/what-your-children-do-will-touch-upon-you-0. Accessed July 26, 2010.

3.7 Countries with the Highest Number of Executions in 2009

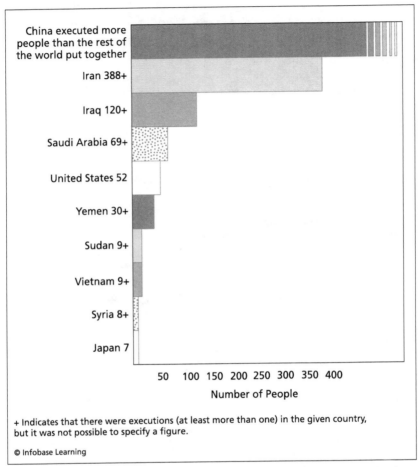

China executed more people than the rest of the world put together

Iran 388+

Iraq 120+

Saudi Arabia 69+

United States 52

Yemen 30+

Sudan 9+

Vietnam 9+

Syria 8+

Japan 7

50 100 150 200 250 300 350 400

Number of People

+ Indicates that there were executions (at least more than one) in the given country, but it was not possible to specify a figure.

© Infobase Learning

This graph shows the number of executions in 2009 by country. China is believed to have the highest number of executions, but no numbers can be confirmed, as the Chinese government refuses to release annual statistics on executions in China. Iran ranks just below China, and the United States has the fifth-highest number of executions in 2009.

Source: Amnesty International. "Death Sentences and Executions 2009." 2010. Available online. URL: http://www.amnesty.org/en/library/asset/ACT50/001/2010/en/17348b70-3fc7-40b2-a258-af92778c73e5/act500012010en.pdf. Accessed July 26, 2010.

IRAN

3.8 Discrepancies between 2005 and 2009 Voter Support for Ahmadinejad in Iran

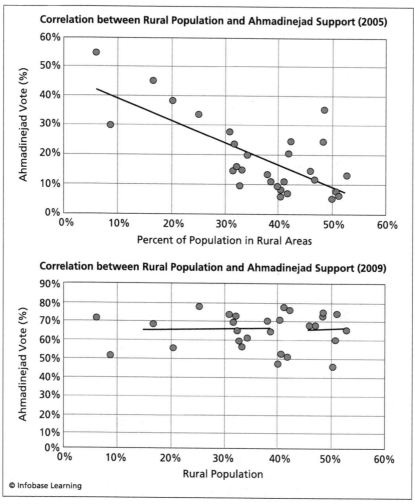

These two graphs chart voter support in the rural population of Iran in 2005 and 2009. As is visible in a comparison of the two tables, the trends from 2005 are virtually flipped upside down in 2009.

Source: Ansari, Ali, Daniel Berman, and Thomas Rintoul. "Preliminary Analysis of the Voting-Figures in Iran's 2009 Presidential Election." Chatham House. June 21, 2009. Available online. URL: http://www.chathamhouse.org.uk/files/14234_iranelection0609.pdf. Accessed March 29, 2010.

3.9 Death Sentences and Executions in 2009: Facts and Figures

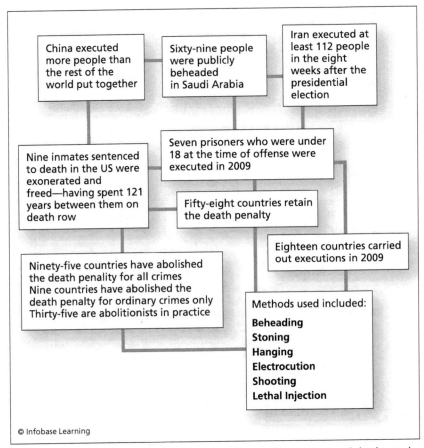

This table is an assemblage of several facts and figures of executions and death penalty sentences in 2009. In Iran, nearly a third of the 388 executions that took place in 2009 occurred in the eight weeks following the presidential elections.

Source: Amnesty International. "Death Sentences and Executions 2009." 2010. Available online. URL: http://www.amnesty.org/en/library/asset/ACT50/001/2010/en/17348b70-3fc7-40b2-a258-af92778c73e5/act500012010en.pdf. Accessed July 26, 2010.

8

Key Players A–Z

AFONSO I (1456–1542/3) Ruler of the Kongo Empire from 1509 to approximately 1543. Born Nzinga Mvemba, Afonso I rose to power after the arrival of the Portuguese and worked diligently with them to bring Christianity to the Kongo Empire. Upon the death of his father, King João I, Afonso was elected king and worked tirelessly to convert the Kongo Empire to Catholicism, establishing schools and financing the church with tax revenues. The slave trade was thriving in the Kongo Empire in the 16th century, and in 1526 Afonso wrote several letters to the Portuguese king about his concerns over the acts of Portuguese slave traders who were allegedly capturing free people to sell as slaves, slowly depleting the nation's population. No action was taken, and Afonso died in 1542 or '43, leaving several descendants who would rule over the Kongo Empire for years to come.

MAHMOUD AHMADINEJAD (1956–) Sixth president of the Islamic Republic of Iran. Ahmadinejad was born the fourth of seven children in Semnan Province of Iran. His mother was a sayyid, or a person believed to be a direct descendant of the Muslim prophet Muhammad. In 1976, he enrolled at the Iran University of Science and Technology, where he studied civil engineering and where he also later taught. In 1997, he received a Ph.D. in transportation engineering and planning from the same university. In 2003, Ahmadinejad became mayor of Tehran, reversing many of the changes made by his moderate and reformist predecessors. In 2005, he was elected president of Iran, but his reelection in 2009 was marred by accusations of fraud, leading to several riots and brutal police crackdowns.

CALIPH ALI (598–661) The cousin and son-in-law of the Muslim prophet Muhammad and ruler of the Islamic Caliphate from 656 to 661. Sunni Muslims believe Ali to be the fourth and last of the Rightly Guided Caliphs, while Shi'a Muslims (the dominant Muslim faction in Iran) consider Ali the first Imam (Supreme Leader) and his descendants as the rightful successors of Muhammad. When Muhammad reported having received a revelation from

God, Ali was among the first to support Muhammad and the development of the Islamic faith. Ali became the fourth caliph in 656, but in 661 he was attacked while praying and died shortly thereafter.

SUSAN B. ANTHONY (1820–1906)   Prominent women's rights leader and suffragist. Susan B. Anthony was born in West Grove, Massachusetts, to progressive parents who were both abolitionists and women's rights advocates. As a teenager, Anthony was an avid abolitionist, and in 1850 she became actively involved in the women's rights movement. Pairing up with fellow suffragist ELIZABETH CADY STANTON, the two toured the United States, delivering speeches on the rights of women. In 1869, Anthony and Stanton founded the National Women's Suffrage Association, of which Anthony became official president in 1892. She died 14 years before the passage of the Nineteenth Amendment, which recognized women's right to vote.

CHARLES LORING BRACE (1826–1890)   Founder of the Orphan Trains and the Children's Aid Society. A social reformer who graduated from Yale and went on to become a Calvinist minister, Brace ministered to the poor of New York City, where he witnessed the plight of homeless, abused, and hungry children who often joined street gangs and were known as the "violent classes." In 1853, he founded the Children's Aid Society, but came to the conclusion that the only way to save the street children from lives of violence was to transport them out of the urban squalor of New York City to the farmlands of the Midwest. Between 1854 and 1929, more than 200,000 children were relocated to family homes in the Midwest.

JIMMY CARTER (James Earl Carter) **(1924–   )** Served as the 39th president of the United States from 1977 to 1981. Jimmy Carter's presidential legacy is best defined by his emphasis on human rights. In 1977, Carter announced that countries that did not respect and defend basic human rights would not receive U.S. aid or arms (though this was truer in theory than in practice). Following his presidency, Carter and his wife, Rosalynn, founded the Carter Center in 1982, a nongovernmental nonprofit organization dedicated to advancing human rights. He has also become a primary figure in Habitat for Humanity, an organization that works to provide quality housing for families living below the poverty line.

ROGER CASEMENT (1864–1916)   An Irish revolutionary and nationalist who wrote about human rights abuses in the Congo and Peru. Casement was born near Dublin to a Catholic mother and a Protestant father who was captain of the Regiment of Light Dragoons. As the British Consul at Boma, Casement was commissioned in 1903 to investigate the state of human rights in the Congo. In 1904, the Casement Report documented the serious human rights violations perpetrated by the Belgian KING LEOPOLD's agents against the Congolese people in Leopold's personal quest to exploit the region's natural resources. The Casement Report was pivotal in forcing Leopold to release his hold on the Congo.

CÉSAR CHÁVEZ (1927–1993)   Mexican American farmworker and civil rights activist who campaigned for the rights of farmworkers. Chávez was born on a farm near Yuma, Arizona, and began working with his family as a migrant farmworker at the age of 10. In 1952, Chávez was trained as an organizer by Fred Ross for the Community Service Organization. Having spent his youth laboring in poverty, Chávez was committed to improving the lives of other migrant laborers, and in 1962 he cofounded the United Farm Workers Association. A vegan who read books on philosophy and economics, Chávez became a nationally renowned figure who led the first successful farm workers' union in history.

CYRUS THE GREAT (576 or 600 B.C.E.–530 B.C.E.)   Founder of the Persian Empire and known for the Cyrus Cylinder. Cyrus II was born in what is now the nation of Iran, and under his reign the Persian Empire expanded to envelop Southwest Asia and much of Central Asia, making it the largest empire in the world. In 1879, the Cyrus Cylinder was discovered. Primarily a tool of propaganda, which highlighted Cyrus's virtues and heroics as a leader, others consider the cylinder to be the first human rights charter in history.

DENG XIAOPING (1904–1997)   Third chairman of the Communist Party of the People's Republic of China from 1978 to 1983. An activist and revolutionary who fought in China's civil war and helped establish the People's Republic of China, Deng Xiaoping became China's leader and reformed many of the policies that had been installed during MAO ZEDONG's regime. He is known for steering China toward a market economy, essentially creating what became known as the socialist market economy, and making China one of the fastest-growing economies in the world. He is also known for his more controversial policies, such as the One-Child Birth Planning policy.

FREDERICK DOUGLASS (1818–1895)   Former slave and prominent abolitionist, writer, orator, and human rights advocate. Born a mixed-race slave (likely the son of his mother's white slave master) in Baltimore, Douglass was separated from his mother as an infant and was later sent to live with a family in Baltimore, where he learned to read. In 1838, Douglass escaped from slavery and married Anna Murray, a free black woman. He went on to publish his memoirs, *Narrative of the Life of Frederick Douglass,* *an American Slave,* and became a highly influential activist in a number of causes, including abolition, women's suffrage, and immigrants' rights.

DZHOKAR DUDAEV (1944–1996) First president of the Chechen Republic of Ichkeria. As the Soviet Union was dissolving, Dzhokar Dudaev and other Chechen militants invaded and claimed many key government buildings in Chechnya and subsequently declared Chechnya's independence from Russia. Under Dudaev's leadership, the Chechen economy crumbled and criminality soared. Dudaev's increasingly erratic and dictatorial behavior resulted in several efforts by opposition groups to forcibly depose him. Dudaev was assassinated in 1996 by two laser-guided missiles while using a satellite phone that allowed a Russian reconnaissance aircraft to locate his position.

OLAUDAH EQUIANO (Gustavus Vassa) **(1745–1797)** Writer, orator, former slave, and abolitionist; also known as Gustavus Vassa. Born in the Benin Empire and believed to be an Igbo, Equiano was kidnapped as a child along with his sister and sold into slavery. Initially enslaved in Africa, he was later forced onto a slave ship and transported overseas to Virginia. He eventually became a skilled seaman and was able to save enough money to buy his freedom, at which point he left America, never to return. As an adult, he penned his autobiography, *The Interesting Narrative of the Life of Olaudah Equiano, or Gustavus Vassa, the African,* and campaigned for the abolition of the slave trade in Great Britain.

DWIGHT D. EISENHOWER (1890–1969) President of the United States from 1953 to 1961. Born in Denison, Texas, as the third of seven sons, Eisenhower served in World War I and World War II before being elected president in 1953. Among his many accomplishments were the cease-fire in the Korean War, the launch of the interstate highway program, and the initiation of the space race. The Eisenhower administration was also responsible for participating in several international coups, including Iran and the Democratic Republic of the Congo, to depose believed-Communist or anti-U.S. leaders in favor of U.S.-friendly leaders.

NATALIA ESTEMIROVA (1958–2009) Russian journalist and human rights activist. The daughter of Russian and Chechen parents and the widow of a Chechen police officer, Estemirova began documenting human rights abuses during the Second Chechen War in 1999, and in 2000 she became a representative of the Chechen rights organization, the Memorial. Her investigative work aroused international attention, and she received several awards, but her journalism also brought her into direct conflict with the Chechen president Ramzan Kadyrov, who allegedly threatened her.

Estemirova was abducted on July 15, 2009, from her home in Grozny, and she was later found dead from gunshot wounds in Ingushetia. Her death has prompted international outcries from human rights organizations around the world concerned for the safety of human rights activists in Chechnya.

BETTY FRIEDAN (1921–2006)   Writer, feminist, author of the book *The Feminine Mystique,* and cofounder of the National Organization for Women. Following her graduation from Smith College, Friedan became a prominent journalist, writing for many union and leftist publications such as the *United Electrical Workers' UE News.* In 1952, she became pregnant with her second child and was consequently dismissed from her job with *UE News.* She went on to write about "the problem with no name," which referred to the dissatisfaction many housewives felt with their lives, which later became the subject of *The Feminine Mystique.* In 1966 she cofounded and became the first president of the National Organization for Women (NOW).

AKBAR GANJI (1960–)   Iranian journalist and prominent political dissident. During the Iran-Iraq War, Ganji served in the Islamic Revolutionary Guards Corps and the Ministry of Intelligence and National Security of Iran, but became disillusioned with the regime and its increasing extremism. He became an investigative journalist and published several reports detailing the actions of corrupt officials. One series of articles that investigated a string of murders known as the Chain Murders of Iran directly accused government officials of murdering dissidents, and in 2000 he was arrested and sentenced to six years in prison. He was released in 2006 and left Iran shortly thereafter.

MARGARET GARNER (?–1858)   African-American slave who became infamous for killing her daughter and attempting to kill her other children to prevent them from being taken back into slavery. In 1856, Margaret Garner, her husband, four children, and her husband's parents fled from Kentucky into the free state of Ohio, where they took refuge with Margaret's uncle and former slave, Joe Kite. The Fugitive Slave Act, however, allowed Southern slaveholders to track down and reclaim slaves that had escaped into the North. The group was located and U.S. marshals and slave catchers surrounded the house. During a violent shoot-out, Margaret killed her two-year-old daughter by cutting her throat, wounded her other children, and attempted to kill herself before being subdued. Her case inspired the 1987 Nobel Prize–winning novel *Beloved* by Toni Morrison and an opera with a libretto by Morrison.

ANGELA GRIMKÉ (1805–1878) and **SARAH GRIMKÉ (1792–1873)** Writers, abolitionists, and women's rights advocates. Born and raised on a plantation in Charleston, South Carolina, Sarah and Angela Grimké later traveled throughout the United States, speaking publicly against slavery and providing firsthand accounts of the lives of slaves on their family's plantation. As two of the first women to become active in such public campaigns as abolitionism and women's rights, they faced much public hostility. Their stirring speeches and powerful literary talents made them nationally renowned.

TENZIN GYATSO (1935–) Fourteenth Dalai Lama of Tibetan Buddhism. Tenzin Gyatso was born in the Tibetan village of Takster in the Chinese province of Qinghai. At the age of two, he was proclaimed the rebirth of the 13th Dalai Lama, and in 1950, at the age of 15, he was officially named the 14th Dalai Lama. That same year, the Chinese army invaded Tibet, and he was pressured to ratify an agreement that would allow China to take control of the region. Tenzin later fled to India, where he established his government with 80,000 other exiles. He was the first Dalai Lama to travel to the West, and in 1989 he received the Nobel Peace Prize.

HAMMURABI (?–1750 B.C.E.) King of Babylon from 1792 B.C.E. to 1750 B.C.E. and known for the Code of Hammurabi. The sixth king of Babylon in Mesopotamia, Hammurabi became known for uniting all of the kingdoms of Mesopotamia under his rule. He also promulgated a code of laws known as the Code of Hammurabi, which included 282 laws that were inscribed on a large stone stele that was erected in a public place for all to see. The laws generally followed the Lex Talionis or "Law of Retaliation" philosophy of "eye for an eye, tooth for a tooth."

THOMAS JEFFERSON (1743–1826) Third president of the United States from 1801 to 1809 and principal author of the Declaration of Independence. Jefferson was born in Virginia, where he was educated and went on to practice law. He became active in politics and, agitated by the abuses inflicted on the American colonies by the British government, wrote *A Summary View of the Rights of British America* in 1774. The following year, he drafted the Declaration of Independence, which was officially adopted by Congress in 1776. From 1785 to 1789, he served as minister to France, where he supported the French Revolution. In 1800, he was elected president of the United States.

LAURENT KABILA (1939–2001) President of the Democratic Republic of the Congo from 1997 until his assassination in 2001. When the Congo declared its independence in 1960, Laurent Kabila was a young deputy commander in the pro-Lumumba General Association of the Baluba People of Katanga. During the Mobutu Sese Seko regime, Kabila established a rebel operation in South Kivu, where he founded the People's Revolutionary Party. The Latin American revolutionary leader Che Guevara came to his assistance with 100 Cuban revolutionaries, but criticized Kabila for being more interested in alcohol and women than in revolution. In 1996, Kabila led his forces into rebellion, beginning the First Congo War. In 1997, Mobutu fled the country, and Kabila assumed power, but proved to be a petty and authoritarian dictator. In 2001, he was shot by a member of his own staff.

RAMZAN KADYROV (1976–) Former Chechen rebel and current president of Chechnya. The Kadyrovs started out as rebels but defected to the Moscow camp during the Second Chechen War in 1999. When Ramzan took office as president in 2007, following the assassination of his father, Akhmad Kadyrov, in 2004, he received much praise from the Russian president VLADIMIR PUTIN and was awarded the Hero of Russia medal. Kadyrov is known for his violent and authoritarian rule, which has included state-sanctioned punitive house burnings to punish the families of rebels. He is also alleged to have orchestrated the murder of the prominent human rights activist and journalist NATALIA ESTEMIROVA.

AYATOLLAH ALI KHAMENEI (1939–) Supreme Leader of Iran since 1989. Following the death of the controversial Ayatollah Khomeini in 1989, Ali Khamenei became the Supreme Leader of Iran, invested with the power of having the final say on any and all political decisions in Iran. Khamenei has been staunchly in favor of MAHMOUD AHMADINEJAD, and when suspicions of election-rigging arose following Ahmadinejad's curious victory in 2009, Khamenei reaffirmed his support for Ahmadinejad and urged Iranian citizens to do the same.

AYATOLLAH RUHOLLAH KHOMEINI (1902–1989) Supreme Leader of Iran from 1979 to 1989. During the shah's dictatorial rule, Ayatollah Khomeini was an openly and vocally oppositional figure. When Shah Muhammad Reza Pehlavi was overthrown in the Iranian Revolution, Ayatollah Khomeini returned from exile to create and assume the position of Supreme Leader of Iran. His political life was highly controversial, as he supported the student hostage takers during the Iranian hostage crisis and effectively erased women's rights in Iran. Khomeini died of a heart attack in 1989 and was succeeded by AYATOLLAH ALI KHAMENEI.

MARTIN LUTHER KING, JR. (1929–1968) Baptist minister and civil rights activist. King was born and raised in Atlanta, Georgia, where he attended Booker T. Washington High School. He skipped the ninth and 12th grades and began college at the age of 15. He received his Ph.D. in systematic theology at Boston University in 1951 and married Coretta Scott in 1953. Best known for his "I Have a Dream" speech, which is considered one of the greatest speeches in history, King is also well known for encouraging nonviolent civil disobedience to campaign for African-American civil rights. In

1964, he became the youngest person to be awarded the Nobel Peace Prize. King was shot during a speech on the balcony outside of his hotel room. Small-time crook James Earl Ray confessed to the murder, but later recanted.

BARTOLOMÉ DE LAS CASAS (1484–1566) Spanish Dominican priest who opposed and documented the abuses inflicted on the indigenous peoples of the Americas by Spanish colonists. As a young man, Las Casas's father and uncles participated in Christopher Columbus's voyages to the Americas, and in 1502 Bartolomé and his father traveled to the island of Hispaniola (today the island of Haiti and the Dominican Republic), where he witnessed the torture, brutality, and outright genocide of the island natives. Las Casas advocated for the rights of the natives and documented the abuses in his book *Historias de las Indias,* but the book was not published until 1875.

KING LEOPOLD II (1835–1909) King of Belgium from 1865 to 1909 and responsible for the Belgian colonization of the Congo. Leopold inherited the throne following the death of his father, Leopold I. Seeing the potential for great financial reward in Africa's natural resources, Leopold II established a private company disguised as a humanitarian organization, known as the International African Society. His quest for the Congo's rich stores of rubber and ivory resulted in the brutal exploitation of the Congolese people through forced labor, rape, torture, and bodily mutilation.

LIU XIAOBO (1955–) Writer and human rights activist in China. Liu received his Ph.D. from Beijing Normal University in 1988 and has been a visiting scholar at several universities around the world. A prominent human rights activist, Liu has been arrested numerous times in connection with human rights protests in China, including the 1989 Tiananmen Square protests. Liu, along with more than 300 other Chinese citizens, signed the Charter 08 manifesto, which called for freedom of expression and protection of individual rights in China. Two days before the release of the charter, Liu was arrested and later sentenced to 11 years in prison for attempting to subvert state power.

JOHN LOCKE (1632–1704) British Enlightenment philosopher whose theories of government influenced the American Declaration of Independence. Born to Puritan parents in Somerset, England, Locke studied medicine and the works of other philosophers at Oxford University. His theories on nature, property, government, society, and the mind influenced other major philosophers such as Voltaire and Rousseau, as well as Thomas Jefferson and the American Revolutionaries. He had a direct influence on America in 1669 when he drafted the Fundamental Constitutions of Carolina.

THOMAS LUBANGA (1960–)   Former rebel leader in the Democratic Republic of the Congo and the first person ever arrested and tried for war crimes by the International Criminal Court (ICC). Born in the Ituri Province of the Democratic Republic of the Congo, Lubanga attended the University of Kisangani, where he earned a degree in psychology. During the Second Congo War, he was the minister of defense for the Uganda-allied Congolese Rally for Democracy-Liberation Movement, before founding another rebel group known as the Union of Congolese Patriots. Under his leadership, his troops committed widespread atrocities, including murder, torture, rape, ethnic slaughter, mutilation, and the kidnapping and conscription of child soldiers. He was arrested in 2006, and his ICC trial began in 2009.

PATRICE LUMUMBA (1925–1961)   First democratically elected prime minister of the Congo, following its independence from Belgium. In the years leading up to Congo's independence, Lumumba was involved in several liberation efforts, most notably as the president of the Mouvement National Congolais (MNC). When Congo declared its independence, Lumumba was elected prime minister, and at a celebratory event attended by King Baudouin of Belgium, who praised the genius of his ancestor, KING LEOPOLD II, Lumumba retaliated in his speech, declaring, "We are no longer your monkeys." Lumumba was notably left-leaning amid cold war tensions, and in a coup that was backed by the United States and Belgian governments, he was deposed and executed.

MALCOLM X (1925–1965)   Civil rights activist and orator. Born Malcolm Little in Omaha, Nebraska, Malcolm X's childhood was marked by much pain and trauma. His father, Earl Little, was active in the Universal Negro Improvement Association and the target of several Ku Klux Klan threats. The family was terrorized by local white supremacist groups, and when Earl Little was struck and killed by a car, many suspected murder. Malcolm's mother was later committed to a mental institution. As a young man, Malcolm became involved in criminal activities in Boston that landed him in jail, where he became interested in Islam. He spent the rest of his adult life campaigning for the rights of African Americans until his assassination in 1965.

JAMES MURRAY MASON (1798–1871)   U.S. senator from Virginia who drafted the Fugitive Slave Act of 1850. Born and raised in the District of Columbia, Mason drafted the Fugitive Slave Act of 1850, which mandated the return of runaway slaves to their masters in the South. The original Fugitive Slave Act, passed in 1793, was largely ignored as many Northerners refused to comply, but Mason's redrafting of it made U.S. marshals and other law enforcement personnel who did not arrest fugitive slaves subject to a $1,000 fine. Previously, fugitive slaves were entitled to a trial, but under the 1850 act, all that was needed was the slaveholder's testimony of ownership.

MAO ZEDONG (1893–1976)   Leader of the People's Republic of China from 1949 to 1976 and First Chairman of the Communist Party of China from 1943 to 1976. When the People's Republic of China was established in 1949, Mao Zedong, who was heavily influenced by Leninist and Marxist philosophy, was named First Chairman. His social and agricultural reforms, such as the Great Leap Forward and the Cultural Revolution, were responsible for widespread devastation to China's agriculture and crippling famine, and his purges and social programs caused the deaths of 50 to 70 million people.

MOBUTU SESE SEKO (1930–1997)   President of Zaire (Democratic Republic of the Congo) from 1965 to 1997. Born Joseph-Désiré Mobutu, Mobutu became president following the overthrows of both PATRICE LUMUMBA and his successor, Joseph Kasavubu. He quickly established a totalitarian dictatorship, and in 1971 he renamed the country the Republic of Zaire. All Congolese citizens were required to stop using their Christian names and adopt African names, and priests faced five years' imprisonment if they were caught baptizing a Zairean child with a Christian name. Despite his practice of publicly executing rivals, as well as embezzling millions of dollars from his own country, he received much support from the United States government. He was eventually overthrown in the First Congo War and died in exile.

MUHAMMAD MOSSADEGH (1882–1967)   Prime minister of Iran from 1951 to 1953. Mossadegh studied law in Paris and Switzerland before his election as prime minister of Iran in 1951, under Shah MOHAMMAD REZA PAHLAVI. As prime minister, he nationalized Iran's oil reserves, which, until that point, had been developed by the British government-owned British Anglo-Iranian Oil Company (BAIOC), which had refused to share half of its profits with Iran. Following the oil nationalization, the British government placed an embargo on all Iranian oil. Mossadegh was deposed in a British- and U.S.-backed coup in 1953.

HOSSEIN MOUSAVI (1942–)   Prime minister of Iran from 1981 to 1989, and presidential candidate in 2009. An architect, painter, and reformist politician, Mousavi is best known for his role as prime minister and, most recently, as MAHMOUD AHMADINEJAD's opponent during the 2009 Iranian presidential elections. Mousavi's campaign color was green, and he has since become the leader of the Green Movement, which seeks the removal of Ahmadinejad. When Ahmadinejad won the presidency in the June 2009 elections, Mousavi supporters took to the streets in protest, often wearing green or bearing green flags and banners.

SHAH MOHAMMAD REZA PAHLAVI (1941–1979)   Shah of Iran from 1941 to 1979. Pahlavi came to power following the forced abdication of his father during World War II. When Prime Minister MUHAMMAD MOSSADEGH was deposed in a CIA-backed coup, sole reign over Iran fell to Pahlavi. His regime was characterized by repression of opposition, and his secret service SAVAK arrested, imprisoned, and tortured many political dissidents. The 1979 Iranian Revolution prompted Pahlavi and his wife to flee the country. Fearing U.S. involvement that would seek to reinstate the shah, a group of Iranian students invaded the U.S. Embassy and took several Americans hostage.

THOMAS PAINE (1737–1809)   Author and American Revolutionary. Born to Quaker and Anglican parents in England, Paine was a failed businessman and excise officer before immigrating to America, where he proved to be a brilliant writer. Beginning his career as editor of *Pennsylvania Magazine*, he went on to anonymously publish *Common Sense*, a pamphlet that called for independence from Britain. The pamphlet was widely influential and is credited with catalyzing the American Revolution. He was also an advocate of abolition, compulsory education, and guaranteed minimum wage. His other written works include *Rights of Man* and *The Age of Reason*.

VLADIMIR PUTIN (1952–)   Second president of the Russian Federation and the current prime minister. As a young man, Putin studied law, graduating from Leningrad State University in 1975 before joining the KGB. Putin became president in late 1999, when the then president BORIS YELTSIN suddenly resigned. Though the Second Chechen War was already under way when Putin became president, he encouraged a major land invasion and seizure of Chechnya. He also declared the Chechen presidency of Aslan Maskhadov illegitimate. In May 2000, Putin appointed Akhmad Kadyrov president of Chechnya, thereby reestablishing Russian control over the country. Guerrilla warfare and Russian counterinsurgencies continued throughout Putin's presidency, which ended in 2008.

ELEANOR ROOSEVELT (1884–1962)   First Lady of the United States from 1933 to 1945 and one of the principal drafters of the Universal Declaration of Human Rights. During and after Franklin Delano Roosevelt's time in office, Eleanor Roosevelt was known for championing the rights of woman and in the 1940s, she was one of the cofounders of Freedom House, an NGO that conducts research on democracy, political issues, and human rights. A delegate in the UN General Assembly from 1945 to 1952, Roosevelt chaired the committee that drafted the Universal Declaration of Human Rights.

JEAN-JACQUES ROUSSEAU (1712–1778) Enlightenment philosopher and writer. Jean-Jacques Rousseau was born in Geneva and spent much of his youth studying and traveling throughout Europe. As a teenager, he was introduced to Françoise-Louise de Warens, who supported him financially and later became his lover. He later took a young seamstress as a lover, with whom he may have had as many as five children, all of whom were abandoned to foundling hospitals. Despite the abandonment of his own children, he is well known today for his theories on education and child rearing. His philosophy of politics and rights heavily influenced the French Revolution.

MARGARET SANGER (1879–1966) Family planning activist and founder of the American Birth Control League. Born the sixth of 11 children, Sanger grew up in Corning, New York, and married William Sanger, with whom she moved to Manhattan. While working as a nurse in the slums of Manhattan's East Side, Sanger became aware of the need for contraceptives for the area's poor women and began writing newspaper columns and pamphlets on family planning. In 1916, Sanger opened a birth control clinic in Brooklyn, for which she was arrested and sentenced to 30 days in prison. Today, she is considered a controversial figure, not only for her views on birth control and abortion, but for her support of eugenics.

DRED SCOTT (1799–1858) A slave who attempted to sue his owner for his freedom in St. Louis, Missouri. The *Dred Scott v. Sandford* case originated when Scott argued that because he and his wife, Harriet, had spent almost nine years traveling with Scott's owner, Dr. John Emerson, throughout Illinois and the Wisconsin Territory, where slavery was prohibited, they were therefore legally free. Dred and Harriet Scott made no claims to freedom during their time in the northern territories, likely because they were not aware of their rights. The case went on for 11 years, and Scott lost, but was eventually sold and freed in 1857, shortly before his death in 1858.

JOSEPH STALIN (1878–1953) Leader of the Soviet Union from 1922 to 1953. Born Joseph Dzhugashvili in Georgia, Stalin (which means "steel") is renowned for his paranoia, which resulted in several purges of members of the Communist Party. His agricultural reform and collectivization campaigns resulted in widespread famine, which is estimated to have killed between 5 and 10 million people. He even went to the extreme of ordering the deportation of entire countries, as was the case for Chechnya. Official records place the number of people who died under Stalin's leadership at 3 million (which accounts only for those who were executed or died in the gulags). Historians estimate that the number of deaths under Stalin's regime may, in fact, be as high as 60 million.

HENRY MORTON STANLEY (1841–1904) Welsh journalist and explorer whose expeditions in Africa helped King LEOPOLD II of the Belgians secure his claim to the Congo. Born to poor, unmarried parents in Wales, Stanley spent his childhood staying with various relatives and eventually ending up in a workhouse for the poor. As a teenager, he traveled to America, where he became a journalist and traveled extensively. Instructed by his employers to search for the missing missionary and explorer Dr. David Livingstone, Stanley traveled to Africa, where, upon finding Dr. Livingstone, he reportedly said: "Dr. Livingstone, I presume?" He later went on to explore the Congo River, and was then approached by King Leopold II to help develop the region.

ELIZABETH CADY STANTON (1815–1902) Abolitionist and women's rights activist. Stanton was born the eighth of 11 children in Johnstown, New York. As a young woman she became involved in the abolitionist movement. However, when she witnessed the sexism that prevented many women from participating in the abolitionist movement, she began to campaign more emphatically for women's rights. She is best known for publishing the "Declaration of Sentiments" and presenting at the Seneca Falls Women's Rights Convention. She and fellow suffragist SUSAN B. ANTHONY caused much controversy when they refused to support the Fourteenth and Fifteenth Amendments, which allowed African-American men the right to vote, but excluded women.

SUN YAT-SEN (1866–1925) Chinese revolutionary and first provisional president of the Republic of China. As a Western-educated dissident, Sun sought to change what he perceived to be the backwardness and repression of Imperialist China, and in 1895 he orchestrated a coup that failed and he fled to London, where he was seized by Chinese diplomats who planned to kill him. The British government intervened, however, and Sun was released. When a successful military uprising overthrew the Qing dynasty, Sun returned to China and became the first provisional president of the new Republic of China. He later cofounded and became the first leader of the Kuomintang.

SOJOURNER TRUTH (1797–1883) Escaped slave, abolitionist, and women's rights activist. Born Isabella Baumfree in New York, Truth spoke only Dutch until she was sold at the age of nine to John Neely, a cruel slaveholder who beat and raped Truth regularly. Truth was sold several times until she came under the ownership of Martinus Schryver, who owned her for 18 years. She was forced to marry an older man, with whom she had five children. In 1826, Truth escaped slavery with her infant daughter and went on to become a prominent rights activist. Her most famous speech, "Ain't I a Woman?" was delivered at the Ohio Women's Rights Convention in 1851.

BOOKER T. WASHINGTON (1856–1915)   Former slave, orator, writer, and civil rights leader. Washington was born shortly before the Civil War, the child of an African-American slave and a white man. After the Civil War, he was educated at the Hampton Institute and went on to head the Tuskegee Institute, a vocational school for freed black men and women. Washington remains a controversial figure in the history of civil rights for his emphasis on developing trade skills in African Americans rather than pressing for formal education, as well as his cooperation with white segregationists.

MARY ELLEN WILSON (1864–1956)   A child-abuse survivor whose case helped establish child-protection laws. As an infant, Wilson's father died, and her mother was forced to board young Mary out so that she could work to support them. When Wilson's mother could no longer afford to pay for child care, Mary was sent to the New York City Department of Charities. Mary was taken in by Mary and Thomas McCormack, but Thomas died soon after and Mary suffered cruel mistreatment under the care of her stepmother. A Methodist missionary and the Humane Society intervened and successfully removed Mary from the home.

BORIS YELTSIN (1931–1997)   First president of the Russian Federation, from 1991 to 1999. Yeltsin was elected president following the fall of the Soviet Union, promising to transform Russia's socialist economy into a free market economy. His presidency, however, was marked by corruption and economic devastation. In 1994, Yeltsin ordered the military invasion of Chechnya to reclaim the country in the First Chechen War, which resulted in the deaths of 15,000 to 100,000 people. Though he won the presidency with 57 percent of the vote, he resigned with an estimated 2 percent approval rating.

9

Organizations and Agencies

The Abdorrahman Boroumand Foundation:
Human Rights and Democracy for Iran
URL: http://www.iranrights.org/
3220 N Street NW, Suite 357
Washington, DC 20007

Named after Dr. Abdorrahman Boroumand, an Iranian lawyer and activist who was assassinated in Paris in 1991, the foundation is a nonprofit NGO that seeks to promote international awareness of the status of human rights in Iran through educational outreach.

ACCION
URL: http://www.accion.org/
56 Roland Street, Suite 300
Boston, MA 02129
Phone: (617) 625-7080

ACCION is a nonprofit microfinance organization that provides microloans, business training, and other financial services to women and men living in poverty who want to start businesses. ACCION's mission is to help relieve poverty and hunger by helping individuals in impoverished communities become self-sufficient.

AIDS.gov
URL: http://aids.gov/
U.S. Department of Health and Human Services
200 Independence Avenue SW
Washington, DC 20201
E-mail: contact@aids.gov

AIDS.gov is a U.S. government Web site designed to provide information on HIV/AIDS, prevention, and treatment, and to educate the public and at-risk communities on HIV/AIDS.

American Civil Liberties Union (ACLU)
URL: http://www.aclu.org/
125 Broad Street, 18th Floor
New York, NY 10004
Phone: (212) 549-2500

Founded in 1920, the American Civil Liberties Union (ACLU) works in courts and legislatures to uphold individual civil rights, including First Amendment rights (freedom of expression, assembly, and religion), equal rights, rights to due process, and rights to privacy.

American Foreign Policy Council
URL: http://www.afpc.org/
509 C Street NE
Washington, DC 20002
Phone: (202) 543-1007

The American Foreign Policy Council (AFPC) is a nonprofit organization that conducts policy analysis and provides information to those creating foreign policy, members of Congress, and the Executive Branch. The AFPC Web site also provides a wealth of information on current issues in foreign policy and U.S. relations with other countries.

AmeriCorps
URL: http://www.americorps.gov/
1201 New York Avenue NW
Washington, DC 20525
Phone: (202) 606-5000

AmeriCorps is a national program that aims to strengthen American communities by partnering trained individuals (either paid AmeriCorps employees or volunteers) with nonprofit organizations throughout the country. Full-time AmeriCorps members commit to one year of service, during which time they are paid a modest living allowance.

Amnesty International
URL: http://www.amnesty.org/
1 Easton Street

London
WC1X 0DW, UK
Phone: (011-44-20) 7956-1157

Amnesty International is a worldwide organization that works to protect human rights and prevent human rights abuses through education and activism. Their areas of focus include violence against women, poverty, the death penalty, torture and terrorism, the global arms trade, and the rights of immigrants and refugees.

Association for Women's Rights in Development (AWID)
URL: http://www.awid.org/
215 Spadina Ave, Suite 150
Toronto Ontario
M5T 2C7
Canada
Phone: (416) 594-3773

The Association for Women's Rights in Development (AWID) is an international feminist network of women and men from various backgrounds and fields devoted to protecting gender equality, sustainable development, and women's rights.

Brookings Institution
URL: http://www.brookings.edu/
1775 Massachusetts Avenue NW
Washington, DC 20036
Phone: (202) 797-6000

The Brookings Institution is a renowned think tank and nonprofit public policy organization that conducts independent research to provide information and recommendations with the goal of strengthening American democracy, improving the social and economic welfare of Americans, and fostering a more open and cooperative international system.

Carnegie Council for Ethics in International Affairs
URL: http://www.cceia.org/index.html
Merrill House
170 East 64th Street
New York, NY 10065-7478
Phone: (212) 838-4120

The Carnegie Council for Ethics in International Affairs is a nonprofit educational institution that strives to address broad ethical themes, including global social justice, war and peace, and religion in politics. Current programs include workshops for ethics in business, public affairs speaking events, global policy innovations, and public ethics radio.

Carr Center for Human Rights Policy
URL: http://www.hks.harvard.edu/cchrp/
John F. Kennedy School of Government
79 JFK Street
Cambridge, MA 02138
Phone: (617) 495-5819

The Carr Center for Human Rights Policy was established in 1999 with the goal of training future leaders for careers in public service and to make human rights issues a central priority in the creation of public policy in the United States and abroad.

The Carter Center
URL: http://www.cartercenter.org/index.html
One Copenhill
453 Freedom Parkway
Atlanta, GA 30307
Phone: (404) 420-5100
E-mail: carterweb@emory.edu

The Carter Center, in partnership with Emory University, is a nongovernmental organization that works around the world in various areas of human rights, conflict resolution, promotion of democracy, and the prevention and eradication of diseases such as river blindness, Guinea worm, and malaria. The program also offers resources in the areas of agriculture and mental health.

Change.org
URL: http://www.change.org/
E-mail: feedback@change.org

Change.org is an organization devoted to gathering and disseminating information on major social and environmental issues, both domestic and international. The aim of the group is to educate individuals and provide materials for becoming involved in issues ranging from health care, education, women's rights, GLBT rights, and climate change.

Organizations and Agencies

Child Labor Coalition
URL: http://www.stopchildlabor.org/
National Consumers League
1701 K Street NW, Suite 1200
Washington, DC 20006
Phone: (202) 835-3323
E-mail: reidm@nclnet.org

The Child Labor Coalition is a project of the National Consumers League that works to raise public awareness of child labor, protect working minors and end child labor exploitation, and promote legislation and policies that will combat child labor.

Children's Defense Fund
URL: http://www.childrensdefense.org/
25 E Street NW
Washington, DC 20001
Phone: (800) CDF-1200

The Children's Defense Fund was established in 1973 to conduct and publish research on child survival, development, and protection in the United States. Current campaigns include providing health coverage for all children, ending child poverty, providing leadership training for youth, and preventing at-risk youth from ending up in prison.

Children's Rights
URL: http://www.childrensrights.org/
330 Seventh Avenue, 4th Floor
New York, NY 10001
Phone: (212) 683-2210

Children's Rights is a nationwide advocacy group that works to reform child welfare systems throughout the United States by releasing policy reports, participating in advocacy efforts, and taking direct legal action.

Children's Rights International
URL: http://www.childjustice.org/html/index.htm
P.O. Box 163, Newtown
Sydney, Australia 2042
Phone: (011-61-2) 9519-9506

Children's Rights International is an international organization that seeks to enforce the United Nations Convention on the Rights of the Child by uniting various specialists across disciplines to protect and advance children's human rights around the world.

Child Rights Information Network (CRIN)
URL: http://www.crin.org/
East Studio
2, Pontypool Place
London, SE1 8QF
United Kingdom
Phone: (011-44-20) 7401-2257

Child Rights Information Network (CRIN) is an international child advocacy organization that bases its goals on the United Nations Convention on the Rights of the Child. Working with 150 countries, CRIN launches advocacy campaigns, leads children's rights coalitions, and works to make children's rights the leading priority of the international community.

Childwatch International Research Network
URL: http://www.childwatch.uio.no/
P.O. Box 1132 Blindern
N-0317 Oslo
Norway
Phone: (011-47-22) 85-4350

The Childwatch International Research Network is an international body of organizations that works to protect children's rights by collaborating on local, regional, national, and international research.

The Cluster Munition Coalition
URL: http://www.stopclustermunitions.org/
2nd Floor
89 Albert Embankment
London
SE1 7TP
England
Phone: (011-44-20) 7820-0222

The Cluster Munition Coalition (CMC) is an international campaign to eliminate the use of cluster munitions (or cluster bombs) through advocacy for anticluster munitions policy and public education. CMC's objectives include pressuring governments to adhere to the 2008 Convention on Cluster Munitions and to build partnerships and facilitate communication.

Organizations and Agencies

Coalition Against Trafficking in Women (CATW)
URL: http://www.catwinternational.org/
P.O. Box 7427
Jaf Station
New York, NY 10116
Fax: (212) 643-9896

The Coalition Against Trafficking in Women (CATW) is an NGO that aims to protect women and children from commercial sexual exploitation and trafficking by creating and supporting antitrafficking projects, addressing the links between prostitution and trafficking, combating the demand for prostitution, and challenging legal acceptance of prostitution and trafficking.

Constitutional Rights Foundation
URL: http://crf-usa.org/
601 South Kinglsey Drive
Los Angeles, CA 90005
Phone: (213) 487-5590

The Constitutional Rights Foundation (CRF) is a nonprofit community-based organization that works to educate America's youth on civic participation and law and government. CRF also develops and distributes educational materials for teachers, coordinates participation projects in schools, and organizes student conferences.

Crimes of War Project
URL: http://www.crimesofwar.org/
1325 G Street NW, Suite 730
Washington, DC 20005
Phone: (202) 638-0230

The Crimes of War Project is a collaborative effort by lawyers, journalists, and scholars to raise public awareness of the legal framework governing armed conflict with the goal of preventing and rectifying war crimes and crimes against humanity.

ECPAT International
URL: http://www.ecpat.net/EI/index.asp
328/1 Phayathai Road
Rachathewi, Bangkok
Thailand 10400
Phone: (011-66-2) 215-3388

ECPAT (End Child Prostitution, Child Pornography, and Trafficking of Children for Sexual Purposes) is a global network of 80 groups in more than 70 countries that seeks to eliminate the commercial sexual exploitation of children by raising public awareness and publishing reports on government efforts to combat child sexual exploitation.

Enough
URL: http://www.enoughproject.org/
1225 Eye Street NW, Suite 307
Washington, DC 20005
Phone: (202) 682-1611

Enough is a project of the Center for American Progress and works to end genocide and crimes against humanity. Created to press the United States and other world powers to intervene in crimes against humanity, the Enough Project focuses on the specific areas of Sudan, the Democratic Republic of the Congo, northern Uganda, Somalia, Chad, and Zimbabwe.

Equality Matters
URL: http://www.equalitymatters.org/
E-mail: info@equalitymatters.org

Equality Matters is a self-described online protest that uses social media and networking sites such as Facebook.com to educate the public and gather support for the issue of gay marriage. Equality Matters comprises only a small group of volunteers, but the Web site offers useful information on the current status of gay marriage and how GLBT families are affected by antigay marriage laws.

Equality Now
URL: http://www.equalitynow.org/
P.O. Box 20646
Columbus Circle Station
New York, NY 10023
Phone: (212) 586-1611

Equality Now is an international organization dedicated to ending violence and discrimination against women and girls. Equality Now primarily focuses on the issues of rape, trafficking, domestic violence, reproductive rights, female genital mutilation, and political participation.

European Court of Human Rights
URL: http://www.echr.coe.int/echr/Homepage_En
Council of Europe

67075 Strasbourg-Cedex
France
Phone: (011-33-3) 8841-2730

The European Court of Human Rights (ECHR) was created in 1959 to uphold the European Convention on Human Rights. As an international body, the court rules on cases brought forth by plaintiffs against countries where human rights violations are alleged to have occurred.

Fair Trade Federation
URL: http://www.fairtradefederation.org/
1718 M Street NW, #107
Washington, DC 20036
Phone: (202) 636-3549

The Fair Trade Federation is an organization that works to build sustainable trade partnerships between North America and other countries for the promotion of equitable trade throughout the world, the alleviation of poverty, and the protection of the environment.

Family Equality Council
URL: http://www.familyequality.org/
P.O. Box 206
Boston, MA 02133
Phone: (617) 502-8700

The mission of the Family Equality Council is to ensure equality for gay and lesbian families by supporting GLBT-headed families, educating the public, supporting equitable policies, challenging discriminatory laws and policies, and partnering with other organizations to maximize resources.

Female Genital Cutting Education and Networking Project
URL: http://www.fgmnetwork.org/index.php
E-mail: http://www.fgmnetwork.org/mail/index.php

The aim of the Female Genital Cutting Education and Networking Project is to raise public awareness of female genital mutilation (FGM), also known as female circumcision, a practice that is pervasive around the world and particularly in African and some Middle Eastern countries.

Free the Children
URL: http://www.freethechildren.com/
233 Carlton Street

Toronto, Ontario
M5A 2L2
Canada
Phone: (416) 925-5894

Free the Children is the world's largest network of children helping children. The organization, which has received the Children's Nobel Prize among many other awards, engages youth and provides leadership training to help eliminate child poverty and exploitation.

Global Aids Alliance
URL: http://www.globalaidsalliance.org/
1121 14th Street NW, Suite 200
Washington, DC 20005
Phone: (202) 789-0432

Global Aids Alliance (GAA) is an international organization that works to stop the spread of HIV/AIDS infection around the world and alleviate its effects on poor countries through policy analysis, advocacy, organizing, and media outreach.

Global Fund for Women
URL: http://www.globalfundforwomen.org/cms/
222 Sutter Street Suite 500
San Francisco, CA 94108
Phone: (415) 248-4800

The Global Fund for Women is an international network that works to protect women's human rights around the world by raising funds and making grants to women-run organizations around the world to promote education, health, leadership, and economic security for women and girls.

Global Health Council
URL: http://www.globalhealth.org/
1111 19th Street NW, Suite 1120
Washington, DC 20036
Phone: (202) 833-5900

The Global Health Council is the world's largest membership alliance for health, made up of health-care professionals, NGOs, corporations, government agencies, and academic institutions committed to improving global health.

Guttmacher Institute
URL: http://www.guttmacher.org/

125 Maiden Lane, 7th Floor
New York, NY 10038
Phone: (212) 248-1111

The Guttmacher Institute is an American nonprofit organization that works toward advancing and protecting sexual and reproductive health and educating the public about reproductive health issues such as pregnancy, sexually transmitted diseases, abortion, and sexual relationships.

Human Rights Campaign
URL: http://www.hrc.org/
1640 Rhode Island Ave NW
Washington, DC 20036-3278
Phone: (202) 628-4160

The Human Rights Campaign (HRC) was founded in 1980 and is today the largest national gay, lesbian, bisexual, and transgender civil rights organization in the United States. HRC works to ensure equality for GLBT individuals and their families through educational outreach, diversity initiatives, media outreach, and publications.

Human Rights Education Associates
URL: http://www.hrea.org/
Postbus 59225
1040 KE Amsterdam
The Netherlands
Phone: (011-31-20) 524-1404

Human Rights Education Associates (HREA) is an international NGO that promotes human rights education, the training of activists, the development of educational materials and programs, and the fostering of relationships through online communication. The services provided by HREA include assistance in curriculum development, group training, research and evaluation, and more.

Human Rights First
URL: http://www.humanrightsfirst.org/
333 Seventh Avenue, 13th Floor
New York, NY 10001-5108
Phone: (212) 845-5200

Human Rights First is an international nonprofit organization that works for the protection of human rights through advocacy, research and reporting, litigation, and coalition building. Current areas of focus include crimes against humanity, discrimination and hate crimes, protection of human rights activists, refugee protection, and fair policies regarding national security.

Human Rights in China
URL: http://www.hrichina.org/public/index
350 Fifth Avenue, Suite 3311
New York, NY 10118
Phone: (212) 239-4495

Human Rights in China (HRIC) works to protect and defend human and civil rights in China by reaching out to international media resources, researching and publishing reports on human rights conditions in China, and working with diverse communities.

Human Rights Watch
URL: http://www.hrw.org/
350 Fifth Avenue, 34th Floor
New York, NY 10118-3299
Phone: (212) 290-4700

One of the leading independent human rights organizations in the world, Human Rights Watch is committed to investigating and calling attention to human rights abuses around the world. By researching human rights conditions on every continent and publishing their findings in thorough reports, Human Rights Watch not only defends the victims of such abuses but holds abusers accountable.

HumanTrafficking.org
URL: http://humantrafficking.org/
Academy for Educational Development
1825 Connecticut Ave NW
Washington, DC 20009-5721
Phone: (202) 884-8000
E-mail: bertone.andrea@gmail.com

Humantrafficking.org is a project of the Academy for Educational Development that facilitates communication between governments and NGOs to pool their resources to help combat human trafficking in East Asia and the Pacific.

Hunger Project
URL: http://www.thp.org/

5 Union Square West
New York, NY 10003
Phone: (212) 251-9100

The Hunger Project is a global organization committed to ending world hunger by working with villages at the grassroots level to help establish self-reliance, educating and empowering women, and working with local governments.

Institute for Local Self-Reliance
URL: http://www.ilsr.org/
2001 S Street NW, Suite 570
Washington, DC 20009
Phone: (202) 898-1610

The Institute for Local Self-Reliance (ILSR) works to provide information, work models, and strategies to support environmentally friendly and equitable community development. The aim of ILSR is to utilize human, natural, and financial resources to benefit local communities.

International Campaign for Human Rights in Iran
URL: http://www.iranhumanrights.org/
Phone: (917) 669-5996
E-mail: hadighaemi@iranhumanrights.org

The International Campaign for Human Rights in Iran aims to protect human rights and human rights activists in Iran by approaching the issue from a non-partisan, nonpolitical perspective and documenting human rights violations to encourage the international community to become active in supporting human rights in Iran.

International Committee of the Red Cross
URL: http://www.icrc.org/
19 Avenue de la Paix
CH-1202 Geneva
Switzerland
Phone: (011-41-22) 734-6001

The International Committee of the Red Cross (ICRC) is a neutral international organization that operates in more than 80 countries to provide assistance to communities that have been affected by armed conflict. The ICRC has a permanent mandate under international law to take impartial action for civilians affected by violence.

International Criminal Court
URL: http://www.icc-cpi.int/
Maanweg, 174
2516 AB, The Hague
The Netherlands
Phone: (011-31-70) 515-8515

The International Criminal Court (ICC) is a permanent, international court that tries individuals accused of heinous crimes, such as genocide, war crimes, and crimes against humanity. The ICC is considered a last resort and will only apprehend and try individuals when a national court has failed to do so.

International Labour Organization
URL: http://www.ilo.org/global/lang--en/index.htm
4 Route des Morillons
CH-1211 Genève 22
Switzerland
Phone: (011-41-22) 799-6111

The International Labour Organization (ILO) works to ensure that all men and women obtain equal and fair employment under safe, equitable, healthy, and secure working conditions.

International Programme on the Elimination of Child Labour (IPEC)
URL: http://www.ilo.org/ipec/
4 Route des Morillons
CH-1211 Genève 22
Switzerland
Phone: (011-41-22) 799-6111

As a project of the International Labour Organization, IPEC operates in 88 countries to eliminate child labor, which the group asserts not only prevents children from acquiring the education and skills needed to ensure a stable future but also depresses the economy and promotes poverty.

International Refugee Rights Initiative
URL: http://www.refugee-rights.org/
866 United Nations Plaza, Suite 4018

New York, NY 10017
Phone: (212) 453-5853

The International Refugee Rights Initiative (IRRI) is an organization that works toward addressing human rights and displacement in Africa, particularly in areas that have been heavily affected by conflict. IRRI strives to protect human rights through research, international collaboration, and information sharing on the regional and international level.

Iran Human Rights
URL: http://iranhr.net/
E-mail: iranhr2007@gmail.com

Iran Human Rights is an organization comprising various activists all over the world, most of whom come from Iran. The aim of their Web site is to call attention to human rights abuses in Iran by publishing articles and news reports that have been screened and verified for their truthfulness and objectivity.

Iranian and Kurdish Women's Rights Organisation (IKWRO)
URL: http://www.ikwro.org.uk/
P.O. Box 65840
London
EC2P 2FS
England
Phone: (011-44-20) 7920-6460

IKWRO is a British organization that provides services, support, and advice for Middle Eastern women living in Britain who are at risk of "honor" killings, female genital mutilation, domestic violence, and forced marriage. The Web site also provides useful information on the current status of women's rights and related issues in Iran.

MADRE
URL: http://www.madre.com/
121 West 27th Street, #301
New York, NY 10001
Phone: (212) 627-0444

Madre is an international human rights organization that aims to effect global equality by helping women become active in their communities. Madre's areas of focus include international peace, women's health, violence against women, and economic and environmental justice.

Minority Rights Group International
URL: http://www.minorityrights.org/
54 Commercial Street
London
E1 6LT
United Kingdom
Phone: (011-41-20) 7422-4200

Minority Rights Group International works in more than 60 countries to support the rights of minority and indigenous peoples and to eradicate discrimination based on class, gender, age, and disability through education, training, and lobbying governments and the United Nations.

Mission for the Establishment of Human Rights in Iran
URL: http://www.mehr.org/
P.O. Box 2037
P.V.P., CA 90274
Phone: (310) 377-4590

Mission for the Establishment of Human Rights in Iran (MEHR) is a global network of activists dedicated to advocating for human rights in Iran through education, reporting human rights violations, and raising public awareness.

National Gay and Lesbian Task Force
URL: http://www.thetaskforce.org/
1325 Massachusetts Avenue NW, Suite 600
Washington, DC 20005
Phone: (202) 393-5177

The National Gay and Lesbian Task Force works to strengthen the GLBT community by training activists, supporting state and local GLBT organizations, and promoting equitable legislation. The Task Force's think tank, the Policy Institute, conducts policy research and analysis to strengthen the cause of gay rights.

National Network for Immigrant and Refugee Rights (NNIRR)
URL: http://www.nnirr.org/
Phone: (510) 465-1984
E-mail: agarcia@nnirr.org

NNIRR is a national organization that works toward promoting equality and respect for the human rights of immigrants and refugees through information sharing and analysis, activism, and educating immigrant communities and the public. The organization consists of local coalitions, immigrant and refugee communities, and religious and civil rights activists.

National Organization for Women (NOW)
URL: http://www.now.org/
1100 H Street NW, 3rd Floor
Washington, DC 20005
Phone: (202) 628-8669

The National Organization for Women (NOW) is the largest organization of feminists in the United States. Among NOW's goals are the elimination of discrimination against women, ensuring reproductive rights for all women, ending sexual violence against women, and combating sexism, racism, and homophobia.

Not For Sale: End Human Trafficking and Slavery
URL: http://www.notforsalecampaign.org/
P.O. Box 371035
122 Seacliff Court
Montara, CA 94037

The Not For Sale campaign is designed to support antitrafficking activism, raise public awareness of human trafficking and slavery, and help individuals identify the hidden epidemic of modern-day slavery.

Open Society Institute
URL: http://www.soros.org/
400 West 59th Street
New York, NY 10019
Phone: (212) 548-0600

The Open Society Institute (OSI) works to promote democracies in which governments are held accountable to their citizens and human rights are respected and protected. OSI creates and supports initiatives to advance education, public health, justice, and independent media around the world.

Peace Corps
URL: http://www.peacecorps.gov/
Paul D. Coverdell Peace Corps Headquarters
1111 20th Street NW
Washington, DC 20526
Phone: (800) 424-8580

The Peace Corps was established by President John F. Kennedy in 1961 to promote world peace and strengthen international relationships by sending American volunteers to countries in need of trained men and women. Peace Corps volunteers commit to approximately two years and work in such fields as education, health, business development, environment, and more.

Polaris Project
URL: http://www.polarisproject.org/
P.O. Box 53315
Washington, DC 20009
Phone: (202) 745-1001

The Polaris Project is the United States's and Japan's largest anti–human trafficking organization. The organization works toward eliminating all forms of human trafficking and modern-day slavery by conducting direct outreach to victims, educating the public on human trafficking, and advocating for stronger antitrafficking laws.

Project for the End of Rape Inc.
URL: http://www.endofrape.org/
P.O. Box 9991
Philadelphia, PA 19118

The Project for the End of Rape Inc. (PERI) is an international group that works to eliminate rape worldwide by encouraging lawmakers, communities, and individuals to transcend the acceptance of rape's inevitability and strive toward the global eradication of rape and sexual violence.

Raise Hope for Congo
URL: http://www.raisehopeforcongo.org/
1225 Eye Street NW, Suite 307
Washington, DC 20005
Phone: (202) 682-1611

The Raise Hope for Congo campaign is a project of the Center for American Progress that focuses exclusively on the problem of sexual violence in the Democratic Republic of the Congo and works to promote greater protections for Congolese women and girls.

Rape, Abuse, and Incest National Network (RAINN)
URL: http://www.rainn.org/

2000 L Street NW, Suite 406
Washington, DC 20036
Phone: (202) 544-3064

Rape, Abuse, and Incest National Network (RAINN) was cofounded by Scott Berkowitz and the singer and rape survivor Tori Amos in 1994. Today, it is the largest anti–sexual assault organization in the United States. The organization promotes education about sexual assault and supports policies to protect survivors of sexual assault. The group also provides a free national sexual assault hotline: (800) 656-HOPE.

Sexual Violence Research Initiative (SVRI)
URL: http://www.svri.org/
Gender and Health Research Unit
Medical Research Council
1 Soutpansberg Road
Pretoria, South Africa
Phone: (011-27-12) 339-8527

The Sexual Violence Research Initiative (SVRI) is a project of the Global Forum for Health Research that strives to promote research and awareness of sexual violence as a public health priority.

Stop Blood Diamonds
URL: http://www.stopblooddiamonds.org/
E-mail: http://www.stopblooddiamonds.org/stop-blood-diamonds-contact.asp

Stop Blood Diamonds is an organization that aims to eliminate the human rights violations that occur in the exploitation of the diamond trade. Stop Blood Diamonds promotes the sale of conflict-free diamonds and provides information on international terror and blood diamonds and U.S., Canadian, and European law.

Stop Child Poverty
URL: http://www.stopchildpoverty.org/
P.O. Box 30-968
Lower Hutt
New Zealand
Phone: (011-64-4) 569-9080

Stop Child Poverty is a global organization that works to raise public awareness of child poverty and to urge world governments to comply with the UN Millennium Development Goals, which strive to halve child poverty by 2015 and eliminate it by 2025.

Stop Rape Now
URL: http://www.stoprapenow.org/
E-mail: anna.tarant@unifem.org

Stop Rape Now is a project of the UN Action Against Sexual Violence in Conflict, which strives to end sexual violence in war by working with peacekeeping operations, raising public awareness, and supporting national efforts to end sexual violence and meet the needs of survivors of sexual violence.

Thomas Jefferson Center for the Protection of Free Expression
URL: http://www.tjcenter.org/
400 Worrell Drive
Charlottesville, NC 22911-8691
Phone: (434) 295-4784

The Thomas Jefferson Center is an organization devoted to the protection of the freedom of expression, including print, mass media, music, the visual arts, and more, through education and participation in legislative and judicial matters.

TransFair USA
URL: http://www.transfairusa.org/
1500 Broadway, Suite 400
Oakland, CA 94612
Phone: (510) 663-5260

TransFair USA is one of 20 members of Fairtrade Labeling Organizations International and the only third-party certifier of fair trade products in the United States. The nonprofit organization audits transactions between U.S. businesses and international suppliers to ensure that farmers are paid a fair, above-market price.

UNAIDS
URL: http://www.unaids.org/en/default.asp
20, Avenue Appia
CH-1211 Geneva 27
Switzerland
Phone: (011-41-22) 791-3666

UNAIDS is a United Nations program that unites 10 UN organizations that work in more than 80 countries worldwide to prevent new HIV infections and provide care and resources for people living with HIV/AIDS.

UNESCO
URL: http://www.unesco.org/new/en/unesco/
7 Place de Fontenoy 75352
Paris 07 SP
France
Phone: (011-33-1) 4568-1000

The United Nations Educational, Scientific, and Cultural Organization (UNESCO) was created after World War II as an organization of peace and international cooperation that fosters global relationships by holding dialogues on education, science, and culture.

United Farm Workers of America
URL: http://www.ufw.org/
P.O. Box 62
29700 Woodford-Tehachapi Road
Keene, CA 93531
Phone: (661) 823-6250

United Farm Workers of America (UFW) was founded by César Chávez in 1962 and became the first successful farmworkers union in the United States. UFW's core values include integrity, nonviolence, innovation, empowerment, and a "si se puede" (yes we can) attitude.

United Nations
URL: http://www.un.org/
405 East 42nd Street
New York, NY 10017-3599
Phone: (212) 308-5092

Established in 1945, the United Nations is an international organization comprising 192 member states (countries). The goal of the organization is to promote international peace and friendly relations among countries, protect human rights, and encourage social progress.

United Nations Children's Fund (UNICEF)
URL: http://www.unicef.org/
UNICEF House
3 United Nations Plaza

New York, NY 10017
Phone: (212) 326-7000

The United Nations Children's Fund is an international organization committed to protecting the rights and well-being of the world's children and their families by researching and publishing reports on child survival and health, education, HIV/AIDS, and child protection in 190 countries.

United Nations Girls' Education Initiative (UNGEI)
URL: http://www.ungei.org/
3 UN Plaza
Programme Division, Education Section
New York, NY 10017
E-mail: ungei@unicef.org

UNGEI is a project of the United Nations to promote worldwide gender equality by encouraging and supporting national governments in their efforts to educate girls and boys alike.

United Nations Population Fund (UNFPA)
URL: http://www.unfpa.org/public/
220 East 42nd Street
New York, NY 10017
Phone: (212) 370-0201

The United Nations Population Fund (UNFPA) is a global agency committed to health and equality worldwide. UNFPA bases its programs on population data to reduce poverty, ensure safe and healthy pregnancies and births, and combat HIV/AIDS.

United Nations World Food Programme
URL: http://www.wfp.org/
Via C. G. Viola 68
Parco dei Medici
00148, Rome
Italy
Phone: (011-39-06) 65139

The World Food Programme is the world's largest organization devoted to combating global hunger. The program's objectives include preparing and responding to emergencies, reducing hunger and malnutrition around the world, and helping individual countries reduce hunger.

Organizations and Agencies

U.S. Agency for International Development (USAID)
URL: http://www.usaid.gov/
Information Center
U.S. Agency for International Development
Ronald Reagan Building
Washington, DC 20523-1000
Phone: (202) 712-0000

USAID is a U.S. governmental agency that assists other countries in recovering from natural disasters, reducing poverty, and reforming government by supporting economic growth, agriculture and trade, global health, democracy, and conflict prevention.

U.S. Campaign to Ban Landmines (USCBL)
URL: http://www.banminesusa.org/
c/o Handicap
6930 Carroll Avenue, Suite 240
Takoma Park, MD 20912
(301) 891-2138

USCBL is a coalition of organizations united to ban the use, production, and exportation of land mines and other antipersonnel weapons in the United States. Currently, the coalition's main priority is to pressure the U.S. government to ratify the 2008 Convention on Cluster Munitions.

V-Day
URL: http://www.vday.org/home
303 Park Avenue South, Suite 1184
New York, NY 10010-3657

Founded by the *Vagina Monologues* author Eve Ensler, V-Day is a global campaign to end violence against women by raising awareness of sexual violence, battery, sexual slavery, and female genital mutilation through performance, initiative gatherings, and benefits.

WhyHungerYear
URL: http://www.whyhunger.org/
505 Eighth Avenue, Suite 2100
New York, NY 10018
Phone: (800) 5-HUNGRY

WHY (Why Hunger Year) is an organization that strives to end global hunger and poverty. WHY works primarily at the grassroots level by supporting community-based programs and connecting those programs to the media, funders, and legislators.

Women's Education for Advancement and Empowerment (WEAVE)
URL: http://www.weave-women.org/
P.O. Box 58
Chiang Mai University
Chiang Mai
50202
Thailand
Phone: (011-66-53) 221-654

Women's Education for Advancement and Empowerment (WEAVE) is an organization that works to support and empower indigenous women, particularly refugees, and protect women's human rights. WEAVE initially focused primarily on refugee women in Myanmar (Burma), but is now expanding their programs to include other displaced women in India, China, and Myanmar.

Women's Rights Information Center
URL: http://womensrights.org/
108 West Palisade Avenue
Englewood, NJ 07631
Phone: (201) 568-1166

The Women's Rights Information Center is a nonprofit organization that provides services for low-income women and their families, such as shared housing for single parents, English as a second language, lawyer consultations, educational workshops, computer training, and career counseling.

World Bank
URL: http://www.worldbank.org/
1818 H Street NW
Washington, DC 20433
Phone: (202) 473-1000

The World Bank was established to provide financial and technical help to impoverished and low-income countries by offering low-interest loans and interest-free credit to invest in education, health, business, agriculture, environmental resource management, and more.

World Health Organization (WHO)
URL: http://www.who.int/en/

Organizations and Agencies

Avenue Appia 20
1211 Geneva 27
Switzerland
Phone: (011-41-22) 791-2111

The World Health Organization (WHO) works with 193 member states to make public health a global priority by promoting development in poverty-stricken countries, focusing on preventative care and security, strengthening health systems, gathering and disseminating information, and fostering partnerships.

World Hunger Education Service
URL: http://www.worldhunger.org/
P.O. Box 29056
Washington, DC 20017
Phone: (202) 269-6322

World Hunger Education Service (WHES) provides information and educational materials about world hunger and facilitates networking among individuals who wish to become involved in the issue of hunger. WHES operates a Web site, Hunger Notes.

World Policy Institute
URL: http://www.worldpolicy.org/index.html
220 Fifth Avenue, 9th Floor
New York, NY 10001
Phone: (212) 481-5005

The World Policy Institute is a nonpartisan organization that conducts policy analysis to address major global challenges, such as creating a sustainable global market, fostering collaboration on national and global security, and engaging civic participation. The World Policy Institute publishes the *World Policy Journal*.

World Vision International (WVI)
URL: http://www.wvi.org/wvi/wviweb.nsf
800 West Chestnut Avenue
Monrovia, CA 91016-3198
E-mail: worvis@wvi.org

World Vision International (WVI) is a Christian relief and advocacy organization that works with families and communities around the world to relieve poverty and hunger. WVI is best known for its sponsor-a-child program, in which individuals commit to sending a certain amount of money each month to provide food and other resources to a specific child.

Worldwide Organization for Women (WOW)
URL: http://wowinfo.org/new/
3 Rue de Varembe
Case Postal 116
1211 Geneva 20
Switzerland

The Worldwide Organization for Women (WOW) is a global network of women committed to advocacy, education, and humanitarian efforts to improve the lives of women and their families around the world.

10

Annotated Bibliography

The resources in this chapter have been grouped into the following categories:

Topics in Human Rights
Global Human Rights
Human Rights in the United States
Human Rights in the Democratic Republic of the Congo
Human Rights in China
Human Rights in Chechnya
Human Rights in Iran

Each category is further divided into the following subcategories:

Books
Studies and Reports
Articles and Factsheets
Documentaries
Other Media

TOPICS IN HUMAN RIGHTS
Books

Agosin, Marjorie. *Women, Gender, and Human Rights: A Global Perspective.* Piscataway, N.J.: Rutgers University Press, 2001. A collection of essays on women's human rights in relation to various topics, including health, activism, displacement, literacy, reproductive rights, and theoretical discussions (women and the private versus public sphere, women and violence, etc.). The essays approach women's human rights from a global perspective to include the rights of various groups.

Alston, Philip, and Euan MacDonald. *Human Rights Intervention, and the Use of Force.* New York: Oxford University Press, 2008. A collection of essays that analyze the complex relations between human rights, national security, and sovereignty, the dilemmas that often arise in attempting to address all three, and ways that such issues can be confronted and dealt with productively. Chapters are divided into eight sections that discuss issues such as armed intervention and international law, state sovereignty, the Kosovo war, and the legality of force.

Bales, Kevin. *Disposable People: New Slavery in the Global Economy.* Berkeley and Los Angeles: University of California Press, 1999. Discusses slavery as the world's oldest social institution and the fact that, despite being illegal, 27 million people are currently enslaved today. From Southeast Asia and the Middle East to South America, Kevin Bales defines "new slavery" and examines its connections to the global economy, from prostitution to multinational corporations. In 2001, Bales cofounded Free the Slaves, a global organization working toward the elimination of human trafficking and slavery.

Ensalaco, Mark. *Children's Human Rights: Progresses and Challenges for Children Worldwide.* Lanham, Md.: Rowman & Littlefield, 2005. A collection of essays from academics and children's rights activists around the world that examine the current state of children's rights and the challenges facing them. While the book focuses on worldwide children's rights, it also discusses the unique situation of children's rights in the United States.

Feer, Kenneth. *Human Rights and Sexual Minorities: GLBT Rights in the Public Eye.* Saarbrücken: VDM Verlag, 2007. Examines why gays and lesbians in some countries enjoy full equal rights while those in others do not. The study explores the struggles and debates over gay rights in Denmark, India, South Africa, and the United States and analyzes levels of development, cultural attitudes, government structures, and rights organizations.

Francioni, Francesco. *Environment, Human Rights, and International Trade.* Portland, Oreg.: Hart Publishing, 2001. A collection of essays by scholars and lawyers on the World Trade Organization process and its effect on human rights and the environment. Essays range from such topics as genetically modified organisms, biosafety, and intellectual property, to trade and labor rights, and child labor.

Gruskin, Sofia, Michael A. Grodin, George J. Annas, and Stephen P. Marks. *Perspectives on Health and Human Rights.* New York: Routledge Taylor and Francis Group, 2005. A collection of essays on the growing field of health and human rights and the overlaps between economic, social, cultural rights and health and well-being. The essays are divided into eight sections, including the links between health and human rights, development, technology, sexual and reproductive health, violence, methods in health and human rights, the right to health, and mobilization for health and human rights.

Kristof, Nicholas, and Sheryl WuDunn. *Half the Sky: Turning Oppression into Opportunity for Women Worldwide.* New York: Knopf, 2009. Two Pulitzer Prize–winning journalists argue for greater investment in the health and education of girls and women in poverty-stricken countries on the grounds that poor countries cannot pull themselves out of poverty unless more female citizens participate in the workforce. Known as the "Girl Effect," Kristof and WuDunn cite the flourishing of China's economy as a result of Chinese women's empowerment and the influx of women into China's factories.

Lumpe, Laura. *Running Guns: The Global Black Market in Small Arms.* New York: Zed Books, 2000. A collection of essays on the illegal small arms trade and its global effects. In association with the International Peace Research Institute, *Running Guns* discusses what constitutes illegal arms trading, who is involved, the role of government and money, and ways in which the illegal arms trade is being fought.

Pogge, Thomas. *World Poverty and Human Rights.* Malden, Mass.: Polity Press, 2002. Examines the discrepancy between wealthy nations and poverty-stricken countries where 18 million people die each year from poverty-related causes. Pogge outlines the way in which the current global order perpetuates this discrepancy, when only 1 percent of the incomes in high-income countries would eliminate global poverty altogether. Pogge also suggests ways in which global economic justice can be attained.

Skaine, Rosemarie. *Female Genital Mutilation: Legal, Cultural, and Medical Issues.* Jefferson, N.C.: McFarland, 2005. Discusses female genital mutilation (FGM) in Africa and other parts of the world, including its various types, cultural practices, global laws, and the intersection of rights, culture, and religion. The book also includes personal interviews.

Uvin, Peter. *Human Rights and Development.* Sterling, Conn.: Kumarian Press, 2004. Discusses development aid and human rights violations and how human rights organizations can reduce conflict. Uvin advocates a rights-based approach to economic development to effect major global change.

Yunus, Muhammad. *Creating a World Without Poverty: Social Business and the Future of Capitalism.* New York: Perseus Books Group, 2007. Written by the Nobel Peace Prize winner and founder of the Grameen Bank Dr. Muhammad Yunus, this book discusses social business, microcredit, and organizations that help individuals in poverty-stricken countries start and manage their own businesses. *Creating a World Without Poverty* is a great resource for anyone wishing to learn more about microfinance and business solutions for combating poverty.

Studies and Reports

Committee to Protect Journalists. "Attacks on the Press in 2009: A Worldwide Survey by the Committee to Protect Journalists." CPJ.org, (2010). Available online. URL: http://cpj.org/AOP09.pdf. Accessed March 4, 2010. Reports on the imprisonment of journalists and photographers around the world, profiling countries from the Americas, Africa, Asia, the Middle East and North Africa, as well as Europe and Central Asia. The report notes that freelance journalists and photographers are in the greatest danger, as they have no major media organization behind them in the event they are detained or threatened.

Human Rights Watch. "The Last Holdouts: Ending the Juvenile Death Penalty in Iran, Saudi Arabia, Sudan, Pakistan, and Yemen" (September 2008). Available online. URL: http://www.hrw.org/en/reports/2008/09/10/last-holdouts. Accessed March 4, 2010. A report that examines the juvenile death penalty in international law and the countries that still execute child offenders. The report includes statistics and analyses of individual cases, and provides recommendations to the countries profiled on ending the practice of juvenile execution.

Strand, Jon, and Michael Toman. "'Green Stimulus,' Economic Recovery and Long-Term Sustainable Development." The World Bank (January 2010). Available online. URL: http://econ.worldbank.org/external/default/main?pagePK=64165259&theSitePK=469372&piPK=64165421&menuPK=64166093&entityID=000158349_20100104121602. Accessed March 4, 2010. A study that examines the trend of short-term "green stimulus" efforts, which are jobs created to boost employment and address environmental issues. The study finds that green stimulus jobs are effective in short-term runs, but generally do not have long-term effects.

UNICEF. "State of the World's Children" (September 2009). Available online. URL: http://www.unicef.org/rightsite/sowc/. Accessed March 4, 2010. Reports on the health and well-being of children around the world with a special focus on the 20th anniversary of the Convention on the Rights of the Child and the progress that has been made in children's rights. The report examines child health and well-being in the areas of nutrition, HIV/AIDS, education, under-five mortality, women, and child-protection.

United Nations, Department for Disarmament Affairs. "The Relationship Between Disarmament and Development in the Current International Context" (2004). Available online. URL: http://www.un.org/disarmament/HomePage/ODAPublications/DisarmamentStudySeries/PDF/DSS_31.pdf. Accessed March 4, 2010. Reports on the major international changes that have occurred since the adoption of the Final Document of the International Conference on the Relationship Between Disarmament and Development in 1987. The report calls for mainstreaming the disarmament-development relationship, raising public awareness of the relationship, and engaging in conflict prevention measures, particularly where illicit small arms and light weapons are concerned.

U.S. Department of State. "Trafficking in Persons Report, 2009" (June 2009). Available online. URL: http://www.state.gov/documents/organization/123357.pdf. Accessed March 4, 2010. Examines the current state of human trafficking and modern slavery around the world, as well as the conditions, policies, and practices that contribute to all forms of human trafficking. The report looks at forced labor, debt bondage among migrant workers, child labor, child soldiers, involuntary domestic servitude, sex trafficking, and child sex trafficking and abuse. The 2009 report also analyzes the impact of the global financial crisis on trafficking.

Articles and Factsheets

Amnesty International USA. "Violence in Post-Conflict Situations" (2010). Available online. URL: http://www.amnestyusa.org/violence-against-women/stop-violence-against-women-svaw/violence-in-post-conflict-situations/page.do?id=1108238. Accessed March 4, 2010. Defines and summarizes violence against women in post-conflict reconstruction. Women are particularly vulnerable to physical and sexual violence during periods of armed conflict, and during reconstruction periods their emotional and medical needs may not be met. This factsheet also addresses domestic violence and economic impacts on women.

World Health Organization. "Violence Against Women" (November 2009). Available online. URL: http://www.who.int/mediacentre/factsheets/fs239/en/. Accessed March 4, 2010. A factsheet that defines violence against women and how it relates to lack of access to education and employment opportunities, as well as low social status for women in many communities. The article also examines statistics, including types of violence (physical, sexual, forced marriage, honor-killings, and child sexual abuse), and incidence of reporting, as well as the health, social, and economic costs and effects of violence against women.

World Hunger Education Service. "World Hunger Facts, 2009." Hunger Notes (2010). Available online. URL: http://www.worldhunger.org/articles/Learn/world%20 hunger%20facts%202002.htm. Accessed March 4, 2010. A factsheet that defines hunger and its causes and effects. Subtopics include poverty, malnutrition, harmful economic systems, armed conflict, and climate change, as well as statistics on malnourished populations.

UNICEF. "Child Protection Information Sheets" (2006). Available online. URL: http:// www.unicef.org/protection/files/Child_Protection_Information_Sheets_(Booklet).pdf. Accessed March 4, 2010. A publication that outlines issues related to child health and welfare and efforts to protect children from violence and exploitation. The document includes statistics and information on violence against children, protecting children during armed conflict, HIV/AIDS, child labor, child marriage, commercial sexual exploitation, female genital mutilation, and trafficking. The document also details UNICEF's goals and efforts to reduce the incidence of such abuses.

Documentaries

Briski, Zana, and Ross Kauffman. Born Into Brothels. Produced by Andrew Herwitz, Ellen Peck, Geralyn White Dreyfous, Jannat Garji, and Lisa Cohen. Directed by Zana Briski and Ross Kauffman. 85 min. Velocity Home Entertainment, 2003. DVD. Documents the lives of eight children born to mothers who work in Calcutta's red-light district. Director Zana Briski teaches the children to shoot and edit photographs, which gives the children a chance to document their own lives. But Briski notes that without help many of the children are doomed to lives of poverty and prostitution, and she works to get the children out of the brothels.

Caldwell, Gillian. Bought and Sold: An Investigative Documentary About the International Trade in Women. Produced by Global Survival Network and WITNESS. Directed by Gillian Caldwell. 42 min. WITNESS, 2009. DVD. A documentary based on a two-year undercover investigation by the Global Survival Network into the illegal trafficking of women from the former Soviet republics. The documentary includes interviews with trafficked women, traffickers, and organizations working to help trafficked women.

Epstein, Abby. *V-Day—Until the Violence Stops.* Directed by Abby Epstein. 73 min. New Video Group, 2005. DVD. Chronicles the development of Eve Ensler's Broadway solo show *The Vagina Monologues* into V-Day, an international campaign to end violence against women. In addition to readings of *The Vagina Monologues,* the film includes interviews with everyday women and celebrities who have experienced or been affected by violence.

Nix, Andrea, and Sean Fine. *War Dance.* Produced by Andrea Nix, Albie Hecht, Andrew Herwitz, Daniel Katz, and Douglas Eger. Directed by Andrea Nix and Sean Fine. 107 min. Velocity/Thinkfilm, 2006. DVD. Follows Nancy, Dominic, and Rose, three young teenagers in Uganda who are students in a refugee camp, preparing to compete in Uganda's national music competition. The children describe the difficult lives they have led as the country's 20-year-long war has torn their families apart and left them orphans, which is contrasted against their passion for music and dance.

Other Media

Yushkiavitshus, Henrikas. "Why Press Freedom Is Disappearing in the Post-Communist World." World Press Freedom Committee, December 2004. Available online. URL: http://www.wpfc.org/sites/default/files/2004%20Henrikas%20 Yushkiavitshus.pdf. Accessed March 4, 2010. Transcript of a lecture on communism, the world after Communist Russia, and disappearing press freedom, including government hostility toward the media and the murders of journalists. The speaker, Yushkiavitshus, served as vice chairman of the Soviet State Committee for Television and Radio for 19 years.

GLOBAL HUMAN RIGHTS
Books

Alston, Philip, Ryan Goodman, and Henry Steiner. *International Human Rights in Context: Law, Politics, and Morals.* New York: Oxford University Press, 1996. A comprehensive textbook that covers various approaches to human rights, including global concepts of human rights, as well as topics within human rights, such as women's rights, capital punishment, torture, economic and social rights, terrorism and national security, cultural conflicts, human rights organizations, and more. This book is intended for a more specialized audience, such as law students and those who wish to pursue careers in the field of human rights.

Beitz, Charles. *The Idea of Human Rights.* New York: Oxford University Press, 2009. Examines the theoretical concept of human rights as it remains couched in human rights language. Beitz addresses controversies within human rights, including the right to freedom from poverty, the right to democracy, and the human rights of women. The book also addresses skepticism and argues for the need for international collaboration to protect human rights.

Donnelly, Jack. *Universal Human Rights in Theory and Practice.* Ithaca, N.Y.: Cornell University Press, 2003. Addresses current topics in international human rights and examines the theoretical and practical issues involved. The book is divided into four parts that discuss the theory of universal human rights (such as morals, human nature, and hegemony), cultural relativism and cultural values, international action, and various essays on theory and practice in human rights.

Freeman, Michael. *Human Rights: An Interdisciplinary Approach.* Malden, Mass.: Blackwell, 2002. An introductory text for students interested in an interdisciplinary study of human rights. The book addresses broad issues, such as historical and religious concepts of human rights, human rights law and theory, and democracy, as well as specific issues within human rights, such as women's rights, minority rights, and cultural relativism. This text is unique in its application of various fields of study to human rights, such as anthropology, political science, sociology, and psychology.

Goodhart, Michael. *Human Rights: Politics and Practice.* New York: Oxford University Press, 2009. A text written specifically for students of politics featuring 20 chapters written by experts from around the world. This book examines basic theoretical issues as well as topics within human rights and devotes a significant section to the political sphere of human rights, addressing normative foundations, international law and relations, comparative politics, and sociological and anthropological approaches.

Hunt, Lynn Avery. *Inventing Human Rights: A History.* New York: W.W. Norton, 2007. Discusses the conceptual development of human rights, including theories from John Locke and Jean-Jacques Rousseau, the influence of the 18th-century novel on human rights, the American Declaration of Independence and Revolution, and the French Declaration of the Rights of Man and Citizen. The book focuses primarily on human rights in France and the United States in modern history.

Ishay, Micheline. *The History of Human Rights: From Ancient Times to the Globalization Era.* Berkeley and Los Angeles: University of California Press, 2004. Traces the history of human rights as a concept and legal topic, beginning with ancient religious and philosophical notions of justice and ethics, to theories of the individual versus the state, the effects of the industrial revolution and the world wars, and globalization.

Lauren, Paul Gordon. *The Evolution of International Human Rights: Visions Seen.* Philadelphia: University of Pennsylvania Press, 2003. Discusses human rights within a global and multicultural framework. Lauren examines philosophies and historical events in human rights, including religious notions of human nature, natural law, and natural rights, justice and the protection of vulnerable persons, war and revolution, the Universal Declaration of Independence, activism and implementation of human rights, and the future of human rights.

McNeill, Desmond. *Global Poverty, Ethics, and Human Rights: The Role of Multilateral Organisations*. New York: Routledge, 2008. Examines the role of human rights organizations in addressing and dealing with human rights abuses. Among the human rights issues the book addresses are global poverty, ethics, development, and global justice, and the organizations discussed include the United Nations, the World Bank, and UNESCO.

Smith, Rhona K. M. *Textbook on International Human Rights*. New York: Oxford University Press, 2010. An introductory book for readers who are new to the issue of human rights. The book devotes considerable space to the work of the United Nations, with a brief history of human rights prior to the formation of the UN, and outlines the work of regional governments, such as Europe, the United States, and the African Union. Several chapters are devoted to specific topics in human rights, such as freedom from torture, the right to self-determination, freedom of expression, and more.

Studies and Reports

Amnesty International. *Report 2009: State of the World's Human Rights* (May 2009). Examines the status of human rights in 157 countries around the world in 2008. Some of the specific issues addressed in the report include violence against women, the death penalty, the work of human rights activists and their need for protection, poverty, counterterrorism, and the way in which the worldwide financial crisis has affected and jeopardized human rights around the world as many people are driven into poverty. The report also addresses the 2008 food crisis in Africa, as well as the rising cost of food and fuel around the world.

Freedom House. "Undermining Democracy: Strategies and Methods of 21st Century Authoritarians" (June 2009). Available online. URL: http://freedomhouse.org/uploads/special_report/83.pdf. Accessed March 6, 2010. Examines the ways in which the regimes of major world powers are adapting their repressive methods to suppress human rights in favor of rapid economic growth. The report discusses sophisticated authoritarianism, clerical authoritarianism, kleptocracies, and more. The individual countries studied include China, Iran, Pakistan, Russia, and Venezuela.

———. "The UN Human Rights Council Report Card: 2007–2009" (September 2009). Available online. URL: http://freedomhouse.org/uploads/special_report/84.pdf. Accessed March 6, 2010. Analyzes the progress of the United Nations Human Rights Council beginning with the conclusion of the institution-building process in June 2007 to the council's 11th session in June 2009. The report looks at the council's ability to take timely action on human rights abuses in specific countries, and its ability to address emerging threats to human rights around the world. The report's primary finding is that a small group of countries with poor human rights records have so far succeeded in preventing the council from protecting human rights.

———. "Worst of the Worst: The World's Most Repressive Societies, 2009" (2009). Available online. URL: http://freedomhouse.org/uploads/specialreports/wow/

WoW2009.pdf. Accessed March 6, 2010. Examines the systematic violations of human rights in 17 countries and four territories out of 42 countries and nine territories that are considered to be Not Free in 2008. The eight countries judged to have the world human rights records of 2008 are Burma, Equatorial Guinea, Libya, North Korea, Somalia, Sudan, Turkmenistan, and Uzbekistan. Territories with the worst human rights records include Chechnya and Tibet.

Human Rights Watch. "World Report 2010." 2010. Available online. URL: http://www.hrw.org/world-report-2010. Accessed March 6, 2010. The 20th annual World Report discussing human rights abuses in 2009. The staff of Human Rights Watch collaborated with activists in more than 90 countries to address the state of human rights around the world, and essays discuss issues such as intensified attacks on human rights activists, health providers complicity in torture, unaccompanied migrant children in Europe, and civilian protection in the Middle East.

United Nations Publications. "State of the World's Population 2009: Women, Population, and Climate." New York: United Nations Publications, 2009. Discusses how population dynamics affect greenhouse gasses and how climate change will affect groups of people, particularly women. This report specifically puts people at the center of the discussion of climate change to ask how urbanization and aging populations will affect climate change, and whether improved reproductive health care and better relations between men and women can fight global warming. This is an ideal resource for individuals wishing to conduct interdisciplinary research on human rights and/or climate change.

UN Watch. "2010 UNHRC Scorecard: With Recommendations for U.S. Leadership" (March 2010). Available online. URL: http://www.unwatch.org/atf/cf/%7B6DEB65DA-BE5B-4CAE-8056-8BF0BEDF4D17%7D/ADVANCE%20VERSION%20-%202010%20HRC%20REPORT%20(RELEASE%20DATE%209%20MARCH%202010).PDF. Accessed March 6, 2010. Reports on the United Nations Human Rights Council's progress in protecting human rights around the world. Of the 47 Human Rights Council member states, only 13 were judged to have positive voting records on 30 key human rights resolutions, including Canada, Germany, Italy, the Netherlands, France, Slovakia, Slovenia, the United Kingdom, Japan, Switzerland, Ukraine, Bosnia, and the Republic of Korea.

U.S. Department of State. "2008 Country Report on Human Rights Practices" (February 2009). Available online. URL: http://www.state.gov/g/drl/rls/hrrpt/2008/index.htm. Accessed March 6, 2010. A collection of reports compiled to examine the status of internationally recognized human rights in countries that receive aid from the United States as well as countries that are members of the United Nations. The Country Reports are gathered by the Department of State and submitted to the U.S. Congress annually.

World Health Organization. "World Report on Violence and Health" (2002). Available online. URL: http://whqlibdoc.who.int/publications/2002/9241545615_eng.pdf. Accessed March 8, 2010. A comprehensive report on trends in violence and health throughout the world. More than 160 international experts participated in the creation of the report, which examines typology of violence and prevention, youth violence, child abuse and neglect, domestic violence, elder abuse, sexual violence, suicide, collective violence, and recommendations for action.

Articles and Factsheets

Cooper, Elise. "Hijacking the UN's Human Rights Mission." FrumForum (March 6, 2010). Available online. URL: http://www.frumforum.com/hijacking-the-uns-human-rights-mission. Accessed March 6, 2010. Discusses a report from the NGO UN Watch that highlights the United Nations Human Rights Council's failure to protect human rights by allowing countries with poor human rights records to become members.

Hines, Holly. "UN Special Rapporteur Manfred Nowak Speaks on Human Rights." *Daily Iowan* (March 5, 2010). Available online. URL: http://www.dailyiowan.com/2010/03/05/Metro/16040.html. Accessed March 6, 2010. Discusses the UN special rapporteur's visit to the University of Iowa's College of Law to discuss torture and human rights concerns. Among the issues addressed was Nowak's stated disappointment in the Obama administration for what he says is its refusal to deal with past human rights violations.

Schlein, Lisa. "UN: Human Rights Violations Rampant in Many Countries." *Voice of America* (March 4, 2010). Available online. URL: http://www1.voanews.com/english/news/africa/Human-Rights-Violations-Rampant-in-Many-Countries-86382077.html. Accessed March 6, 2010. In her annual report to the United Nations Human Rights Council, the United Nations high commissioner Navanethem Pillay says that too many countries continue to abuse the rights of their own people and prevents a broad overview of some of the basic rights being violated by racism, sexism, and intolerance.

UN News Centre. "Ban Marks 40th Anniversary of Landmark Global Pact on Nuclear Weapons Control" (March 5, 2010). Available online. URL: http://www.un.org/apps/news/story.asp?NewsID=33990&Cr=nuclear&Cr1=. Accessed March 6, 2010. On March 5, 2010, the UN secretary general Ban Ki-moon marked the 40th anniversary of the United Nations–backed Nuclear Non-Proliferation Treaty, which has since remained the cornerstone of nuclear disarmament and the encouragement of peaceful nuclear development.

———. "Impunity for Domestic Violence, 'Honor Killings' Cannot Continue—UN Official" (March 4, 2010). Available online. URL: http://www.un.org/apps/news/story.asp?NewsID=33971&Cr=violence+against+women&Cr1=. Accessed March 6, 2010. The UN high commissioner Navanethem Pillay calls on world governments to address domestic violence and "honor killings," which she describes as an extreme symptom of discrimination against women. Pillay states that such violence is facilitated and perpetuated by cultures of impunity and governments that fail to act.

United Nations Cyber School Bus. "Human Rights Factsheet" (2010). Available online. URL: http://www.un.org/cyberschoolbus/humanrights/resources/factsheet.asp.

Accessed March 6, 2010. Provides a broad overview of global human rights facts and statistics for young students wishing to learn more about human rights. Facts listed include the most pervasive violations of human rights in the world (violence against women and girls), poverty statistics, child labor statistics, and more. The factsheet is written in clear, accessible language for children, but it also cites its sources from major world reports and provides links.

Documentaries

Human Rights Watch. *Human Rights Watch Box Set.* Directed by Anthony Giacchino, John Scagliotti, Kief Davidson, Richard Ladkani, Ritu Sarin, Tenzing Sonam, Rithy Panh, Sabiha Sumar, Ana Carrigan, and Bernard Stone. 570 min. First Run Features, 2009. DVD. A collection of Human Rights Watch–endorsed films produced by First Run Features. Films include "The Khmer Rouge Killing Machine," "The Devil's Miner," "Dreaming Lhasa," "Silent Waters," "Dangerous Living," "The Camden," and "Roses in December."

HUMAN RIGHTS IN THE UNITED STATES
Books

Anderson, Carol. *Eyes Off the Prize: The United Nations and the African American Struggle for Human Rights, 1944–1955.* New York: Cambridge University Press, 2003. Discusses the NAACP's mobilization following the end of World War II and the world's realization of the horrors of racism in Nazi Germany. Anderson examines the formation of the United Nations and the development of human rights language that the NAACP attempted to utilize to bring attention to African Americans' human rights and the needs for equal education, employment, and housing in the black community. With the onset of the cold war, however, such notions were recast by white supremacists as Soviet-inspired, and the NAACP refocused its agenda on civil rights rather than human rights.

Fineman, Martha Albertson, and Karen Worthington. *What is a Right for Children?* Burlington, Vt.: Ashgate, 2009. Explores the concept of children's rights and contrasts discussions of children's rights in the United States against other countries, concluding that children's rights are more readily accepted and implemented in the United States. The authors examine the human rights of children as balanced against the rights of parents and families, the role of the state in intervening in cases of abuse, and how certain fundamentalist religious notions of the natural authority of the parent over the child is at odds with human rights philosophy, which sees the child as an individual with rights.

Glendon, Mary Ann. *A World Made New: Eleanor Roosevelt and the Universal Declaration of Human Rights.* New York: Random House, 2001. Examines the historical context of the Universal Declaration of Human Rights and the role that Eleanor Roosevelt played in its drafting. Glendon explores the way in which Roosevelt and the other drafters argued and negotiated from their various political, moral, and intellectual positions to arrive at a declaration that could be applied to all nations, religions, and cultures. This book is particularly pertinent in researching cultural relativism and claims from nations today of Western hegemony in the declaration.

Jackson, Thomas F. *From Civil Rights to Human Rights: Martin Luther King, Jr. and the Struggle for Economic Justice.* Philadelphia: University of Pennsylvania Press, 2007. Researches the deeper implications of Martin Luther King, Jr.'s nonviolent campaign against racism and injustice to explore the influences of Gandhian philosophy, African-American gospel, socialism, and Popular Front internationalism on King's concept of human rights and how to secure them. Jackson argues that King was not only campaigning for racial equality but also for a radical redistribution of economic and political power in America.

Kinzer, Stephen. *Overthrow: America's Century of Regime Change from Hawaii to Iraq.* New York: Times Books, 2006. Chronicles America's 110-year-old history of intervening in and toppling foreign governments, usually with disastrous results. Beginning with the overthrow of the Hawaiian Queen Liliuokalani in 1893, Kinzer details the ways in which the United States thwarted independence movements in Cuba, Puerto Rico, the Philippines, and Nicaragua, orchestrated coups in Iran, South Vietnam, Chile, and Guatemala, and invaded Afghanistan, Iraq, Grenada, and Panama. Kinzer notes that U.S. intervention in foreign governments has almost always left those countries worse off than they were before.

Rowland, Debran. *The Boundaries of Her Body: A Troubling History of Women's Rights in America.* Naperville: Sphinx Publishing, 2004. Recounts the history of women's rights in the United States, beginning with the signing of the Mayflower Compact in 1620. Rowland discusses women's historical status as wives and mothers, and how common notions of women's biological and intellectual inferiority prevented them from exercising and enjoying their basic human rights until the 1960s.

Zinn, Howard. *A People's History of the United States: 1492 to Present.* New York: HarperCollins, 2003. Provides a comprehensive history of politics, justice, and rights in the United States, beginning with Christopher Columbus's first expedition to the Americas. Operating on the premise that history is often told from the dominant group's perspective, this book researches and discusses American history from the perspective of minority groups, including Native Americans, indentured servants, the poor, African-American slaves, and women.

——. *The Twentieth Century: A People's History.* New York: HarperCollins, 2003. Using *A People's History of the United States* as his foundation, Zinn compiles all of the chapters on the 20th century in this book, along with two new chapters. Starting with Theodore Roosevelt's presidency, Zinn discusses the experiences and struggles of the United States's minority groups up through the Clinton administration, the 2000 election of George W. Bush, and the war on terror.

Studies and Reports

Amnesty International. "Investigation, Prosecution, Remedy: Accountability for Human Rights Violations in the War on Terror" (December 4, 2008). Available online. URL: http://www.amnesty.org/en/library/info/AMR51/151/2008/en. Accessed March 8, 2010. Examines the cases of detainees suspected of terrorism in the United States's war on terror and the need for accountability in human rights violations. The report discusses human rights abuses committed by the U.S. military, including enforced disappearances, torture, inhumane treatment that has resulted in death in custody, incommunicado detention, arbitrary and indefinite detention, and secret international transfers of detainees without due process (rendition).

————. "United States of America: Report 2009" (2009). Available online. URL: http://www.amnesty.org/en/region/usa/report-2009. Accessed March 8, 2010. An account of the status of human rights in the United States in 2008. The report addresses specific issues relevant to the United States, such as counterterror and the rights of prisoners in the U.S. naval base in Guantánamo Bay, Cuba, military commissions and the number of years prisoners are spending in Guantánamo Bay before a trial is even scheduled, torture and inhumane treatment, electroshock weapons, health care and maternal mortality, migrants rights, violence against women, and the death penalty.

Amnesty International USA. "Maze of Injustice: The Failure to Protect Indigenous Women from Sexual Violence in the USA" (2007). Available online. URL: http://www.amnestyusa.org/women/maze/report.pdf. Accessed March 8, 2010. Discusses the pervasive sexual abuse of indigenous women in the United States. Findings include statistics that reveal that indigenous women are 2.5 times more likely to be sexually assaulted than women in the general U.S. population, that one in three indigenous women will be raped during her lifetime, and that the majority of perpetrators (86 percent) are non-Native men.

Department of Justice, Federal Bureau of Investigation. "Hate Crime Statistics, 2008" (November 2009). Available online. URL: http://www.fbi.gov/ucr/hc2008/index.html. Accessed March 8, 2010. A compilation of statistics on hate crimes in the United States in 2008, including specific incidents and offenses, victims, perpetrators, location type (schools, businesses, residences, etc.), and jurisdiction. In 2008, there were a reported 9,160 hate crimes committed, 51.3 percent of which were racially motivated, 19.5 percent were motivated by religious bias, and 16.7 were motivated by sexual orientation bias.

Human Rights Watch. "Impairing Education: Corporal Punishment of Students with Disabilities in U.S. Public Schools" (August 2009). Available online. URL: http://www.hrw.org/en/reports/2009/08/11/impairing-education-0. Accessed March 7, 2010. A 70-page report in which the ACLU and Human Rights Watch found that students with disabilities constituted 18.8 percent of all students who received corporal punishment in public schools in the 2006–07 school year, even though they only comprise 13.7 of the total nationwide student population.

————. "Jailing Refugees: Arbitrary Detention of Refugees in the U.S. Who Fail to Adjust to Permanent Resident Status" (December 2009). Available online. URL: http://www.hrw.org/en/reports/2009/12/29/jailing-refugees-0. Accessed March 7, 2010. Explores the detention of refugees for failing to apply for permanent resident status. Detentions are selective and arbitrary, which is in violation of international human rights law, and the report recommends the U.S. government change the law to end the arbitrary detention of refugees and grant them permanent resident status upon granting them asylum in the United States.

———. "Locked Up Far Away: The Transfer of Immigrants to Remote Detention Centers in the United States" (December 2009). Available online. URL: http://www. hrw.org/en/reports/2009/12/02/locked-far-away-0. Accessed March 7, 2010. Examines the detention and transfer of noncitizens by Immigration and Customs Enforcement officials within a network of 300 facilities throughout the United States. While noncitizens are often initially detained near their place of residence, many have been subsequently transferred to remote detention facilities thousands of miles away as part of ICE's use of detention as a form of immigration control.

U.S. Department of Health and Human Services, Administration for Children and Families, Children's Bureau. "Child Maltreatment, 2007" (2009). Available online. URL: http://www.acf.hhs.gov/programs/cb/pubs/cm07/cm07.pdf. Accessed March 8, 2010. Reports on the incidence of child abuse in the United States in 2007 (the report was published in 2009), including statistics on types of abuse, perpetrators, abuse victims, and the individuals who reported abuse. Findings reveal that in 2007, 794,000 children were determined to be victims of abuse or neglect, the majority of whom were under one year of age, and that approximately 1,760 died from abuse and neglect.

Articles and Factsheets

Amnesty International USA. "Daily Injustice, Immeasurable Damage" (March 5, 2010). Available online. URL: http://www.amnestyusa.org/document.php?id=ENGUS A20100305002&lang=e. Accessed March 8, 2010. Reports on the 180 detainees held at the Guantánamo Bay naval base 400 days after President Obama ordered his administration to resolve each case and close the detention facility as soon as possible. In early 2010, an interagency review determined that 50 detainees would continue to be held indefinitely, without charge or trial.

Centers for Disease Control and Prevention, National Center for Injury Control and Prevention. "Understanding Child Maltreatment Factsheet" (2009). Available online. URL: http://www.cdc.gov/violenceprevention/pdf/CM-FactSheet-a.pdf. Accessed March 8, 2010. Provides a basic overview of child maltreatment, including definitions of abuse and neglect, statistics on child abuse in the United States, health concerns, who is at greatest risk of being abused, and how the CDC approaches prevention.

Ide, William. "Google Urges US Lawmakers to Make Open Internet Key Part of Diplomatic, Trade Policy." *Voice of America* (March 2, 2010). Available online. URL: http://www1.voanews.com/english/news/usa/Google-Urges-US-Lawmakers-to-Make-Open-Internet-Key-Part-of-Diplomatic-Trade-Policy-86054082.html. Accessed March 8, 2010. Discusses efforts of the search engine company Google to press Congress to make an open Internet a key part of foreign and trade policy, arguing that Internet censorship stifles business and investment for U.S. companies.

Lee, Elizabeth. "Gay Marriage Law Takes Effect in Washington." *Voice of America* (March 3, 2010). Available online. URL: http://www1.voanews.com/english/news/usa/-Gay-Marriage-Law-Takes-Effect-in-Washington--86287977.html. Accessed March 8, 2010. Reports on a new law in Washington, D.C., that allows same-sex couples the right to marry. The law took effect on March 3, 2010 amid a storm of controversy. Opponents protested, arguing that D.C. residents should have been allowed to vote on the issue, but Chief Justice John Roberts of the U.S. Supreme Court rejected the argument on the grounds that local issues are deferred to local courts.

Malone, Jim. "Possible Shift on US Terror Trial Alarms Human Rights Groups." *Voice of America* (March 5, 2010) Available online. URL: http://www1.voanews.com/english/news/usa/Possible-Shift-on-US-Terror-Trial-Alarms-Human-Rights-Groups-86673597.html. Accessed March 8, 2010. Reports on the efforts of human and legal rights groups to urge the Obama administration not to change its decision to try the alleged 9/11 terrorists in the U.S. civilian court system rather than military commissions. The possible decision change comes after large-scale controversy throughout the United States regarding whether or not alleged terrorists should be brought into the United States for trial.

Richey, Warren. "Supreme Court: Does Part of Patriot Act Violate Citizens' Rights?" *Christian Science Monitor* (February 22, 2010). Available online. URL: http://www.csmonitor.com/USA/Justice/2010/0222/Supreme-Court-Does-part-of-Patriot-Act-violate-citizens-rights. Accessed March 8, 2010. Discusses a lawsuit filed by the Humanitarian Law Project challenging a specific section of the Patriot Act that makes it a crime to provide material support to a known terrorist group. Some, however, have criticized the law for being too broad, as "material support" can also include peace activists working with terrorist groups to persuade them to use nonviolent means of political protest.

Documentaries

Beauchamp, Keith A. *The Untold Story of Emmett Louis Till.* Directed by Keith Beauchamp. 70 min. Velocity/Thinkfilm, 2004. DVD. Recounts the gruesome lynching of 14-year-old Emmett Louis Till in a small town in Mississippi in 1954 and the events surrounding his death, including the actions of his family members and a highly publicized court battle that ended in the acquittal of Till's murderers by an all-white, all-male jury. Interviews with Till's family and footage of the event highlight the brutality of the Jim Crowe–era Southern racism that resulted in the brutal death of an African-American teenager.

Burns, Ken, and Paul Barnes. *Not for Ourselves Alone: The Story of Elizabeth Cady Stanton and Susan B. Anthony.* Produced by PBS. Directed by Ken Burns. 180 min. PBS Paramount, 1999. DVD. A documentary of the women's suffrage movement and the work of Elizabeth Cady Stanton and Susan B. Anthony. The film also recounts the relationship between Stanton and Anthony and their lifelong struggle for women's rights.

Dupre, Jeffrey. *Out of the Past: The Struggle for Gay and Lesbian Rights in America.* Produced by Jeffrey Dupre, Andrew Tobias, Eliza Byard, Kevin Jennings, and Michael Huffington. 97 min. Allumination, 1998. DVD. Examines the struggles of the gay community to fight ignorance, hatred, and intolerance to secure their human rights. The documentary combines accounts of past struggles by major gay and lesbian historical figures, as well as modern-day efforts to protect one's rights, including those of a Utah teenager who attempts to start a Gay-Straight Alliance at her high school.

Lee, Spike. *4 Little Girls.* Produced by Spike Lee, Daphne McWilliams, Jacqueline Glover, Michele Forman, and Samuel D. Pollard. Directed by Spike Lee. 102 min. HBO Home Video, 1997. DVD. A documentary recounting the bombing of a black Baptist church in Birmingham, Alabama, in 1963 that killed four young girls. Interviews with the girls' friends and families not only reveal the intimate pain caused by the crime but also how the bombing was, itself, symptomatic of the larger issue of institutionalized racism in the United States.

Newnham, Nicole, and David Grabias. *Sentenced Home.* Directed by Nicole Newnham and David Grabias. 76 min. Indiepix, 2005. DVD. Follows the lives of three Cambodian-American immigrants in Seattle, Washington, who came to the United States as child refugees fleeing the brutal Khmer Rouge in the 1980s. Now, as adults, they are being deported back to Cambodia as part of the U.S. immigration policy that resulted from the confusion and fear of the 9/11 terrorist attacks.

Other Media

Jefferson, Thomas, and Congress. *The Constitution of the United States, Bill of Rights, Declaration of Independence, and Articles of Confederation: The Essential American Papers.* A collection of primary sources to aid research on the development of human and civil rights in the United States. Available online. URL: www.archives.gov/exhibits/charters/.

Von Garnier, Katja. *Iron Jawed Angels.* Produced by Denise Pinckley, James Bigwood, and Laura McCorkindale. Directed by Katja von Garnier. 123 min. HBO Home Video, 2004. DVD. A film starring Hilary Swank and Frances O'Connor as suffragists Alice Paul and Lucy Burns, who campaigned for the addition of the Nineteenth Amendment to the U.S. Constitution. The film is a fictionalized account of the true story of the women's suffrage movement and the lives of the activists who fought for women's rights.

HUMAN RIGHTS IN THE DEMOCRATIC REPUBLIC OF THE CONGO
Books

Clark, John F. *The African Stakes of the Congo War.* New York: Palgrave Macmillan, 2002. A collection of essays that examines the conflict in the Democratic Republic of the Congo, its historical origins, and the interests of neighboring countries that have intervened or offered support. The book also discusses the political climate that has contributed to the crisis, including rebel groups, military coups, and the Mobutu kleptocracy.

Conrad, Joseph. *Heart of Darkness.* New York: W.W. Norton, 2005. A novel that was originally published in 1902 about a man named Marlow who accepts a foreign assignment from a Belgian trading company to Africa. His assignment is to transport ivory down the Congo River, but his real mission is to retrieve the rogue ivory dealer Kurtz, who has established a new life in the jungles of the Congo. The novel addresses such themes as racism, savagery versus civilization, and 19th-century Western notions of Africa as the "Dark Continent."

Hochschild, Adam. *Leopold's Ghost: A Story of Greed, Terror, and Heroism in Colonial Africa.* New York: First Mariner Books, 1998. A thorough examination of the 19th-century colonization of the Congo by the Belgian King Leopold II. Hochschild discusses the imperialistic scramble among the European world powers and Leopold's own desperation for a Belgian colony that later became his own private enterprise. Much of the book draws on eye-witness accounts of the colonization that resulted in the deaths of millions of Congolese people, and the torture, mutilation, and rape of millions more.

Nzongola-Ntalaja, Georges. *The Congo: From Leopold to Kabila: A People's History.* London: Zed Books, 2002. A comprehensive analysis of Congolese history and the events that have led up to the current conflict that has already killed millions of civilians. Beginning roughly from the Congo's introduction to Portuguese explorers, Nzongola-Ntalaja outlines the subsequent devastation wrought by the slave trade, which was later compounded by the Belgian King Leopold's colonization. The book goes on to examine the political chaos that erupted following the country's declaration of independence, and the various world powers that intervened to protect their own interests, all of which contributed to the current crisis.

Prunier, Gérard. *Africa's World War: Congo, the Rwandan Genocide, and the Making of a Continental Catastrophe.* New York: Oxford University Press, 2008. Examines the specific role that Rwanda has played in inaugurating and perpetuating the Congo Wars. Prunier discusses the way in which the Rwandan genocide acted as a catalyst that later provided grounds for justifying Tutsi leaders' incursion to clear out refugee camps populated by Hutus on the border between Rwanda and Congo, which had the effect of sparking off a major armed conflict that embroiled eight neighboring countries.

Turner, Thomas. *The Congo Wars: Conflict, Myth, and Reality.* London: Zed Books, 2007. Provides a detailed analysis of armed conflict in the Democratic Republic of the Congo, tracing the complexity of the current situation back to the legacy of Belgian colonialism. Turner discusses the large-scale violence that has engulfed the nation, yet remains widely underreported outside of Africa, as well as the self-interested military interventions by Uganda, Rwanda, Angola, Zimbabwe, and Namibia that have led to the Congo Wars being redubbed Africa's World War.

Wrong, Michela. *In the Footsteps of Mr. Kurtz: Living on the Brink of Disaster in Mobutu's Congo.* New York: HarperCollins, 2001. Provides an account of the decadent and greedy Mobutu regime from Wrong's perspective as a foreign correspondent who lived in Zaire (today's Democratic Republic of the Congo) for six years. Wrong describes Mobutu's excesses, such as his claim that he needed $10 million a month to live off of, but more revealing is her exploration into how and why Mobutu received so much support from the CIA, the World Bank, the International Monetary Fund, and the French and Belgian governments.

Studies and Reports

Human Rights Watch. "The Christmas Massacres" (February 2009). Available online. URL: http://www.hrw.org/en/reports/2009/02/16/christmas-massacres-0. Accessed March 9, 2010. Reports on the devastating slaughter of more than 865 people and the abduction of 160 children in the Haute Uele district of the Democratic Republic of the Congo between December 24, 2008, and January 17, 2009. The most brutal attacks occurred between December 24th and 25th, when villagers had gathered for the Christmas festivities. The Lord's Resistance Army (LRA) killed their victims with axes, machetes, and clubs.

———. "Soldiers Who Rape, Commanders Who Condone" (July 2009). Available online. URL: http://www.hrw.org/en/reports/2009/07/16/soldiers-who-rape-commanders-who-condone-0. Accessed March 9, 2010. Examines the systematic use of rape as a weapon of terrorism against civilians by the Congolese army. The report focuses specifically on the 14th Brigade, which has been accused of many acts of sexual violence in North and South Kivu Provinces, along with reports of looting. The report notes that despite such widespread reporting, little if any action has been taken by political and military authorities to prevent rape.

———. "You Will Be Punished" (December 2009). Available online. URL: http://www.hrw.org/en/reports/2009/12/14/you-will-be-punished-0. Accessed March 9, 2010. Examines a political alliance shift that took place in January 2009 that saw the Congolese and Rwandan armies collaborate to oust the abusive Democratic Forces for the Liberation of Rwanda (FDLR) army, a Rwandan Hutu militia whose leaders participated in the Rwandan genocide. The shift has resulted in even more death and violence as Congolese soldiers have looted villages and killed and raped villagers as punishment for allegedly collaborating with enemy soldiers. Between January and September 2009, 1,400 people were killed and 7,500 rapes were reported, double the number from the previous year.

International Crisis Group. "Congo: Five Priorities for a Peace-Building Strategy" (May 2009). Available online. URL: http://www.crisisgroup.org/home/index.cfm?id=6095&l=1. Accessed March 9, 2010. Examines the recent collaboration between the Congolese and Rwandan militaries and the problem of the Rwandan Hutu rebels in the Kivu Provinces. The report recommends implementing an effective strategy for disarming and neutralizing the FDLR, refocusing the Security System Reform on results in eastern Congo, encouraging reconciliation and human security, improving governance, and stabilizing and maintaining regional relationships.

Annotated Bibliography

Mowjee, Tasneem. "Humanitarian Agenda 2015: Democratic Republic of Congo Case Study." Feinstein International Center (October 2007). Available online. URL: https://wikis.uit.tufts.edu/confluence/display/FIC/Humanitarian+Agenda+2015+--+Democratic+Republic+of+Congo+Case+Study. Accessed March 9, 2010. Reports on the conflicts in the Democratic Republic of the Congo and contextualizes humanitarian goals within the larger project undertaken by the Feinstein International Center at Tufts University, entitled "Humanitarian Agenda 2015," which examines humanitarian values and action on a global scale, the effects of terrorism and counterterrorism on humanitarian activism, the coordination of humanitarian and political agendas, and the security and safety of humanitarian activists.

United Nations. "Security Council Committee Established Pursuant to Resolution 1533 (2004) Concerning the Democratic Republic of Congo" (2010). Available online. URL: http://www.un.org/sc/committees/1533/. Accessed March 9, 2010. Reports on the arms embargo placed on the Democratic Republic of the Congo by the United Nations Security Council. In 2003, the adoption of resolution 1493 placed an arms embargo on all foreign and Congolese armed militias in North and South Kivu and Ituri, but the adoption of resolution 1533, along with several others between 2004 and 2009, has extended the arms embargo to all of the Democratic Republic of the Congo.

Articles and Factsheets

Abiola, Seratu. "Marching for Women of Congo." AllAfrica.com (March 9, 2010). Available online. URL: http://allafrica.com/stories/201003090274.html. Accessed March 9, 2010. Discusses the march led by activists in the Enough Project and Women for Women as a part of International Women's Day to raise public awareness to sexual violence against women in the Congo. The march was one of 103 events in 18 countries in which women from around the world gathered on bridges to mark International Women's Day.

Amnesty International. "UN Forces Must Remain in the Democratic Republic of Congo" (March 5, 2010). Available online. URL: http://www.amnesty.org/en/news-and-updates/un-forces-must-remain-democratic-republic-congo-2010-03-05. Accessed March 9, 2010. A statement released by Amnesty International urging the Congolese government to allow MONUC, the UN's Congo peacekeeping mission, to remain in the Democratic Republic of the Congo. MONUC is the largest UN peacekeeping mission in the world, with 20,500 personnel, and Amnesty International argues that it is the only force in the DRC capable of providing protection to civilians.

Honan, Edith. "U.N. to Start Troop Withdrawals from Congo in 2010." *Reuters* (March 5, 2010). Available online. URL: http://www.reuters.com/article/idUSTRE62507V20100306. Accessed March 9, 2010. Reports on the UN announcement that it would begin withdrawing troops in its MONUC peacekeeping mission from the relatively peaceful western regions of the DRC in June 2010. Troops will remain in the more unstable eastern regions until at least June 2011.

The 2010 withdrawals coincide with the 50th anniversary of the country's independence and come at the request of the Congolese government.

International Monetary Fund. "Public Information Notice: IMF Executive Board Concludes Article IV Consultation with the Democratic Republic of Congo" (December 16, 2009). Available online. URL: http://www.imf.org/external/np/sec/pn/2009/pn09136.htm. Accessed March 9, 2010. Examines the economic crisis in the Democratic Republic of the Congo and how the International Monetary Fund is getting involved. The article provides a detailed overview of the Congo's economy, as well as a table that charts the DRC's financial fluctuations between 2005 and 2009.

United Nations Development Programme. "Human Development Report 2009: The Democratic Republic of Congo" (2009). Available online. URL: http://hdrstats.undp.org/en/countries/country_fact_sheets/cty_fs_COD.html. Accessed March 9, 2010. The 2009 report measures the Human Development Index (HDI) in the Democratic Republic of the Congo over the course of 2007. The HDI provides a composite measure of three different areas of life that indicate overall well-being: health and life expectancy, education, and standard of living (income). The 2009 report provides graphs and tables that visually capture the Congo's HDI and contrast it against that of other African countries.

U.S. Department of State. "The Democratic Republic of Congo" (January 2010). Available online. URL: http://www.state.gov/r/pa/ei/bgn/2823.htm. Accessed March 9, 2010. A detailed factsheet that provides information on the Democratic Republic of the Congo, including geography, population demographics, government, economy, and historical background. This is an ideal first stop for those with little to no familiarity with the Democratic Republic of the Congo.

Wakabi, Wairagala. "Lubanga Witness Says ICC Agents Paid Him to Tell Lies." AllAfrica.com (March 8, 2010). Available online. URL: http://allafrica.com/stories/201003090074.html. Accessed March 9, 2010. Examines recent reports that a witness in the Thomas Lubanga ICC trial was paid to falsely identify himself as a former child soldier. The witness, whose face and name have not been disclosed for his protection, claims that he and others were paid by intermediaries, who also gave them the names of former commanders in the Patriotic Forces for the Liberation of Congo (FPLC), which Lubanga led.

Documentaries

ABC News Nightline. *Heart of Darkness: The Democratic Republic of Congo.* 150 min. ABC News, 2006. DVD. A five-part series that examines the armed conflict in the Democratic Republic of the Congo. Part one focuses on the actual fighting in the DRC. Part two looks specifically at the town of Shabunda, which has been devastated by the wars. Part three focuses on the economic center of Kinsangani. Part four follows the life of a woman who is supporting 10 children by working as a porter. Part five provides an overview of the Congo as the most mineral-rich region in Africa and what that means for the Congolese people.

Balluff, Dan. *Children in the Congo: From War to Witches.* Produced and Directed by Dan Balluff. 67 min. Light Beam Productions, 2008. DVD. Documents the devastation brought on by years of warfare in the Democratic Republic of the Congo and how Congolese children have been the most affected. The film documents the lives of street children in Kinshasa who have become targets of accusations of witchcraft, torture, and child prostitution.

Bate, Peter. *Congo: White King, Red Rubber, Black Death.* Produced by Nick Fraser, Bill Binnemans, Iikka Vehkalahti, Olaf Grunnert, and Paul Pauweis. Directed by Peter Bate. 84 min. Art Mattan, 2003. DVD. A documentary that recounts how King Leopold II of Belgium colonized the Congo and instituted a regime of cruelty and barbarity that killed and mutilated millions of Congolese people in the name of profit. The documentary has been denounced by the Belgian government for depicting Leopold as a genocidal tyrant.

Scott, Pippa. *King Leopold's Ghost.* Directed by Pippa Scott. 103 min. Direct Cinema Limited, 2006. DVD. A documentary based on the book by Adam Hochschild about the brutal colonization of Congo and the reign of King Leopold II. The documentary involved four years of research and includes archival materials, such as letters, secret reports, and photographs. Filmed in the Congo, Belgium, United States, Canada, and the United Kingdom, the documentary stars Don Cheadle, Alfre Woodard, and James Cromwell.

Other Media

The Lubanga Trial at the International Criminal Court. Available online. URL: http://www.lubangatrial.org/. Accessed March 9, 2010. 2010. Web site. Provides a wide range of news reports, legal analysis, and commentary on the Thomas Lubanga trial at the International Criminal Court. Lubanga, a former rebel leader in the Democratic Republic of the Congo who is charged with conscripting and using child soldiers, is the first person to be tried for war crimes by the International Criminal Court, which was established in 1998 through a collaboration of 120 countries. This Web site provides up-to-date reporting on the progress of the Lubanga trial.

HUMAN RIGHTS IN CHINA

Books

Becker, Jasper. *Hungry Ghosts: Mao's Secret Famine.* New York: Henry Holt, 1996. Examines the 1958–62 famine that came as a result of China's "Great Leap Forward" and Mao's collectivization vision that forced untrained peasants to bear the weight of China's industrial and agricultural expansion. Becker reports on the many catastrophic failures of the Great Leap Forward despite the governmental propaganda claiming large-scale success, and the famine that caused millions of people to starve to death.

Brook, Timothy. *Quelling the People: The Military Suppression of the Beijing Democracy Movement.* Palos Altos, Calif.: Stanford University Press, 1992. Explores the events of the Tiananmen Square Massacre of 1989, including the student hunger strikes, the imposition of martial law, the thousands of people killed by the People's Army, and the civil war that nearly erupted as armies turned against one another. Through eye-witness reports, hospital records, and student accounts, Brook outlines a vivid picture of the violent massacre, the details of which the Chinese government is still trying to repress.

Chang, Leslie T. *Factory Girls: From Village to City in a Changing China.* New York: Random House, 2008. Chang, a former Beijing correspondent for the *Wall Street Journal,* explores the movement of 130 million Chinese workers from rural villages into factories, focusing specifically on two teenage girls and their hardships and successes as they begin new lives as assembly-line workers in the factory city of Dongguan. Chang, a first-generation Chinese-American, provides excerpts from the girls' diaries and text messages, as well as details from her own family's immigration from China to America, to shed light on this phenomenon.

Evans, Karin. *The Lost Daughters of China: Adopted Girls, Their Journey to America, and the Search for a Missing Past.* New York: Penguin Putnam, 2000. Discusses observations on Chinese history and culture during the author's journey to adopt her daughter from a Chinese orphanage. As her daughter was abandoned as an infant by her birth mother in a market, Evans examines women's history in China and the cultural and political practices that have led to the abandonment of 1.7 million infant girls annually.

Goldman, Merle. *From Comrade to Citizen: The Struggle for Political Rights in China.* Cambridge, Mass.: The President and Fellows of Harvard College, 2005. Details the way in which the economic shift to the market and more open communication with other countries has allowed Chinese intellectuals and other individuals and groups formerly associated with the Communist Party to shed their allegiances and assert their political rights. Many are now even calling for a new political system (as is the case in the Charter 08).

Johnson, Kay Ann. *Wanting a Daughter, Needing a Son: Abandonment, Adoption, and Orphanage Care in China.* St. Paul, Minn.: Yeong & Yeong, 2004. Examines infant abandonment and adoption in China as a product of cultural son-preference and strict governmental birth policies. Johnson also explores the rising number of families—especially in urban centers—who do want daughters. This book explores the complex cultural and political processes that promote infant abandonment and at one time had China sending more children overseas for adoption than any other country in the world.

Pan, Philip P. *Out of Mao's Shadow: The Struggle for the Soul of a New China.* New York: Simon & Schuster, 2008. Provides a unique and intimate look at post-Mao China and the individuals struggling to rebuild their lives and communities despite local government corruption, authoritarian brutality, and an unfair judicial system. Pan, a former bureau chief in China for the *Washington Post,* weaves together interviews with artists, peasants, and entrepreneurs to draw an outline of corruption and human rights violations in China.

Williams, Philip F., and Yenna Wu. *The Great Wall of Confinement: The Chinese Prison Camp Through Contemporary Fiction and Reportage.* Berkeley and Los Angeles: University of California Press, 2004. A comprehensive study of China's prison camp network, known since 1951 as the laogai system. The book draws from a wide range of primary sources, including literary depictions of the prison camps, to piece together the life of a prisoner, from arrest and interrogation to release.

Yang, Guobin. *The Power of the Internet in China: Citizen Activism Online.* New York: Columbia University Press, 2009. Explores the way in which the debut of the Internet in the 1990s sparked a new wave of expression and activism in China by allowing users to organize and protest despite state efforts to police the Internet. Yang's book outlines a new era of informational politics and social change in China.

Studies and Reports

Amnesty International. "2008 Annual Report for China" (2009). Available online. URL: http://www.amnestyusa.org/annualreport.php?id=ar&yr=2008&c=CHN. Accessed March 10, 2010. A report that examines various areas of human rights and how they have been addressed or violated in China. Topics include the death penalty, minority rights, freedom of the press and censorship, torture and ill treatment of prisoners, the targeting of human rights activists, violence and discrimination against women, including reports of forced abortions, repression of religious groups, refugees, Tibet, and discrimination against gays and lesbians.

Human Rights Watch. "An Alleyway in Hell: China's Abusive 'Black Jails'" (November 12, 2009). Available online. URL: http://www.hrw.org/en/reports/2009/11/12/alleyway-hell-0. Accessed March 10, 2010. A report that documents how government officials abduct Chinese citizens and hold them incommunicado in secret detention facilities for extended periods of time, often depriving them of food, sleep, and medical care. Despite prisoners' reports of the facilities, journalists' visits, and academic research that has proven the existence of such jails, the Chinese government continues to deny the existence of these black jails.

———. "We Are Afraid to Even Look for Them: Enforced Disappearances in the Wake of Xinjiang's Protests" (October 20, 2009). Available online. URL: http://www.hrw.org/en/reports/2009/10/22/we-are-afraid-even-look-them-0. Discusses the Xinjiang protests in July 2009, during which a number of Uighurs, an ethnic minority group in China, protested the deaths of Uighur workers at a toy factory in Guangdong. The protests became violent, and hundreds of people have been detained under suspicion of participating in the protest. Approximately 43 Uighur men and teenage boys who were detained have simply disappeared, although Human Rights Watch suspects that the number may be higher, as many families have been reluctant to come forward for fear of government reprisals.

———. "Where Darkness Knows No Limits: Incarceration, Ill Treatment, and Forced Labor as Drug Rehabilitation in China" (January 7, 2010). Available online. URL:

http://www.hrw.org/en/reports/2010/01/07/where-darkness-knows-no-limits-0. Accessed March 10, 2010. Reports on China's Anti-Drug Law and the routine incarceration of suspected drug users without trial or judicial oversight. Suspected drug users may be incarcerated for up to six years with little to no medical care and no rehabilitative support to help them stop using drugs. Furthermore, many are forced to perform unpaid labor.

U.S. Department of State. "2008 Human Rights Report: China (Includes Tibet, Hong Kong, and Macau)" (February 25, 2009). Available online. URL: http://www.state. gov/g/drl/rls/hrrpt/2008/eap/119037.htm. Accessed March 10, 2010. The most recent U.S. report on human rights in China, with sections addressing arbitrary or unlawful deprivation of life, enforced disappearance, torture, arbitrary arrest or detention, denial of fair and public trial, arbitrary interference with privacy, family, or home, freedom of speech and press, and freedom of assembly, among others.

Articles and Factsheets

Al Jazeera. "Tibetans Storm Chinese Embassy" (March 9, 2010). Available online. URL: http://english.aljazeera.net/news/asia/2010/03/201039123118107311.html. Accessed March 10, 2010. Reports on recent protests in New Delhi, India, marking the anniversary of the 1959 Tibetan uprising. Several Tibetan exiles stormed the Chinese embassy, reportedly chanting "Tibet belongs to Tibet" and "Free Tibet." The protest was organized by the Tibetan Youth Congress.

Associated Press. "Lawyers Ask UN to Help Find Missing Chinese Lawyer" (March 10, 2010). Available online. URL: http://www.google.com/hostednews/ap/article/ ALeqM5i8Atiz2R14DxsAwNVNpPNa7ZBwPwD9EBOBNG1. Accessed March 10, 2010. A brief article reporting on an international group of lawyers who are asking the United Nations to declare the arbitrary detention and disappearance of the Chinese lawyer Gao Zhisheng a violation of international law. The group says that Gao is being held incommunicado.

BBC News. "'Uighur Spy' for China Jailed in Sweden" (March 8, 2010). Available online. URL: http://news.bbc.co.uk/2/hi/asia-pacific/8556736.stm. Accessed March 10, 2010. Provides details on the sentencing of Babur Maihesuti to 16 months in prison for spying on Uighur expatriates for the Chinese government. The court reported that Maihesuti had infiltrated the World Uighur Congress, a political body for Uighur expatriates, and from January 2008 to June 2009 he collected information on Uighur expatriates that he passed along to the Chinese government.

Corbin, Kenneth. "China Says Google Never Filed Complaint in Hacking Case." *Datamation* (March 8, 2010). Available online. URL: http://itmanagement.earthweb. com/secu/article.php/3869201/China-Says-Google-Never-Filed-Complaint-in-Hacking-Case.htm. Accessed March 10, 2010. Reports on Google's January 2010 claims that it was the target of a Chinese hacking attack and its threat to pull its operations from China altogether if the government continues to censor certain Web sites and attempts to hack into the Gmail accounts of Chinese dissidents.

The Chinese government has since responded that Google never reported the attack or sought negotiation regarding China's censorship practices.

Foster, Peter. "Chinese Poet Liao Yiwu Blocked from Going to German Festival." Telegraph.co.uk (March 2, 2010). Available online. URL: http://www.telegraph. co.uk/news/worldnews/asia/china/7351771/Chinese-poet-Liao-Yiwu-blocked-from-going-to-German-festival.html. Accessed March 10, 2010. Reports on the Chinese writer Liao Yiwu, who had already boarded an airplane in Chengdu when he was ordered to get off. He was later interrogated for four hours by security officials who demanded to know why he was going to speak in Germany. Liao was arrested in 1990 and imprisoned for four years after recording a poem called "Massacre" about the Tiananmen Square Massacre, during which he screamed and wailed while reading his poem aloud.

Kurczy, Stephen. "Is Internet Access a Human Right? Top 10 Nations That Say Yes." *Christian Science Monitor* (March 9, 2010). Reports on a recent survey that finds that 87 percent of Chinese respondents see Internet access as a fundamental human right, compared to 76 percent of Americans. Worldwide, 79 percent of respondents believe that the Internet is a basic human right. This comes after Secretary of State Hillary Clinton's January 2010 condemnation of the Chinese government's restrictions on Internet access.

Mysinchew.com. "Writers, Scholars Call for Release of Top China Dissident" (March 10, 2010). Available online. URL: http://www.mysinchew.com/node/36202. Accessed March 10, 2010. Reports on a letter submitted to China's parliament calling for the release of the dissident and human rights activist Liu Xiaobo. Liu, a writer and former professor, was sentenced in December 2009 to 11 years in prison following his co-authoring of Charter 08. The letter to the Chinese parliament was signed by more than 100 writers and scholars, including Salman Rushdie, Nadine Gordimer, and Ma Jian.

Schatz, Amy. "Web Firms Under Fire to Protect Human Rights." *Wall Street Journal* (March 2, 2010). Available online. URL: http://online.wsj.com/article/SB1000142 4052748704548604575097603307733826.html?mod=googlenews_wsj. Accessed March 10, 2010. Discusses the recent announcement made by Senator Dick Durbin that he plans to introduce legislation that will require internet companies to take reasonable steps to protect human rights or face criminal liability. Several Internet companies have argued that some of the countries in which they operate sometimes mandate Web site restrictions.

Documentaries

ABC News Nightline. *Soul Searching in China.* 22 min. ABC News, 2007. DVD. Documents religious intolerance in China and the government's crackdown on the outlawed religion known as Falun Gong. The Chinese government has stated that there are no underground churches in China, but like Falun Gong practitioners, Chinese Christians have reported having to worship in secret for fear of government retaliation.

Ban, Zhongyi. *Gai Shanxi and Her Sisters*. Produced by Yamagami Tetsujiro. Directed by Ban Zhongyi. 80 min. dGenerate Films, 2009. DVD. Tells the story of Hou Dong-E, who was kidnapped from her village in the Shanxi along with several other women and forced into sexual slavery to the Japanese army during World War II. Fifty years later, Hou joined several other women to seek justice and reparations, but she died before she could see justice served. The documentary comes together from the stories of survivors as well as former Japanese soldiers.

History Channel. *Declassified: Tiananmen Square*. 50 min. A&E Home Video, 2005. Documents the Tiananmen Square Massacre of June 1989. Using previously unseen footage and declassified diplomatic sources, the History Channel documentary provides a new perspective on the events of the massacre and the students who were killed for protesting for democracy.

Huffman, Brent E., and Katerina Monemvassitis. *Frontline: Tank Man*. Produced by Katerina Monemvassitis and Marsha Bemko. Directed by Brent E. Huffman and Katerina Monemvassitis. 60 min. PBS, 2006. DVD. Documents the events of the Tiananmen Square Massacre with a central focus on a photograph of a man standing in front of the People's Army tanks. Though the man, to this day, remains unknown, the photograph has since become an iconic image of the student protest for democracy and its brutal quashing by the government.

Stanek, Carolyn. *Found in China*. Directed by Carolyn Stanek. 82 min. Tai-Kai Productions, 2007. DVD. Follows six families with adopted Chinese daughters as they take a Heritage Tour through China to gain a better understanding of Chinese culture and the circumstances that led to their adoptions. The documentary focuses special attention on the girls, who, at the ages of nine to 13, are part of the first cohort of infant girls to be adopted overseas after being abandoned by their birthparents.

HUMAN RIGHTS IN CHECHNYA
Books

Gall, Carlotta, and Thomas de Waal. *Chechnya: Calamity in the Caucasus*. New York: NYU Press, 1999. Gall and de Waal, two *Moscow Times* correspondents, provide a detailed picture of the conflict in Chechnya, beginning with the historical presence of Russia in the Caucasus and Chechnya's centuries-old tradition of fighting Russian imperialism. The authors then focus in on the first Chechen war (1994–97), beginning with Chechnya's bid for independence and Boris Yeltsin's ill-fated decision to recapture Chechnya by force. The book was written before the second Chechen war, which began in 1999, but this book highlights the events that led up to the first outbreak of fighting.

Gammer, Moshe. *The Lone Wolf and the Bear: Three Centuries of Chechen Defiance of Russian Rule*. Pittsburgh: University of Pittsburgh Press, 2006. Explores the development of Chechen self-perception and national identity over the course of three centuries of resistance against Russian imperialism. Despite many of Chechnya's historic documents having been systematically destroyed by the Russian government, Gammer pieces together the history of a region that claims more than 70 different ethnic groups, all of which remain united in their determination for a national identity.

Gilligan, Emma. *Terror in Chechnya: Russia and the Tragedy of Civilians in War.* Princeton, N.J.: Princeton University Press, 2010. Explores Russia's violent response to Chechnya's demands for independence, focusing primarily on the second Chechen war, which was started by Boris Yeltsin in 1999 and maintained by Vladimir Putin when he became prime minister in 2000. Drawing her evidence from eyewitness accounts and interviews with refugees and humanitarians, Gilligan outlines a conflict that involved torture, disappearances, executions, and other human rights abuses against the Chechen people.

Hughes, James. *Chechnya: From Nationalism to Jihad.* Philadelphia: University of Pennsylvania Press, 2007. Examines the Chechen conflict within the larger contexts of nationalism, ethnic politics, imperialism, and independence. Hughes explores Chechen nationalism within the movement for self-determination and probes the outbreak of fighting following the failed negotiations of the 1990s that coincided with rising Islamic radicalism. The conflict in Chechnya is thus outlined as a polarized struggle between imperialistic might and radical resistance.

Jagielski, Wojciech. *Towers of Stone: The Battle of Wills in Chechnya.* New York: Seven Stories Press, 2009. Examines the current conflict in Chechnya by focusing attention on two historical figures in Chechnya's long history of resistance against Russian rule: Shamil Basayev, a renowned Chechen hero and warlord, and Aslan Mashadov, a politician who is viewed by some as a national hero and others as an opportunist. The two men and their personal struggles under and against Russian rule serve to provide a clearer outline of the current crisis in Chechnya.

Meier, Andrew. *Chechnya: To the Heart of a Conflict.* New York: W.W. Norton, 2004. Provides a thorough account of the Chechen wars and locates the conflict in a historical context of Russian expansion into the Caucasus, the nationwide Chechen conversion to Islam in the 17th century, mass deportation under Stalin, repatriation under Khrushchev, and the brutal suppression of the Chechen bid for independence. Meier was *Time*'s Moscow correspondent from 1996 to 2001, during which time he witnessed the military bombardment of Grozny. This book provides a firsthand account of the conflict, as well as interviews with Chechen civilians.

Oliker, Olga. *Russia's Chechen Wars 1994–2000: Lessons from Urban Combat.* Santa Monica, Calif.: Rand, 2001. A brief overview of the tactics and planning of the Russian military as it fought to take control of the Chechen capital of Grozny and other outlying towns and villages during the first and second Chechen wars. Oliker notes that while the Russian military's second attempt to take Grozny was more successful than the first, its decision to ignore certain problems in the urban mission were ignored, with devastating results.

Politkovskaya, Anna. *A Small Corner of Hell: Dispatches from Chechnya.* Chicago: University of Chicago Press, 2007. Recounts the second Chechen war by focusing on those caught in the crossfire: the Chechen civilians. Politkovskaya incriminates those on both sides who stand to profit from the war, how ordinary civilians have been affected, and how the war has damaged Russian society. Politkovskaya was a journalist in Moscow and an outspoken critic of the Chechen war before she was murdered in 2006.

Smith, Sebastian. *Allah's Mountains: The Battle for Chechnya.* New York: Tauris Parke Paperbacks, 2008. Author and journalist Sebastian Smith gives a first-hand account of the crisis in Chechnya and the struggle over the mountainous region in the Caucuses between the outnumbered ethnic group of Chechens and the Russian military. Smith recounts his travels with Chechen guerrillas and provides an eyewitness account of the first Chechen war, which devastated Grozny, destroyed a number of villages and towns, and killed thousands of people.

Tishkov, Valery. *Chechnya: Life in a War-Torn Society.* Berkeley and Los Angeles: University of California Press, 2004. A Russian ethnographer examines the war-ravaged region of Chechnya and probes the various factors and circumstances that have contributed to the country's instability, such as militant Islam, nationalism, and blood feuds. Early on in the book, Tishkov admits that as a Russian intellectual, his perspective on Chechnya is not neutral.

Studies and Reports

Amnesty International. "Rule Without Law: Human Rights Violations in the North Caucasus" (June 30, 2009). Available online. URL: http://www.amnesty.org/en/library/info/EUR46/012/2009/en. Accessed March 11, 2010. Reports on Amnesty International's concerns for human rights in Chechnya, Ingushetia, Dagestan, and Kabardino-Balkaria. The report looks specifically at such human rights violations by law enforcement officials, including deaths in custody, torture and ill treatment, extrajudicial killings, abductions and disappearances, arbitrary detentions, and threats made to human rights activists.

Committee to Protect Journalists. "Attacks on the Press 2009: Russia" (February 16, 2010). Available online. URL: http://cpj.org/2010/02/attacks-on-the-press-2009-russia.php#more. Accessed March 11, 2010. Reports on the 19 journalists who were murdered for their work in or about Russia since 2000, including Natalia Estemirova in Chechnya. The top developments emphasized in the report are the responses from the international community and Russian authorities' decision to reopen investigations into the unsolved 2006 murder of the journalist Anna Politkovskaya.

Hammarberg, Thomas. "Report" (November 26, 2009). Available online. URL: http://www.unpo.org/images/26-11-2009%20chechnya%20coe%20report.pdf.Accessed March 11, 2010. A report by the Commissioner for Human Rights of the Council of Europe following his visit to the Chechen Republic and the Republic of Ingushetia in September 2009. The report addresses the persistent challenges of protecting human rights in the North Caucasus and focuses on such issues as the murder of Natalia Estemirova and the protection of human rights defenders, counterterrorism, abductions and disappearances, and impunity for Russian authorities.

Human Rights Watch. "Special Report: Anatomy of Injustice: The Unsolved Killings of Journalists in Russia" (September 15, 2009). Available online. URL: http://cpj. org/reports/2009/09/anatomy-injustice-russian-journalist-killings.php. Accessed March 11, 2010. Examines the murders of 17 (at the time of the report's publication) journalists in Russia since 2000 for their open criticism of the Russian government. Only one of the cases has seen the murderer identified and prosecuted. The report includes a special section on journalists who have been murdered for reporting on Chechnya and neighboring republics in the Caucasus.

———. "What Your Children Do Will Touch Upon You: Punitive House-Burning in Chechnya" (July 2, 2009). Available online. URL: http://www.hrw.org/en/ reports/2009/07/02/what-your-children-do-will-touch-upon-you-0. Accessed March 11, 2010. Reports on systematic punitive house-burnings by Russian authorities to punish the families of suspected terrorists. In 2008, the Chechen president Ramzan Kadyrov stated unequivocally that the families of insurgents should expect to be punished if they do not turn their relatives in or convince them to surrender. If a family does not turn in an insurgent relative, they are automatically assumed to be providing food and assistance to the insurgents.

———. "'Who Will Tell Me What Happened to My Son?': Russia's Implementation of European Court of Human Rights Judgments on Chechnya" (September 27, 2009). Available online. URL: http://www.hrw.org/en/reports/2009/09/28/who-will-tell-me-what-happened-my-son-0. Accessed March 11, 2010. Discusses Russia's response to the European Court's rulings on cases regarding Chechnya. In nearly all 115 cases brought against Russia, the Russian government was found guilty of extra-judicial killings, tortures, and disappearances, yet in the 33 cases specifically examined by Human Rights Watch, Russia had failed to prosecute a single perpetrator.

Articles and Factsheets

Badkhen, Anna. "From Chechnya, a Cautionary Tale." *Boston Globe* (March 11, 2010). Available online. URL: http://www.boston.com/bostonglobe/editorial_opinion/ oped/articles/2010/03/11/from_chechny a_a_cautionary_tale/. Accessed March 11, 2010. Reports on the reconstruction of the Chechen capital of Grozny since Russian troops withdrew from Chechnya. The author compares the situation between Russia and Chechnya to that of the United States and Iraq and notes that as in Chechnya, Iraqi insurgents are likely to continue their acts of violence even after the war is declared officially over.

Barry, Ellen. "Investigator Says Killer of Rights Worker Identified." *New York Times* (February 25, 2010). Available online. URL: http://www.nytimes.com/2010/02/26/ world/europe/26chechnya.html. Accessed March 12, 2010. A news report claiming that Russian authorities have determined with certainty who killed the journalist and human rights activist Natalia Estemirova, but that they have been unable to arrest the suspect, who has gone into hiding. Statements from global human rights organizations such as Human Rights Watch point to high-ranking officials in the Chechen government.

Freedom House. "Country Report: Chechnya 2009" (2009). Available online. URL: http://www.freedomhouse.org/template.cfm?page=22&year=2009&country=7 753. Accessed March 11, 2010. Provides an overview of human rights developments in Chechnya in 2008, paying special attention to recent rulings against Russia in favor of Chechens by the European Court of Human Rights, President Ramzan Kadyrov's authoritarian rule over Chechnya, and the rebel groups that continue to use brutal violence against civilians. The report determines Chechnya to be "Not Free."

Ognianova, Nina. "Why a Killing in Chechnya Is an International Issue." Committee to Protect Journalists (February 16, 2010). Available online. URL: http://cpj.org/2010/02/why-a-killing-in-chechnya.php. Accessed March 11, 2010. Probes the significance of the murder of Natalia Estemirova in 2009 and why it is relevant to the rest of the world. As one of the few journalists to write her own eyewitness accounts of the human devastation in Chechnya, Estemirova had gathered a significant amount of evidence directly linking tortures, disappearances, arsons, murders, and punitive violence directly to the Chechen government and President Ramzan Kadyrov.

Reuters. "Russia Urges Sweden to Extradite Chechen 'Bandits'" (March 9, 2010). Available online. URL: http://www.reuters.com/article/idUSTRE6283PH20100309. Accessed March 11, 2010. Reports on Sweden's refusal to extradite two Chechen separatists accused of kidnapping and murder. In March 2010, the Swedish prime minister Frederik Reinfeldt met with the Russian president Dmitry Medvedev and discussed the issue of human rights in the Caucasus, where human rights activists say young people are being pushed through corruption, poverty, and oppression by authorities to join Islamic militant groups.

VOA News. "Russian Human Rights Activist Found Dead in Chechnya." *Voice of America* (July 15, 2009). Available online. URL: http://www1.voanews.com/english/news/a-13-2009-07-15-voa26-68804912.html. Accessed March 12, 2010. Reports on the U.S. response to the 2009 abduction and murder of the human rights defender Natalia Estemirova. The news article also includes responses from the Russian and Chechen presidents, each of whom expresses indignation and outrage and promises to find the killers, while the human rights group Memorial, for whom Estemirova reported, holds the Chechen government responsible.

Documentaries

Gordon, Michael. *Deadlock: Russia's Forgotten War.* Produced by Stephen Sapienza. Written by Michael Gordon. 40 min. Azimuth Media, 2009. DVD. Explores the second Russo-Chechen war from the perspective of the *New York Times* Moscow bureau chief Michael Gordon. Vladimir Putin had just become president of Russia when the second war in Chechnya began, and he made public statements of his desire to bring stability to Chechnya. While the U.S. president George W. Bush and other world leaders supported Putin's determination to fight Chechen terrorists and rebuild Chechnya, Michael Gordon argues that other, more complex issues were underlying the invasion.

Sokrianskaia, Ekaterina, and Zarema Mukusheva. *Crying Sun: The Impact of the War in the Mountains of Chechnya.* Produced by Memorial and WITNESS. Directed by Ekaterina Sokrianskaia and Zarema Mukusheva. 26 min. WITNESS, 2009. DVD. Documents the lives of people in the mountainous Chechen village of Zumsoy as they struggle to maintain their cultural and community identity despite two devastating wars, military raids, enforced disappearances, and attacks by guerrilla fighters.

HUMAN RIGHTS IN IRAN
Books

Afary, Janet. *Sexual Politics in Modern Iran.* New York: Cambridge University Press, 2009. Explores the Iranian cultural, social, and political attitudes toward sexuality, from pre-modern history up through Iran's sexual revolution. Afary's comprehensive study of Iranian sexual politics examines at the ancient practices of slave concubinage, harems, formal and temporary marriage, and rituals of courtship, and explores their movement toward a Westernized modernity. She also looks at how Iran's sexual politics were affected by the Islamic Revolution, particularly where birth control, female sexuality, and same-sex love were concerned.

Esfandiari, Haleh. *Reconstructed Lives: Women and Iran's Islamic Revolution.* Baltimore, Md.: Johns Hopkins University Press, 1997. Charts the profound upheaval that Iranian women experienced following the 1979 Islamic Revolution. Esfandiari explores the way in which the rights that many women had won over the years were suddenly reversed and the state assumed control over what women could study, wear, and do in public. Interviews with businesswomen, professionals, and other working women provide detailed firsthand accounts of the many strategies Iranian women have used to manage and to subvert state authority in their own lives.

Keddie, Nikki R. *Modern Iran: Roots and Results of Revolution.* New Haven, Conn.: Yale University Press, 2006. Provides a comprehensive look into the social, political, and cultural development of Iran since the Islamic Revolution. Keddie, a scholar on Iran who writes about 19th- and 20th-century Iranian history, examines Iran's nuclear and foreign policy, its international relations, particularly with the United States and the United Nations, its economy, the increasing conservativism of the government, and developments in intellectual life and human rights.

Kinzer, Stephen. *All the Shah's Men: An American Coup and the Roots of Middle East Terror.* Hoboken, N.J.: John Wiley, 2008. Researches and reconstructs the 1953 coup Operation Ajax, which was orchestrated by the American and British governments to overthrow the elected prime minister of Iran, Mohammad

Mossadegh. The coup had the effect of inaugurating a cruel dictatorship by Mohammad Reza Shah, who, despite his brutal regime, had the full support of the United States and the United Kingdom until his overthrow in 1979.

Pollack, Kenneth. *The Persian Puzzle: The Conflict Between Iran and America.* New York: Random House, 2005. Examines the current tension between the United States and Iran as the Iranian government pursues its nuclear program. Pollack, the former director for Gulf Affairs at the National Security Council and a military analyst for the CIA, cautions against invading Iran despite his 2002 support for the invasion of Iraq in his book *The Threatening Storm: The Case for Invading Iraq,* for which he has since apologized. Pollack posits that Iran's acquisition of nuclear would not pose a significant threat.

Saberi, Roxana. *Between Two Worlds: My Life and Captivity in Iran.* New York: HarperCollins, 2010. Recounts Saberi's ordeal of being arrested and detained in Iran on accusations of espionage. In January 2009, Saberi, an Iranian-American journalist, was taken from her home by four men and detained in Iran's Evin Prison, where she was held incommunicado for several days. After a mock trial, she was found guilty of espionage and sentenced to eight years in prison, but worldwide uproar from politicians and major media organizations prompted the Iranian government to release her in May 2009.

Taheri, Amir. *The Persian Night: Iran Under the Khomeinist Revolution.* New York: Encounter Books, 2009. Examines the Iranian Revolution under Ayatollah Ruholla Khomeini and Iran's political and social disintegration. According to Amir, the Republic of Iran has three phobias: women, Jews, and America, and he outlines the way in which the ayatollahs mobilized hatred of Israel, women, and the West. Amir was the editor of Iran's largest newspaper until the mullahs came to power, and he now lives in Paris and London.

Studies and Reports

Ansari, Ali, Daniel Berman, and Thomas Rintoul. "Preliminary Analysis of the Voting Figures in Iran's 2009 Presidential Election." Chatham House (June 21, 2009). Available online. URL: http://www.chathamhouse.org.uk/files/ 14234_iranelection0609.pdf. Accessed March 15, 2010. Scrutinizes and compares the province-by-province breakdown of voting statistics in Iran in the 2005 and 2009 presidential elections. The study finds a number of discrepancies, including two provinces that had a turnout that exceeded 100 percent, a number of provinces where Ahmadinejad won a landslide victory despite being widely unpopular in previous years, and the fact that in one-third of all provinces Ahmadinejad would have had to win the votes of all conservative, centrist, and new voters, as well as nearly half of all reformist voters.

Human Rights Watch. "Iran: Freedom of Expression and Association in the Kurdish Regions" (January 9, 2009). Available online. URL: http://www.hrw.org/en/ reports/2009/01/08/iran-freedom-expression-and-association-kurdish-regions. Accessed March 15, 2010. Details the way in which Iranian authorities use security and press laws, along with other legislation, to arrest Kurds for attempting to peacefully assemble and express their dissent. The report notes that following the election of Mahmoud Ahmadinejad in 2005, the government began cracking down on dissidents by citing "security concerns" and imprisoning journalists and activists for inciting racial and ethnic conflict.

———. "The Islamic Republic at 31: Post-Election Abuses Show Serious Human Rights Crisis" (February 11, 2010). Available online. URL: http://www.hrw.org/en/reports/2010/02/11/islamic-republic-31-0. Accessed March 15, 2010. A 19-page report that examines the state of human rights in Iran since the Islamic Revolution in 1979. The report documents a number of human rights violations, including torture, rape, extra-judicial killings, suppression of the rights to freedom of speech and assembly, and arbitrary detentions, particularly in the aftermath of the June 2009 election protests.

———. "The Last Holdouts: Ending the Juvenile Death Penalty in Iran, Saudi Arabia, Sudan, Pakistan, and Yemen." Available online. URL: http://www.hrw.org/en/reports/2008/09/10/last-holdouts-0. Accessed March 15, 2010. Documents the practice of executing juvenile offenders in five countries, where more than 100 juvenile offenders are awaiting execution. The report also examines individual cases among the 32 juvenile offenders who have been executed since 2005. Among these, 26 executions have occurred in Iran, two in Saudi Arabia, two in Sudan, one in Pakistan, and one in Yemen.

Iran Human Rights Documentation Center. "Forced Confessions: Targeting Iran's Cyber Journalists" (September 2009). Available online. URL: http://www.iranhrdc.org/httpdocs/English/pdfs/Reports/Forced%20Confessions%20-%20Targeting%20Iran's%20Cyber-Journalists.pdf. Accessed March 15, 2010. Examines the cases of three Iranian bloggers and cyber-journalists who were arrested and detained by the Iranian government in 2004 and 2005. The report details how Roozbeh Mirebrahimi, Omid Memarian, and Arash Sigarchi were arrested, tortured, forced to confess, and were eventually convicted of moral, press, and national security crimes.

———. "Violent Aftermath: The 2009 Election and Suppression of Dissent in Iran" (February 2010). Available online. URL: http://www.iranhrdc.org/httpdocs/English/pdfs/Reports/Violent%20Aftermath.pdf. Accessed March 15, 2010. A 122-page report that documents the Iranian government's brutal crackdown on protestors following the June 2009 presidential election. The report notes that hours before Ahmadinejad was declared the victor, authorities began arresting dissidents, opposition politicians, and activists. The report also notes allegations of rapes and sexual abuse of male and female detainees by authorities.

Articles and Factsheets

CNN.com. "State Department Criticizes Iran for Persecuting Religious Minorities" (March 13, 2010). Available online. URL: http://www.cnn.com/2010/WORLD/meast/03/13/us.iran.religious.persecution/. Accessed March 15, 2010. Discusses the State Department's criticism of Iran's persecution of religious minorities, namely followers of the Baha'i and Christian faiths. According to the State Department, the Iranian government has detained more than 45 Baha'is and more than a dozen Christians in the last four months. As many as 60 Baha'is are currently imprisoned in Iran because of their faith.

Ghaemi, Hadi, and Aaron Rhodes. "U.N. Must Stand Up for Rights of Iranians." CNN.com (March 13, 2010). Available online. URL: http://www.cnn.com/2010/OPINION/03/13/ghaemi.iran.un.rights/. Accessed March 15, 2010. The article's authors, both of whom work for the International Campaign for Human Rights in Iran, examine the fact that the U.N. Human Rights Council has yet to take action on the human rights violations in Iran, despite many protestors of the 2009 election having been jailed or killed. Iran is currently seeking to gain a seat on the Human Rights Council, and the authors argue that if the Human Rights Council agrees to seat Iran, it will effectively condone the Iranian government's actions.

Human Rights Watch. "Crackdown's Torrent of Abuses: Rights Violations Mounting as Government Celebrates Revolution's Anniversary" (February 11, 2010). Available online. URL: http://www.hrw.org/en/news/2010/02/10/iran-crackdown-s-torrent-abuses. Accessed March 15, 2010. Discusses the human rights abuses detailed in the Human Rights Watch report "The Islamic Republic at 31." According to the report, the human rights abuses during the governmental crackdown on protestors following the controversial 2009 presidential election are broader and more extreme than previously thought. The article calls for the release of all peaceful protestors and for those responsible for human rights abuses to be held responsible.

Knowlton, Brian, and Nazila Fathi. "U.S. Report Describes Worsening Human Rights in Iran and China." New York Times (March 11, 2010). Available online. URL: http://www.nytimes.com/2010/03/12/world/12rights.html. Accessed March 15, 2010. Discusses the recent U.S. State Department's statement that the human rights situation in Iran has degenerated since the presidential election of 2009. In its human rights report, the State Department cited killings of protestors and politically motivated torture, beatings, and rapes.

Ragan, Steve. "Iran Takes Down Human Rights Web Sites—Accuses Them of Espionage." Tech Herald (March 15, 2010). Available online. URL: http://www.thetechherald.com/article.php/201011/5378/Iran-takes-down-human-rights-websites-%E2%80%93-accuses-them-of-espionage. Accessed March 15, 2010. Reports on an announcement made by the Islamic Revolutionary Guards Corps in Iran that its cyber teams hacked into and dismantled 29 Web sites with links to U.S. espionage efforts. Thirty people were arrested on charges of assisting the United States in waging a cyber-war. According the Tehran Public and Revolutionary Prosecutor Office, the Web sites were part of a CIA operation launched in 2006 to destabilize Iran.

Reuters. "Iran Said to Ban Activities of Largest Reformist Party." Radio Free Europe Radio Liberty (March 15, 2010). Available online. URL: http://www.rferl.org/

content/Iran_Said_To_Ban_Largest_Reformist_Party/1984541.html. Accessed March 15, 2010. Discusses reports that Iran's judiciary has banned the activities of the leading reformist party in efforts to quash the reformist movement in Iran. The party had been planning to hold its annual meeting on March 11, 2010, but released a statement claiming to have been banned from holding the meeting.

Documentaries

Karandish, Makan. *Iran: The Forgotten Glory.* Directed by Makan Karandish. 95 min. Mystic Films International, 2009. DVD. A two-part documentary that was shot in more than 60 locations over the course of five years, documenting the ancient Persian civilization. Part I, "Birth of a Nation," looks at the rise of the Achaemenid Empire, which extended from India to the outskirts of Europe, and details the lives of such historical heroes as Cyrus, Darius, and Xerxes. Part II, "Renaissance of Glory," examines the Seleucid and Parthian dynasty up through the emergence of Islam.

Manouchehri, Nezam. *Iran/America: A World Between.* Produced and directed by Nezam Manouchehri. 56 min. CreateSpace, 2008. DVD. Follows the story of an Iranian American who was raised in the United States and travels to Iran to gain a better understanding of his father's homeland. As the young man travels through Iran toward the city of Mashhad, he meets his father's friends and relatives who provide information and a different perspective on Iran.

———. *Letters from Iran.* Produced and directed by Nezam Manouchehri. 33 min. Paradisa Productions, 2008. DVD. Documents an Iranian exile's return to his homeland. Narrated through a series of letters written to a friend in the United States, the filmmaker provides a detailed look at modern life in Iran in the decades following the revolution, including the perspectives of suppressed intellectuals, other Iranian exiles, and Western-educated Iranians who have returned.

Other Media

Maccarone, Angelina. *Unveiled.* Produced by Markus Fischer and Ulrike Zimmermann. Directed by Angelina Maccarone. 97 min. Wolfe Video, 2005. The fictional story of Fabria, an Iranian woman who flees Iran when faced with the death penalty for her love affair with another woman. Her application for asylum in Germany is rejected, but when a fellow exile commits suicide, she assumes his identity and is able to take refuge in Germany. The film navigates the converging lines of sexual, gender-based, and racial discrimination.

Majidi, Majid. *Children of Heaven.* Produced by Amir Esfandiari and Mohammad Esfandiari. Directed by Majid Majidi. 89 min. Miramax, 1999. DVD. A fictional story of a young Iranian brother and sister. When the boy accidentally loses his sister's only pair of shoes, the children decide to secretly share the brother's shoes, since their parents are too poor to afford another pair. The children trade off every day as they hurry to and from school, and when the boy finds out that the prize in a student footrace is a new pair of shoes, he aims to win. *Children of Heaven* was the first Iranian feature film to earn an Oscar nomination for best foreign film.

Chronology

2112–2095 B.C.E.

- The Sumerian Code of Ur-Nammu is written in present-day Iraq, making it the earliest known legal code. While the code makes provisions for vulnerable members of society, such as orphans and widows, it is primarily concerned with protecting social order. Murder, theft, and rape are punishable by death, but the severity of both the crime and the punishment are considered relative to the context of the crime, including the respective classes of the perpetrator and the victim.

1780 B.C.E.

- King Hammurabi of Babylon commissions the Code of Hammurabi, the oldest complete code of laws in the world. The code, like many other ancient law codes of this time and region, operates on the *lex talionis* or "eye for an eye" principle, meaning that the perpetrator of a crime will be punished with equal or more severity to that of the crime committed. Most crimes in the Code of Hammurabi are punishable by death.

600–530 B.C.E.

- The Persian king Cyrus the Great founds the Persian Empire under the Achaemenid Dynasty, which covers the states of the ancient Near East and much of Southwest and Central Asia. He becomes historically renowned for respecting the religions and customs of his conquered subjects and for establishing a government that works for the benefit of the people. Around 539 B.C.E., he drafts a declaration of his claim to power over his new subjects, as well as a rough outline of their own rights. The declaration is inscribed in Akkadian cuneiform script on a clay cylinder that is erected in public; later, it will be considered the first human rights charter in history.

380 B.C.E.

- The ancient Greek philosopher Plato collects a series of dialogues between Socrates and other philosophers on the nature of society and the state, the meaning of justice and morality, and political theory.

384–322 B.C.E.

- Aristotle, Plato's own pupil who would later become tutor to the Macedonian king Alexander, theorizes that human beings are not equal. Rather, Aristotle emphasizes functionality and posits that an individual human being is only as valuable as his or her function in society. Thus, a slave has inherently fewer rights than his master because his social function is that of a tool or object. He also theorizes that women's bodies are less orderly and logical than men's, thus making women an inferior life-form. Aristotle's philosophies will later go on to heavily influence Christian theology.

43 B.C.E.

- The Roman writer Cicero theorizes that law is the inherent reason or logic that guides every human being's actions. Thus, Cicero equates natural reason with natural law.

10–67 C.E.

- The Christian writer and proselytizer Saint Paul travels and writes extensively on the tenets of the Christian faith, which include an emphasis on unity, fraternity, and equality. He also adapts notions of natural reason and law to the Christian faith by suggesting that those who have not been instructed in the Christian teachings (such as the ancient Greek philosophers Socrates, Plato, and Aristotle) can still be morally upright because every human being is inscribed with natural reason.

622

- The Muslim prophet Muhammad drafts the Constitution of Medina to settle and prevent disputes between the warring Muslim, Jewish, and pagan tribes in the region of Medina in modern-day Saudi Arabia. The constitution outlines laws for civil and social interaction in addition to defining and establishing individual rights, which includes the rights of Jews and other non-Muslims.

630s

- Muhammad and his followers conquer the city of Mecca, which Muhammad names the holiest site in Islam.

Chronology

632

- Muhammad dies, and his followers are divided concerning his successor. Those who believe Abu Bakr to be Muhammad's successor become organized as the Sunnis, while those who believe Muhammad's cousin and son-in-law, Ali, to be the true heir become the Shiites.
- Muslim Arabs wage war on Persia in the Islamic conquest of Persia.

636

- Iran is captured in the Battle of al-Qâdisiya, marking the beginning of the Islamic conversion of Iran.

1215

- A series of failures in England prompts a group of barons to draft a document to limit the king's power. The document becomes known as Magna Carta, which translates to "Great Charter," and outlines the rights of free men under the king's rule. The barons force King John to sign the document, which becomes a significant historical milestone in the development of constitutional law. Magna Carta later goes on to influence the common law and the American Constitution. The 61st clause is the weightiest of the document. Known as the Security Clause, it establishes the right of a group of barons to overrule the will of the king through force, if necessary.

1225–1274

- The Italian priest Thomas Aquinas (known in the Catholic Church as Saint Thomas Aquinas) develops Christian theology under the influence of Aristotelian philosophy. According to Thomas, *ius* (justice) is a natural good inherently understood by human beings, and written law is the human expression of that natural good.

1482

- Portuguese explorers make first contact with the Kongo Empire in Africa. With 3 million subjects, an army of 80,000 men, and six major provinces, the Kongo Empire is a highly structured and complex society.

1492

- Christopher Columbus and his crew sail into the Bahamas on October 12. At the island of Guanahani, they are greeted by Arawak Indians, several of whom Columbus kidnaps and takes back to Spain. Spain will later go on to colonize the islands of Cuba and Hispaniola.

1501

- Shia Islam becomes Iran's state religion.

1508

- The Spanish priest Bartolomé de Las Casas arrives in Cuba and is horrified by the brutality of the Spaniards and the suffering of the enslaved Cuban natives. Las Casas documents the grotesque abuses and theorizes that between 1494 and 1508 more than 3 million Cuban natives had been killed, though some scholars later dispute this number. He proposes the use of African slaves instead of Indians, believing Africans to be stronger and constitutionally heartier, but he later retracts this suggestion.

1517

- The Catholic priest and theology professor Martin Luther nails the Ninety-five Theses to the door of the Castle Church in Wittenberg, Germany, to protest the abuses of the Catholic Church. The document denounces the sale of indulgences, which are essentially penances that can be purchased to atone for one's sins, but it is also considered the founding moment of Protestantism. Luther goes on to argue that human nature is unstable and prone to vice, and thus is not a reliable foundation for notions of law and justice.

1525

- Several German peasant groups meet to come to an agreement on their stance toward the Swabian League, an association of German cities that consists of nobles, knights, and royalty. The peasant groups adopt the Twelve Articles, a document that outlines their rights, including the right to freedom and equality, the right to elect and dismiss a local preacher, the right to hunt, fish, and gather timber, and the right to freedom from excessive taxation.

1526

- The Kongo's King Afonso writes distressed letters to the Portuguese king João III, begging him to intervene in the slave trade that was ravaging the Kongo Empire. While the slave trade existed in the Kongo prior to contact with Portugal, the Portuguese slave traders are now kidnapping and selling free citizens.

1559

- The Russian emperor Ivan the Terrible founds Tarki, an urban settlement in present-day Dagestan. The Cossack army is stationed in Tarki and develops a strained relationship with the neighboring Chechens, as the two groups frequently raid each other's villages.

Chronology

1583–1649

- The Dutch jurist Hugo Grotius writes extensively on his theory of natural law, which he divides into primary and secondary laws of nature. Primary laws of nature are those that express the will of God, while secondary laws of nature are those that can be derived purely from human reason. He also develops a theory on the just war, in which he maintains that war is cruel and violent but often a necessary evil and thus should be used only to protect rights and punish crimes. Additionally, he develops international law based on natural law and castigates Christian states that use violence and brutality in wars to obtain their own ends.

1607

- Jamestown is founded on land belonging to a tribe of Algonquin Indians led by Chief Powhatan. The settlement is established on a swamp, and as they are too late to plant crops, the future of the British explorers is tenuous.

1610

- The winter of 1610 becomes known as the Starving Time. A number of British soldiers desert to the Native Americans and beg Powhatan for food and shelter. Such an act of desertion carries heavy penalties in the British settlement, and when Governor Thomas West de la Warr demands that Powhatan return the men, Powhatan refuses and war ensues. Several Algonquin natives are killed, including the queen and her children. Powhatan orders a truce when his daughter, Matoaka (otherwise known as Pocahontas), is captured.

1619

- The first African slaves are brought to New England. Approximately 1 million have already been shipped to the Caribbean and South America.

1632–1704

- John Locke develops several historically significant theories of the mind, society, and government. In his *Two Treatises of Government*, he posits that all men are fundamentally equal under God and that no man has any natural claim to power over another. Every man, according to Locke, has the innate power to govern himself and his neighbors, who, in turn, have the same power. Thus, government becomes necessary to maintain order to ensure that one man does not infringe on the rights of another.

1665

- The Portuguese army goes to war with the Kongolese army, and the Kongo's King António is killed. With no heir to the throne, rival factions claim power, and the empire dissolves in civil war. While warring Kongo groups battle for power, an increasing number of Kongo slaves are being kidnapped and sold.

HUMAN RIGHTS

1675–1676

- Building tensions between the British colonies and various Native American tribes over tribal lands come to a head in King Philip's War. Eight hundred of the 52,000 British colonists and 3,000 of the 20,000 Native Americans are killed in battle, making it (proportionally) one of the deadliest wars in American history.

1689

- The British Parliament adopts the Bill of Rights following the Glorious Revolution, wherein King James II was overthrown and William of Orange became king of England. The Bill of Rights includes the right to freedom from royal interference with the law, freedom from arbitrary taxation, the right to petition the monarch, the right of Protestants to bear arms, the right to elect members of Parliament without royal interference, and freedom of speech.

1712–1778

- Jean-Jacques Rousseau writes on political philosophy and his theories of child-rearing and education. In his 1762 book *The Social Contract*, Rousseau contrasts man's natural freedom as an amoral animal against the confines of society and civilization. His notions of nature and primitive man are highly romantic and sentimental, characterizing nature as divine, simple, and majestic, and he imagines a long-since erased human past when human beings lived in a state of total freedom, which changed when men saw the need to protect their possessions and thus saw the necessity of entering into a social contract.

1722

- Tsar Peter the Great lands on the shores of Dagestan and sends his men inland to explore the area. The men are repelled by the native Chechens, but the episode marks the beginning of Russian imperial expansion into Chechnya.

1750

- The British government passes the Iron Act, which seeks to suppress the iron manufacturing industry in the American colonies to protect the iron industry in England.

1763–1767

- The Mason-Dixon Line is surveyed by Charles Mason and Jeremiah Dixon to resolve border disputes. The line forms the borders of Pennsylvania, Maryland, Delaware, and West Virginia and becomes the line of demarcation between Northern free states and Southern slave states.

Chronology

1764

- British Parliament passes the Sugar Act, which exclusively taxes the American colonies for all sugar imports, with revenues going to fund the British military.

1770

- In America, British soldiers fire their muskets on an unruly but unarmed mob in Boston, Massachusetts, killing five civilians and wounding six others. Two of the soldiers are found guilty of murder, but the verdict does little to mollify anger among the Americans. The incident, known as the Boston Massacre, becomes one of the key events to ignite the American Revolution.

1773

- The Tea Act imposes a tea tax on all British colonies, and the American colonies boycott British tea, often leaving the tea on the import ships or demanding that the import ships take the tea back to England. When the royal governor in Boston insists on keeping the ships in the harbor to press the people of Boston to take the tea, a group of Americans dressed as Mohawk Indians board the ships and dump 342 containers of tea into the harbor. This event is later known as the Boston Tea Party.

1775

- British troops march out to destroy military supplies in Concord, Massachusetts, for which Paul Revere rides through the streets at midnight, shouting to alert the town. An unarmed militia meets the approaching troops and a fight breaks out in which eight Americans are killed and 10 others are wounded. This event reportedly inspires Thomas Paine to write *Common Sense.*
- Thomas Paine writes an article entitled "African Slavery in America." It is the first written argument advocating abolition published in the United States.

1776

- Thomas Paine anonymously publishes *Common Sense,* in which he calls for a break from England on the grounds of protecting Americans' natural rights. With echoes of Rousseau, Paine examines man's natural state of freedom and theorizes that in an ideal society the people will run the government. Thus, he frames his argument in the context of human rights, rather than political or civil rights. *Common Sense* becomes an international best seller.
- Thomas Jefferson drafts the Declaration of Independence. After several revisions and rewrites, including one in which an entire section on the slave trade is eliminated, the Declaration is adopted by Congress.

HUMAN RIGHTS

- The Chechen rebel Sheikh Mansour organizes an uprising against Russian rule, which is temporarily successful but ends in failure when Mansour is captured and imprisoned in Russia.

1789

- In France, a financial crisis and poor harvest lead to nationwide poverty and starvation among the French peasants, which breeds resentment toward the nobility and royalty, who continue to partake in grandiose displays of consumption. The National Assembly, a body representing the common classes of France, convenes to draft a declaration. Marquis de Lafayette, a friend of Thomas Jefferson's who also served under George Washington during the American Revolution, helps draft the Declaration of the Rights of Man and Citizen.

- Following the king's dismissal of a popular minister, a mob of Parisians storms and overwhelms the Bastille, once a symbol of the French monarchy. The Declaration of the Rights of Man and Citizen is officially adopted by the National Assembly.

- The former slave Olaudah Equiano publishes his memoirs, *The Interesting Narrative of the Life of Olaudah Equiano, or Gustavus Vassa, the African, Written by Himself,* detailing his abduction from Africa as a young child and his painful life of slavery in Europe and America.

1791

- The French playwright and activist Olympe de Gouges writes the Declaration of the Rights of Woman and the Female Citizen, which mirrors the tone and format of the Declaration of the Rights of Man and Citizen, but with particular emphasis on women's rights. For this, she is executed as a counterrevolutionary and an unnatural being.

- The Bill of Rights takes effect in the United States.

1792

- The successful revolutionary movement in France culminates in the declaration of a republic. Feudal privileges held by the nobility and clergy are abolished, all church property is seized, and religious orders as well as inherited aristocratic titles are eliminated.

- In England, Mary Wollstonecraft writes *Vindication of the Rights of Woman,* in which she argues for stronger and more thorough education for girls and women. The book addresses the theories of such major philosophers as John Locke and Jean-Jacques Rousseau and argues that women need better education to transcend their ornamental status, be equal companions to their husbands, and raise responsible, intelligent children.

Chronology

1804

- After winning their freedom, the slave population of Saint-Domingue rises up in rebellion when the French army returns to reenslave them. The successful revolt results in Haiti's independence and its establishment as the first nation of freed slaves.

1807

- The Slave Trade Act ends the kidnapping and importation of slaves throughout the British Empire.

1817–1864

- Russia's expansion into the Caucasus becomes known as the Caucasian War, during which Russian troops meet fierce resistance from native Chechens and other ethnic groups of the Caucasus.

1820

- When Missouri petitions for statehood, the U.S. Congress is faced with a potential imbalance as there are 11 free states, and the admission of Missouri would make 12 slave states. Debates rage over the Northern states' right to exclude slavery from their territories versus the Southern states' rights to own slaves. As Maine is also petitioning for statehood at this time, a deal is struck in which Maine will be admitted to the Union as a free state and Missouri will be admitted as a slave state. The deal becomes known as the Missouri Compromise.

1832

- The New England Association of Farmers, Mechanics, and Other Working Men releases a statement condemning child labor as harmful to children's well-being.

1836

- The state of Massachusetts passes the first child labor law, which requires factory-working children under the age of 15 to attend school a minimum of three months out of the year.

1839

- Pressured by England, the Portuguese government ends its involvement in the slave trade in Africa.

1842

- Massachusetts passes a law that prohibits children from working more than 10 hours per day.

1843

- In Chechnya, the Dagestani imam Shamil Basayev becomes ruler of Dagestan and Chechnya following a successful resistance campaign against the Russian army. He proves to be a ruthless and repressive leader who despises Chechens as bandits.

1848

- Elizabeth Cady Stanton writes the Declaration of Sentiments, in which she outlines the oppressions under which U.S. women were living and demands the right to vote. The Declaration of Sentiments is read at the Women's Rights Convention at Seneca Falls the same year.

1850

- To address the problem of runaway slaves, Senator James Murray Mason of Virginia drafts the Fugitive Slave Act, which allows the owner of a runaway slave to enter into a Northern state to retrieve him or her and prosecute anyone found harboring or aiding a runaway slave. The act causes a great deal of controversy as Northerners see it as a way for Southerners to force their slave-owning ideology onto free states.

1852

- Harriet Beecher Stowe publishes *Uncle Tom's Cabin,* a novel that highlights the suffering of slaves and reportedly convinces Abraham Lincoln to abolish slavery.

1853

- Appalled by the state in which many urban street children live, the minister and humanitarian Charles Loring Brace founds the New York Children's Aid Society with the immediate goal of getting children off the streets and the larger overarching goal of getting children out of the urban slums altogether.

1854

- Charles Loring Brace establishes the Orphan Trains in a mass relocation effort to move children west, out of the urban slums and onto the farms of midwestern families. Children are literally loaded onto the trains and taken to various towns throughout the Midwest, where they are displayed on the platforms for farmers to choose their pick. The movement is not without controversy, as record keeping is shoddy and no inquiries are made into the backgrounds of the adopting farmers.

1857

- In the United States, the *Dred Scott v. Sandford* case is found in favor of Sandford. Dred Scott is an African-American slave suing for his freedom on the grounds that he and his wife spent nine years in the North where slavery is prohibited. The U.S. Supreme Court's decision not only finds in favor of his owner but also overturns the Missouri Compromise, stating that Congress has no authority to prohibit slavery in the Northern states.

1859

- In an effort to maintain power, Imam Shamil allows Chechnya and Dagestan to be reincorporated into the Russian Empire.

1861

- Abraham Lincoln becomes the 16th president of the United States, and the Civil War breaks out immediately thereafter.

1863

- President Lincoln issues the Emancipation Proclamation, declaring free all of the slaves living in the states that have seceded from the Union.

1865

- Slavery is officially abolished in the United States following the Union victory in the Civil War, which has taken the lives of 620,000 soldiers.
- Emancipation of the slaves is declared with the passage of the Thirteenth Amendment, which states that neither slavery nor involuntary servitude shall exist within the United States.

1866

- Sun Yat-sen is born to a tenant-peasant family in rural China.

1869

- In the United States, Elizabeth Cady Stanton and fellow suffragist Susan B. Anthony create the National Woman Suffrage Association.

1870

- African-American men are granted the right to vote with the passage of the Fifteenth Amendment, which prohibits the U.S. government from denying a citizen the right to vote based on his race or previous condition of servitude.
- The Great Persian Famine kills approximately 2 million people.

1874

- The case of 10-year-old Mary Ellen Wilson becomes the first to highlight the rights of abused children in the United States. When the Methodist missionary Etta Wheeler finds Mary Ellen, she is badly injured and malnourished from years of abuse and neglect, but New York City authorities are reluctant to get involved for fear of setting a precedent in which the state overrules the rights of parents. With the help of the American Society for the Prevention of Cruelty to Animals (ASPCA), Etta Wheeler is able to get Mary Ellen away from her abusive parents and publicize the need for state involvement in child protection.

1875

- In the United States, the Civil Rights Act is passed, granting equal rights to African Americans and maintaining that all persons are equally entitled to full participation in civic life and enjoyment of public facilities. The act is later ruled unconstitutional on the grounds that the state cannot prohibit discrimination among private businesses and citizens.

1876

- The Belgian king Leopold II organizes an expedition into the Congo basin, one of the most mineral-rich regions in the world, to convince or force African leaders to relinquish their land to Leopold's sham humanitarian organization, Association du Congo.

1881

- The former slave and author Booker T. Washington becomes the first leader of the Tuskegee Institute, a vocational training school in Alabama for African Americans. Washington emphasizes the need for African Americans to build their skill sets to compete in the job market and gain financial stability.

1883

- Sun Yat-sen returns to China after studying in Hawaii and is dismayed by what he perceives to be a backward society that maintains outmoded traditions, heavy taxation, and a poor education system.

1884

- The Berlin West African Conference is organized by the German chancellor Otto von Bismarck to officially partition the continent of Africa into colonial regions. Leopold II presents and wins support for his project to colonize the Congo region under the guise of wishing to save the Congolese people from Arab slave traders.

1885

- Leopold II declares the Free State of Congo under his authority and initiates a brutal regime of forced labor that includes systematic rape and mutilation against those who do not meet their quota.

Chronology

1889–1930

- A total of 3,700 black men and women are lynched in the United States, reaching the highest peak in 1890.

1895–1911

- Ten uprisings take place in China, finally achieving success with the Wuchang uprising that overthrows the Qing Emperor. Sun Yat-sen becomes the first elected provisional president of the Republic of China. Sun, as the leader of the Chinese Nationalist Party (also known as the Kuomintang [Guomindang] or KMT), espouses three principles of government: nationalism, democracy, and equalization.

1903

- Roger Casement, the British consul in Boma, writes a report detailing the inhuman practices of Leopold's agents against the Congolese people, including the practice of cutting off the hands of those who do not fulfill their quota and shipping the dried hands to Belgium to prove to the commissioner that they are enforcing Leopold's regime.
- Vladimir Lenin becomes the leader of the Soviet Union

1906

- Upton Sinclair publishes *The Jungle,* a novel that depicts the struggles of working-class families and immigrants and the dangerous conditions of factory work in Chicago. The book's description of the use of tainted food in mass food production leads to the passage of the Pure Food and Drug Act.

1908

- As Leopold's cruel practices in Congo are publicized, worldwide outrage eventually forces him to give up control of the Congo to the Belgian state. Compulsory labor in the Congo continues for another 40 years under Belgian rule, with a required number of days that every citizen is required to labor without pay.

1909

- The National Association for the Advancement of Colored People (NAACP) is founded by W. E. B. DuBois and other activists campaigning for the rights of African Americans. DuBois publicly challenges Booker T. Washington's support for "separate but equal" segregation policy, as well as his emphasis on vocational training over education. DuBois encourages African Americans to seek a liberal arts education.

1911

- A fire breaks out on the ninth floor of the Triangle Shirtwaist Factory in New York City, killing 146 of the 500 employees. The high death toll is a direct result of the factory managers' habits of locking the emergency exits to prevent theft, as well as the poor safety measures in the building, including a flimsy fire escape that is not able to support the weight of the girls climbing down. Many jump to their deaths, and the catastrophe results in a statewide overhaul of safety regulations.

1917

- The National Woman's Party is established in the United States with the specific aim of winning a constitutional amendment that will grant women the right to vote.

1919

- Pro-war rhetoric justifying World War I as a war for democracy generates discussions about U.S. women's rights. Congress passes the Nineteenth Amendment, granting women the right to vote.

1920

- U.S. women are granted the right to vote with the passage of the Nineteenth Amendment, which prohibits the government from denying a citizen the right to vote because of that citizen's sex.

1921

- Margaret Sanger founds the American Birth Control League in New York City.

1922

- The dissolution of Tsarist Russia results in Chechnya's emergence as an Autonomous Oblast.

1924

- Vladimir Lenin dies, and Joseph Stalin, an ethnic Georgian, becomes leader of the Soviet Union.

1925

- In China, Sun Yat-sen dies and leadership of the KMT passes to Chiang Kai-shek, who purges all Communists from the KMT and ignites the Chinese Civil War.
- In Iran, Reza Khan overthrows the Qajar Dynasty to become shah.

Chronology

1933

- The German president Paul von Hindenburg appoints Adolf Hitler as chancellor of Germany.

1934

- Chechnya and Ingushetia are merged together to form the Chechen-Ingush Autonomous Republic in the Soviet Union (ASSR).

1937–1938

- The Russian dictator Joseph Stalin is becoming increasingly fearful of spies and enemies, and arrests for espionage leap from 10 percent in 1937 to 27 percent in 1938.

1939

- Germany invades Poland, and Great Britain and France declare war on Germany, initiating World War II.

1941

- Fearful of the shah's ties to Germany, and with an aim to utilize Iran's railway system during the war, Great Britain and the Soviet Union invade Iran and force Reza Khan to abdicate in favor of his son, Mohammad Reza Pahlavi.

1944

- As Nazi troops approach the Caucasus, Joseph Stalin fears that the Chechens will conspire with Germany to invade Russia, and he makes the decision to deport the entire country to Siberia and Kazakhstan on charges of mass collaboration with the Germans. Those deemed "untransportable," including children, the sick, the elderly, and pregnant women are killed. In Russia, Chechnya is erased from history as Chechen becomes a prohibited language and Chechnya is eliminated from Russian textbooks.

1948

- In response to the human rights atrocities of Nazi Germany, the United Nations General Assembly appoints the Canadian John Peters Humphrey director of the Division of Human Rights and gives him the responsibility of drafting a universal declaration of human rights. Along with several other politicians and activists from around the world, Humphrey helps draft the Universal Declaration of Human Rights, which is adopted by the United Nations in December 1948, and is the first document to declare universal equal rights among all human beings in every country.

1949

- The Chinese Communist Party comes to power in China and installs Mao Zedong as chairman of the new People's Republic of China. Mao supports the abolition of the Four Authorities: political authority, authority of the clan, theocratic authority, and patriarchal authority.

1950

- In China, the Agrarian Reform Law abolishes land-ownership in China and redistributes land and agricultural responsibility among the peasantry, beginning the process of collectivization.

1951

- In Iran, Dr. Mohammad Mossadegh is elected prime minister, but he quickly becomes a target of international anger when unfair pricing that profits Great Britain but not Iran prompts him to nationalize Iran's oil. Britain responds by placing an embargo on Iranian oil.

1953

- Joseph Stalin dies.
- The United States and Great Britain coordinate in a coup d'état called Operation Ajax to remove Mossadegh from power, leaving sole rule of Iran to the shah, whose authoritarian reign is guaranteed support from the United States and Britain.

1954

- In the United States, the landmark *Brown v. Board of Education* is instrumental in proving the harmfulness of "separate but equal" segregation by revealing the way in which the segregation of white and black schools naturally resulted in inferior resources and funding for black schools.

1956

- In China, all farms have become completely collectivized into farming communes.
- In the Hundred Flowers Campaign, Mao Zedong encourages intellectuals and dissidents to voice their concerns about his policies. When millions of responses pour in to criticize the government, Mao quickly halts the campaign and systematically persecutes all those who spoke out against him. 550,000 people are labeled as rightists and punished.

1957

- Nikita Khrushchev's restoration of the Chechen-Ingush Autonomous Soviet Socialist Republic allows the deported Chechens to finally return to their homeland after 13 years of exile.

- In Iran, the shah establishes an internal and secretive security system known as SAVAK, which brutally crushes opposition groups through beatings, imprisonment, torture, death, and exile.

1958

- The Chinese government announces its Great Leap Forward campaign, which encourages mass productive output. Grain and steel production are of primary importance, along with agricultural modernization. In his drive to produce massive quantities of crops, Mao attempts to revolutionize agricultural methods based on shoddy science that has the ultimate effect of devastating crops throughout the country. Grain production collapses, and the resulting famine kills 16 to 30 million people.

1959

- Anticolonial riots in the Congolese city of Kinshasa results in the Congo's independence from Belgium, and Patrice Lumumba becomes Congo's first elected prime minister. Before the Belgian government relinquishes control, it robs the Congolese treasury and transfers the debt to the Congolese government. Insurrection and riots result in widespread rape and violence against white Europeans living in the Congo.

1960

- The birth control pill is approved by the U.S. Food and Drug Administration (FDA).

1961

- A coup d'état organized by the CIA results in the overthrow of Patrice Lumumba and in the installation of Joseph-Désiré Mobutu (Mobutu Sese Seko) as the new leader of the Congo.

1962

- César Chávez founds the National Farm Workers Association in California to organize farmworkers. The National Farm Workers Association later merges with the Filipino American Agricultural Workers Organizing Committee (AWOK) to become United Farm Workers of America.

1963

- Betty Friedan publishes *The Feminine Mystique,* which explores the roots and effects of American patriarchy and urges American women to demand their human rights.
- The Equal Pay Act is passed in the United States, requiring employers to pay female employees the same wages as male employees for the same work.

- In Iran, Ayatollah Khomeini publicly criticizes the shah and is immediately imprisoned and then exiled.

1964

- The Civil Rights Act is the most sweeping civil rights bill in U.S. history. Title VII focuses specifically on job discrimination and prohibits employers from refusing to hire any individual based on race, religion, sex, or national origin.

1966

- In China, Mao Zedong announces the need to wage war against the Four Olds: old habits, old customs, old ideas, and old culture. The campaign becomes known as the Cultural Revolution, and Mao encourages all Chinese citizens to denounce friends and family members suspected of clinging to old traditions. Denounced individuals are made to wear placards with their mistakes written on them and march in public. In the meantime, the Red Guards scour the countryside, destroying monuments to old religions and traditions.

1968

- A group of Mexican-American students in Los Angeles, California, organize a series of walkouts to protest inequality and discrimination in the Los Angeles Unified School District high schools.

1971

- The Congolese president Mobutu renames the country Zaire.

1973

- The landmark *Roe v. Wade* case results in the nationwide legalization of abortion in the United States on the grounds that prohibiting a woman from aborting a pregnancy is in violation of due process clause of the Fourteenth Amendment, which protects the right to privacy.

1975

- Mao Zedong dies, leaving China in economic disarray. Under his leadership, tens of millions of people have died.

1977

- The U.S. president Jimmy Carter announces that foreign governments found to be in violation of the basic human rights of their people will not receive U.S. aid or arms. Reluctant to criticize the shah, the United States does not discontinue providing aid and arms to Iran.

Chronology

1978

- Deng Xiaoping assumes control of the Chinese government and institutes reforms that will repair China's devastated economy and bring it into the world market.

1979

- China constitutes 25 percent of the world's total population, but constitutes only 7 percent of its arable land. In an attempt to reduce population and encourage productive output, the Chinese government implements the One-Child-Per-Family policy, which limits urban families to one child and rural families to two children.

- In Iran, demonstrations against the shah's repressive regime prompts the shah to flee the country, allowing Ayatollah Khomeini to return from exile. Iran becomes an Islamic republic, and a theocratic constitution is created. Believing the United States to be harboring the shah, a group of Iranian students seizes the U.S. Embassy and takes all those inside hostage.

- Ayatollah Khomeini revokes many of the rights Iranian women have won over the years and enforces *hijab,* the female practice of completely covering one's body except for the face and hands. Women who appear in public without a full-body covering may be punished by up to 75 lashes. Khomeini also reduces the marriage age among girls from 18 to 13 years.

1986

- Ayatollah Khomeini dies and is succeeded by Ali Khamenei as Supreme Leader of Iran.

1989

- Pro-democracy protests by students and intellectuals in China's Tiananmen Square lead to a government crackdown that kills several hundred protesters. The number of the dead and wounded is unclear, as the government and the Red Cross have provided different figures.

- World leaders gather to discuss children's human rights at the Convention on the Rights of the Child, where they agree upon a set of nonnegotiable standards and minimum entitlements for children. The convention sets forth 54 articles and two optional protocols that outline the basic rights of children under the age of 18, including the right to survival and the right to protection from abuse and exploitation.

1991

- Under the leadership of Dzhokar Dudaev, the All-National Congress of the Chechen Nation seizes the building of the Supreme Soviet and forces President

Doku Zavgayev to abdicate. Dudaev is elected president of Chechnya and declares Chechnya independent of Russian rule. The Russian president Boris Yeltsin refuses to recognize Chechnya's independence.

- The Soviet Union collapses.

1993

- Following the end of the cold war and the fall of the Eastern European Soviet Bloc, 171 countries and 800 NGOs gather in Vienna, Austria, for the Vienna World Conference on Human Rights, with the aim of resolving disparities in human rights among different countries.
- The Bangkok Declaration is drafted and signed by several Asian countries to represent all Asian states at the Vienna World Conference. The Bangkok Declaration stirs controversy at the World Conference for its insistence on culturally relative human rights and the authors' accusations that Western countries have fashioned their concept of human rights on Western ideals.
- In his increasingly dictatorial behavior, the Chechen president Dudaev disbands parliament in favor of sole, unmitigated rule.

1994

- Rwanda is engulfed in mass genocide as ethnic Hutus begin killing all ethnic Tutsis. When the Tutsi rebels regain power, more than 1 million Hutus flee to Zaire, where they are housed in squalid refugee camps.
- Russian troops invade Chechnya and capture the capital of Grozny. This marks the beginning of the first Russo-Chechen war, which lasts until 1996 and results in the deaths of tens of thousands of Chechen civilians and the displacement of 500,000 more.

1996

- The Chechen president Dzhokar Dudaev is killed in a rocket attack.

1997

- Due to President Mobutu's profligate spending and the theft of state funds for his family's private use, Zaire is 12 billion dollars in debt.
- Allied with the anti-Mobutu group, the Alliance for Democratic Liberation, the Rwandan army invades Zaire, attacks the refugee camps, and takes the capital of Kinshasa, ousting President Mobutu. The Rebel leader Laurent Kabila declares himself president and renames the country the Democratic Republic of the Congo (DRC).
- Mobutu dies of prostate cancer in exile.

Chronology

1998

- The Congolese president Laurent Kabila attempts to distance himself from the Rwandan army by purging all Tutsis from his administration. The Rwandan army responds by invading the DRC with the backing of the Ugandan army. Kabila gains the support of Namibia, Angola, and Zimbabwe to fight off the invasion. As other countries become involved, the fighting becomes the largest war in African history.

1999

- In the Democratic Republic of the Congo, a cease-fire agreement is signed in Lusaka, Zambia, which becomes known as the Lusaka Agreement, but it fails to stop the fighting. The United Nations makes further attempts to secure peace by deploying a peacekeeping mission known as MONUC to the DRC.
- The bombing of apartment buildings in Moscow is thought to be the work of Chechen terrorists. Russia responds by launching a massive counterterrorist campaign against Chechnya. Leaflets are dropped over Grozny warning civilians to leave the city or be killed as presumed terrorists. Human Rights Watch reports widespread human rights abuses committed by Russian soldiers, including looting, arson, beatings, and murder.
- In Iran, the former interior minister Abdullah Nuri criticizes the ayatollah's Special Clerical Court as illegal. Ayatollah Khamenei goes on live television to defend the court, which punishes dissenting Muslim clerics in Iran.

2001

- The Congolese president Laurent Kabila is assassinated.
- The Iranian journalist Akbar Ganji publishes a series of stories on the murder of 80 dissidents throughout the 1990s. The murders, often staged to look random and even accidental, are known as the Chain Murders of Iran. Ganji is arrested and imprisoned for five years.

2002

- A UN report lists 85 international businesses that have profited from the conflict in the Congo, 21 of which are Belgian.
- Chechen rebels take 700 people hostage in a Russian theater. The Russian authorities respond by gassing the entire building, killing 130 of the hostages. Many survivors later report health problems, but the Russian government insists that they are not related to the gassing incident.

2003

- The Former separatist Akhmad Kadyrov is elected president of Chechnya.

HUMAN RIGHTS

2004

- The Chechen president Akhmad Kadyrov is assassinated when a landmine detonates beneath his stage during a parade in Grozny.
- The European Court of Human Rights begins to hear cases brought forth by Chechen civilians against the Russian government. The judges declare that Russia violated several human rights laws.

2005

- In China, sex-selective abortion and female infanticide results in an imbalanced sex ratio. Males now exceed females by 32 million.
- Mahmoud Ahmadinejad, a former teacher and the mayor of Tehran, is elected president of Iran. In a speech, he makes the internationally controversial statement that Israel should be wiped off the map and replaced with a Palestinian state. He later denies that he is threatening Israel.

2007

- Ramzan Kadyrov, son of former president Akhmad Kadyrov, assumes the presidency of Chechnya with the support of the Russian president Vladimir Putin.
- Since Mahmoud Ahmadinejad's election to the office of president, executions in Iran have increased by 300 percent, from 86 people in 2005 to 317 people in 2007, making it second only to China in the number of people it executes each year.
- Mahmoud Ahmadinejad is invited to speak at Columbia University in New York City, where the university president Lee Bollinger calls him a "petty and cruel dictator."

2008

- Human rights concerns come to the world's attention during the Beijing Olympics, when many foreign journalists complain of Internet censorship and heavy restrictions. During the games, news of the accidental poisoning of thousands of infants due to melamine-tainted infant formula leads to a total news blackout to suppress the spread of information.
- Hundreds of Chinese citizens sign Charter 08, demanding reform in China. Liu Xiaobo, one of the authors of the charter, is arrested and imprisoned.

2009

- In January, the Congolese militia leader Thomas Lubanga becomes the first person to be tried by the new International Criminal Court (ICC) in The Hague since its founding as the world's first war crimes tribunal. Lubanga is on trial for conscripting and using child soldiers.

Chronology

- The UN's peacekeeping mission MONUC partners with the Congolese army in an attempt to disarm the Rwandan rebel group, the Democratic Forces for the Liberation of Rwanda. The operation, known as Kimia II, results in the deaths of more than 1,000 Congolese civilians between March and October 2009.
- The U.S. president Barack Obama visits China and gives a televised address to an audience of Chinese students, in which he emphasizes the importance of freedom of expression, access to information, and political participation. His visit is not widely publicized in China, and the televised address is censored.
- China is named the world's worst jailer of journalists for the 11th year in a row.
- Russia announces the end of its counterterrorist campaign and withdraws its troops from Chechnya.
- The Chechen human rights group Memorial identifies 25 cases of punitive house-burning.
- The Chechen human rights journalist and activist Natalia Estemirova is murdered.
- The European Court of Human Rights has issued 115 judgments on cases brought forth by Chechen civilians against Russia. Russia has been found guilty of extra-judicial killings, enforced disappearances, and torture. To date, no perpetrator has been prosecuted in Russia.
- Three Iranian men await execution for allegedly engaging in homosexual acts as children.
- One hundred thirty juveniles await execution in Iranian prisons.
- The Iranian president Mahmoud Ahmadinejad is elected to a second term, defeating his popular opponent, Hossein Mousavi. At the announcement of Ahmadinejad's victory, hundreds of thousands of people take to the streets of Tehran in protest, many believing the election to have been rigged. The Iranian government admits to detaining 4,000 people, and international reporting groups place the death toll at 150. In the 50 days following the protests, 115 people are executed for crimes related to the protests. Reports later emerge of abuse of detainees by Iranian authorities, including beatings, rape, and torture. Ayatollah Khamenei declares the election valid and urges Iranian citizens to unite behind Ahmadinejad, but studies later reveal discrepancies in voter turnout, suggesting voter fraud.
- Women constitute two-thirds of the world's 800 million illiterate people.

2010

- In early 2010, Iranian officials admit to having arrested 6,000 protestors following the June 2009 reelection of Mahmoud Ahmadinejad—2,000 more than the previously stated 4,000 arrests.

- After failing to come to an agreement with the Chinese government to allow Google to display uncensored search results, Google shuts down its Chinese search engine and begins redirecting search queries to its Hong Kong–based site.

- In a televised interview in July, Chechen president Ramzan Kadyrov describes human rights activists, specifically those affiliated with Memorial, as "enemies of the state, enemies of the people, enemies of the law." Russian president Dmitry Medvedev fails to respond.

- Iranian authorities begin targeting lawyers en masse, particularly those representing human rights officials. Officials prepare cases of tax irregularities against 30 lawyers, including Nasrin Sotoudeh, who has represented the Nobel Prize laureate Shirin Ebadi. Sotoudeh is arrested in September and sentenced to 11 years in prison.

- Liu Xiaobo, the activist for human rights reform in China, is awarded the Nobel Peace Prize, but he is unable to be present to receive his award, as he is serving an 11-year sentence in a Chinese prison. At the awards ceremony, he is represented by an empty chair. In an attempt to stifle the news of Liu's award from spreading in China, the Chinese government puts Liu's wife, Liu Xia, under house arrest and targets other human rights activists as well.

- In December, defense lawyers representing Congolese militia leader Thomas Lubanga apply to have the ICC case against him thrown out, based on allegations that the prosecution coached and bribed witnesses. After considering the application, the judges rule in February that the trial will continue.

2011

- In early January, 26-year-old Tunisian street vendor Mohamed Bouazizi dies from injuries he suffered after dousing himself in gasoline and setting himself on fire in front of a local government building. Bouazizi's desperate act comes after years of government harassment and extortion, culminating in the confiscation of his wares after he is unable to pay a bribe, leaving him penniless and stranded in debt. The suicide ignites nationwide protests, which result in the ouster of President Zine El Abidine Ben Ali after 23 years of rule.

- The protests in Tunisia spark similar actions across several countries throughout the Middle East and North Africa, including Egypt, Yemen, Jordan, Iraq, Iran, Bahrain, Oman, Morocco, Algeria, Syria, and Libya. Pro-democracy demonstrations in Egypt result in the removal from power of President Hosni Mubarak.

- On February 14, tens of thousands of protestors take to the streets of Tehran and other major Iranian cities in the largest demonstrations since the protests following the disputed 2009 reelection of President Mahmoud Ahmadinejad. The protests continue into March, and security forces crack down on demonstrators with teargas, batons, and guns, resulting in three confirmed deaths as of March 6 and several dozen injured, as well as hundreds of arbitrary arrests.

Chronology

- In the month of January alone, authorities executed 73 Iranian prisoners, averaging three executions per day.
- In the United States, the Obama administration declares the Defense of Marriage Act unconstitutional. The 1996 law previously prohibited the federal government from granting marital privileges, such as Social Security payments and immigration sponsorship, to same-sex couples.

Glossary

abolitionism a movement in the United States and Europe to end the slave trade and emancipate the slaves. The abolitionist movement gained in popularity after the U.S. Declaration of Independence, and by the mid-19th century most countries around the world had abolished slavery.

aid a donation of resources from one country to the other, with the aim of providing assistance to the struggling recipient country. Humanitarian aid may come in the form of food, money, medicine, or on-the-ground help. Development aid consists of funds and other resources to support long-term development. Military aid often takes the form of arms to support a national ally.

arbitrary detention the arrest and detention of an individual without evidence of a crime. In authoritarian governments, arbitrary detention may be used to silence opposition.

arms trafficking the smuggling of illegal weapons and ammunition. Also known as gunrunning, arms trafficking is often responsible for providing arms to major conflict zones.

antipersonnel weaponry weapons that are designed to destroy soft targets, such as soldiers and light or unarmored vehicles. Common antipersonnel weapons include cluster bombs, hand grenades, and other weapons designed for human targets.

capitalism an economic system that is run by a competitive free market and in which goods and services are privately owned. This system can be contrasted against state-owned means of wealth.

censorship the act of limiting, suppressing, editing, or blocking access to any individual's or group's act of expression, whether that is in the form of speech, writing, music, or performance. In the United States, materials may be censored if they are considered offensive or harmful, while in more authoritarian governments, materials may be censored if they object to governmental policies.

child abuse   the act of harming or mistreating a child physically, emotionally, or sexually. Abuse may also be committed by a failure to act, such as neglect and/or complicity with an abuser.

child prostitution   the commercial sexual exploitation of a minor under the age of 18. Children may be prostituted by a pimp, by their parents, or they may be abducted and trafficked for purposes of prostitution.

children's rights   outlined by the 1989 Convention on the Rights of the Child as the right to survival, full development, protection from harm and abuse, and the right to participate fully in family, cultural, and social life.

civil rights   rights that protect an individual from oppressive action by the state and ensure a person's ability to participate fully in civic and political life. Such rights include the right to physical safety, freedom from discrimination, the right to justice, and the right to vote.

cluster munitions   an explosive weapon that releases and disperses a cluster of bomblets. Cluster munitions are often antipersonnel weapons, and they do not discriminate between civilians and soldiers.

colonialism   the organization of a country or territory into colonies by another country's government, typically for financial or investment purposes, such as the production of goods or the exploitation of natural resources.

collective farming   the pooling together of agricultural resources and labor to form a farming commune rather than individual farms. Collectivization may be voluntary or forced, as exemplified by the farming communes of the Soviet Union and China.

communism   a social and political system that aims to ultimate equality among individuals by abolishing classes and private property and distributing resources evenly.

constitution   a body of rules or basic principles that define a government and outline its reach and limitations.

constitutional amendment   a change to a constitution. Some governments require a complex legal procedure to ratify or approve an amendment, while others, such as the U.S. government, can ratify an amendment based on a majority vote.

corporal punishment   physical or bodily punishment, such as caning, whipping, striking, or, in the case of children, spanking. Judicial corporal punishment is used in some countries to punish offenders, while corporal punishment in the home is commonly used by parents to correct children.

counterterrorism the acts and strategies taken by governments and militaries in response to terrorist acts or threats. Counterterrorism differs from antiterrorism in that it is offensive, which means one country or group moves into another group's territory to disarm them.

coup d'etat the forceful, unlawful, or unconstitutional deposition of a government, usually by a group within the state, such as an opposition group or the military to establish a new government. Occasionally, though, a coup may be arranged by an outside government.

cult of personality the political phenomenon that occurs when a country's leader uses media and propaganda to disseminate an idealized image of himself as a hero, father, or savior figure. Two of the most well-known cases are Joseph Stalin of the Soviet Union and Mao Zedong of the People's Republic of China.

democracy a political system in which the people or citizens of a country determine the future and direction of the country through voting, or through elected officials. The word *democracy* is derived from the Greek word *demokratia,* meaning, "rule of the people."

developed nation typically refers to nations that have achieved a certain standard of living, measurable by health, life expectancy, literacy, education, income, and overall well-being. Some define a developed nation by its per capita income.

developing nation refers to countries in which not all citizens enjoy a certain standard of living, such as access to health care, medicine, and education, as well as freedom from hunger and poverty. The development of a nation today is measured by the UN's Human Development Index (HDI), which looks at factors including life expectancy, literacy, and per capita income.

dictatorship an autocratic form of government in which a single leader or a small group of people makes all of the decisions for a country. In 20th-century examples, such as Hitler's Germany or Stalin's Soviet Union, a dictator's power is often unrestricted and unaccountable.

dissident an individual who contests or challenges the principles and policies of a governmental regime or institution. A political dissident is a person who publicly disagrees with governmental policies.

enforced disappearance the secret abduction, incommunicado detention, deportation, or murder of an individual by the state without notifying family members or allowing the detainee to make contact with outsiders such as a lawyer.

exile   refers to both a self-imposed and a state-enforced deportation from an individual's homeland. In a state-enforced exile, an individual may face the threat of imprisonment or death if he or she attempts to return.

exploitation   the act of using a person, object, or resource for one's own personal benefit, usually to the detriment of the person or object being used. Common usage of the term as applied to people refers to commercial sexual exploitation, such as prostitution and pornography, but may also refer to people forced into labor or forced to work for unfair wages.

extrajudicial killing   refers to the execution of a person or group by the state without legal proceedings or the approval of a court.

fair trade   a movement to improve the lives and working conditions of producers in developing countries by paying higher prices for goods. The Fair Trade movement also seeks to promote sustainability and environmentally friendly agriculture and production.

female genital mutilation (female circumcision)   a surgical procedure in which the external female genitalia is partially or completely removed. Female genital mutilation (FGM) is categorized into three types: Type I is the removal of the clitoris; Type II is the removal of the clitoris and the labia minora; and Type III, or Infibulation with Excision, consists of the removal of the clitoris, labia minora, and parts of the labia majora, as well as the suturing together of the labia majora, leaving a small opening for the passage of urine and menstrual blood.

freedom of expression   the right to speak, write, or produce art without censorship. Freedom of expression is included as a human right in the Universal Declaration of Human Rights under Article 19, and Thomas Jefferson believed freedom of expression to be tantamount to a fair and just society.

gay/lesbian/bisexual/transgender (GLBT) rights   a movement for social and civil equality for lesbian, gay, bisexual, and transgender people, which includes freedom from discrimination, challenges to heteronormativity, recognition of the rights of gay and lesbian families, and the right of same-sex couples to marry.

global health   refers to health concerns on a broad, global scale, emphasizing such issues as hunger, poverty, disease, pregnancy and childbirth, and child mortality. The World Health Organization (WHO) is the leading organization addressing global health.

habeas corpus   a writ that brings a detainee before a court to determine if he or she is being detained legally. A detainee may file a petition for a writ of habeas corpus to be released on the grounds that he or she is being held unlawfully.

hijab refers to the head and body covering that Muslim women wear so that only the face and hands are visible. The *hijab* differs from a burqa, which covers the entire body completely.

homophobia refers to a fear or hatred of homosexual individuals, but the term generally encompasses all negative attitudes or actions toward people who are not identified as heterosexual.

honor killing the killing of a female family member by male family or clan members based on the perceived dishonor that that individual has brought upon the family by being accused of having extramarital sex, refusing to comply with an arranged marriage, or seeking divorce. Women may also be accused of bringing dishonor on the family by being raped.

human rights a set of irreducible, universal entitlements to which every individual human being is endowed by virtue of being human. The U.S. Declaration of Independence outlines the most basic, all-encompassing rights as the right to life, liberty, and the pursuit of happiness.

human trafficking the act of abducting, tricking, or coercing a person into prostitution, forced labor, or involuntary servitude in another country. This also includes the sale of infants and children for adoption. Human trafficking is the fastest-growing crime industry in the world and is particularly effective in keeping victims vulnerable by not telling them where they are, or taking them to a country where they do not speak the language.

hunger a general term that refers to the state in which an individual, group, or society continually experiences persistent malnutrition or starvation due to poverty or famine.

imam a Muslim leader who acts as an authority figure in the Muslim community. The early Islamic imams are believed to have been chosen by God and free of all sin.

imperialism a relationship of dominance and subordination wherein one state controls other states or regions in an empire. Through expansion, the dominant state may gain access to resources, ports, trade routes, or strategic war locations. Imperialism also has the corollary of reinforcing ideologies of racial, religious, and gender supremacy.

indentured servitude refers to the practice of contracting one's service to another individual for a fixed period of time. In Colonial America, indentured servitude was typically agreed upon in exchange for transport to America. An indentured servant became the legal property of his or her master and had no legal protection from mistreatment. Furthermore, the servant could not travel or marry without the master's permission, and at any time the master could extend the term of servitude by claiming that the servant had committed an infraction of some sort.

insurgency an armed rebellion, insurrection, or uprising against a recognized authority, such as a state or government, by a group that is not considered a belligerent (a state or nation at war).

justice a term that generally refers to equitableness in a moral context. To behave justly is to behave righteously. To bring a perpetrator to justice or see that justice is served refers to the administration of a punishment commensurate with the crime.

juvenile offenders a person under the age of 18 who has committed a crime, or who was under the age of 18 at the time the crime was committed. In discussions of executions of juvenile offenders, this term does not always suggest that the offender is under the age of 18 at the time of execution, but rather that he or she is being executed for a crime committed as a juvenile.

microfinance a movement to alleviate poverty by providing loans, credit, savings, insurance, and funds transfers to low-income individuals or communities who are interested in starting businesses.

natural law the theory of law as natural, God-given, or self-evident. Natural law often coincides with natural reason and natural rights and has often been used to argue for human rights. Natural law is the basis of the U.S. Declaration of Independence.

natural rights entitlements that are not based on culture, religion, or law, but are universal and naturally governed. Natural rights are distinct from human rights in that natural rights are considered distinct from social or civil rights, while human rights encompasses both natural and civil rights.

natural resources environmental or raw materials such as land, minerals, and animals. Biotic resources refer to plants and animals, while abiotic resources are nonliving things such as minerals, soil, and water.

negative rights rights to noninterference or to not be subjected to a certain condition. For example, freedom of speech is the right to not be censored, and freedom of religion is the right to freedom from state-mandated religious belief.

nongovernmental organization (NGO) an organization that is free from any governmental participation or representation. Several different types of NGOs exist, such as international NGOs and community-based NGOs, and some accept partial government funding.

Glossary

positive rights   rights to certain benefits, such as health care, education, or equal pay.

poverty   a state of existence in which an individual, family, or community does not have the means to afford basic necessities for survival, such as food, clean water, medicine, clothing, or housing. One-third of all deaths around the world are due to poverty-related causes, and there is a correlation between poverty and educational underachievement in children.

press freedom   freedom of expression through various media outlets, such as electronic media (television, radio, Internet) and print media (newspapers, magazines). Freedom of the press is protected by the U.S. Constitution as a necessary component to the maintenance of a free society.

prostitution   the exchange of money for sexual services. When adults or children are forcibly prostituted, the practice becomes known as sexual slavery or human trafficking. There are many arguments for and against decriminalizing prostitution. Proponents argue that it will protect people from being forced into prostitution, while opponents argue that the trade is fundamentally exploitative.

racism   an attitude of fear or hatred toward an individual based on his or her perceived race. Racism does not always manifest itself in open hostility, but may function at more subtle levels, such as racial stereotypes or generalizations.

rebel   an individual who resists authority. In the context of conflict, a rebel group may also refer to insurgents.

reproductive rights   the rights of individuals and couples to decide how many children, if any, they will have, as well as when to have them. Reproductive rights are commonly referenced in the context of women's rights to contraception and abortion, but they also include reproductive health and rights to maternal and neonatal health care.

separatist   an individual who separates from an established body, or who advocates the secession of one group from a larger political, cultural, or religious body.

sexism   discriminatory acts or attitudes based on a person's sex. Sexism may be exhibited in overt hostility, such as violence, or it may manifest in the promotion of gendered stereotypes. Sexism is commonly considered in the context of sexist or misogynistic attitudes toward women, but sexism may also be used by women toward men.

slavery   a state of involuntary bondage or servitude, which may or may not be based on race ideology, such as American slavery and the transatlantic slave trade. In ancient Greece and other cultures, slaves were prisoners of war or simply people who had been abducted from other regions.

social contract   a philosophical theory that posits that individuals give up full autonomy when they join society in exchange for protection and provisions. The theory operates on the belief that prior to civilization as we understand it today, man enjoyed ultimate freedom and self-determination.

socialism   a system of social organization that distributes ownership, production, land, capital, and the means of production equally throughout the community. In Marxist theory, it is the imperfect stage of transition from a capitalist society to a communist society.

suffrage   the right to vote. The American women's suffrage movement of the late 19th and early 20th centuries not only sought the right to vote but also rights to divorce and landownership.

terrorism   the use of violence or threats of violence to coerce or rebel against a government. Often, a terrorist attack does not have a concrete objective, but rather serves as a political and ideological show of rebellion.

theocracy   a system of government that is founded upon a specific religious faith, such as Christianity or Islam. Laws and social organization are consequently couched in religious laws and beliefs.

torture   the systematic infliction of pain on a prisoner to either coerce a confession or elicit the names of coconspirators. Torture methods vary in severity, from such practices as breaking on the wheel to relatively milder tortures, such as sleep deprivation or exposure to extreme temperatures. During the U.S. war on terror, many questions arose regarding the difference between torture and extreme interrogation practices.

unlawful imprisonment   the detention of an individual without legal justification or evidence of a crime. In repressive governments, political dissidents may be unlawfully imprisoned to silence opposition, as is believed to be the case in the arrest and imprisonment of the Chinese dissident Liu Xiaobo.

Wahhabism   a branch of Islam that follows the teachings of Muhammad ibn Abd-al-Wahhab, an 18th-century Muslim scholar who advocated the violent purgation of infidels and *kafir,* or those who reject God and truth.

women's rights   a broad range of universal rights and freedoms to which all girls and women are entitled, such as the right to vote, work, own property, obtain an education, marry at one's discretion, and decide if and when to have children. Women's rights movements throughout history have commonly shared the goal of securing rights equal to those of men.

Index

Index

Index

Index

Raise Hope for Congo 324
rape 4, 73
    of Congolese women 73, 77, 80, 81, 82–84,
        211–214, 285, 380c
    of Iranian dissidents 108
    of prisoners 61
Rape, Abuse, and Incest National Network
    (RAINN) 324–325
reason, natural 7–8, 370c
rebels 396g
Reflections on the Revolution in France (Burke)
    18–19
Reformation, Protestant 10, 372c
regional supranational bodies 26
Rehabilitation Act (1973) 59, 160–161
relativism, cultural vii, **30–31,** 33
religious rights 32, 71
Renaissance 9
Reporters Without Borders 106
reproductive rights
    abortion 55–56, 57, 386c
    birth control 55, 57, 382c, 385c
    definition of 396g
Republic (Plato) 6–7
Revere, Paul 14, 375c
Reza Khan Pahlavi (shah of Iran) 382c, 383c
Rice, Condoleezza 98–99
rights. *See* human rights; specific types
Rights of Man (Paine) 18, 19–20
Ring of Gyges 6–7
Robinson, Mary 208
Roe v. Wade 55–56, 386c
Rome Statute 26
Roosevelt, Eleanor 27–28, 179, 303b
Roosevelt, Franklin D. 27, 53, 179
Roth, Kenneth 230
Rousseau, Jean-Jacques 12, 22–23, 304b, 374c,
    376c
RU486 57
Rushdie, Salmon 230
Russia (Soviet Union)
    and Chechnya 25, **93–101,** 242–246
    and China 89
    and Congo 78–79
    and international agreements 28–30
Rwanda, and Congo 79–80, 83, 388c, 389c

S

Sadulayeva, Zarema 100
Saint Tammany Parish, prisoners in 167–169
same-sex marriage 62–63, 393c
Sanger, Margaret 55, 304b, 382c
Sanjabi, Karim 103

Sassanian Empire 102
SAVAK (Iranian security service) 102–103,
    385c
Save the Generation 100
"School Siege: Eyewitness Accounts"
    (Chechnya, 2006) 238–242
Scott, Dred 48, 304b, 378c–379c
Scott, Harriet 48
Security Clause, of Magna Carta 371c
segregation 53–54, 381c, 384c
self-evident rights 3, 15
Senate Bill 1070 (Arizona) 60, 173–178
Seneca 8
Seneca Falls convention 50, 378c
separate but equal 54, 381c, 384c
separatist 401c
servitude, indentured **43–44**
Seven Years' War 45
severitas 8
sexism 401c
Sexual Violence Research Initiative (SVRI) 325
Shamil (Dagestani imam) 94–95, 379c
Shepard, Matthew 61–62
Shepherd, William 52
Shiites 101–102, 371c
Shi Tao 92
Sierra Leone 73
Sinclair, Upton 52–53, 381c
slavery 401c–402c. *See also* forced labor
    in Americas **42–43, 47–50**
        abolition of **20–22,** 46, **47–50,** 375c
        American Revolution and 46–47
        beginnings of 40, 373c
        Declaration of Independence and
            15–16
        Douglass (Frederick) and 134–141
        Dred Scott decision 48–49, 378c–379c
        Emancipation Proclamation on 49–50,
            141–144, 379c
        official end of 50, 379c
        Truth (Sojourner) and 133–134
    in Congo 74–75, 76, 78, 373c
    property rights in 32
Slavery Abolition Act (1833) 21
Slave Trade Act (1807) 21, 377c
Smith, Howard W. 148
Smith, John 41
social contract 12, 402c
Social Contract, The (Rousseau) 12, 374c
social groups vii, 34, 74
socialism 402c
social movements **20–25.** *See also* specific
    movements

Index